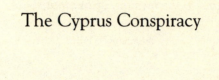

The Cyprus Conspiracy

THE CYPRUS CONSPIRACY

◆ ◆ ◆ ◆

America, Espionage and the Turkish Invasion

Brendan O'Malley
and Ian Craig

I.B.Tauris *Publishers*
LONDON • NEW YORK

Published in 1999 by I.B.Tauris & Co Ltd
Victoria House, Bloomsbury Square, London WC1B 4DZ
175 Fifth Avenue, New York NY 10010
Website: http://www.ibtauris.com

In the United States and Canada distributed by St. Martin's Press
175 Fifth Avenue, New York NY 10010

ISBN 1 86064 439 2

A full CIP record for this book is available from the British Library
A full CIP record for this book is available from the Library of Congress

Library of Congress catalog card: available

Typeset in Goudy by Dexter Haven, London
Printed and bound in Great Britain by CPD, Ebbw Vale

CONTENTS

LIST OF ILLUSTRATIONS

PREFACE

The trigger for our search for the real story behind the Cyprus crisis – which has left the island divided to this day – was an unguarded remark made by James Callaghan. Sipping a glass of wine on the terrace of the House of Commons, Callaghan, who was Foreign Secretary in 1974, spoke emotionally of his role in the dramatic events to a fellow MP: 'It was the most frightening moment of my career,' he said. 'We nearly went to war with Turkey. But the Americans stopped us.'

Our curiosity aroused, we asked Callaghan to elaborate, but he insisted on seeing our questions in advance and, when he saw them, declined to be interviewed. Harold Wilson and then Defence Secretary Roy Mason also declined. That set us off on a long hunt for the truth. We wanted to know why Greece staged a coup against Cyprus and tried to assassinate its President, why Turkey retaliated with a full-scale invasion, and why Britain sent a military task force but took no action – when all three powers were supposed to be guarantors of Cyprus's independence.

The more we looked into it, the more complex the Cyprus jigsaw became, and at every important turn there was the hand of the CIA or the US State Department.

Our investigation involved deep research through top secret files, released in Britain and America, including Defence, Foreign Office and Colonial Office papers, Cabinet minutes, State Department and CIA papers, and interviews with a number of those closest to the crisis. History records that Cyprus was divided because of a Greek-inspired coup and a Turkish invasion. We discovered that the truth was considerably more complex. It was a conspiracy by America, as Britain stood by, to divide the island. And the reason, ignored by previous studies of the Cyprus crisis, was the island's strategic value as a military and intelligence base as well as America's considerable military interests in Turkey. These swamped all other considerations as far as America was concerned. In fact they have done so in all British and American policy over Cyprus in the past 50 years.

This book explodes the myth that Cyprus is divided today purely because of ethnic hatred. It reveals an astonishing international plot, developed from a blueprint evolved first under British rule, then by US President Johnson's officials, the goals of which were finally realised in 1974 even as the Watergate scandal reached its climax.

There are many people, too numerous to mention, who have helped us with this investigation, but we would like to offer our special thanks to the staff of the Public Records Office at Kew, the British Library in London, Colindale and Leeds and the House of Commons library, whose service and resources were invaluable to our research; to former US Secretary of State Dr Henry Kissinger, the Cypriot leaders on both sides including Glafkos Clerides, Rauf Denktash, the late Ezekias Pappiannou, Vassos Lyssarides and Kenan Attakol, and Callaghan's former political aide Lord McNally, who allowed us to interview them; to the press offices of the Cypriot Government in Nicosia, the Turkish Republic of North Cyprus and the Ministry of Defence in Whitehall; to electronic intelligence experts Professor Jeffrey Richelson and Professor Desmond Ball, and investigative journalist Duncan Campbell; and to distinguished Turkish journalist Mehmet Ali Birand for their help.

Brendan O'Malley
Ian Craig
London, March 1999

INTRODUCTION

There is one legacy of the Cold War which continues to haunt the West: a European country that remains cut in two, its capital split like Berlin before the Wall came down, with a corridor of no-man's land preventing 200,000 refugees from returning to their homes. To visitors it is a popular holiday island, but away from the resorts it is bristling with troops, military hardware and electronic spying bases. Situated at the strategically crucial meeting point of three continents, it is for its size one of the most heavily armed countries in the world, with more foreign agents per head of population than anywhere else.

It is 25 years since the Greek military dictators in Athens staged a coup in Cyprus, dramatically ousting its Greek-Cypriot leader, Archbishop Makarios, and Turkey retaliated by seizing more than a third of the island in a two-phase invasion.

Greek Cypriots have long believed the Americans were to blame for failing to prevent the bloody events of 1974, which left the island 'ethnically cleansed' long before the phrase was ever conjured up. In Washington, congressmen demanded to know why their country, as the main supplier of arms to the two NATO partners, had allowed one country to usurp democracy in a friendly state and the other to occupy a major slice of its territory, bringing both of them to the brink of a disastrous war.

In London, MPs cross-examined Foreign Secretary James Callaghan on why Britain, as a guarantor of Cyprus's independence, with a major air base, numerous spying facilities and thousands of troops on the island, took no military action to prevent the crisis erupting. But no-one could cut through the shroud of secrecy that descended on the subject.

US Secretary of State Henry Kissinger fought long and hard to prevent key officials releasing documents or answering questions on the period, and in his memoirs, *Years of Upheaval*, he was uncharacteristically reticent. He said, 'I must leave a full discussion of the Cyprus episode to another occasion'.[1] Callaghan was similarly evasive when pressed on Britain's role, leaving MPs to conclude: 'The full truth will never be known unless, and until, all official papers of the period can be seen'.[2] Only this year did Kissinger return to the subject more fully in his latest memoirs, *Years of Renewal*. Late in the production of this book, he

ix

agreed to be interviewed by us on the subject – but only for 15 minutes (see Appendix and all references to Appendix in the text).

When we investigated James Callaghan's private admission[3] that Britain came close to war with Turkey during the crisis, but America vetoed military action, we discovered that Prime Minister Harold Wilson had sent a potent military task force to the Mediterranean and pleaded with Kissinger to take joint military action to stop the Turks.[4] But the Americans were working to a grander design. This book argues that the Cyprus crisis was no failure of American diplomacy, but a deliberate Cold War plot to divide the island and save the top secret spying and defence facilities from the twin threats of a communist takeover or British withdrawal.

Behind the plot is a secret world of intelligence and intrigue on Cyprus, an island bristling with radar and electronic intelligence hardware that made it a major military prize for the superpowers at a time when tracking advances in enemy nuclear missile technology, providing early warning of nuclear attack and monitoring military threats to the oil fields of the Middle East were critical to winning the nuclear arms race and the Cold War. During the inquiry into the costly Cyprus secrets trial in London in 1985 – in which seven British servicemen were wrongly accused of passing 2000 top secret documents to the Soviets – David Calcutt QC declared that the signals intelligence units on Cyprus handled very large amounts of highly classified material which were fundamental to the safety and interests of the United Kingdom. Under intelligence-sharing arrangements with Washington they were fundamental to the defence of the West too.

Nobody should underestimate the role that traditional enmities between Greeks and Turks, savage ethnic killings, and Turkey's need to protect its southern flank have played in the division and continuing tension over Cyprus, where in 1998 Turkey threatened to blow up Russian air-defence missiles ordered by the Greek-Cypriot President, risking war with Greece and Russia, and to annex northern Cyprus.

But our story sets out to show how for decades Britain and America, at times collaborating, at other times vying with each other, rode roughshod over the aspirations of the majority of Cypriots in pursuit of their own military interests. The story tracks how first the British denied the Cypriots self-determination because of their military interests; then Eisenhower forced Harold Macmillan to give up sovereignty but denied the Cypriots real independence; and finally Washington began plotting to partition the island between Greece and Turkey – by force.

One fascinating aspect of the Cyprus problem is the way, as if cutting through the trunk of a tree and examining the rings of history, it sheds light on one major episode after another during the Cold War and the story of America's special relationship with Britain – from Eden's failure at Suez to Kissinger's triumph during the Yom Kippur war – and highlights the extent to which success in the nuclear arms race and the battle against communism, or imagined communists, dominated all other considerations.

For this reason our book starts not in 1974 but with the creation of the last 'new world order', when the Cold War began and Britain and America were competing for influence in the oil-rich Middle East. It tracks how the Americans forced Britain to give up sovereignty over Cyprus against the will of its military Chiefs of Staff and then forced Archbishop Makarios to accept a severely restricted form of independence that allowed the West's military and spying bases to carry on as before.

When fighting between Greek and Turkish Cypriots threatened to destroy this arrangement, and there were fears that Makarios would try to turn Cyprus into a Soviet satellite, President Johnson's officials first tried to divide the island by diplomacy then devised plans to split it by force. Ten years later, as electronic spying became critical to keeping the West ahead in the nuclear arms race, Harold Wilson – himself suspected by some elements of American and British intelligence services of being a Soviet agent – threatened to pull Britain out of Cyprus altogether.

When Makarios fired off a warning that 'the invisible hand' of the Athens junta was at work in Cyprus conspiring to assassinate him, it triggered retaliation in the form of a coup. Within five days Turkish troops landed on the island, and 25 years later they are still there. What was America's involvement in those events? Did they know about them in advance? Did the Americans encourage them? Was there a motive?

In 1964, US Assistant Secretary of State George Ball told a British officer who was working to end the growing ethnic separation by bringing both sides together, 'You've got it wrong son. There's only one solution to this island, and that's partition.'[5] The officer, Lieutenant Commander Martin Packard, confirmed that the maintenance of the military facilities on Cyprus was deemed of paramount importance by the British and American governments and their military advisers at the time, and they thought this would more easily be achieved in a divided Cyprus.[6] Did they finally achieve their aim in 1974? That is what this book seeks to prove.

CHRONOLOGY

Cyprus has been inhabited since the early Neolithic Age, circa 3700BC. During the following 5000 years, the island was colonised by Phoenicians and later by Achaeans, who brought their Greek language and religions, and came under Assyrian, Macedonian, Egyptian, Persian, Roman, Byzantine and Saracen rule.

1191 – King Richard of England, the Lionheart, took possession of Cyprus.

1489 – Cyprus fell to the Venetians.

1571 – Famagusta fell to the Turks. Cyprus became part of the Ottoman Empire.

1878 – The British Government signed a defensive alliance with Turkey and assumed administration of Cyprus, which remained part of the Ottoman Empire.

1914 – Britain annexed Cyprus after the outbreak of war with Turkey.

1915 – Britain offered Cyprus to Greece if it would aid Serbia. Greece declined.

1923 – Under the Treaty of Lausanne, Turkey and Greece recognised British annexation of Cyprus.

1925 – Cyprus became a crown colony. The High Commissioner was replaced by a Governor.

1931 – The Legislative Council was abolished following widespread disturbances linked to enosis, the movement for union with Greece. Government House was burned down.

1947 – A British plan for a limited degree of self-government on Cyprus was rejected by Greek Cypriots.

1950 – The election of Makarios, then Bishop of Kitium, as Archbishop.

1954 – Further British proposals for limited self-rule were rejected. The Greek Government raised 'self-determination' for Cyprus at the UN. A Greek Colonel, George Grivas, returned to the island and organised EOKA to fight for enosis.

1955 – The EOKA campaign of violence began. A conference between Britain, Greece and Turkey was held in London. A state of emergency was declared on Cyprus by the Governor, Field-Marshal Sir John Harding.

1956 – In March, Archbishop Makarios was deported to the Seychelles. Between September and November, Cyprus was prepared for and used as a launchpad for the Suez operation. In December, Lord Radcliffe's constitutional proposals for Cyprus were rejected.

1957 – In March, Harold Macmillan held talks with Eisenhower, at which Cyprus was raised. Makarios was freed from the Seychelles (but barred from Cyprus). Macmillan considered giving up sovereignty of Cyprus, and retaining only military bases. In September, the Foreign Office held secret talks with the United States, at which the Americans proposed a settlement based on guaranteed independence. Britain accepted it could no longer keep the whole of the island against the will of its people. The Soviets launched satellites into space.

1958 – Cyprus was used in American and British military intervention in the Lebanon and Jordan. The Macmillan Plan was made public: most of Cyprus would be put under rule by a tridominium, while Britain would keep sovereign base areas. In November, Makarios proposed that Cyprus be independent of Greece, Turkey and Britain. The Cyprus question was taken to NATO. Greece and Turkey rejected British plans, and Washington over-ruled London.

1959 – In February, after pressure from the Americans, the Greeks and Turks agreed to guaranteed independence for Cyprus. Macmillan said Britain was prepared to hand over sovereignty, providing it could retain its bases.

1960 – On 15 August, the Union Jack was lowered from Government House in Nicosia for the last time. Makarios was President, Turkish Cypriot Dr Fazil Kuchuk Vice President. Treaties of Establishment, Guarantee and Alliance gave independence to the new Republic of Cyprus.

1962 – The Cuban missile crisis took place.

1963 – Makarios demanded 13 changes to the constitution. Inter-ethnic violence erupted. The system of government established in 1960 collapsed. In December, a British truce force tried to keep the peace.

1964 – In January, acting US Secretary of State George Ball suggested partition. President Johnson resisted calls for the United States to send in troops. In February, a US contingency plan to allow a 'controlled' Turkish occupation in northern Cyprus was discussed with Britain. Turkish ships were on the move, but the plan was abandoned at the last minute. In March, a UN peace-keeping force took over from the truce force. The Greek National Guard was created. Up to 18,000 Turkish Cypriots withdrew to enclaves, which Makarios block-aded. In June, a plan for the UN to escort Turkish Cypriots back into mixed villages was abandoned. During inter-ethnic fighting, Turkey threatened to invade, but Johnson vetoed it in a 'brutal diplomatic note'. Turkey backed down. In August, former US Secretary of State Dean Acheson proposed enosis, with a military base for Turkey and autonomous cantons for Turkish Cypriots. When this failed, Acheson and Ball considered forcing Greece and Turkey to split Cyprus between them. Grivas returned to Cyprus.

1967 – In April, there was a military coup in Greece. Turkish Cypriots were killed in an attack by the Cypriot National Guard, led by Grivas. Turkey threatened military action. Greece backed down and pulled out excess troops, and Grivas was withdrawn. The Arab-Israeli Six Day War took place. In

November, Harold Wilson devalued the pound and ended Britain's worldwide defence commitments.

1968 – Nixon was elected US President, and made Henry Kissinger National Security Adviser.

1970 – In March, Makarios's helicopter was shot down, but he survived. The Soviets overtook the Americans in numbers of ICBMs, and by 1974 had 50 percent more.

1971 – Grivas returned secretly to Cyprus, and started a renewed campaign for enosis under the name EOKA-B.

1972 – The SALT I nuclear arms limitation agreement was signed.

1973 – Henry Kissinger became Secretary of State as well as National Security Adviser. In October, an attempt to blow up Makarios failed. The Yom Kippur War took place between Arabs and Israelis. Western allies refused to help the US airlift to Israel. Kissinger issued a nuclear alert to deter Soviet intervention. In November, Greek junta leader Colonel Papadopoulos was ousted by strongman Brigadier Ioannides in Athens.

1974 – In January, Grivas died. In February, Wilson won the British election and announced sweeping defence cuts. There was tension in the Aegean between Greece and Turkey over oil rights. In July, Makarios issued an open letter warning of the junta's threats to his life. On 15 July, a Greek coup toppled President Makarios; Nicos Sampson was declared President. On 16 July, Makarios, earlier reported dead, escaped and was airlifted by the RAF to London. On 20 July, Turkey landed troops, creating a beachhead. On 22 July, a ceasefire was brokered by Kissinger. On 23 July, the Greek junta fell and Sampson resigned. Glafcos Clerides became acting President of Cyprus. Between 25 and 30 July, and between 8 and 13 August, peace talks were held in Geneva. On 9 August, Nixon resigned over Watergate. On 14 August, the Turks lauched a full-scale invasion, seizing 37 percent of the island. Greece pulled its forces out of NATO. In October, the British withdrew a plan to pull out of Cyprus after pressure from the Americans. In December, Makarios returned to Cyprus.

1975 – In February, US congressmen imposed an arms embargo on Turkey, defying Kissinger. US installations in Cyprus and Turkey were closed in retaliation.

1977 – In August, Makarios died.

1978 – US arms embargo ended. US installations in Cyprus and Turkey were re-opened.

1980 – Greece resumed full role in NATO.

1983 – Turkish Cypriots unilaterally declared a 'Turkish Republic of Northern Cyprus'.

1990 – Cyprus applied to join the European Community.

1997 – Greek Cypriots ordered £400 million worth of Russian missiles. Turkey warned they would shoot them down on arrival, and Cyprus agreed to leave them on a Greek island. Turkey also threatened to annex northern Cyprus.

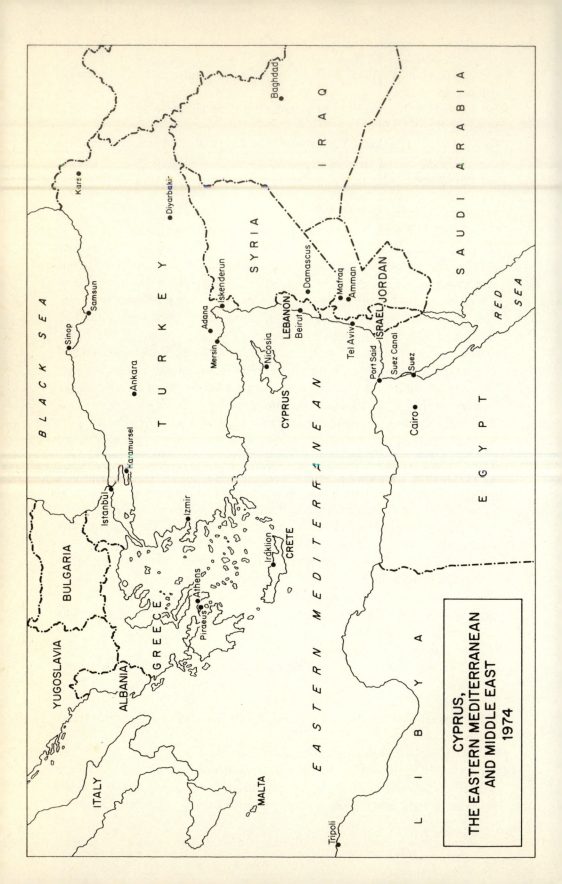

CYPRUS,
THE EASTERN MEDITERRANEAN
AND MIDDLE EAST
1974

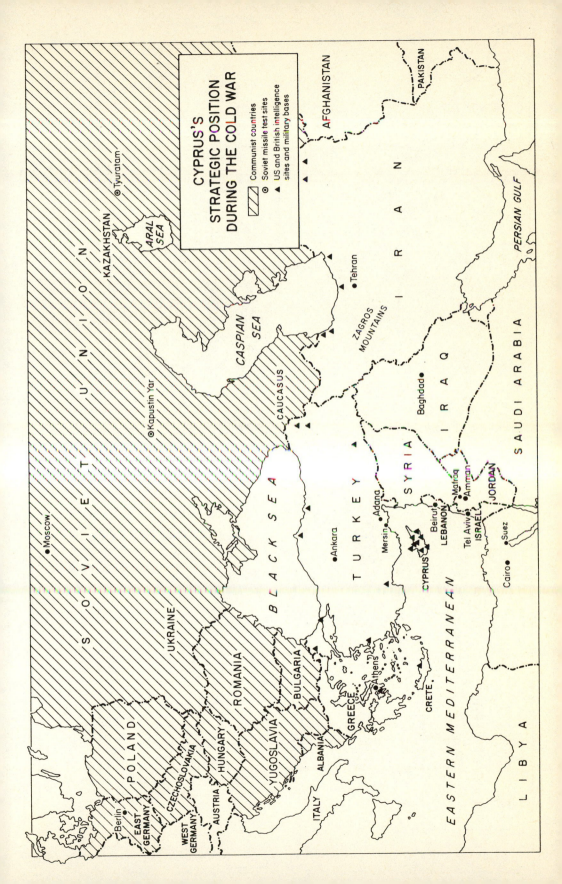

CYPRUS'S
STRATEGIC POSITION
DURING THE COLD WAR

Communist countries
⊙ Soviet missile test sites
▲ US and British intelligence
sites and military bases

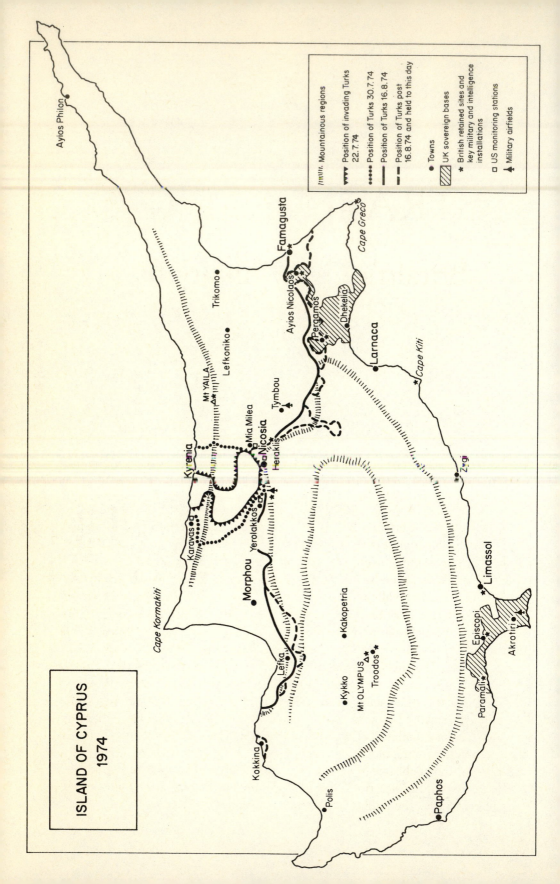

ISLAND OF CYPRUS
1974

Ayios Philon

Cape Kormakiti

Kokkina

Polis

Paphos

Kyrenia

Karavas

Yerolakkos

Morphou

Lefka

Kykko

Mt OLYMPUS

Troodos

Paramali

Akrotiri

Episcopi

Limassol

Kakopetria

Mia Milea

Nicosia

Heraklis

Trikomo

Lefkoniko

Mt YAILA

Tymbou

Ayios Nicolaos

Pergamos

Dhekelia

Famagusta

Cape Greco

Larnaca

Cape Kiti

Zygi

⋀⋀⋀⋀	Position of invading Turks 22.7.74
••••	Position of Turks 30.7.74
——	Position of Turks 16.8.74
– – –	Position of Turks post 16.8.74 and held to this day

ʌ̓ʌ̓ʌ̓ Mountainous regions

● Towns

★ British retained sites and key military and intelligence installations

▨ UK sovereign bases

▫ US monitoring stations

⚓ Military airfields

~1~
STRATEGIC PRIZE
Britain's Vital Military Base

In a top secret briefing note in 1950, British military chiefs of staff spelled out the importance of Cyprus to Britain. They warned defence ministers that if Britain wanted to keep its position in the Middle East, Cyprus must remain British; moreover, even in peacetime the popular communist movement on the island must never be allowed to win control. It was, they said, the only way to ensure the future of Britain's military facilities there, and any weakening of this commitment would alarm Britain's key allies, since Cyprus was a vital link in the chain of British bases running through the Mediterranean to the Middle East and beyond. 'The effect on Turkey and other Middle East countries, and indeed the United States, of any abrogation of British sovereignty is likely to be so serious that it is strategically necessary for Cyprus to remain British,' they said.[1]

Their remarks followed Cabinet concern that the nationalist emotions which had long rumbled below the surface in Cyprus were being channelled into a potentially powerful movement under a new Greek-Cypriot leader, Archbishop Makarios, and might one day erupt. But, when ministers asked if the heat could be taken out of the situation by promising a review of the island's status in ten or 12 years' time, the military chiefs were adamantly opposed.

During the First World War Britain had offered to hand Cyprus over to the Greeks if they joined the battle against the Kaiser. But since then the strategic value of the island as a military base had risen dramatically due to Western Europe's fast-deepening dependence on Middle East oil and the threat to that lifeline from nationalism and the Soviets. Situated 40 miles from the southern coast of Turkey and 70 miles from the Lebanon, Cyprus was also seen as a vital base from which to prevent the right flank of NATO being turned by Eastern Bloc forces in a Third World War.

The production of crude oil in the Middle East increased from 6 million tons in 1938 to 163 million tons by 1955. Oil from the two other significant producers, the United States and Venezuela, was mainly consumed in the Americas. The Soviet Union, too, produced its own oil, but there was little exportable surplus. Consequently, Europe relied heavily on Middle East supplies to fuel its economic recovery. The region supplied two-thirds of Britain's needs and contained 65 percent of the world's known reserves, which implied that Western economies would come to rely on it still further as they expanded in the future. Though the oil was produced mainly in Kuwait, Saudi Arabia, Iraq and Iran, the export of oil from the region involved other states – Syria, Lebanon, Jordan, Egypt and Israel – through which supplies were carried by pipeline (41 million tons a year by 1956) or, in the case of Egypt, by ship via the Suez Canal (77 million tons a year) and on through the Mediterranean to Europe. The production, transportation and sale of Middle Eastern oil were important for Britain's balance of payments and the gold and dollar earnings of the sterling area. Even US companies carried out their work in sterling, so the uninterrupted operation of their work was also important to Britain.[2]

It was fortunate for Britain that such an important resource was being developed in a region over which it had extensive influence. Britain had controlled Egypt since 1881 and, after the rolling back of the Ottoman empire in the First World War, secured League of Nations mandates over Iraq, Transjordan and Palestine, while France was given mandates over Syria and Lebanon. Though not making them colonies, the mandates made the Arab states subordinate to British and French interests – and the Arabs felt cheated of their independence. By degrees Britain made formal concessions to nationalist pressure, but did not give up its real influence. Iraq, for instance, gained independence in 1932, but Britain kept two military bases at Habbaniyah and Shaibah, near Basra. Transjordan was given independence in 1946, but under a king who had been installed by the British and an army led by British officers. Britain was also given the use of two air-bases at Amman and Mafraq.

Britain's relationship with Iraq, Jordan and a handful of Persian Gulf states – Kuwait, Bahrain, Qatar and the Trucial sheikhdoms – was therefore one of mutual dependence. The Arab rulers gave Britain the use of military facilities or, in the case of the Gulf states, control over foreign relations and the granting of oil concessions, in return for guarantees of military protection against aggressors or internal agitators.[3] This afforded Britain the means of maintaining a stable, if undemocratic, order in which its economic interests could continue to operate and develop unhindered, and in which British assets could be safeguarded.

Up to the early 1950s, the flagship of this system of overseas defence was the Middle East military headquarters at Suez. In addition to guarding the Suez Canal, a vital strategic waterway, the Suez base maintained a strategic reserve of up to 80,000 troops, which could be rapidly redeployed to reinforce British garrisons and airfields in the Levant and the Persian Gulf. But, at the very time when Britain's influence and economic interests were being threatened by a rising tide of nationalism, the agreement which permitted the British presence at Suez was coming up for renewal and was unlikely to be renegotiated. The only alternative site was Cyprus.

After oil, the second factor which gave Cyprus a new military significance was the threat of Soviet expansion. During and since the war, a huge swathe of Europe had fallen to the communists, creating a bloc of pro-Soviet regimes, many of them established through brutal oppression, which extended from the Baltic to the Balkans, virtually cutting the continent in two. The Soviets began with the annexation of Estonia, Latvia, Lithuania, Belorussia, the remainder of Ukraine, and Moldavia. By 1950, Poland, East Germany, Czechoslovakia, Hungary, Rumania, Bulgaria and Albania had become Stalin's satellites. In 1948 the Soviets challenged the West directly by blockading Berlin and, most alarming of all, in 1949 they exploded their first atomic bomb. As Britain's wartime leader Winston Churchill had warned, an 'iron curtain' was descending across Europe, and the Soviets seemed bent on 'indefinite expansion of their power and doctrines' wherever the opportunity arose. The British feared that the Soviets would next try to sweep through southern Europe, dealing a death blow to western democracy and shrinking British influence irretrievably. The next in line for communist takeover in the south was Greece, where after the Second World War a civil war raged for four years between communist forces, backed by Albania, Bulgaria and Yugoslavia, and nationalist forces, supported first by 16,000 British troops and later by the Americans. Turkey was also in Soviet sights, because of its enormous strategic value: in the West it straddled the Dardanelles, the only sea passage between the Soviet Union and the Mediterranean, and in the east it blocked one of two routes by which the Soviets could advance into the oil fields of the Middle East (the other being through the Zagros mountains of western Iran).

In a secret memo to the British Cabinet's Defence Committee in 1946, Foreign Secretary Ernest Bevin stressed that the British presence in the Mediterranean was vital to the country's position as a great power.

> The Mediterranean is the area through which we bring influence to bear on southern Europe, the soft under-belly of France, Italy, Yugoslavia, Greece and Turkey. Without our physical presence in the Mediterranean, we should cut little ice with those states

which would fall, like eastern Europe, under the totalitarian yoke. We should also lose our position in the Middle East (including Iraq oil, now one of our greatest assets).[4]

The Soviets had already been at work in Iran, a major oil supplier, where they tried to set up a communist government in the northern part of the country in 1945 and backed an attempt to assassinate the Shah in 1949. If Stalin controlled the Middle East, he would have had the power to bring Western Europe to its knees by cutting off its oil lifeline, as Adolf Hitler had secretly planned to do if Russia had fallen in the Second World War.[5]

Cyprus had a key role to play in keeping the Russians out of the Mediterranean and the Middle East through Britain's commitment to the defence of Turkey, under the Anglo-French-Turkish treaty of 1939 and, from 1951, under the North Atlantic Treaty. The chiefs of staff noted in 1951: 'Both on land and in the air Turkey is an integral part of the Middle East strategical area; a rapid collapse of Turkey in the face of Russian aggression would be disastrous to Allied plans for the defence of Egypt.'[6] They were anxious to build up a Middle East defence alliance under British auspices, of which Cyprus would be the hub, as Suez was too far south to support defence facilities in the Northern Tier, the rim of mountainous countries to the north of the Levant and the Persian Gulf which provided a land barrier between them and the USSR.[7]

Bevin recognised that the Americans, while important allies, represented an additional threat to British influence in the region as economic rivals. However, Britain's straitened circumstances after the Second World War forced an ambivalent policy towards the United States, encouraging the Americans to take responsibility for defending Western capitalism where Britain could not afford to, while trying to maintain maximum British influence over areas of key interest such as the Middle East. The Americans had their own agenda. They were happy to spend billions of dollars propping up Western European economies that provided a captive market for American exports, and to lead their collective defence under the newly-formed North Atlantic Alliance. However, while in some places they saw the British empire as a useful barrier to the spread of communism,[8] in other parts of the world they rejected it as an undesirable obstacle to free trade, and encouraged political nationalism by championing self-determination on the world stage.

Part of the price Washington exacted for supporting Britain in the Second World War was the joint declaration in 1941 by British Prime Minister Winston Churchill and the US President Franklin D Roosevelt, known as the Atlantic Charter. In it they declared their respect for 'the right of all peoples to choose the form of government under which they will live; and... to see sovereign rights and self-government restored to those who have been forcibly deprived of them'. The charter was seen by many colonies – which were contributing troops and resources to the war effort – as a firm commitment to self-government for 'all peoples'. However, a month after the declaration Churchill disingenuously claimed that the references to the rights to self-government were meant to apply only to the states occupied by Nazi Germany, not the crown colonies. The resentment this caused only inspired more support for nationalism. Churchill seemed to expect the colonies to accept that the principles they were helping Britain fight for during the war would be denied them once victory was achieved.[9]

By 1947 Britain was forced to quit India. Independence for Burma and Ceylon followed a year later. The new-found freedom in Asia inspired nationalist movements in the Arab world, challenging Britain's control of oil and the oil routes. A campaign of violence forced the British to abandon their mandate over Palestine in 1948, leading to the establishment of a Jewish state. This provided no satisfaction for the Arabs and, alarmingly for Britain, the next thrust of their nationalism came in Egypt.

Since the Anglo-Egyptian Treaty, signed by Foreign Secretary Anthony Eden in 1936, Britain had kept a large number of troops in Egypt and retained exclusive control of the Suez Canal Zone, giving her an important strategic base and ensuring free passage along the canal, essential as a trade route to the Far East and, more recently, as a shipping route for oil. But the Wafd movement was voted into office in 1950 on an anti-British ticket and the new prime minister, Nahas Pasha, opposed the Treaty. Cyprus was the only other base suited to the task.

Hard on the heels of Pasha's victory, Britain lost its virtual control of the oil industry in Iran (or Persia as it was still known by many), which supplied most of the West's oil. The new nationalist leader, Dr Muhammad Musaddiq, nationalised the Anglo-Iranian Oil Company (AIOC), in which the British Government was the majority shareholder. The company ceased operations, virtually bringing Iranian oil exports to a standstill.

Musaddiq's action also emboldened Pasha. In October 1951, he decided unilaterally to end the Anglo-Egyptian Treaty governing the Suez base without negotiations. At the same time Fedayeen guerrillas carried out attacks on British garrisons in the canal zone. In one counter-attack, British troops killed 50 Egyptians and wounded 100, which led to anti-British riots by violent mobs in Cairo. It seemed clear Britain would not now secure even its limited goal of permission to use the base in international emergencies once the troops had gone and to leave a skeleton force there to keep the installations ready. The West took this setback so seriously that the Americans, despite their professed anti-imperialism, intervened six months later, secretly using the CIA to help General Neguib topple the Cairo regime, and King Farouk. Nevertheless, Egypt and other Arab states spurned the offer to join a proposed regional military alliance against Russia similar to NATO. As the storm clouds of Arab nationalism gathered, the realisation dawned in London that Cyprus, as Britain's only colony in the region, and with its airforce base and military facilities, would soon be the only guaranteed means of protecting Britain's position in the Middle East and the

Persian Gulf. At the end of 1952, the Cabinet agreed to switch the headquarters of Britain's Middle East forces from the Suez base to Cyprus.

Even as preparations for the changeover got under way, the Cyprus facilities proved vital during a covert operation against Musaddiq in Iran in 1953. The operation had been left in the hands of the CIA in Tehran. A wireless link via RAF Habbaniyah in Iraq kept the agents in contact with British military head-quarters on Cyprus. The plan, suggested to the United States by Britain, involved the recruitment by the CIA of around 6000 anti-Musaddiq Iranians for a $20 million pay-off. But it was betrayed, and the US State Department lost its nerve, sending orders for its men to get out quick. All would have been lost, had it not been for British intelligence, which controlled the communications link with the CIA agents from facilities on Cyprus. MI6 agent Christopher Woodhouse received the State Department's pull-out signal, but delayed sending it on to Iran. The CIA officers did not move out, and chaos reigned until 19 August, when the CIA's agents stormed Tehran Radio and announced that General Zahedi was the new Prime Minister. After violent pro-Shah demonstrations, Musaddiq fled.[10] A compromise was reached in which Iranian oil remained officially nationalised but a consortium of eight Western oil companies was able to buy all the oil it wanted for 25 years.

The West had got its oil back. But the fact that the nationalisation, on whatever terms, had been upheld was yet another green light for nationalists elsewhere and, ironically, the biggest challenge came from Colonel Nasser, the real leader behind the US-backed coup in Cairo in 1952. He took control of the Government from General Neguib in February 1954, and by July had forced Britain to agree a total withdrawal from the Suez Canal base within 20 months.

The switching of Britain's Middle East military headquarters to Cyprus had to go ahead swiftly. The island was also to become the new home for MI6's regional base, controlling MI6 stations at Beirut, Tel Aviv, Amman, Jeddah, Baghdad, Tehran, Basra, Damascus, Cairo and Port Said.[11] The island also housed important early-warning radar and electronic spying stations. The intelligence gathered was shared with the Americans under a secret pact drawn up in 1947 called the UKUSA Agreement. Australia, Canada and New Zealand were also members of the UKUSA pact, each member being allotted a different area of the world to gather intelligence from – to avoid duplication. By 1955, Cyprus assumed even greater importance as the dream of a British-led strategic alliance in the Middle East was realised with the signing of the Baghdad Pact, comprising Britain, Turkey, Iraq, Iran and Pakistan.

The pact formally committed Britain to the forward defence of the region, a defence in which nuclear bombs and the Cyprus air-bases played a crucial part in deterring Soviet expansion. A Russian attack on the strategically vital oil fields could come from one of two directions: through Turkey and northern Syria into Iraq, or via Iran and through the mountains separating it from Iraq. Britain was now committed to countering both threats under its obligations to NATO and the Baghdad Pact and Cyprus – geographically better placed than the Suez Canal base, which was too far south – provided the headquarters and platform from which such operations would be launched. *The Times* reported, 'In the event of a Russian invasion through Persia, the Cyprus airfields would be necessary for the support of the ground forces in Iraq. The Middle East Land and Air Forces HQ and the brigade group being formed in Cyprus would become the nucleus of our defence against such an invasion.'[12] The vital element in those forces was the bomber squadrons operating from Cyprus, which secret British Cabinet minutes said would be capable of delivering a heavy counter-blow with nuclear weapons.[13] Nuclear bombs could be used to hold back attacking forces in the mountains long enough to allow a defensive front to be set up in Iraq. An attack on Iran and then Iraq, which Britain was pledged to defend and with whom Turkey was allied, would inevitably start a major war. That likelihood was the deterrent to open aggression in the region.

Cyprus was also needed to aid the enforcement of the 1950 tripartite declaration by which the United States, Britain and France agreed to keep the balance of arms between the Arabs and the Israelis. These tasks required good intelligence facilities and a mobile riot squad such as the strategic reserve in Cyprus would provide.

The British military presence on Cyprus – the key logistical, intelligence and air support for such operations, and the base from which the nuclear deterrent would be launched – therefore became the most important visible sign of British power and determination to keep the current order in the eastern Mediterranean and Middle East.[14] Its military facilities were needed more than ever to protect Britain's oil supplies and shipping, which, in a year without disruptions, was able to import all of Europe's oil requirements from the region.[15] As Eden succinctly put it, 'No Cyprus, no certain facilities to protect our supply of oil. No oil, unemployment and hunger in Britain. It is as simple as that.'[16]

~2~

THE ENEMY WITHIN

The Rise of the Enosis Campaign

The enthusiasm for turning Cyprus into Britain's command centre was not shared by the Cypriots. The same groundswell of nationalism that had driven Britain out of Egypt had been gathering pace in Cyprus, and the Government soon found its sovereignty over the island being challenged at the very time when it had invested so much in not letting go.

The desire for enosis – union with Greece – among the mainly Greek-Cypriot population was nothing new. Their ancestors had come to the island from the Bronze Age onwards. Since the fall of Alexander the Great, they had been invaded or controlled by the Romans, the Crusaders and the Venetians before three centuries of Ottoman rule, which had lasted until Cyprus was put under British protection in 1878, by which time about one sixth of its people were Turkish. Since the Greek war of independence in 1821 other Greek islands had one by one achieved union with the Hellenic motherland, and Cyprus hoped to do the same. In 1915, Britain offered to give Cyprus to Greece in return for immediate military support for Serbia during the First World War, but King Constantine, who was married to the Kaiser's sister, refused. When he was temporarily overthrown, the Greeks entered the war on the side of the allies in

1918, but Lloyd George ruled this too late to warrant the prize of Cyprus. Under the post-war settlement, the 1923 Treaty of Lausanne, Britain annexed the island, dashing Greek Cypriot hopes that foreign rule would end with the defeat of the Turks and the central powers. Pro-enosis sentiment boiled over in the 1930s, after a Greek-Cypriot delegation in London, asking for Cyprus to be ceded to Greece, was abruptly rebuffed. On the island, riots broke out when taxes were increased, and the Governor's house was burned down. The colonial power sent in troops and warships from Egypt, and tried to crush the nationalist movement by deporting its leaders, outlawing any mention of enosis, and abolishing the legislative council in favour of rule by decree.

It was a short-sighted response that later British leaders came to regret. Ernest Bevin, the British Foreign Secretary, pointed out to Cabinet colleagues in a secret memo in 1946 that if Britain was to develop Cyprus as a strategic base, 'our whole policy towards Cyprus will have to be reviewed, for we have starved the Cypriots, treated them very badly, and must mend our ways'.[1]

By then the world had changed. Colonised nations everywhere which had helped fight the Germans and Japanese for the freedom of the world now wanted freedom for themselves. And the Greeks on Cyprus were no exception. When British Prime Minister Clement Attlee offered them self-government under a liberal constitution in 1948, they rejected it precisely because it did not allow for self-determination. No half-measure would do, and from then on Britain faced a protracted liberation struggle on two fronts: a campaign of violence led by a battle-scarred Greek colonel, George Grivas, and relentless political pressure from a leader highly skilful in mobilising new world opinion against the colonial rulers, Makarios. If the Russians were the external threat to Britain's economic and political interests in the eastern Mediterranean, these were the enemy within.

Makarios, born Michael Mouskos in a village in western Cyprus in 1913, had the leadership of the enosis movement thrust upon him. As a novice in the Orthodox church he went to Nicosia in 1933, where he could see at first hand the effects of Britain's switch to direct rule: two of the three bishops were deported, the third was restricted to the Paphos area as a punishment for sedition, and no election was permitted for a successor to the late Archbishop. After taking the name Makarios at his ordination in 1938, the young cleric enrolled at theology college in Athens, moving on to Boston University in the United States in 1946. It was there, according to Makarios's biographer, Dr P.N. Vanezis, that he mixed with Greek nationalists, and his mind became clear on the Cyprus issue. 'He could not be proud of that part of the history of Cyprus dependent on the Crusaders, Venetians, Turks and British. They were all, in one way or another, foreign oppressors of his Hellenic homeland,' said Vanezis.[2] The election of a Labour Government in Britain gave the nationalists fresh hope – only for it to be dashed by Attlee's 1948 offer, which fell short of self-determination. The Greek Cypriots – who had fought alongside British troops in the Second World War – were bitterly disappointed.

Makarios was elected Bishop of Kitium in his absence, and returned to Cyprus, where the Archbishop, Makarios II, asked him to play a key role in re-establishing the church's political leadership of the Greek community. That role had been developed in the days of the Byzantine empire and revived under Turkish rule. But Britain's suspension of elections for Archbishop from the 1930s until 1947 had given the communist-led party, AKEL, a free rein to build up its influence, and an AKEL-led coalition won control of four out of the six town councils in 1946. In 1948 the Ethnarchy council was revamped and its leader, the young Bishop Makarios, was given responsibility for re-uniting Greek Cypriots under the church banner. He pitched himself into the emotionally-charged campaign for enosis. At a popular rally in October 1949 in Nicosia, he roused the Greek Cypriots by calling for freedom for his 'enslaved people' from the 'British yoke', and entreating them to join the 'noble struggle for union with the Motherland'.[3]

Three months later, Makarios organised a referendum of Greek Cypriots on the issue of enosis. Turkish Cypriots were excluded by virtue of the vote being taken in Greek Orthodox churches. With Greek Cypriots reportedly threatened with excommunication if they did not sign up to the cause, the yes vote was 95.7 percent, giving impetus to the campaign. No doubt it helped Makarios win the election for Archbishop, in October that year, with 97 percent of the Greek-Cypriot vote. As Archbishop, he assumed the mantle of political and spiritual leader of the Greek-Cypriot majority on Cyprus. Britain now faced a political force to be reckoned with.

Meanwhile in Athens, the first steps towards a military confrontation were being plotted by George Grivas, a 52-year-old Cypriot-born retired Greek colonel and experienced guerrilla fighter. A small wiry former lecturer in military tactics, he was a rigidly self-disciplined soldier, fanatically fit, daring and brutally single-minded. During the Second World War, Grivas had fought against the Italians and Germans in the Greek army, a campaign which is said to have caused Hitler fatefully to have delayed his invasion of Russia by six weeks. Later he formed his own private army, which fought with the British to stop the main resistance movement led by the communists from taking over once the Germans had been defeated. Like many other Cypriots who had battled alongside Allied forces in the war for 'Greece and freedom', he believed he was also fighting for the freedom of Cyprus. But after the refusal of the post-war Labour Government to consider a change in sovereignty, Grivas became convinced that only a revolution would liberate his homeland.[4]

Having spent five years systematically studying the techniques and organisation of the communist guerrillas in Greece, Grivas thought it was time to mount a military campaign in Cyprus, and sounded out the Greek Chief of General Staff, General Kosmas, on the idea. Kosmas agreed that Cyprus had to be freed by force. Two months later Grivas visited the island for the first time in 20 years and met Makarios. The Archbishop had grave doubts about whether an effective campaign could be mounted. But the Greek colonel was convinced that guerilla warfare by small groups in the mountains and saboteurs in the towns would bring results, and he returned to Athens to create a revolutionary committee.

Grivas and Makarios met again at a secret session of the committee chaired by the Archbishop on 2 July 1952 in Athens. The collaborators around the table included George Stratos, a former Greek war minister; two members of Makarios's Ethnarchy Council; a Cypriot general; Colonel Alexopoulos, a former member of Grivas's army; two Athens University professors and a lawyer. Makarios still seemed sceptical about whether enough men would be found to carry out a military struggle, and the meeting ended inconclusively. But they met again that month, without the Archbishop, and in October Grivas returned to Cyprus, against Makarios's wishes, to begin planning a series of guerrilla attacks on British installations. He spent five months studying the logistical possibilities of the island in near total secrecy, and prepared a gun-running operation to provide arms and explosives for the attacks.[5] His tactics were designed to cause 'so much confusion and damage in the ranks of the British forces' as to show the world that they were no longer in complete control. He planned to fight on three fronts: sabotage against installations and military posts; attacks on British forces by a large numbers of armed groups; and organised passive resistance by the population. Deeds of heroism and self-sacrifice would focus international attention on Cyprus until the aims were achieved. 'The British must be continuously harried and beset until they are obliged by international diplomacy, exercised through the UN, to examine the Cyprus problem and settle it in accordance with the desires of the Cypriot people and the whole Greek nation,' he said. Copies of the plan were given to Makarios. Grivas brought out of store guns which had been hidden by his private army during the Greek civil war, and weapons hoarded by others. But he knew he had to find more arms, enough to dig in for a long campaign.[6]

Makarios, meanwhile, worked to consolidate pro-enosis support on the island, and whipped up international backing from Greece and a number of non-aligned countries. In Cyprus, for instance, he denounced an attempt to 'de-Hellenise' secondary schools, by which he meant the Government's offer to pay teachers' salaries if the schools would let it choose the curriculum and the teachers, an attempt to replace enosis propaganda in the classroom with its own. He put at the head of the Church's youth movement, OHEN, a zealous supporter of enosis, Papastravos Papagathangelou, under whom religious instruction had come to include anti-British propaganda. A political youth movement, PEON (Pancyprian National Youth Organisation), was also set up, it soon becoming a recruiting ground for Grivas's guerrillas, slogan-painters and leaflet-distributers. It was outlawed in 1953.

The first thrust of Makarios's campaign to internationalise the enosis question took place in Greece. The Greek Foreign Minister, Evangelos Averoff, had in

November 1951 offered Britain four bases in Greece and any facilities it wanted in Cyprus if it would hand over the island. But British Foreign Secretary Eden flatly turned down the offer. The Greek Government, he believed, was too weak, and it would therefore be too high a risk to entrust Britain's long-term defences to it. The danger of upsetting Turkey was also too great. Neither, though he did not mention it, did he want the use of military facilities to be limited to NATO purposes. This did not discourage Makarios, who pressed the Greeks to get the Cyprus question inscribed on the UN agenda. He visited Egypt, Lebanon and Syria in the spring of 1952 to lobby for support. When Greek leaders rebuked him for demanding an initiative at the UN, he appealed over their heads. With the help of the Greek primate and trade unions, popular demonstrations were organised, and Makarios publicly warned the Greek people that their leaders were pursuing a devious course and that Britain had slammed shut all doors on any idea of talks. He told them they must demand that the issue be brought before the UN.

The moral argument behind Makarios's case was boosted in November when, though not mentioning Cyprus, the UN passed a resolution calling on all member states to apply the principle of self-determination to peoples in non-self-governing territories under their control. But when the Greek Government, headed by Field-Marshal Papagos, who had led the nationalist forces in the Greek civil war, refused to act on enosis, Makarios told Grivas it was time for dynamic action.[7] His only concern was that it should be sabotage, not armed revolt, and he sent a message to the guerrilla leader asking him to supply mines and hand grenades. Papagos was reluctant to upset Britain and Turkey, Greece's military partners in NATO, of which it had just become a full member, by challenging British sovereignty in Cyprus. But Makarios twisted the knife. Addressing a meeting attended in force by AKEL, he said, 'In our effort to win the freedom we desire we shall stretch out both our right hand and our left to take the help offered by East and West'. Thus Papagos was caught between his country's defence allegiance and the political need to back the popular campaign for enosis – which Makarios was threatening to turn into an anti-Western movement.

Papagos pinned his hopes on a meeting with Eden, who visited Athens in September 1953 while he was supposed to be convalescing after a series of operations. However, when the Greek premier asked Eden for a sign that Britain would help by moving on Cyprus, Eden erupted, telling him that enosis 'would never happen'. He even enquired sarcastically why the Greeks did not ask for Alexandria or New York, where there were so many of their countrymen.[8] The bilious outburst enraged Papagos, who resolved to punish Eden's arrogance by bringing the matter before the UN, as Makarios wished, thus internationalising the problem.[9] Eden's ill-temper may have been just that. He was suffering from a botched operation on his gall bladder and two further operations to unblock his bile duct, all since the beginning of April. He remained prone to bouts of fever.

For years the British policy had been simply to keep Cyprus out of the news as much as possible, but in a memo prepared for the Cabinet in July 1954, the Colonial Secretary, Oliver Lyttleton, and Foreign Minister, Selwyn Lloyd, warned that this negative line was no longer adequate. In Athens, Papagos had taken up the Cyprus question with 'great energy', they said, and threatened to raise the whole issue at the UN on 22 August. British diplomats had warned the Greeks that nothing but harm could result from such action, but Lyttleton admitted that a 'deterioration in our relations with Greece is the price we must pay if we are to keep Cyprus. The point may even come at which we shall have to decide whether Cyprus is strategically more important to us than Greece'.[10]

The new Governor of Cyprus, Sir Robert Armitage, told the ministers that the containment of the enosis movement was long overdue. He believed this called for a dispelling of any notion that the Government might allow self-determination for Cyprus. The problem was that the absence of local representatives on the Governor's Executive Council in Cyprus was 'difficult to defend'. Lyttleton recommended an offer of a limited form of self-government under a 'more restricted' constitution than the 1948 offer, but coupled with a firm statement that sovereignty was not going to be abandoned by Britain in the foreseeable future. The Cabinet seemed oblivious to the impact this less generous offer might have on the Cypriots.[11] During a statement on the proposals on 28 July 1954, Churchill's Colonial Minister, Henry Hopkinson, duly told the House of Commons that some Commonwealth territories could 'never' expect to be fully independent, and that the question of the abrogation of British sovereignty 'cannot arise'.

In the eyes of the Greek-Cypriot population this blew the lid off any pretence that Britain would eventually move towards self-determination. It seemed Britain viewed Cyprus above all as a strategic base, and democratic ideals could not be allowed to get in the way. Secret documents, released under the 30-year rule, show their suspicions were true. Just two days before Hopkinson's devastating and fateful pronouncement, the Cabinet discussed its approach to the Cyprus question in the light of the growing pressure from Papagos at the UN and a firm decision to transfer the Middle East Land Forces HQ from Suez to the island. The Cabinet was told that nothing less than continued sovereignty over the island could enable Britain to carry out its strategic obligations in Europe, the Mediterranean and the Middle East.[12] The day before Hopkinson's speech, Britain signed the agreement with Egypt for a total evacuation of British troops over 20 months. Without Suez, the chiefs of staff believed, there was no question of letting Cyprus go. But by telling the world this, Hopkinson was denying the Greek Cypriots the chance even to dream of achieving their goal. Politically, it handed Makarios the backing of the Greek-Cypriot people on a plate. But it was no fool's blunder. The policy had been agreed in advance by the Cabinet.

Lyttleton added insult to injury by publicly repeating the argument Eden had used privately in 1951 against Greek rule in Cyprus: 'I cannot imagine any policy more disastrous for Cyprus than to hand it to an unstable power, however friendly,' he said, ensuring his gloomy prediction of deteriorating relations with Greece came true.

Makarios, furious at Hopkinson's statement, rejected the new constitutional plan out of hand and gave the go-ahead for a campaign of sabotage. He warned, 'We shall consider as enemies of our national cause those who may give in to the Government's constitutional pressure. We shall brand such persons as traitors, and we shall be unable to protect them from the people's rage and shame.' He paid for a boat to take Grivas to Cyprus, and he urged the colonel to speed up the dispatch of arms to the island. He wanted action before the debate at the UN in December, to persuade the Americans that an adverse attitude would start trouble in Cyprus, and thus in the Middle East. Though Grivas thought this schedule was unrealistic, on 26 October he left his house in Athens without telling even his wife where he was going, embarked on a ship at Piraeus and sailed for Rhodes, from where a fishing boat took him the remaining 200 miles to a rocky stretch of Cyprus's western coast, near Paphos.

Operating at first from safe houses in Nicosia, Grivas began recruiting and training members of his guerrilla organisation in the use of automatics and the art of sabotage. The organisation was to be called EOKA (the initial letters of the Greek words for National Organisation of Cypriot Combatants). Its aim was to use terrorism to provoke the British into acts of oppression that would turn world opinion against the colonial power and force it to withdraw from the island. First, police stations and other installations were to be sabotaged to show that there was a nationalist force prepared to oppose British rule. At the same time schoolchildren would be encouraged to protest, inspiring nationalist pride in their parents. Second, Greek-Cypriot collaborators or opponents of EOKA would be severely punished, or even executed, to deter potential informers and assist the exacting of funds. Then British troops would be killed with the aim of provoking severe counter-measures that would unite the Greek Cypriots against the British.[13]

At the United Nations, the Cyprus issue was voted onto the agenda by the General Assembly, but the Political Committee passed a resolution putting off a decision on it 'for the time being'. In Greece, there were violent protests. In Cyprus, there was widespread anger, culminating in the proclamation of a general strike and riots, in which three youths were shot by British troops. The conditions were perfect for Grivas to begin his activities. At the end of December, he sent out a sabotage group to reconnoitre targets, including the Cyprus broadcasting service at Athalassa and two military wireless stations nearby.

Grivas built up EOKA to a force of 300 fighters, organised in small bands or cells of between five and ten men. Members of each cell graduated to the role of assassin only after training by stages, involving slogan-painting and bomb-throwing. The central HQ was secret and mobile and, to avoid detection by British intelligence, all orders were communicated by hand through an elaborate system of couriers. A political organisation called PEKA was set up, and many of its members were teachers and priests.[14] Its role was to indoctrinate the villagers and children with pro-enosis propaganda.

In January 1955, a sudden impetus was given to the planned struggle when Makarios, arriving back from the United States, met Grivas and told him that Papagos, having failed to win the support of the UN, wanted action too.[15] The Archbishop offered to put up the money to smuggle more arms. Earlier that month, EOKA had received 600kgs of dynamite, 2200 detonators, 18 pistols and 12 hand grenades. Grivas speeded up the preparations, even threatening to 'execute all those who will not conform to my instructions'.[16]

Expecting trouble, the British created a Special Branch on Cyprus, which achieved its first success on 26 January when HMS *Comet*, acting on intelligence information, intercepted a fishing boat on which 10,000 sticks of dynamite were found, along with arms, hand grenades and ammunition. Thirteen Cypriots were arrested. The boat and its arms had been paid for by Makarios, but its capture did not put him off. In a sermon in Nicosia on 14 February, he said, 'We are more determined than ever to put an end to British sovereignty over Cyprus. Strict British laws and imprisonments will not prevent our campaign from ending in enosis.'[17] Grivas, meanwhile, was busy organising mountain gangs so that he could be ready to shift the centre of his operations into the hills for greater security. He trained them in bomb-making with the help of funding from Makarios – £200 a month – and supplies of explosives from mines and quarries. On 2 March another arms cargo landed, this time successfully. It comprised three BREN guns, four sub-machine-guns, some automatics, seven revolvers, 47 rifles, 20kgs of explosives, around 300 hand-grenades and some 400,000 rounds of ammunition. Three weeks later, Grivas told Makarios that he was ready to start the struggle, and on 29 March the Archbishop gave him his blessing.[18]

In the early hours of 1 April 1955, 16 bombs went off across the island, and the Cyprus Broadcasting Corporation (CBC) transmitters were attacked as EOKA began a campaign of bomb attacks and sabotage. The heavily guarded secret wireless interception base at Ayios Nikolaos, home of 9 Signal Regiment, was rocked by an explosion. Other targets hit were the radio tower at Wolseley barracks, the two CBC transmitters at Athalassa and Lakatamia outside Nicosia, government offices, police stations and military installations. The Episkopi power plant was sabotaged. One bomb exploded outside a Nicosia hotel which the Governor, Sir Robert Armitage, had just left. Another was placed in the house of a Turkish-Cypriot official in Larnaca. One EOKA man was electrocuted as he tried to cut off the electricity supply to Nicosia. Grivas drew up his first revolutionary proclamation calling on the Greek Cypriots to throw off the English yoke and 'be worthy of the Greek heroes'. He warned that the struggle would be hard, but said, 'If our rulers refuse to give us back our freedom, we shall claim it with our own hands and with our own blood'.[19]

Over the next four years, 600 people were to be killed, the majority of them Greek-Cypriot, and 1260 wounded. Of 238 civilian casualties, 203 were Greek Cypriots; 156 British servicemen died. Four thousand seven hundred and fifty-eight bombs were to be manufactured, of which 1782 exploded, causing millions of pounds' worth of damage.[20]

On 6 May, the Colonial Secretary repeated the British position on Cyprus in the House of Commons. Athens Radio reported that the British Government had once more said 'never' to negotiations, and called on all Cypriots to be ready to rise up in arms if the new British Government, to be elected on 26 May, adopted the same policy. The day before the election another attempt in Cyprus to blow up the Governor failed as a bomb exploded in a cinema after he left. In a sermon in Athens, Makarios told the Greeks, 'Stand by your Greek-Cypriot brothers to the end. I give you an assurance that the Cypriots have reached the decision – an irrevocable decision – to be free of foreign rule. We shall not be afraid, we shall not be intimidated, we shall not bow to illiberal laws, oppression, imprisonment, exile or even death. All for freedom. Long live freedom!'[21] The British election returned the Government of Eden, Churchill's successor as Tory leader. The urgent task before him was to find a way of preventing the situation in the last safe haven in the eastern Mediterranean exploding in his hands.

~3~

THE SECRET ALLIANCE

Eden Stokes Turkish Violence

The Cabinet was divided over how to defuse the threat to British sovereignty. Foreign Secretary Harold Macmillan and Colonial Secretary Alan Lennox-Boyd warned ministers in June 1955 that the Greek Government would raise the Cyprus issue at the next UN General Assembly, and that this time it was unlikely that Britain could defeat or outflank them with procedural tricks. Neither could Britain rely on the same support from the Americans, unless some forward move was made. At the same time, they added, '… the situation in Cyprus itself will become still more intractable. Terrorism may take root and lead to outrages which would make any political settlement even more difficult.'

Eden favoured trying to trick the Greek Cypriots into co-operation with self-government in return for a pledge to discuss the status of the island at some future stage. This would be no more than an empty promise, as he planned to tell the Turkish Government in secret that 'we contemplate no change of sovereignty in the foreseeable future' and 'we intend to stay in Cyprus as long as the world situation makes it necessary for us to do so'.[1] But he thought the offer would give the Greek Government the chance to back down without losing face, and might swing American support in Britain's favour. Lennox-Boyd and Macmillan opposed trying to clamp down on the enosis movement without offering a new initiative. They called for three-way talks with Greece and Turkey to break the deadlock. But Eden insisted that Greek claims to Cyprus were ill-founded, and that the policy of firmness had already had some effect on Greek public opinion, whereas agreeing to discuss the matter with Greece would make Britain look weak. He put off a decision.[2]

However, international pressure against Britain's intransigence mounted. First Argentina gave its support to Greece's appeal to the UN over Cyprus. Then Britain was put on trial at the first international congress of jurists in Athens, where one professor sought to prove that self-determination was a principle of elementary justice, and as such should be applied to the Cypriots as much as anyone else. When he was ruled out of order, the case was taken up by the Americans, who wanted self-determination to be set down as a fundamental principle of justice for all people, and a motion was carried which repudiated the non-application of that principle, citing Cyprus as an example. Jurists from 48 countries backed a declaration reaffirming their faith in the rights of the individual, including freedom of speech, freedom of the press, of worship, of assembly, and of association, and the right to free elections – rights that were severely limited in Cyprus by the unelected British administration.[3] Only a week later, schoolchildren on the island were fined for tearing up a picture of the Queen, and Greek communist magazines were ruled seditious, and banned.

The intervention of the American jurists was a worrying sign for Eden: if their views were echoed in the Washington administration, any vote in the forthcoming UN session might go against Britain. Ideologically, American foreign policy was strongly influenced by the pursuit of individual liberty; economically, it used its superpower status to expand its trading interests worldwide. In its denial of self-determination, the British empire was the enemy of the first; in its economic control of the colonies, an obstacle to the second. During and since the Second World War, America had pushed for self-determination everywhere, and had used this moral crusade partly to stave off communism, but also to prise Britannia's ageing fingers off the trinket boxes of the empire, the colonies. America had her own plans for the soft markets and cheap resources they offered. In the Middle East, the prize was oil, and Washington stood to boost its influence at the expense of Britain's if it was seen to oppose Britain's undemocratic approach to the Cyprus question.

President Eisenhower's address to the UN's tenth anniversary meeting on 20 June caused acute embarrassment in London. Speaking in the same San Francisco building where the UN Charter was signed a decade earlier, he made an impassioned plea to all member nations to reaffirm the principles on which the UN had been established. These were 'That every people has the inherent right to the kind of government under which it chooses to live and the right to select in full freedom the individuals who conduct that government'. The

Charter declared 'That on every nation in possession of foreign territories there rests the responsibility to assist the peoples of those areas in the progressive development of free political institutions so that ultimately they can validly choose for themselves their permanent political status'. Eisenhower called on all member nations to rededicate themselves to these ideals.[4] Four days after Eisenhower's speech, Britain's permanent representative at the UN, Sir Pierson Dixon, warned that time was running out to secure US support at the UN. Eden himself feared that defeat at the hands of the Greeks would lead to perennial trouble, such as the riots in French North Africa that followed the 'annual row' at the UN.[5]

That risk was underlined by a new outbreak of violence on Cyprus. The day before Eisenhower's speech, British soldiers became the target of EOKA attacks for the first time. Bombs exploded in two British-owned bars in Nicosia and the south-western port of Famagusta, putting at risk the lives of dozens of servicemen and their friends. Two days later, four bombs went off in Nicosia, another four in Famagusta, and one each in Larnaca and Limassol. Elsewhere on the island, two bombs were set off outside the Kyrenia home of General Sir Charles Keightley, Commander-in-Chief Middle-East Land Forces, and masked men attacked a police station at Lapithos. The next day there were nine explosions, five of them in the homes of British army officers. Dynamite was thrown on to the balcony of a house in Famagusta, seriously wounding a British military wire operator.[6]

Armitage warned Eden that he might have to declare a state of emergency on the island within days – and put Makarios under lock and key.[7] Police commissioner George Robins announced plans for a 1500-strong mobile reserve police force, and the biggest rewards ever offered in Cyprus were put up for information leading to the arrest of killers who had shot dead a sergeant at Amiandos police station, and for news about terrorists or illicit arms and explosives. But crowds took to the streets to support arrested EOKA suspects.

The disorders gave Greece a new pretext for taking up the issue at the next session of the UN. Eden had to decide now whether to give the go-ahead for a conference – to offset further criticism at the UN – or a crackdown. The latter would jeopardise any chance of the conference succeeding. On 28 June, Eden brought the issue to Cabinet himself. He decided the conference would provide a chance to change the international perception of the Cyprus problem as a purely anti-colonial struggle and put the spotlight on the antagonism between Greece and Turkey instead. This would put pressure on Athens to accept a compromise plan that suited Britain.[8]

The Cabinet agreed, on condition that the invitation avoided publicly conceding that foreign governments could have a say in the future of Cyprus. No invitations were to be sent to the Cypriots, and the NATO allies, Greece and Turkey, were to be told that after giving further consideration to strategic issues in the area, the Government was inviting them to 'a conference in London on the political and defence questions affecting the Eastern Mediterranean, including Cyprus'. It was as if the island's problems were merely one item on the agenda. This was meant to send reassuring signals not only to MPs in London but also to those members of UKUSA – the international network for collecting and sharing intelligence information – which might be worried about the implications of any changes in the status of Cyprus, or the facilities there. The UKUSA countries – the United States, Canada, Australia and New Zealand – were told about the conference initiative a day before it was made public. Unfortunately, not everyone in Whitehall was aware of the real subject-matter of the talks. One meeting of defence chiefs was told that the Foreign Office felt that, in view of the title of the talks, a representative of the chiefs of staff should be in the British delegation. The matter was hurriedly put right. The chiefs-of-staff committee minuted that this would be unsuitable 'as they understood the title of the talks was a political cover and the talks were in fact intended to be purely political'.[9]

The gleeful reaction of the Papagos Government to the conference invitation gave way rapidly to suspicion. They suspected (correctly) that it was a British trap to undermine Greece's new appeal to the UN. It would also mean letting the old enemy, Turkey, have a say in the future of Cyprus, raising an obstacle to enosis potentially more lasting than even British control of the island.[10]

Shortly after Eden's decision, the Defence Minister, Lloyd asked for the views of the chiefs of staff on the military importance of Cyprus, the threats to internal security, and the likely effects of possible political solutions which might be reached at the conference. A top secret report was drawn up by the military chiefs' close advisers, senior diplomats, and top intelligence and security advisers. They warned Lloyd against conceding any real power to the Cypriots. They said that Britain's military needs on the island could only be met if the control of defence, external affairs and internal security remained in British hands. Anticipating that the questions of self-government and self-determination would be raised at the talks, they warned that retaining all Britain's military facilities was strategically essential, and that without them British prestige and influence in the Middle East would be lost. It would destroy the attempts to create a Middle East defence organisation. 'We must therefore have full control of the island in all respects in war,' they said.[11] Furthermore, long-term plans to expand the facilities on Cyprus to match its new strategic role were already well underway. The army and RAF were scheduled to complete by 1959 the headquarters of the Middle East Land Forces and of the Middle East Air Force at Episkopi, and permanent barracks at Dhekelia housing three infantry battalions and a brigade headquarters. Also by then, the airfield at Akrotiri, earmarked for a nuclear bombing role, would be operational.[12]

They warned that if EOKA violence continued it would escalate into attacks on British servicemen, and that bloodshed at the hands of British soldiers would inspire a widespread campaign of passive resistance, hindering the efficiency of the military facilities and diverting soldiers from important strategic tasks. But the biggest worry was the potential for deliberate violence between Greek and Turkish Cypriots, which would 'seriously impair the efficiency of Cyprus as a base'. This danger would grow if the Turkish Cypriots and the Turks came to believe that Britain seriously intended to hand the island over to Greece.[13]

The military men discounted a number of the political options available. Granting an elected assembly, they said, could lead to victory for the communists, who would force the British off the island. The introduction of a constitution with provision for eventual self-determination would stimulate agitation for a speedier hand-over of the island, leaving Britain leasing bases from Greece and dependent on Athens' goodwill. The best option, they thought, was to declare a firm intention to retain sovereignty over Cyprus, while offering a liberal constitution under which the Greek and Turkish Governments would have some association with the administration of the island. They admitted this would lead to more intense violence, but believed this could be quelled through a costly, substantial and possibly sustained military and security commitment. The United States would be hostile, and relations within NATO would be strained. But it would benefit Britain's defence relations in the Middle East. Those countries – like Turkey, Iraq and Jordan – which supported Britain and respected military strength 'would be encouraged to rely on us in their own defensive alignments'.[14]

On 23 July, Lloyd, leading a Cabinet discussion on tactics for the conference, employing the defence chiefs' arguments, suggested Britain should use Turkey's opposition to enosis to help protect Britain's defence interests on Cyprus. 'Throughout the negotiations our aim would be to bring the Greeks up against the Turkish refusal to accept enosis and so condition them to accept a solution which would leave sovereignty in our hands.' He wanted the participants to be kept talking for as long as the UN Assembly was in session.[15]

Eden agreed that Turkish anger was the key to protecting British interests. Turkey needed the British military presence on Cyprus, which was committed to the defence of Turkey's southern flank as well as the Middle East.[16] He decided to turn Turkish fears of any British pull-out to his advantage by collaborating secretly and continuously with them on the island's future. First, it was essential to win Turkey's trust by demonstrating that Britain would not let itself be stampeded off the island.[17] In the run-up to the talks he ordered a raft of new measures against the enosis movement on Cyprus to show that Britain was serious about keeping control. A law was passed enabling the detention without trial of suspected EOKA supporters. The security forces were empowered to stop and search vehicles for explosives and weapons. Reconnaissance aircraft began making routine flights from Nicosia's RAF station, and naval patrol boats began patrolling Cyprus's waters for arms smugglers. Restrictions were placed on the possession of firearms, and the penalty for illegal possession was doubled to six months in prison. An auxiliary police force was also formed, made up entirely of Turkish Cypriots.[18]

The Greek Cypriots protested against the new detention law with a 24-hour general strike. In Nicosia, hundreds rioted, setting fire to the British Council building, and police fired shots and tear gas to break them up. Grivas also went on the offensive, now terrorising Greek Cypriots in the local police to force them to turn a blind eye to EOKA activities. By the end of August, five policemen had been shot. There were also guerrilla raids on police stations and several incidents of sabotage – including explosions at two British military installations in Famagusta.

Confident that the tacit alliance with Turkey would work, Macmillan warned ministers two weeks before the talks that they were likely to end in deadlock, and that firm action would have to be taken to handle the disorders that would break out.[19] Police pay was increased, steps were taken to appoint a director of operations to co-ordinate the activities of the police and armed forces, and the Governor demanded police reinforcements with experience in colonial hot-spots such as Malaya and Kenya.[20] By 18 August, 57 men had been arrested under the detention law, and just days before the conference opened, troops practised an island-wide road-block exercise in readiness for any emergency. Makarios remained defiant. He said, 'We shall not yield, and we shall not lose heart'. But the British Government's unflinching approach was providing satisfaction in Ankara. Turkish Foreign Minister Nuri Birgi told American Secretary of State John Foster Dulles that, as Britain was now taking a tough line towards the terrorists, the Cyprus problem was on the way to a solution.[21]

Eden let it be known to the British Embassy in Ankara that he was sure it was 'in our interest' if Turkey spoke out on the issue, even if this meant being rigid and 'violently' anti-Greek at the conference.[22] The Turkish newspapers issued a fierce warning that Greek-Cypriot autonomy would mean the end of the Turkish alliance with Britain. In London, the Turkish Prime Minister, Adnan Menderes, arriving for the talks, said that Ankara wished to see no change in the Cyprus status quo, but publicly warned that if there were to be a change, the island should revert to Turkey. The Turks, Eden confidently concluded, 'would never let the Greeks have Cyprus'. He was prepared to risk the serious rift this policy might cause in the south-eastern wing of NATO. Britain's Middle East defence position came first.

The conference opened in London on 29 August, and proceeded according to plan. The Greeks, while offering safeguards to the Turkish Cypriots, demanded an immediate plebiscite on self-determination for Cyprus. The Turks vehemently opposed them. They threatened to treat any changes as an abandonment of the Treaty of Lausanne and counter-claim against Greece in Thrace and the Dodecanese. They insisted that if Britain gave up control, sovereignty must return to Ankara, since in a war Turkey could be supplied only through her southern ports, and whoever controlled Cyprus was in a position to control those ports, making the island strategically vital.[23] Stunned by Turkey's hard-line stance, the Greeks dropped their insistence on an immediate plebiscite, but still argued that self-government should lead to self-determination for Cyprus within five years. The Turks would only accept self-government if they were fully satisfied that Britain would not yield on the island's international status.[24]

Macmillan, under orders to make no concessions on self-determination, proposed to the conference that it record that since it was unable to agree on the future status of the island, proceedings were being adjourned and would be reconvened at some time in the future. He hoped it might then include elected representatives from Cyprus, as he was offering them a constitution providing for an elected majority and a quota of seats and ministerial portfolios for Turkish Cypriots. In case they had not grasped the full implication of what he was saying, Macmillan added in a statement the next night, 'We do not accept the principle of self-determination as one of universal application. We think that exceptions must be made in view of geographical, traditional historical, strategic, and other considerations'. And in reply to a Turkish question as to whether Britain intended to maintain the status of the island, he said, 'I am bound to say that there is no prospect of any change in the foreseeable future'.[25]

Days later, Eden's prediction that raising Cyprus's future with the Turks would be explosive proved remarkably accurate. Turkish anger boiled over into savage anti-Greek riots in Istanbul, Izmir and Ankara. Greek homes and property were smashed up, and churches were ransacked. *The Times*[26] reported suspicions that the riots were organised. They appeared carefully synchronised, taking place simultaneously in districts far apart from each other. The usually efficient Turkish police were apparently unable to cope with the emergency, and the rioters acted with little interference for three-and-a-half hours. The reason given for the delay in police action was the fact that both President Bayar and Prime Minister Menderes were in a train on the way to Ankara, and no-one could order extraordinary measures in their absence. The violence shocked Athens.

A fortnight later, Eden used the Turkish outburst to ask the Americans for help at the UN. He claimed the Greeks had started the trouble and that it would continue until the agitation for enosis ended.[27] The only thing that would stop the unrest was a clear majority at the UN against the Greek motion, and this could not be achieved without US support. The Americans reluctantly consented. At the UN, Macmillan's deputy, Minister of State at the Foreign Office Anthony Nutting, argued that, given the inflamed situation on Cyprus, 'quiet diplomacy' would do more good than international debate. On 23 September the Assembly voted by 28 to 22, with 10 abstentions, to leave the issue off the agenda.[28]

Playing the Turkish card had worked: it had relieved the international pressure on Britain, temporarily at least. But for Eden this was not merely a short-term policy. In October he told his Cabinet that Turkey was pivotal to the Northern Tier defence arrangements, and that this factor must be kept in mind in *all* considerations of the Cyprus question.[29]

~4~

MILITARY CRACKDOWN

Harding Gets Tough

Two days after the vote at the UN, on 25 September 1955, Eden removed Armitage as Governor of Cyprus. The replacement was a top military commander, Sir John Harding, and he was given a powerful mandate to crush opposition to British rule with all the forces at his disposal. The fifty-nine-year-old Harding was the retiring Chief of the Imperial General Staff (CIGS), and had a distinguished military career and a keen understanding of Cyprus's strategic value. During the Second World War, he had commanded the Seventh Armoured Division in the Western Desert and become Chief of Staff to Field Marshal Alexander in Italy. He rose to Commander-in-Chief Far East and later Germany, and was made CIGS in 1952, a post which brought him into contact with the military leaders of Greece and Turkey. One of his last tasks as CIGS was to impress on ministers the need to keep a firm grip on Cyprus for military reasons. It was, he said, a place of 'outstanding importance… for the British military effort in the area and for Middle East defence as a whole'.[1] After a recent visit to Cyprus to see the situation at first hand, Harding had warned that the EOKA threat was so serious that it could develop into a full-scale rebellion, and advised Eden to concentrate all the security operations on the island in the hands of one man. Though Macmillan opposed a military appointment, Eden gave Harding a free hand to get tough with the guerrillas and a powerful mandate to crush opposition to British rule. Political talks soon became less of a priority, except to drive a wedge between Makarios and Grivas on the issue of co-operating with self-government.

The importance of Harding's task was underlined by the announcement on 27 September 1955 of an arms deal between Colonel Nasser of Egypt and the Eastern Bloc. For weeks weapons had been secretly dispatched to Cairo from Czechoslovakia and the Soviet Union. They included 50 MiG 15 fighters, 45 Illyushin bombers and 115 heavy tanks as good as the Soviet Union's best, and better than any the Israelis possessed.[2] In a single move, the Russians had given the Egyptians a dangerous superiority in weapons over the Israelis. This was exactly the type of threat which Britain's military presence in Cyprus was intended to counter. Macmillan told the Cabinet that the Soviets were also making overtures to supply arms to Saudi Arabia, Syria and possibly others. There was a serious danger that they would try to entice all the Arab states away from the West. It was essential, therefore, to keep the situation in Cyprus, the home of Britain's most important base in the Middle East, under control.

But Makarios had other ideas. He launched a campaign of passive resistance to British rule to cause as much disruption as possible. He called on all Greek Cypriots to withdraw from serving on public bodies, and told a 4000-strong meeting that the Cypriot people 'will not abandon the struggle, even if the whole island is converted into a prison camp'. He even worked with communist trade union leaders for the first time in a general strike in protest at the UN's decision not to debate the Cyprus question.[3]

Harding flew in battalions of troops and police reinforcements, imposed curfews on troublesome villages, and held private talks with Makarios, trying to persuade him to co-operate on self-government with the prospect of further talks on self-determination at a future date if self-government was successfully implemented.

British troops began to impose night curfews on Cyprus in the run-up to the Greek and Turkish national holidays on 28 and 29 October, and demonstrations were banned on the days themselves. But the passing of a death sentence on an EOKA gunman led to the the first death of a British soldier, when EOKA retaliated with a grenade attack. On Greek national day itself there was rioting in Famagusta, some of the thousands who took part threw dynamite and stones, and 500 people were held by the police. There were clashes with troops and police in Larnaca, where schoolchildren stoned the security forces, and at Limassol, where there was a 24-hour general strike in protest at the curfew.

Seeking to break the deadlock, Eden secretly agreed a new policy formula with Harding. It stated that Britain no longer believed the principle of self-determination could 'never' be applicable to Cyprus, but it was 'not now a practicable proposition' due to the 'present strategic importance of the island' and 'consequences on relations between NATO powers in the Eastern Mediterranean'.[4] There was no real intention behind it of granting self-determination. With Nasser agitating against the West, the main priority was to protect Britain's oil interests in the region, and for this the strengthening of ties with Turkey, which was crucial to the Baghdad Pact, had to be kept constantly in mind. He wrote to the Turkish premier, Adnan Menderes, to reassure him that the purpose of the new initiative was not to abandon Britain's or Turkey's interest in Cyprus.[5]

Harding presented the new formula to Makarios in secret on 21 November, during an explosion of EOKA violence. On 18 November, there were 30 bombings at British Army camps and installations across the island. One killed a sergeant and seriously wounded a warrant officer at Kykko camp near Nicosia. The bomb was hidden in the saddle-bag of a bicycle left against a wall, and blew the roof off the sergeants' mess. Another destroyed Nicosia's General Post Office. Others were tossed into bars frequented by servicemen and officers' homes, and one into the headquarters of 51 Brigade. The attacks continued for three days. There were gun battles in the mountains. In Famagusta, 200 soldiers fought with EOKA men in the streets after guerrillas sprayed an army patrol with bullets. There were also demonstrations in the towns, which were broken up by tear-gas and baton charges, and pupil protests in schools.[6]

Makarios was not hoodwinked by the formula. Even Harding, expecting an *impasse*, drew up his own contingency plans to deport him to the Seychelles, along with the Bishop of Kyrenia.[7] Eden, however, had not given up hope of gaining Makarios's co-operation, and the details of the talks and their failure were kept under wraps.

As there was no halt to EOKA's violence – Grivas claimed several hundred acts of sabotage were carried out in the first week of his new bombing campaign[8] – Harding declared a state of emergency. He announced the death penalty for possessing arms or explosives, and life imprisonment for sabotage. Even the carrying of stones could be punished with two years' imprisonment. Political protest strikes were outlawed. All assemblies, with the exception of cinema and theatre audiences and religious services, were banned. Long-term prison sentences could be given for wearing a uniform, drilling, and sheltering suspects. Convicted males under eighteen could be whipped. Entire villages could be fined, shops and houses closed down, and property confiscated. Harding could silence church bells, ban flags, restrict the movements of individuals, censor mail and control telephone calls.

The draconian measures did not deter a planned attempt on Harding's life. At a ball at the Ledra Palace Hotel, a waiter switched off the lights and threw two hand-grenades across the crowded dance floor, injuring the wife of the Cyprus Police Commissioner and others. Fortunately for Harding, he had not been able to attend.[9]

Armed with his new powers, Harding put 10,000 British troops on a war footing, detained church leaders, and punished troublesome villages. At

Lefkonico on 3 December 1955, the first collective fine was imposed after youths burned down the post office. The men of the village had to pay £2000 between them towards reconstruction, and Harding closed down the high school. Over 1000 men, from shepherds to businessmen, were taken from their homes in police vans to the police station. The payments ranged from four shillings to £35, and a curfew was imposed until the £2000 had been collected.

The tough measures played into Makarios's hands, enabling him to win more support, not just in Cyprus but in Greece and internationally. Indeed, they were exactly the type of measure Grivas had tried to provoke through EOKA's violent resistance. Eden appealed personally to the new Greek Prime Minister, Constantine Karamanlis, to recommend his formula to the Archbishop. But Karamanlis thought it so qualified by strategic considerations that it made the implied promise of self-determination worthless. The Americans were ambivalent.

Eden was dismayed. He could not understand why neither the Greeks, nor the Americans, nor the UN, would take the Turkish position seriously. For him, the moral argument in favour of self-determination came low on the list of priorities – it doesn't surface in any of the minutes of Cabinet discussions. It was simply a matter of recognising the relative strength of British and Turkish interests: 'In geography and in tactical considerations, the Turks have the stronger claim in Cyprus; in race and language, the Greeks; in strategy, the British, so long as their industrial life depends on oil supplies from the Persian Gulf'.[10]

After more EOKA raids, Harding sent masses of troops on large-scale sweeps in the mountains of western Cyprus, where Grivas was based. As dawn broke on 8 December, 1000 troops, including Marine Commandos, searched 25 monasteries throughout the island for weapons. Detonators, Sten guns and army clothing were found. Over the next few days, security operations were extended into surrounding villages in a bid to flush out EOKA activists.[11] On 11 December, army lorries carrying hundreds of troops roared into the village of Spilia, situated down the mountainside from Grivas's dugout, which had been serving as his headquarters. According to the EOKA leader, the operation, which was the first large-scale attempt to root him out, ended in chaos when hundreds of confused soldiers opened fire on each other in the mist. Grivas had escaped the pincer movement by fleeing five miles west across unguarded roads. Five days later he and his group were passed by another convoy looking for him, which he estimated at 50 trucks and 1000 men.[12]

While these operations were underway, Harding turned on the other 'enemy within', the communists. He outlawed AKEL and its youth, women's and farmers' organisations, seized its printing equipment, and shut down its newspaper. In dawn raids, security forces arrested 135 AKEL members, including its general secretary, Ezekias Papaiannou, who had pressured Makarios to demand immediate self-determination and an end to the use of Cyprus as a base. Defence chiefs feared the communists more than EOKA because they believed they had the greater potential power, and could ultimately do more damage to British defence interests by switching the island's allegiance to the Soviet Bloc. When news of the ban reached the factories many workers downed tools and joined protests. The strikers included thousands engaged in construction work at the expanding military camps at Dhekelia and Akrotiri, part of the programme of upgrading the island's facilities for its enhanced military role. The demonstrations were broken up by commandos firing tear gas.

Trouble brewing in the Middle East made the situation more critical. Nasser's agents were stirring up opposition to Western influence in the Arab states and, with each instalment of Eastern Bloc arms, he grew more confident of being able to take revenge on Israel for the defeat of 1948. The most immediate concern for the British was that this might provoke a pre-emptive strike from Israel, which could exploit internal unrest in Jordan by invading the West Bank. In Jordan's capital, Amman, the Government had resigned after violent protests against plans to join the Western-backed Baghdad Pact, in which the rioters called for the withdrawal of the British officers who commanded Jordan's infantry division, mobile armoured force and airforce. The trouble was being fomented by Egypt and Saudi Arabia. British defence chiefs feared that at any moment Israel might attack Egypt or Jordan to prevent Nasser creating a new enemy, unrestrained by British influence, on her doorstep. Such a conflict would threaten oil interests and might escalate into a global war. Plans were approved to use Cyprus as the command centre and launch-pad for the defence of Jordan and the prevention of an Arab-Israeli war.[13]

In January 1956, over 100 aircraft were sent to Nicosia as a precaution, many of them to airlift troops to Jordan in the event of conflict. If Israel attacked Egypt and Jordan, the generals planned to launch an immediate air offensive to knock out the Israeli airforce and slow down and paralyse any forces advancing into the Sinai desert against the Egyptians or into the West Bank against the Jordanian Arab Legion. More than 90 bombers, fighters and ground-attack aircraft would be rushed to Cyprus to fight alongside aircraft already stationed on the island and in Iraq. US air forces would operate from British airfields, and British and American carrier strikes would hit Israeli airfields and set up a blockade.[14]

But, as Nasser's arms build-up increased, the greatest danger was of a combined Arab attack on Israel led by Nasser. This would mean sending in fighters from Cyprus and from carriers in the Mediterranean to destroy the Egyptian airforce and strike at Nasser's lines of communication through the Sinai desert. A full-scale blockade of Egypt would be mounted to end the war. The Americans, it was hoped, would join in by sending a fighter/bomber force to a British base, and by using the Sixth Fleet. In the meantime, the British sent a brigade of 2200 paratroops and infantrymen to Cyprus in the hope of deterring Israeli aggression.[15]

Deterrence, though, depends heavily on the credibility of the threat, and Harding knew his failure to control EOKA undermined the strategic task. He went on radio to warn rivals in the Middle East that the island would be 'fully usable' if war broke out. Shortly afterwards, the airfield at Akrotiri became operational, and the navy and RAF made a show of strength with the Americans in the eastern Mediterranean. The aim was to impress on Israel and Egypt 'our will and capacity to use overwhelming force' to stop them fighting.[16]

Nasser was not in the mood to be impressed by British or Israeli threats. He was growing steadily bolder, thanks to massive aid from the Soviet Union, which over the previous year had increased its trade with Egypt by 65 percent. In early February, Moscow agreed to help build an atomic energy station in Egypt. He continued to stir up trouble in Jordan, and vowed to repel any Israeli attack. *The Times* warned prophetically (on 15 February 1956) that were it not for the deal between Egypt and the World Bank on the funding of the Aswan Dam project – which looked big enough to absorb Egypt's surplus energies for many years – one would say that events in the Middle East were moving rapidly towards a showdown.

In this atmosphere, Harding restarted his talks with Makarios. He offered to hold a conference on self-government, provided the Archbishop first renounced violence, but he made no concessions on the issue of self-determination. Makarios refused to sign an agreement without a date for self-determination.[17] But, in a significant concession, he offered to set that issue aside for the time being and co-operate in establishing self-government. But he also demanded an end to the state of emergency and an amnesty for all political prisoners. Communist leaders accused him of conceding too much, and organised a protest strike of 1000 workers engaged in constructing the new British bases.

When Harding kept a tough line on self-government – refusing to allow an assembly that could elect a Greek-Cypriot majority, or a quick handover of power to Cypriot ministers – Makarios made another major compromise. Against the explicit wishes of Grivas, he agreed to the Governor retaining control of internal security until order was restored, and asked only for only an early end to the state of emergency.[18]

The compromises fell on deaf ears. Lennox-Boyd, arriving in Cyprus to take part in the talks, was ordered by Eden to give no more concessions.[19] An hour before the final negotiations between Makarios and Harding were due to resume, 19 bombs exploded across the island. The talks broke down, triggering a new wave of violence. On 3 March, EOKA blew up a Hermes troop-carrying aircraft at Nicosia airport which, but for a delay in take-off, could have killed up to 68 passengers – all members of servicemen's families.[20] At the same time, Nasser achieved an anti-British coup in Jordan. The British head of Jordan's army was dismissed. With him went the senior British officers in charge of the Legion's intelligence and infantry, just as Nasser had planned. British policy in the region seemed on the point of collapse.[21]

Suddenly, on 9 March, Makarios was seized while attempting to board a plane to Athens, taken to the Seychelles along with the Bishop of Kyrenia and two others, and placed under house arrest. The British public was told that

Makarios had 'slammed the door' on the talks. Harding said in an official state-ment that he had been aware for a long time that Makarios was implicated in EOKA terrorism, but that he was 'now so far committed to the use of violence for political ends that he either cannot or will not abandon it'. Evidence that Makarios had provided cash for arms smuggling came from parts of Grivas's diaries captured by the security forces. Labour MPs condemned the deportation as 'an act of madness', and suggested that nothing new had emerged about Makarios during the talks.[22] The Americans expressed shock and dismay.

Eden tried to pin the blame for the breakdown in the talks firmly on Makarios. He told the MPs, 'The Archbishop would only in the end agree to terms which gave him virtual control of the island'. But acting Labour leader Aneurin Bevan questioned whether the Government had ever intended to reach a negotiated settlement, given that the major issue of self-determination had already been resolved. On the three sticking-points, he said Makarios's demand for majority representation was in line with liberal democratic traditions, the request for an amnesty was understandable since he could not possibly commend an agreement that left his comrades in the hands of their enemies, and it should have been possible to agree to hand over internal security once reasonable order had been established. He suspected that not only did Eden not want to give away sovereignty for the foreseeable future, but that he did not want to offer genuine self-government either. At the heart of the matter was the question of whether the Government wanted to have the whole of Cyprus as a base, or have a base on Cyprus. It had been widely assumed that the talks were aimed at securing Cypriot self-government and retaining a British military base on the island. 'If it is a fact that the Government wish to have Cyprus as a base, the negotiations with the Archbishop have been dishonest from the beginning,' said Bevan.[23]

Secret defence papers, now released, show that defence chiefs did indeed believe that Britain needed to retain the whole of Cyprus as a base, and there-fore had to keep control of internal security not merely until law and order had been restored, but for as long as the island was militarily important. This view was stated clearly to ministers in July 1955, and spelt out in more detail on 23 February 1956, less than a week before the negotiations with Makarios ground to a halt for the same reason.[24] The papers also show that Harding completely agreed with this view.[25] The Government's claim to be offering a 'wide measure of democratic self-government', the basis on which Makarios had entered the talks, had therefore been, as Bevan suggested, a sham from beginning to end.

In the papers, defence chiefs detailed what military facilities were needed on Cyprus and what level of control had to be exercised there to meet Britain's mili-tary commitments in peace and war in the region. They concluded that the facilities required would impinge on every aspect of government – therefore precluding full self-government for the Cypriots – and must be safeguarded.[26]

The defence chiefs said the role of British forces in Cyprus was: to defend the Arab states, Turkey and Israel from a Russian invasion of the Middle East; to protect Britain's commercial interests and British nationals; and to collaborate with members of the Baghdad Pact. In a local war, they might be needed to defend Jordan, prevent or end an Arab/Israeli conflict, and ensure the free use of the Suez Canal to British shipping. In a global war, they would be used to hold the Russian advance beyond the Zagros mountains in Iran. This would require nuclear intervention by V-bombers based on Cyprus. In any war, the island would be used 'as a base' for British ships, for operating aircraft, and for providing administrative support. Nothing less than a catalogue of sweeping powers would be needed. These included control over: civil aircraft; public services; shipping and ports; cable, wireless and telephone communications and radio transmissions; exit and entry into Cyprus; the power to set up radar, anti-aircraft and seaward defences; the requisitioning of land, buildings, transport and commodities for military use; and the classification of military installations as 'prohibited areas'. Further requirements would be: control over publicity, propaganda, broadcasting and the press; a censorship organisation; a civil defence organisation; control over customs, imports and exports; provision for the detention and deportation of undesirables; provision for the conscription and direction of labour and the introduction of wartime legislation.[27]

The form of self-government on offer in the talks therefore had to leave foreign affairs, defence and internal security in the hands of the Governor. Ultimately he had to have the power to dismiss obstructive ministers or revert to direct rule.[28]

The reality was that Britain had no intention of giving up control of internal security, or freeing EOKA's most dangerous men, or handing over power to an elected Greek-Cypriot majority that might be led by Makarios or, worse, the communists. Aneurin Bevan concluded that the Government was trying to protect Britain's interests by using old-fashioned colonialism instead of modern methods and, as a consequence, was damaging Britain's name the world over. 'We stood alone in 1940 but it was a noble isolation. We are almost standing alone today, but it is an ignoble loneliness we are achieving,' he said.[29]

~5~

HAMSTRUNG AT SUEZ

Grivas Sabotages Military Preparations

Harding was running out of time. His tough tactics had failed to kill off the EOKA campaign of sabotage or prevent political strikes slowing down the contruction of the bases, and Cyprus was not ready to play the crucial role it had been designated in the case of a conflict in the Middle East. The British intelligence network, which included electronic spying facilities on Cyprus, provided more evidence of close links between Egypt and Eastern Bloc countries, particularly Czechoslovakia, and in April 1956 the Soviet leaders, Nikita Kruschev and Marshal Bulganin, on a visit to Britain, boldly revealed their intention to cause as much trouble for Britain in the Middle East as they could.[1] An MI6 agent in the Egyptian Embassy in Prague gave detailed reports of shipments of Eastern Bloc arms to Nasser. It was feared that the Egyptian leader was aiming to create a league of Arab republics, stretching from the Magreb to the Middle East, under his leadership. If he succeeded, he would gain control over the lucrative oil fields on which Western economies depended and would be able to strangle Europe at will.[2] In April, Egypt began massing forces inside the Gaza strip and the Sinai desert, and launched commando raids into Israel, drawing retaliatory shelling. Israeli intelligence said similar attacks were

32

being planned from Jordan, where the Arab Legion, without its British officers, no longer provided a restraining influence. In June, Soviet Foreign Minister Shepilov visited Cairo and joined Nasser in watching with satisfaction the last British soldiers leave the Suez base. The Egyptian leader celebrated his 99 percent vote in the recent 'election' with a parade of Russian weapons and planes and token forces from a string of Arab countries. Senior British ministers believed that before long Egypt would launch a full-scale attack on its Jewish neighbour. That would draw British troops and planes on Cyprus into war.[3]

British generals foresaw grave economic, political and military problems involved in any action against Egypt. It would drag Britain into a war against all the Arab states. It would endanger the lives of British nationals throughout the Arab world. British troops would have to go into battle against Jordanian forces, breaching the 1948 armistice line with Israel. Even the Iraqis, Britain's close allies, would face enormous pressure to enter the war on the side of the Arabs, or risk destroying their own position in the Arab world. This would leave the Baghdad Pact in tatters, with a 'devastating effect' on Britain's strategic position.[4] Oil supplies would be dramatically cut – none could be expected to pass through the Suez Canal or the pipelines terminating in the Levant, as Arab countries such as Syria, the Lebanon and Jordan would be forced by popular pressure and outside agitation to join Egypt in blocking oil supplies. This would cause 'grave dislocation' and 'permanent damage' to the economy of Britain and Western Europe. The region provided 70 percent of Britain's oil imports. Up to 110 million tons a year flowed through the canal, or was piped through Arab states under Nasser's influence. With such high stakes, preventing Arab aggression in the first place was paramount.[5]

Crucial to all the military's contingency plans were the air facilities on Cyprus, where the Middle East Air Force was based, following the move of the Levant headquarters from Iraq to Episkopi in 1955. It was now the largest RAF overseas command with an operational area covering some 2.5 million square miles. The headquarters in Cyprus controlled units in Jordan, Iraq and Libya, and the RAF retained staging rights in the Suez Canal Zone.[6] Once completed, the Akrotiri base was expected to be the best on British-controlled territory between home and the Far East, its 3000-yard runway capable of taking nuclear bombers.[7] But the airfield was not ready, and neither were many of the other facilities planned for the island after the switch of the Middle East headquarters from Suez. The island was not expected to be fully equipped for its new role until 1959, and even the work on some of the key air facilities, hampered by the intermittent political strikes and sabotage, was behind schedule. After Makarios's deportation, for instance, there were strikes at the bases at Dhekelia, Akrotiri and Episkopi, and the RAF station at Famagusta.

The sheer numbers of troops and RAF units on Cyprus tied down in internal security tasks, and the equipment and back-up facilities that went with them, meant if air action had to be taken there would be overcrowding and refuelling problems at the Nicosia and Akrotiri airfields.[8] Vehicles and equipment for Middle East action would have to be sent to the island well in advance, and because of the limitations on air-lift capacity, there would be a worrying eight-day gap between the departure of troops to the field of battle and the arrival of replacements to tackle EOKA.[9] Military chiefs had already been forced to scrap plans to deploy two Canberra squadrons in Nicosia, bombed-up to deter Israeli aggression, because, with the stationing of additional troops to meet the internal security situation and construction delays at Akrotiri, there was nowhere to put them. Air Marshal Sir Claude Pelly said no more Canberras could be deployed on Cyprus for at least nine months – until November 1956, when they were eventually used against Nasser in the Suez crisis – except under war emergency conditions.[10] The anti-British campaign on Cyprus was taking its toll. Each of the plans to take military action in the Middle East was complicated by limited capacity on Cyprus or the clogging up of facilities with forces and equipment assigned to the operation against EOKA, and this gravely impaired the strategic value of the island.[11]

The chiefs of Staff were warned in March that the troubles on Cyprus might at any time deplete the forces available to fight in the Middle East, and that troops from the British strategic reserve would have to be shipped to the scene of battle. Even with the existing level of unrest, only one battalion could be spared from Cyprus without replacement from Britain.[12] Furthermore, if an Arab/Israeli war did break out, EOKA could be expected to take advantage by intensifying its activity, which would mean no troops could be drawn from Cyprus to fight elsewhere without a deterioration in the situation on the island.[13]

This left Harding working against the clock to try to stamp out the EOKA threat. He dropped all attempts at finding a political solution and concentrated on trying to break the back of EOKA and flush out its leader. In areas where there was suspected EOKA activity, British forces imposed curfews, closed down shops, cleared people from their homes for months at a time, made mass arrests, and enforced collective fines of up to £40,000. Harding put a reward of £10,000 on Grivas's head and £5000 on a number of known EOKA gang leaders.

But there was no let-up in the attacks on troops, police stations and military facilities. There was another attempt on Harding's life, this time by a cleaner at Government House who smuggled in a time-bomb strapped to his chest and hid it under Harding's mattress. Harding survived only because the cool night air coming through his open window affected the timing mechanism. When the Governor refused clemency for two EOKA gunmen – who were hanged on 10 May – a further wave of violence on Cyprus and anti-British riots in Athens was unleashed.[14]

Harding did not have time to worry about public opinion. The essential task, he told his troops, was to ensure the island's military facilities were 'protected and secure, and always ready for use'.[15] He pitched all the resources he could muster into rooting out the guerrillas and their leader throughout May and

June. Following tip-offs, thousands of commandos, paratroops and police with tracker dogs, backed up by RAF helicopters, were sent on a sweep of the country-side in north-west Cyprus, while Navy ships patrolled the coast. Their task was made difficult by the ease with which EOKA men could fade into the shadows. Grivas and his followers, operating in small groups, had built hundreds of hides in the mountains – cavities hewn out of rock, or underground passages away from footpaths and often hidden by trees – where men could remain undiscovered for weeks at a time, despite searches by troops. In the villages, there were numerous priest-holes behind walls or under the floorboards in houses, where EOKA members concealed themselves. Grivas minimised intelligence leaks by using as much as possible his secret network of human messengers rather than radio or telephone. Nevertheless, by marching up to 20 miles at night, the British troops were able to surprise a number of EOKA gangs at daybreak, capturing two wanted leaders on 20 May. Three hundred people in the village of Milikouri were rounded up for questioning, and Grivas's main communications base at the Kykko monastery nearby was discovered.[16]

Using the intelligence gained, the operation closed in on Grivas's principal area of operation in the mountains west and south of Mount Olympus. In early June they began to concentrate on the Paphos forest, where they knew Grivas was hiding, and where they hoped to corner more of his gangs. The guerrilla leader ordered diversionary bombings and political demonstrations in the towns as he tried to escape along the chain of EOKA hides leading to Limassol. Twice he was nearly caught by patrols as he fled down the steep mountain slopes, once leaving parts of his diary and his Sam Browne belt by a stream in the rush. The search area was narrowed down to a 25-square-mile stretch of dense woodland, which was cordoned off and patrolled feverishly. Another EOKA gang and two leaders on the wanted list were captured. But when the net finally closed in on Grivas, disaster struck the operation. A fire broke out in the trees behind him, and the flames streaked through the wood and up the nearby slopes, setting ablaze an army lorry. Nineteen soldiers died and 18 others were injured. Helicopters buzzed in to rescue the injured, and in the commotion the guerrilla leader vanished.[17]

One effect of Grivas's terror tactics and Harding's indiscriminate oppression was the increased risk of ethnic conflict. EOKA's murder of informers had fright-ened many Greek Cypriots away from joining the police, and the new auxiliary force was made up almost entirely of Turkish Cypriots, making them appear increasingly on the British side. It was inevitable that Turkish Cypriots would be killed in action taken against the security forces. Defence chiefs had warned that interethnic fighting could prove explosive, and 'seriously impair the efficiency of Cyprus as a base'.

In late April, when a Turkish-Cypriot police sergeant who had come to the aid of a Greek-Cypriot colleague was murdered, Turkish crowds surged into the Greek sector of Nicosia and attacked shops, looting and burning.[18] In May, several Turkish-Cypriot policemen and auxiliaries were killed in daily shooting incidents and clashes between the two communities. In one village near Nicosia, there was a pitched battle with knives and sticks. Haystacks and buildings were set alight. A Turkish-Cypriot policeman on a motorbike was killed with a shovel. That day the Nicosia fire service was called out 15 times to put out fires in Greek-Cypriot shops. The Commissioner of Nicosia announced that the city was to be divided into two parts by a permanent wire fence so that the two sides of the town could be rapidly isolated if further trouble broke out between Greek and Turkish Cypriots. Another shooting of a Turkish-Cypriot policeman, in a coffee shop, led to fights with clubs and knives. The funeral on 29 May turned into a riot, and the angry crowd, armed with pick-helves and stakes stormed a factory, beating to death the Greek-Cypriot watchman.

The Americans were alarmed by the impact of the ethnic tension on relations between Turkey and Greece. In Athens, the Foreign Minister resigned in the face of pressure for a stronger stance on Cyprus and Prime Minister Karamanlis pledged to take the issue to the UN in the autumn. Eisenhower pressed for talks with Makarios to be reopened. But Eden believed he could not concede any more if he was to keep the tacit alliance with Turkey intact.[19] He told Eisenhower that the Turks were violently opposed to enosis, and to offer more would have serious repercussions on Middle-Eastern security. The Americans were suspicious of Britain's use of Turkey to bolster its position in the Middle East, where it rivalled American influence.

Perceived changes in the long-term strategic needs on Cyprus gave Eden some room to manoeuvre. The chiefs of staff admitted that, though Cyprus was militarily 'indispensable' at present, it might not always be so.[20] The development of nuclear power might cut Britain's reliance on Middle-East oil, and the development of long-range nuclear bombers and ballistic missiles might change requirements for the base in the long term.[21]

The opportunity was seized on by Harding, who was losing confidence in his ability to crush EOKA. He wanted an offer of self-determination at a future date to be made to ease the pressure.[22] Ministers agreed that Turkey should be sounded out confidentially on a proposal that ten years after a liberal constitution had been successfully put into operation, a two-thirds majority vote of NATO would decide whether a change to the international status of Cyprus could be reconciled with Western defence obligations in the region. Athens was not consulted. But following talks with Turkey the proposal was modified to give Britain permanent sovereignty over two base areas, which Turkey would be allowed to use, and any extra facilities it needed for its defence commitments in the region. But even this failed to win Ankara's support, because Turkey's interest was not just long-term, but permanent.[23] While Britain's Middle-East interests might diminish, the island would always be the gateway to Turkey's southern flank. The Turks were not prepared to risk the island falling into Greek, or other enemy, hands. Not wishing to cross them, Eden abandoned all efforts to secure international agreement on the island's status. On 12 July, it was announced that Lord Radcliffe would go to Cyprus to consult with representatives of both communities and draw up a constitution regardless.

In the meantime, events in the Middle East were sliding towards war. The turning-point was the abrupt withdrawal of American funds from Colonel Nasser's prized development project, the Aswan Dam, on 19 July. The Americans were angered by Cairo's courting of the Soviets, and World Bank funds for the project depended on the United States and Britain backing it. Two days later, the British also pulled out. Nasser had placed the prestigious project at the heart of his political programme, and was stung into retaliation. On 26 July, he nationalised the Suez Canal, arguing that it would pay for the dam instead. The nightmare Britain dreaded was coming true. An Arab power had taken control of the most important oil route.

Eden feared that if Nasser's coup went unchallenged all the British and other Western interests in the Middle East would crumble. He thought that, like Hitler's march into the Rhineland, this was a crucial moment in history: if the forces of Arab expansion were not turned back at its first breach of the international order, Nasser would subvert his neighbours, destroy Israel, and create an Arab empire that could control the oil routes, leaving Europe at his mercy. It was precisely this kind of trouble which the strategic presence in Cyprus was deployed to deter and counter. Macmillan, now Eden's Chancellor of the Exchequer, believed that if the canal was surrendered, Europe's fate would be left in the hands of 'satellites of Russia', it would mean pan-Arabism, dominated by communism, and the right flank of Europe turned.[24]

Nasser threatened to meet force with force if his grip on the canal was challenged, though he did promise to keep it open. But Eden told the MPs that the canal could not be allowed to fall under the control of one state (even though legally it was due to come under Egyptian control in 1968 anyway). Ministers began contemplating war. They knew that they would get no support from Washington, but found willing allies in Paris. The French viewed Nasser as a menacing threat to their interests in the Magreb, where armed resistance by Algerian rebels, trained by his forces, was threatening to develop into a full-scale war. On 2 August, the British and French announced that a conference was to be held in London later in the month to arrange international control of the canal. But despite the diplomatic initiative, the French fleet began to mass at Toulon, and the British called up reserve forces and sent three aircraft-carriers to Cyprus. The French Prime Minister, Guy Mollet, suggested that another ally be brought into the military plans – Israel. On 7 August, British and French defence chiefs set up a joint military command to prepare for an assault on Egypt, using 50,000 British and 30,000 French troops.

Cyprus was chosen as the obvious headquarters, the launch-pad for war. But it was plainly still not ready. At the outset of the planning, the Nicosia airfield was the only one in operation on the island and, still under reconstruction, it was not working to full capacity.[25] In September, Sir Charles Keightley, commander in charge of the Suez operation, warned Cabinet ministers that of the three airfields in Cyprus, the only one available for certain parts of the air operation was Nicosia and it was overcrowded and 'most vulnerable'. The EOKA campaign had disrupted the development of Cyprus as the main Middle East base, and Keightley warned that the air defence arrangements had grave shortcomings and suffered from out-of-date equipment and lack of space for dispersal of aircraft. 'There is an inherent difficulty owing to the Cyprus situation in organising passive air defence,' said Keightley. The Akrotiri and Tymbou airfields had to be hurriedly developed during September and October. Keightley was very concerned that the Egyptians might catch them off guard if they persuaded the Russians to launch a heavy air attack against Cyprus, using the Soviet 'volunteer' force in Egypt, or perhaps even from Syria.[26]

Cyprus had other limitations too. It lacked harbours or anchorages for naval ships, or facilities for landing craft, which meant any sea-borne assault had to be launched from Malta, over 900 miles away. The paratroops had received no recent training, and there was no mobile parachute packing station – they had to be packed in Britain – despite the fact that a parachute brigade had been nominated as the strategic reserve based on the island. According to historian Hugh Thomas, one commander reported that there were not even enough trained pilots available, the infantry was preoccupied with EOKA, and there were no amphibious specialists. Furthermore, because they had been tied up with the anti-EOKA operations, the marines had not taken part in an amphibious assault exercise for almost a year, and the paratroops had gone without a training air drop for a similar period.[27]

Nasser later claimed he knew, through spies working secretly in Cyprus, Aden and Malta, that Britain would not be able to react militarily to nationalisation for between three and four months. 'We thought at that time that it would be possible to reach a sort of a settlement during these three months.'[28] He tried to stir up more trouble in Cyprus by directing broadcasts in Greek at the island. Grivas could see from the heightened activity in the bases that Britain was heading for a military confrontation in the Middle East, and took advantage of the distraction it caused to the security operation against EOKA.

In the first half of August, EOKA bombed military and security targets on Cyprus virtually every day. On 7 August, for instance, a bomb exploded at the CBC station on the outskirts of Nicosia, and another blew up in the customs house at Kyrenia. The next day, bombs were found in a hotel used by police officers in Larnaca and in the Dhekelia army camp, two exploded in the ordnance depot at Larnaca, another exploded in a contractor's yard at Akrotiri, in Episkopi two bombs exploded in an army building under construction, and another exploded at a Paphos police station. Bombs weren't the only action damaging the efforts to get the bases ready. There were political strikes in the bases. On 10 August, when three EOKA men were hanged – and bombs exploded in the Garrison Club at Nicosia and sank a launch at Famagusta – most of the contractors' labour in the big service installations went on strike. At the crucial air-base and army installations at Episkopi and Akrotiri, the majority of Greek labourers failed to turn up for work. At the Dhekelia base, there was a complete standstill. The Paphos dock workers were also on strike.[29]

Grivas's forces ceased fire from 16 August, but on 27 August the ambushes, shootings and sabotage began again. In five days a bomb exploded at an army officer's house and another officer was shot in Nicosia; a limpet mine damaged a tank landing ship, spilling five tons of oil; a fire destroyed the new officers' and sergeants' mess at Episkopi; an explosion started a fire in the new camp area there too; in Famagusta a time-bomb wrecked the engineers' stores depot; and at Paphos the power lines were sabotaged, causing a four-hour power failure. Harding admitted the Suez problem had set back attempts to eliminate EOKA by up to three months.

In August, the London conference on the canal arrangements, boycotted by Egypt, supported an American proposal for an international operating board, and agreed to put the plan to Nasser.

Meanwhile, the British and French military build-up continued. Three French ships carrying 600 troops were sent to Cyprus. An emergency airfield five miles from Nicosia, at Tymbou, was rapidly made fit for use by the French transport aircraft. Akrotiri was to be made ready for use by late September, but because of delays it did not become operational until October as the continuous bombing, sabotage and arson by EOKA, and political strikes among the base's labourers, took their toll.

Nasser rejected the London proposals. He insisted that Egypt was entitled to own the canal, but said that other nations would not be barred from using it. American Secretary of State Dulles put forward an alternative plan for a Suez Canal Users' Association, in which the users would pay dues to SCUA, but Egypt would receive a fair share of the dues. Some on the British and French side thought they could use SCUA to force Nasser into a climbdown by challenging him to prevent SCUA ships from passing through the canal, though the French were worried about the lack of air defence readiness on Cyprus if hostilities began. France's Admiral Barjot stressed to British commanders that Nasser was a 'madman' who might take the setting up of SCUA as an act of war and 'do a Pearl Harbour' on Malta and Cyprus.[30] But Dulles made clear his strong opposition to the use of military or economic force. When Eisenhower learned that Britain and France had ordered an evacuation of their nationals from Egypt, Jordan, Syria and the Lebanon, he wrote privately to Eden to warn him against military action: 'I am afraid, Anthony, that from this point onward our views on the situation diverge,' he said.[31] Soviet leader Marshal Bulganin also told Britain and France that he knew they had troops on Cyprus, and warned that the USSR could not stand aside if they moved. British MPs, on the other hand, were kept in the dark.

In the meantime, Grivas kept up his relentless campaign against military targets. Between 7 August, when the joint Anglo-French command was established, and 15 September, the allies' planned D-day for a Suez offensive, Grivas's men carried out 56 bomb attacks against military targets. There were 18 attacks – bombings, arson and acts of sabotage – inside or directed at the major bases and facilities at Akrotiri, Episkopi and Dhekelia; 14 against the camps and soldiers based in Nicosia, and nearly 20 against naval and storage facilities and equipment and pipelines at the ports of Famagusta, Limassol and Paphos. There were 20 incidents of military vehicles or vehicles owned by servicemen being ambushed, mined or bombed. A further 20 unexploded bombs aimed at military targets were discovered.[32]

The Suez D-day – when, according to the plan, 80,000 men were to land at Alexandria, defeat Nasser's army and topple his government – had to be continually postponed, even though the chiefs of staff warned that after 6 October 'Operation Musketeer' would not be a sound operation of war. As the international negotiations dragged on, the risk of an intelligence leak became too great and a new plan was drawn up, for an assault landing at Port Said.[33]

By now the fuse lit by Nasser was burning short. In mid-October, an Israeli raid on Jordan was followed by the election in Jordan of a pro-Egyptian, anti-British and anti-Iraqi Government. In the negotiations on Suez, which continued until 12 October, Nasser accepted SCUA's right to collect dues, but not the principle that the canal should be held under international control. The UN Security Council motion endorsing international control was vetoed by the Soviets. British, French and Israeli leaders secretly struck a deal in which Israel agreed to attack Egypt through the Sinai desert and across the Mitla Pass, leading to the Suez Canal. In return, British and French forces would wipe out the Egyptian airforce to prevent Nasser bombing Tel Aviv in retaliation. Britain and France would then issue ultimatums to Israel and Egypt demanding that they withdraw their forces from 10 miles either side of the canal and accept occupation of the canal by Anglo-French troops, to guarantee passage through it. If Egypt resisted, they would impose their will by force.[34]

Nasser, meanwhile, set up a joint army command with Syria and Jordan, and Jordan's Chief of Staff declared that the Arabs should set a date for Israel's 'destruction'. The two sides were set on collision course. But on Cyprus, the British and French forces had already been under fire for some time – from the enemy behind their own lines. Between the first planned D-day, 15 September, and the end of October, EOKA carried out a further 63 bombing attacks on military targets, a large number of them inside the bases and installations that were gearing up for the war against Nasser. More strikes, acts of arson and sabotage hampered the construction work in the bases. Since the Suez preparations began, more than 60 bombs had been used to ambush patrols, buses carrying troops, or the cars of servicemen, and 13 servicemen had been killed at the hands of EOKA.[35]

At the end of October the 16th Paratroops were suddenly relieved of their anti-guerrilla duties in the mountains. They had been closing in on a number of EOKA gangs hiding in a densely wooded area, but were told they had to report back to base for a 'training exercise'. Only the brigadier and his major knew that Egypt was in their sights. Just one battalion was chosen because the airfields on Cyprus simply could not cope with transport aircraft in sufficient numbers to lift a greater force.[36] The most devastating piece of sabotage by Grivas's forces was the explosion of four bombs that gashed the runway at Akrotiri and delayed the military action at Suez for two weeks. One of his men, a civilian worker at the base, had crawled through a storm drain under the runway to plant them.[37]

The RAF established a communications centre at Akrotiri, and the naval task-force set up a combined headquarters on its flagship off the coast. On 27 October, Anglo-French aircraft-carriers set sail from Malta for Cyprus. Within two days, 20 squadrons of Canberra and Valiant bombers left British shores for the island. On Cyprus were the Royal Horseguards, eight infantry battalions, the 3rd Commando Brigade, and three paratroop battalions. There were now 17 RAF bomber squadrons on Malta and Cyprus, seven detachments of fighters, and several transport squadrons, with their French counterparts, in Cyprus.

Eisenhower, kept in the dark about the European allies' plans, feared Israel was about to attack Jordan. But at 4pm on 29 October, Israel broke out of her borders not eastwards but southwards into Egypt. Israeli paratroops landed on the Mitla pass and French-supplied Mysteres patrolled the Suez Canal. That night the French secretly flew transport planes from Cyprus to drop food and arms for the Israelis behind their lines.[38] The collusion, breaching the 1950 Tripartite Declaration, was spotted by US intelligence. Eisenhower demanded to know from Eden what was going on. At the UN the Americans introduced a Security Council motion demanding Israeli withdrawal and an end to hostilities, but to Eisenhower's dismay Britain and France vetoed it.

The European allies issued their planned ultimatum, ordering both sides to pull back ten miles from the Suez Canal, effectively sanctioning Israel's 100-mile advance into Egypt, and declared that their forces would invade if the conditions were not met. Three aircraft-carriers arrived within striking distance of Egypt on 31 October. The bulk of the British assault armada was due to arrive on 6 November. Eisenhower felt personally betrayed by Eden, whose telegram informing him of the ultimatum arrived after the news broke on press tapes at the White House. On the evening of 31 October, 200 Canberras, Venoms and Valiants and 40 French Thunderstreaks roared down the runways on Cyprus, Malta and several aircraft-carriers, and headed for Egypt. They bombed a dozen airfields, dropping nearly two thousand bombs in 18 waves of attacks.

Nasser pulled his army out of the Sinai desert to bolster his defences around Cairo, and ordered the blocking of the Suez Canal. Over the next two days 47 ships filled with concrete were deliberately sunk in the canal. This caused dismay in London and Paris, since keeping the tanker route open was a principal aim of the allied military action. In the early hours of 2 November, an emergency meeting of the UN General Assembly overwhelmingly voted down the Anglo-French veto and called for an immediate ceasefire, but the European allies ignored it. Radar stations and anti-aircraft crews on Cyprus, meanwhile, scoured the skies for counter-attacks by Nasser's Russian-supplied Ilyushin bombers. But the Egyptians had not yet been trained to fly them. By the end of the day, British and French airforces achieved their target of neutralising the Egyptian airforce. Attempts to turn the air-power on Egyptian naval units had to be put off because the US Sixth Fleet interposed warships for the evacuation of US civilians. The next step was the allied assault landing. French paratroops on Cyprus were put on alert as Admiral Barjot pressed General Keightley, the British Commander-in-Chief based on the island, for an immediate airborne operation to land troops along the canal. But the short time the British paratroops had had to prepare since dropping their operations against EOKA, the limit on the numbers that could be involved due to the overcrowding, disrepair and building work at the Cyprus airfields, and the fact that supporting naval firepower was not yet available weighed heavily against such a move.[39]

While British bombers and French ground-attack aircraft were taking off and landing at Cyprus at the rate of one a minute, Grivas struck again. On 2 November, 23 bombing raids were carried out across the island against targets inside military bases and military camps, and against military patrols.[40] Airforce personnel preparing bombers for their raids on Egypt, troops billeted, ready to go into action, and communications staff monitoring enemy radar and signals did not know where EOKA bombers or snipers would strike next.

On 3 November, as invading Israeli forces finished mopping up the remaining Egyptian troops in Egypt's Sinai peninsula, Britain and France announced their conditions for complying with the UN ceasefire call. These included agreement that a UN force should be sent to keep the peace until both the Arab-Israeli and canal disputes were settled. Israel agreed to the ceasefire on 4 November, but the Egyptians held out until the next day. Intelligence reports from Cyprus revealed that the Egyptians were pulling their forces back from Port Said to bolster the defence of Cairo until a UN force arrived. Their retreat embarrassed the British and French Governments because it meant the Israelis could achieve all their objectives before the allies were ready to invade. Ben Gurion had to be pressed to withdraw Israel's consent to the UN's conditions for the ceasefire.

That evening, Eden telegraphed Eisenhower to inform him that the allies were going to invade. He pleaded with the President to understand why he had to risk a breach in the special relationship with America – to prevent Nasser becoming a 'Moslem Mussolini'.[41]

At 4.15am on 5 November, RAF Valettas laden with paratroops lurched into the air from the runway at Nicosia, and French transport planes took off from Tymbou. They massed above the south coast of Cyprus and set off for Egypt to drop more than 1000 paratroops around Port Said and the nearby Gamil airfield, at the northern end of the Suez Canal. Sea-borne forces joined them the next day from Malta. The Americans punished Britain by furiously selling sterling. The Bank of England desperately tried to prop up the pound, draining Britain's reserves in the process. At the same time, the Soviets threatened rocket attacks on London, Paris and Tel Aviv. But the colonial powers were defiant. At dawn on 6 November, Anglo-French naval forces bombarded Port Said, shelling Egyptian positions. British commandos and tanks landed on the beaches, and the troops stormed the port under cover of tank fire, while French commandos moved into neighbouring Port Fuad, cleared of Egyptian forces by their paratroops the night before. Arms supplies were dropped by planes from Cyprus, and casualties were flown back to the island for medical attention. Allied commanders masterminding the operation from Cyprus prepared for the advance down the canal to take Ismailia and Suez, but by now there had been a run on the pound and the ground had been cut from under Eden.[42]

At 9.45am on 6 November, ministers were told that Israel had agreed to accept a ceasefire. Though allied troops were still 75 miles from Suez, Macmillan, once the hawk, pressed for an end to the fighting on economic grounds, while other ministers feared further action might trigger a Soviet invasion of the Middle East. Allied Command on Cyprus had been told by NATO headquarters that Soviet jets were flying over Turkey and heading for Egypt or Syria, and French intelligence had spotted six Russian submarines approaching Alexandria. The French were ordered to prepare their fleet to face Soviet aircraft and warships. Fighters in Cyprus were scrambled to intercept an unidentified aircraft, which turned out to be an American spy plane. If the Russians became involved there was a real danger of widespread, or even world, war. Eden and Mollet reluctantly agreed to a ceasefire.[43] The Egyptians had lost up to 3000 men, the Israelis 200, the British 27, and French only three. But Nasser was still in place, and Eden was despondent.

The UN ordered British, French and Israeli troops out of the canal zone. Eden insisted that first the canal should be cleared by Anglo-French forces, and there should be an effective UN force in place. On 10 November, British troops arrived to replace the marines and paratroops in Egypt as an occupying force. The paratroops were shipped out of Suez and back to Cyprus. During the Suez operation, the military build-up to it, and the occupation of Egyptian soil, more British troops died at the hands of EOKA than in fighting Nasser's troops. Since the Anglo-French joint military preparations began, on 7 August, there had been 174 separate bomb attacks on British military targets on the island, and 124 bombs had been thrown at, detonated under or planted in, vehicles of the armed forces, threatening, maiming and killing servicemen. There were 33 deaths in the first three weeks of November alone.

Harding privately admitted that the Suez crisis had been a major blow to his campaign to break EOKA. He told the Ministry of Defence that the paratroops had brought EOKA near to defeat in May, June and October: 'I have little doubt that if it had been possible to continue active operations against them on that scale for several months, their defeat would have been completed'.[44] Instead, the very war against EOKA – back on the UN agenda on 12 November – had jeopardised the use of Britain's most important Middle East base at its most crucial hour.

The commander of the Suez operations, General Sir Charles Keightley, privately singled out the failure to secure American co-operation or international backing, and the limitations on the military capacity – brought about by the delays in the building work caused by political strikes, damage wreaked by EOKA, and the high levels of manpower and equipment taken up in countering the guerilla threat – as vital factors hindering the operation. Keightley told the chiefs of staff, 'We suffered badly from a shortage of airfields and ports in Cyprus. When operations started both the airfields in use in Cyprus were under construction or repair. There were no ports, anchorages or hards capable of holding an assault force. Our Cyprus bases were dangerously vulnerable to even a single bomber. Aircraft had to stand wing tip to wing tip with insufficient dispersal area and the limited port facilities were overcrowded. We did not have a really effective radar cover deployed at the outset.' But he also said Suez had shown that carrying international opinion was now an absolute principle of war. 'It was the action of the United States which really defeated us in attaining our objective. Her action in the UN is well known, but her move of the Sixth Fleet which is not so generally known, was a move which endangered the whole of our relations with that country. It is most difficult to appreciate the effect of the shooting down of a US aircraft or the sinking of a US sub, but both these might easily have happened. The situation with the US must at all costs be prevented from happening again.'[45]

~6~

MACMILLAN'S PACT

Eisenhower Deal Frees Makarios

For Britain, the Suez crisis did not end with the ceasefire, and the endgame had far-reaching consequences for Britain's position on Cyprus. While Eden refused to pull British troops out of Egypt until the canal had been cleared – because only then could Britain claim it had achieved its aim in the operation of keeping the canal open to international shipping – Washington frantically sold sterling, blocked Britain's rights on IMF funds and refused to help with its shortfall in oil supplies. By mid-November 1956, the British economy had reached a critical condition. Macmillan feared Britain's foreign reserves would be drained within weeks, and that the economy would be paralysed for want of oil. Half of the country's oil supplies had been halted. Only American co-operation and financial support could pave the way for replacements from the Western hemisphere. Otherwise a disastrous fall in foreign reserves, to $1300 million, down from $2400 million before the crisis, would be needed to pay for supplies and diversions around the South African Cape over the next three months. But when Eden sent Lloyd to Washington to win support for London's position, Eisenhower refused to meet him. Unwilling to risk damaging relations with the Arabs, he had banned all

45

communication with Eden's Government until Britain and France pulled their forces out of Suez.[1]

This perilous situation proved a watershed in Anglo-American relations. It demonstrated that no British premier could go it alone militarily in the Middle East in the face of US opposition, and it forced Britain to reappraise its military role in the region, including on Cyprus. The first to grasp that point was Harold Macmillan. He decided there was only one way out of the deadlock at Suez. Without telling Eden or Lloyd, or indeed most of the Cabinet, he secretly met the US Ambassador, Winthrop Aldrich, and asked for a meeting with Eisenhower. Britain, he told Aldrich, had reached the crossroads – it would have to decide between a withdrawal from Suez or seizing the whole canal area. But he offered a way forward for the President. He said Eden would soon be out of the way because he was about to stand down due to ill health, though in fact the prime minister's doctor had told Macmillan only that Eden would be taking a rest from work.[2]

Eisenhower swallowed the bait and arranged for Aldrich to contact in strict secrecy the two men the Americans thought most likely to succeed Eden – Macmillan and Rab Butler – and offered to furnish them with 'a lot of fig leaves' if Eden was forced out and there was an immediate withdrawal from Suez. The secret understanding with Washington paved the way for Macmillan to take over the premiership and was the first of several personal pacts with Eisenhower which, among other things, led Britain to give up sovereignty over most of Cyprus. Eden, unaware of the conspiracy, flew out to Jamaica on 23 November to convalesce. With the Prime Minister absent, the Egypt Committee suspended, and Butler chairing Cabinet meetings, Macmillan told ministers that Washington's support was crucial for the securing of a UN peace-keeping force in Egypt and for preventing hostile resolutions being passed at the UN. On 24 November, the United States kept up the pressure by abstaining in a UN vote. British amendments to a motion calling for their immediate withdrawal from Suez were defeated.[3]

On 28 and 29 November, Macmillan warned ministers that the announcement, due on 4 December, of the losses of gold and dollars sustained in November would be a 'considerable shock to public opinion and international confidence in sterling' unless they were also able to announce clear measures to remedy the situation. Otherwise employment and production levels might plummet. They had to be able to say at once that they were proceeding to exercise drawing rights on funds from the IMF – rights which were being blocked by America – and to seek dollar loans. This would not be possible without the good-will of the United States, which could only be obtained by an immediate and unconditional undertaking to withdraw Anglo-French forces from Port Said.[4]

But ministers were dismayed to discover that the Ambassador in Washington had already been authorised to inform the State Department that Britain intended to pull out of Suez within 14 days. They feared they could not carry the support of MPs for what amounted to a devastating admission of failure in the Suez operation.[5] On 1 December, Macmillan tightened the screw, warning that the drain on reserves was even more serious than previously thought, and that no improvement could be expected unless the Government established normal political relations with the United States. The Cabinet conceded defeat.[6]

When Lloyd announced in parliament that British troops would begin withdrawal in mid-December if a competent UN peace-keeping force was in place, America lifted the financial constraints, tankers carrying oil supplies left the Persian Gulf bound for Europe and US Vice-President Richard Nixon stressed the need for a close Anglo-American alliance. On 11 December, the Cabinet was told that the United States had strongly supported its application for an immediate withdrawal of $561 million from the IMF, almost half Britain's quota.[7]

When the French insisted that they could not complete the withdrawal until 22 December, a worried Butler told the Cabinet this breached the 'understanding' with America on this subject, on the strength of which they had given Britain their support in the IMF.[8] But by 22 December the last British troops had been evacuated from Port Said and Port Fuad, and America had passed $2 billion to Britain, The codeword 'Lobster' advised Allied HQ in Cyprus that the Anglo-French forces were now clear of Egyptian soil. The Suez operation was over.

So, too, was Eden's career. By the time he returned from Jamaica on 20 December, the key decision to pull out had been taken without consulting him; his power had evaporated, and all that was left was for him to go.[9] When Eden announced his resignation to the Cabinet on 9 January, Macmillan – with no hint of his part in Eden's downfall – said it grieved him deeply that his political association with the Prime Minister over 30 years must now be broken. Butler said for him personally it was a bitter blow. And the following day Macmillan took over the premiership.[10]

While this astonishing political coup was underway, the last act of Eden's policy on Cyprus was played out when the constitutional proposals developed for the island by Lord Radcliffe were sabotaged in December 1956. Eden had charged Radcliffe with developing an acceptable system of purely internal self-government for the Cypriots. Radcliffe proposed that the legislative assembly should allow for a Greek majority, while laws exclusively affecting the Turks would require a two-thirds majority for approval. He suggested that the hand-over of power to Cypriot ministers on all internal affairs should immediately follow agreement on self-government. But the Foreign Office was anxious to keep Ankara 'on our side', and pledges made to the Turkish Foreign Minister, Nuri Birgi, at a private lunch in London on 30 November destroyed any chance of Radcliffe's proposals being accepted by the Greeks. Birgi and his officials insisted that the only way of ending Greek oscillation over Cyprus was to devise a solution that was practical and final – and that meant partition. Lloyd asked him if the Turks would be satisfied with an arrangement that provided for eventual partition if and when self-determination were to come about. Birgi said that the sooner there was a definitive settlement the better.[11] When Lennox-Boyd announced the Radcliffe proposals in the Commons, he raised for the first time in public the possibility of settling the Cyprus question by dividing the island. Lennox-Boyd told MPs that when the conditions were right for self-determination, it would be exercised in such a way that the Turkish community, no less than the Greek community, would be free to decide their own future status. 'In other words... it must include partition among the eventual options,' he said.

This was another attempt to play Ankara off against Athens in order to buy Greek acquiescence in continuing British rule on Cyprus. On the same day as the Birgi meeting, General Keightley and other members of the Middle East Defence Co-ordinating Committee had warned the chiefs of staff that there was an 'overwhelming military argument *against* (authors' italics) partition',[12] and Lennox-Boyd himself had told the Cabinet confidentially[13] that the question of partition 'would not arise until the island was no longer needed as a base'. Even then, partition would not be put to the Cypriots as an option before they had been invited to remain under British sovereignty. With the help of the new constitution – and by implication the threat of partition – he thought they might well express such a preference. As expected, the Greeks were enraged by Lennox-Boyd's partition statement, and rejected the Radcliffe proposals outright. EOKA denounced them as an Anglo-Turkish conspiracy. Equally predictably, the affair fuelled Turkish ambitions. The Turks pressed their case further by demanding equal representation for the two communities in the proposed assembly, and on 28 December said partition was the only solution because Turkey needed an outpost in Cyprus for her own security.

Few could have predicted that come the new year there would be a fundamental shift in the British stance on Cyprus. The inglorious end to the Suez crisis had left Britain impotent and bereft of authority in the Middle East, and economically dependent on America. So damaging was Britain's loss of prestige that elder statesman Winston Churchill wrote to his former wartime ally, Eisenhower, warning him that the crisis had created a 'dangerous vacuum' in the Middle East which the Soviet Union would move into. 'The very survival of all that we believe in may depend on our setting our minds to forestalling them. If we do not take immediate action, it is no exaggeration to say that we must expect to see the Middle East and the North African coastline under Soviet control and Western Europe placed at the mercy of the Russians.' He pleaded for a return to the special relationship between Washington and London to remedy the situation.[14]

Eisenhower responded by broadcasting to the world that America was asserting its leadership in the Middle East. On 5 January, announcing what became known as the Eisenhower Doctrine, the President pledged to come to the aid of 'any nation or group of nations requesting assistance against armed aggression from any country controlled by international communism'. He made available up to $500 million for economic aid to any country in the Middle East whose independence needed to be bolstered. It contrasted starkly with Macmillan's private warning to the Cabinet on 8 January that Britain could no longer afford its £1550 million defence budget, and would probably have to cut it by £200 million.[15] As a result of the Suez debacle, Britain had lost its dominant role in the Middle East for good. From now on it was forced to let the Americans take the lead, even in the settlement of the Cyprus problem. The situation was summed up pointedly by Henry Brandon, the respected *Sunday Times* correspondent, who had access to senior American leaders: 'The basic postwar assumption had been that in the event of another conflict, Britain would hold the Middle East while the United States would take on the Soviet Union. That division of responsibility, after Suez, was upset.'[16]

The British chiefs of staff admitted privately that the events of the past year had 'destroyed our own dominant position in Jordan. The Egypt-Syria-Soviet nexus is well on the way to replace us'.[17] They feared the only way to keep the effectiveness of the nuclear deterrent to Russian aggression was to keep possession of a number of air-bases, of which the only one in the Middle East apart from Akrotiri on Cyprus was Mafraq in Jordan. They feared they would not now be able to keep that open for British use and thereby maintain the value of the RAF medium-bomber force against Russian targets.[18] Two Canberra squadrons on Cyprus were not enough to convince the Baghdad Pact allies of Britain's intention and capability to provide a nuclear defence for them. The nuclear strike force needed to be doubled in size. In the meantime, 23 major army units, in addition to fighter and bomber aircraft, were to be retained in Cyprus – the most the facilities could take – to keep up the appearance of strength in the Middle East.[19]

But though Cyprus was left bristling with troops and planes, Macmillan knew the days of British action in the region without the support of America were over – the country's dire economic circumstances and his deal with Eisenhower had seen to that. The Ministry of Defence was asked to cut world-wide troop levels from 760,000 to 460,000. Instead of competing with the United States in the region, Britain needed to concentrate on taking its share of responsibility for the defence of Western, rather than its own, interests. This included finding a solution on Cyprus that would allow Britain to keep its facilities for NATO and anti-Soviet use, and enable the United States to keep the peace between Greece and Turkey while allowing it to use facilities in those countries for the same purpose. This was the price of Britain losing its position of influence in the Middle East to Washington. In March 1957, Macmillan flew to Bermuda for talks with Eisenhower which heralded the closest period of co-operation between the two countries since the war, and one of the key subjects discussed was Cyprus.

America had long been pressing Britain to change its policy on Cyprus. In 1954, Eisenhower wrote to Churchill personally to voice his concern about the effects of Britain's Cyprus policy on the American public, who believed Greece was being 'reasonable and conciliatory'. In June 1956, Dulles resisted Eden's plans to offer Turkey a veto over self-determination.[20] British diplomats learned that at least one senior American military source believed the strategic importance of Cyprus after the Suez debacle was virtually limited to NATO purposes; that the British could no longer use it as a base for operations on their own, and that even its value to the Baghdad Pact was questionable. Certainly, the Americans did not want to see the island used in ways which conflicted with their own interests, as at Suez.[21]

As soon as he had become Prime Minister, Macmillan had asked Lloyd and the Ministry of Defence to urgently look into alternative arrangements on the island. Lloyd looked at the possibility of partition, the Ministry of Defence at whether Britain's military needs could be served by retaining a slice of Cyprus as a base. Macmillan soon became convinced by the American argument that there was no reason why Britain could not make do with an airfield, whether on long lease or with sovereignty, as with Gibraltar. 'Then the Greeks and Turks could divide the rest of the island between them,' he noted in his diary on 15 March.[22]

When Greece brought the Cyprus question before the UN in February, Evangelos Averoff, the Greek Foreign Minister, warned Grivas that American backing for Greece's hard line was falling away. He appealed to him to call a ceasefire on the island. Grivas agreed only to keep things quiet for the time being. It wasn't enough to swing the vote. With Washington's support, a non-committal motion was conclusively passed which called for a 'peaceful, democratic and just' solution.[23]

In the eyes of the Greek public, the vote spelled failure, and left Karamanlis fighting for his political life. Facing a vote of no confidence, and knowing there was no hope of regaining the initiative on Cyprus through new talks unless the fighting on the island was stopped, he appealed once more to Grivas to hold his fire. The EOKA leader would only do so if Makarios was freed and allowed to negotiate on behalf of all the Cypriots. According to Christopher Woodhouse, who had access to Karamanlis's personal papers, the Greek Prime Minister, desperate for a political lifeline, wrote to Eisenhower on 15 March asking for help. He reminded the President of their face-to-face meeting during the Suez crisis, when Eisenhower had promised to press Britain for the release of Makarios.[24]

In London, the British Cabinet was aware that it had to make some response to Grivas's offer to satisfy public opinion, but it was not prepared to let Makarios go unless he first denounced EOKA violence, an unrealistic demand, since Makarios was in the Seychelles for refusing to do just that. However, on 22 March, the second day of the crucial Bermuda summit between Eisenhower and Macmillan, a message was relayed to the Cabinet in London telling them that the US President was offering to take up the Cyprus question with the Greek Government, and that Macmillan was 'anxious to keep the US informed of our intentions and the terms of the announcement on the release of Makarios'.[25] Macmillan had come to the talks to cement the new relationship with America, and the last thing he wanted was to fall out with Eisenhower over Cyprus. The Prime Minister felt the offer of mediation between Greece, Turkey and Britain from outgoing NATO Secretary General Lord Ismay neatly side-stepped the need to respond to Grivas's ceasefire condition, providing a face-saving excuse for the adoption of a new position. And he telephoned Ismay to ask him to put his offer in writing to the Greek, Turkish and British representatives at the North Atlantic Council.[26] Athens was thought likely to oppose NATO involvement, but Macmillan was told in Bermuda that the US Ambassador was under orders to deal with that problem.[27] That day, Eisenhower sent a message to Karamanlis informing him that he had put the pressure on the British Prime Minister, and that Macmillan had consented to the Archbishop's release.[28]

The Cabinet in London threatened to mar the arrangement by insisting that Makarios denounce EOKA violence, which he refused to do unless the British ended the state of emergency in Cyprus. From Bermuda, Macmillan, after consulting Lloyd, let his ministers know that he favoured letting the Archbishop go anyway, despite having previously agreed with them on setting the precondition, and on his return he overruled dissent in the Cabinet.[29]

It was a small price to pay for what was on offer from Eisenhower at Bermuda. During the four days of talks, they reached agreement on three key defence issues. The United States was to join the Military Committee of the Baghdad Pact; Washington was to supply Britain with 60 Thor intermediate-range ballistic nuclear missiles (IRBMs); and both would continue nuclear tests. The Thor deal was a breakthrough in the development of Britain's nuclear deterrent, providing a rocket delivery system long before it could have manufactured one itself, and was proof of America's restored trust in Britain. The Baghdad Pact commitment contrasted sharply with the row a year earlier, when America dragged its heels on providing the nuclear weapons needed to prime the Cyprus bomber force, the agreed deterrent against a Soviet invasion of the Middle East.[30] The two leaders also promised to keep in close touch on current issues, and to work together at the UN to secure majorities in their common interests. They would do this by bringing their policies closely into line before they were raised at the UN. This was to prove invaluable to Britain on the Cyprus issue in the coming years. On his return, Macmillan said the talks went a long way to restoring and strengthening relations with America as 'cornerstone to world peace'. Eisenhower later wrote that the meeting was the most successful international conference he had attended since the Second World War.[31]

On 29 March, Makarios was freed, though he was barred from returning to Cyprus. Lord Salisbury, Chairman of the Conservative Party and a distinguished minister, immediately quit the Cabinet in protest. He had resigned in 1938, with Eden, over the appeasement of Mussolini. Eisenhower sent a personal message to Macmillan sympathising with him at having lost such a senior colleague over the decision. At Westminster, the Prime Minister lied to MPs, who suspected he had struck a deal with Eisenhower over the release of Makarios. He maintained, 'No reference was made either by me or the President to a decision which must rest wholly within the responsibility of the British government and with no one else'. He would only admit, 'The position and importance of Cyprus in the strategy of the Middle East was, of course, referred to, as was the NATO initiative for conciliation, since the United States, as a member of NATO, is concerned'.[32]

~7~

SOUNDING THE RETREAT

NATO Allowed to Mediate

Macmillan came back from Bermuda looking for a down-grading of Britain's military commitment on Cyprus. From April 1957, he sought to persuade his Cabinet that the island's strategic importance would decline over the next ten years, and that the scale of facilities required 'would not justify the indefinite continuance of repressive measures which were becoming increasingly repugnant to public opinion'. He ordered a re-examination of the future military value of the base to see what scope there was for reducing forthwith further spending on military works on the island. He also set up a committee headed by the Cabinet Secretary to consider whether partition outside the required military areas might be a feasible solution. This followed a series of American diplomatic interventions, and proposals for a Cyprus settlement from NATO Secretary General Paul-Henri Spaak, which represented an extraordinary interference in Britain's affairs, especially as the British Cabinet had yet to agree in principle that it should give up its sovereignty over any part of Cyprus. But these can be explained by Macmillan's agreement at Bermuda to co-operate closely with the Americans, and his admission that he discussed, with Eisenhower, NATO's offer to mediate.

Church bells rang out in Cyprus to celebrate Makarios's release. Barred from his homeland, he headed for Greece, on his way denouncing the idea of NATO mediation in the Cyprus problem. In Athens on April 17, he received a hero's welcome. Well-wishers lined the streets as he drove to Constitution Square to deliver a robustly anti-British speech denouncing Harding's tactic of turning Cyprus into an armed camp. Pledging to continue the struggle, he said, 'Neither Middle East oil, nor Western defence, nor Turkish opposition shall deter the Cypriots' claim to determine their own present and future'. Police tried to hold back the crowd as they chanted 'EOKA' and 'Death to Harding'. But despite his public defiance, the wily Archbishop scented collusion between Britain and America. In an attempt to head off a possible agreement over the Cypriots' heads by the NATO partners, he urged Grivas to check the armed struggle to create an atmosphere in which bilateral talks with the British could take place. Makarios was ready to accept a period of self-government before enosis, which could be accompanied by international guarantees to protect Turkish-Cypriot rights. The Turks were now saying that nothing short of partition would do, and Turkish-Cypriot militants were being armed. Makarios believed further action by EOKA would only play into Turkey's hands, by causing an inter-ethnic blood-bath. That would pave the way for partition on the grounds that it was the only safe option for the Turkish Cypriots. His flexibility enraged Grivas, who shared none of the Archbishop's political sophistication, and feared he was giving up the fight – he later discovered that the Archbishop had halted arms consignments to EOKA from Greece. Nevertheless, he suspended guerrilla activities. Makarios wrote to the Government to express his willingness to negotiate on how to apply self-determination.[1]

But Macmillan's more pressing concern was how to persuade his ministers and chiefs of staff of the need to cut Britain's commitment on Cyprus. His readiness to give up sovereignty over the bulk of the island shocked the military top brass, who were adamant that Britain must keep the whole island as a base.[2] General Keightley, who commanded the Suez operation from Cyprus, had insisted that continuing British sovereignty was the only way to guarantee the rights and facilities which had proved essential in the Suez campaign, and doubted Britain could play its essential role in combatting the spread of communism through NATO and the Baghdad Pact without it. He said any partition scheme would fail to meet the military requirements for the use of Cyprus in either limited or global war.

The generals were further alarmed when they heard of rumours in Washington that Britain was considering pulling out of Cyprus altogether. Defence officials fired off a missive to American defence chiefs, putting the case for British retention of the island in the strongest terms. They stressed heavily the strategic importance of Cyprus to both NATO and the Baghdad Pact. They said the island's bomber base, soon to provide a nuclear strike capacity, its electronic spying facilities, and the crucial new NATO early-warning radar made it vital to the defence of NATO's otherwise weak right flank. Baghdad Pact forces were also 'gravely inadequate' and – though Britain was not able to offer rapid military support by land forces – 'the nuclear air effort which could be deployed from Cyprus would be of considerable significance'. They warned their Washington counterparts of dire consequences if Cyprus was to fall into pro-Soviet hands.[3] The fact that they felt the need to plead the case for their presence in their own colony showed how far they believed Britain had become subordinate to America in the region – and in the special defence relationship generally. But Macmillan believed it would take 'more troops than we can afford' to hold the island through the next few years, and since his deal with Eisenhower it had become for him personally a question not of whether to abandon the concept of retaining the whole island as a base, but how.

The Americans' main concern was to remove a damaging source of conflict between their NATO partners and preserve the island's usefulness to the Western alliance. As both partition and enosis brought with them the risk of war between Greece and Turkey, the solution they favoured most was a form of guaranteed independence. In June, Spaak – newly appointed NATO Secretary General, a socialist, and former Prime Minister of Belgium – opened his attempts to mediate by mooting the idea that Cyprus should become independent – but be barred from joining with other countries – for a fixed period, after which its status would be looked at again. Foreign office officials complained that Spaak seemed to have been 'nobbled' by the Americans, who admitted talking to him and gave wholehearted support to his plan.[4] The Foreign Office strongly opposed independence because it would mean rule by Makarios or, worse, the communists, who were popular.[5]

The Americans tried to scare the Greeks into making concessions. The American Ambassador in Athens, George Allen, told Greek Foreign Minister Evangelos Averoff that there were indications that Britain had decided to pull out of Cyprus, and would leave Greece and Turkey to divide the island between them. 'The Americans wondered whether the Greek government had realised just how likely this was; and, in view of the very real danger, they could not help thinking that something ought to be done to forestall it,' Averoff recalled. But Karamanlis could not afford to oppose nationalist sentiment at the time.

In London, Macmillan worked out his own plan for Cyprus, designed to 'secure our essential military needs and to reduce our colonial commitment'. He believed it necessary to retain the use of an air-base, to support the Baghdad Pact and for general Middle East and Persian Gulf defence purposes, and keep hold of intelligence and propaganda facilities which could not be provided elsewhere. But he felt these needs could be met by retaining exclusive British sovereignty over small enclaves at Akrotiri-Episkopi, Dhekelia-Pergamos, Cape Greco and a number of establishments elsewhere that would be needed to house early-warning radars, electronic spying equipment and communications facilities. Guided by economic considerations and pressure from America, the Cabinet made the fundamental policy switch from insisting on sovereignty over the whole island to retaining sovereignty only over military base areas.[6]

The difficult part was to find a way to share the burden of keeping the peace in the rest of the island, while keeping it in safe hands from Britain's military point of view. Macmillan proposed surrendering the area outside the bases to a condominium of Britain, Greece and Turkey, under a governor nominated by the three sovereign powers. The governor, who would not be a national of Britain, Greece or Turkey, would control internal security, defence and external relations. If disputed, NATO could have the last say on who was appointed. Responsibility for defence would rest with the three sovereign powers, but since they were all in NATO, 'it would be reasonable that they should look to the [North Atlantic] Council to interest themselves in its defence'. For internal security, the governor would be able to call on a force comprising equal numbers of British, Turkish and Greek troops. Radcliffe's constitutional proposal would form the basis of self-government of the non-British part of the island.[7]

At one point, Macmillan even suggested that the island might be run by the British under a mandate from NATO, since this would strengthen Britain's hold on the airfield at Nicosia, and the communications between the vital strategic points on the island and Famagusta, the main entry point for seaborne supplies. But he feared MPs would not back this, because it would imply a complete surrender of British sovereignty and might appear as a move by Britain to transform the whole island into a NATO base.[8] He did suggest, however, that if there was an internal crisis after a tridominium had got off the ground, it might be better to resign Britain's share of the tripartite sovereignty outside the base areas and 'allow the Greek and Turkish governments to restore order as best they could'. He acknowledged, however, that this would involve a grave risk of open conflict between Greece and Turkey and widespread bloodshed on the island.[9]

Macmillan knew his plan could only succeed if Spaak and Eisenhower gave it their backing. Greek acceptance could be won 'only by American pressure', while it was up to Britain to convince the Turks that they would gain nothing by rejecting the plan in the hope of achieving partition.[10] He suggested using the device of tripartite talks – which had worked in the London conference of 1955 – to win the support of Greece and Turkey. He hoped it would be possible to present all the options, this time including the US-favoured one of guaranteed independence, to be examined and one-by-one dismissed in favour of his own plan once it was clear that the others would be opposed by one side or the other.[11] But Karamanlis was wary, and the British Ambassador in Ankara, Sir James Bowker, warned that if the Greeks showed any sign of accepting the talks, the Turks were likely to reject them. The project was aborted.

In the absence of co-operation from Greece and Turkey, the Foreign Office held detailed secret discussions with American officials at the US Embassy in London on 12 September 1957, to review the options available for a Cyprus inititative. Macmillan hoped that he could secure American support for his plan, but the Americans had serious doubts.[12] They thought that in the condominium plan there would be uncertainty about where ultimate authority would lie, given that sovereignty was to be shared and that in disputes appeals could be made to NATO. They argued instead for a system of guaranteed independence, to be approached through an interim period of Radcliffe-style self-government. Radcliffe had proposed an assembly with a Greek-Cypriot majority, but requiring a two-thirds majority on issues affecting Turkish Cypriots exclusively. The arrangement would be guaranteed by a number of NATO powers, and could be altered only by mutual agreement. The British thought that because of its interim nature it would encourage Greece and Turkey to develop it by intrigue. This would perpetuate tension, and British commitments would not be much reduced. They also thought a tridominium offered a more certain barrier against communist subversion than a democratic government.[13]

This point was underlined by a crisis centring on Cyprus's neighbour, Syria. At the end of August 1957, the Soviets furnished Syria with a massive military and economic aid package, thus presenting exactly the kind of communist threat to American interests which the Eisenhower Doctrine was designed to deter. Western arms were rushed to Jordan, Lebanon and Iraq, all on Syria's border, and Turkey called up its reserves and engaged in manoeuvres close to its southern frontier. The Russians dispatched a naval squadron to the Syrian port of Latakia and held manoeuvres close to the Turkish border in Bulgaria and the Caucasus. The crisis dissipated in late October, but was a sharp reminder to Turkey, America and Britain of the need to keep the communists out of Cyprus, which lies 70 miles off Syria's coast and guards Turkey's southern ports. For Turkey, in particular, it also underlined the need to have a military presence on the island in case the British ever left.[14]

Though they did not reach agreement in September, the private talks showed how Britain and America were moving closer together over Cyprus, leaving the positions of Turkey and Greece exposed as extremes. Britain had accepted that it could no longer afford to keep the whole of Cyprus against the population's will, and the Americans were now more concerned with reaching an agreement that would satisfy Western military interests than pleasing the Greek lobby at home. They helped Britain at the next big test, a renewed attempt by Greece to win support for its position at the United Nations.[15]

The first public sign of Macmillan's change of policy on Cyprus was the replacement of Harding by a non-military governor. Harding embodied a policy of retaining sovereignty through military occupation and repression. The appointment of Sir Hugh Foot, a respected liberal diplomat who had served as Chief Secretary in Nigeria and Governor of Jamaica, pre-empted criticism of Britain's military tactics at the UN. On 26 October, Dulles added to the pressure on the Greeks, by warning that the UN – because it gave a free hand to communist and non-aligned countries to influence the outcome – was not the right place to resolve the Cyprus question. He said it should be sorted out in direct talks between Greece and Turkey. But Karamanlis was under pressure at home to stand firmly behind a demand for independence within a fixed period of time. In Cyprus, Grivas organised mass demonstrations on Greek independence day, and warned against 'the immoral bargainings of the British, Americans and Turks'. He underlined his message with a spectacular show of force, as his men blew up four Canberras and a Venom, worth £4.5 million, at the Akrotiri RAF base.

At the UN in early December 1957, Makarios circulated to delegates copies of his 'Black Book', containing details of alleged tortures by the British. The Soviets attacked British colonialism and repression in Cyprus. The Greeks pressed ahead with their resolution demanding self-determination. But the Americans used all their influence behind the scenes to lobby for a neutral motion that merely called for talks between 'those concerned' to achieve a 'peaceful, democratic and just solution'. The Greek resolution failed to obtain the two-thirds majority needed when it came before the the General Assembly, for which Macmillan thanked the Americans. Foreign Office officials reported that both the Greeks and Turks were now 'rather suspicious' of the US role on Cyprus.[16]

As soon as Foot took over in Cyprus, he freed 100 Cypriots, and lifted restrictions on the movements of another 600. He also toured villages on horseback, despite the obvious security risks, dropping in to cafés to chat with local people, in an attempt to win the support of Greek-Cypriots for self-government and isolate EOKA. Grivas played into his hands with some macabre attacks on left-wing opponents.[17] The murder of trade unionists – one was tied to a tree in a churchyard and beaten to death in front of his wife – led to large street demonstrations and island-wide protest strikes by left-wingers.

Foot brought with him to Cyprus his own plan to get self-government off the ground. It involved ending the state of emergency, allowing Makarios to return, offering some communal autonomy, giving the Cypriots dual nationality and postponing any final decision on the island's future status until after a fixed period of five or seven years. Foot said any final decision would have to be acceptable to both Greeks and Turks, and admitted this gave Ankara, as well as Athens, a veto on long-term policy.[18] According to John Reddaway, who worked as an administrative secretary under Foot in Cyprus, one condition of self-determination after the fixed period was the provision of NATO bases on the island – possibly including a Turkish one, though the Foreign Office denied this.[19]

Foot failed to foresee the impact that allowing a Greek veto on the island's future status would have on the Turks. Angered and alarmed, they telegrammed their objections to every aspect of the plan. Britain was sounding the retreat to sovereign base areas without first guaranteeing them partition, the mininum they would concede if the British relinquished control. Riots ignited the Turkish-Cypriot quarter of Nicosia. Crowds carrying banners with the slogans 'Partition or death' and 'British murderers kill our people' filled the streets. At least five

Turkish Cypriots were killed as security forces moved in to break them up. Foot warned they would all 'go to hell for no purpose' if they missed the chance of settling the dispute among allies.[20]

However, when Foot and Lloyd visited Ankara in January 1958 for a Baghdad Pact meeting, and then Athens, they saw there was no future for the Governor's plan. In Ankara, the Turks insisted on a federal constitution before agreeing to any political developments, and demanded a base on Cyprus immediately.[21] Ministers feared such a base would be used to bring more arms onto the island, and fuel more strife. The Turkish right of veto on the island's future status made the plan unacceptable to Karamanlis too, and the initiative failed.[22]

Macmillan was running out of patience. In a conversation with Foot at Nicosia airport on 14 February, he decided it was time to choose a plan and try to force it through, regardless of opposition from Athens or Ankara or violence on the island. He realised this could not now be achieved without American support.[23]

A re-opening of EOKA's military and political campaign made matters urgent. Grivas began his long-nurtured plan for a campaign of passive resistance, including the boycott of British goods, from soap to alcohol and even the football pools. He also pressed ahead with a campaign of sabotage. In the first ten days of April there were more than 50 explosions as EOKA guerrillas bombed and burned government buildings. A British police officer was shot and fatally wounded. In the third week of April there were more than 40 acts of sabotage. The fighting only stopped when Foot made a dramatic offer to meet Grivas in secret, alone and unarmed. But Grivas feared a trap, and did not reply. In May, two British military policemen in plain clothes were shot dead. Troops rounded up more than 700 youths for questioning.

All the signs were there that the violence – and the cost of containing it – would escalate. Foot recalled, 'I feared that at any time some EOKA outrage would set off Turkish resistance and that civil war between the Greeks and Turks which we most dreaded would result'.[24] Yet the Cabinet, meeting in mid-May, was warned that it was 'militarily unacceptable' to commit British forces to keep the peace on Cyprus for even the seven-year interim period envisaged in Foot's proposals if troop numbers were reduced as planned. The Government was due to make a full statement on the future of Cyprus on 19 May, but Macmillan had run out of options to propose, and the statement was put off to allow time for a plan to be put confidentially to the North Atlantic Council, and their approval secured.

Lloyd was instructed to ask Dulles for his backing for the original tridominium plan at the NATO meeting in Copenhagen, and to help put pressure on Greece to co-operate. Macmillan told Lloyd to impress on Dulles that he was prepared to 'risk a great deal and put all the effort that I can command into persuading both our countrymen and the rest of the world that this is a good and even a noble plan – an example of how Western countries should be able to sink their old differences in the light of much greater dangers'.[25] He wanted the Foot plan to serve as the basis for internal self-government in the interim period before tridominum, to cool the troubles on the island. But the Americans favoured guaranteed independence, and the power to influence Greece and Turkey lay in their hands.

~8~

NORTH ATLANTIC AGENDA

Eisenhower Rejects the Macmillan Plan

The Cyprus question was taken to NATO at a jittery time for the West. Over the previous year, the Soviets had taken a giant leap in the arms race, beating the Americans to the next stage of missile technology, with the successful testing of an intercontinental ballistic missile (ICBM) system and a new type of hydrogen bomb. Symbolic of the Soviets' technological achievement was the launch of Sputnik, the first man-made satellite in space, in October 1957 and, shortly afterwards, the sending of a bigger satellite into orbit with a dog on board. The nation which many thought technologically backward had beaten the Americans into space, and the military implications were devastating: it was only three years since the Russians had first developed long-range bombers which could deliver nuclear bombs to the American mainland. Now they were capable of launching missiles which could hit American cities within 30 minutes of take-off. American planners did not think they would be able to match this before the early 1960s. Defence hawks called for a speedy rearmament and a massive fall-out-shelter programme. Some even called for a preventive war on the Soviet Union.[1]

In the Eastern Mediterranean and Middle East, Soviet advances appeared equally threatening. The Russians were building five bases for guided missiles and nuclear weapons in Bulgaria and two in Albania, on the borders of Turkey and Greece respectively. Missiles in the two Soviet satellite states were said to be capable of striking Athens, Ankara, Nicosia or any British bases in the region – though the accuracy of missiles was very unreliable by modern standards.[2] And next door to Turkey, in Syria, the Soviet Union encouraged a purge of non-left-wing officers in the army. The purge backfired, because Syria's ruling pan-Arab nationalist Ba'ath movement feared a complete communist takeover, and pressed Nasser into forming a United Arab Republic of his Moscow-backed Egypt with Syria. This was of little comfort to NATO members, as Nasser appeared to be making much ground on his quest for a pan-Arab state, and had the power to persuade Syria to cut off the flow of oil from Iraq – 25 million tons a year – if he wished. A month later, pro-communist Yemen joined Nasser's federation and rebels tried to force Britain's strategically important Aden protectorate to follow suit. The unrest spread with alarming speed to the West's traditional allies, Jordan, Iraq and the Lebanon.

The Turkish premier, Menderes, said if Syria fell under Soviet influence it would lead to the encirclement of Turkey and endanger Iraq, Jordan, Lebanon, Saudi Arabia and Iran. 'The conquest of the Middle East by Russia, even without armed intervention, after establishing herself in Syria, would be extremely easy,' he said. North Africa and the Mediterranean would become a Russian field of action – and Europe would be encircled. He urged as many NATO countries as possible to stock up with intermediate-range missiles and atomic weapons.

With Soviet missiles threatening Turkey from the north, and political upheaval on its border, the Turks could not afford any uncertainty over Britain's commitment to stay on Cyprus. If the island fell into the hands of Turkey's enemies, whether Greeks or communists, it would leave her totally surrounded and vulnerable from the south.

During the delay in the announcement of Macmillan's plans, these fears reached fever-pitch. A Turkish spokesman in Cyprus said they would oppose any compromise over their future with arms and that the Turkish Government had promised support by 'all means', including troops and ships.[3] Turkish-Cypriot leaders Dr Fazil Kutchuk and Rauf Denktash issued dire warnings that Macmillan was about to hand self-determination to the Greek-Cypriots. The Turks used the tactics encouraged by Eden in 1955 – talking loudly of violence. On 7 June 1958, as Macmillan flew to Washington for more talks with Eisenhower, the Turkish information centre in Nicosia was bombed, sparking off two months of massacre, riot and arson. It is believed the bomb was thrown by a Turkish *agent provocateur*. A British investigation found that the furniture in the front of the office had been removed to a safe place before the explosion occurred. After the bombing, hundreds of Turkish Cypriots took to the streets armed with sticks, cudgels and other weapons, and began to attack police cars, burn Greek buildings and loot shops in the old quarter of Nicosia. The tactics bore all the hallmarks of pre-planned concerted action. The violence quickly spread to other towns. The first night's clashes left four dead and scores injured, and factories and offices ablaze.[4]

The following day, 200,000-strong crowds gathered in Istanbul to protest against British policy on Cyprus. As they moved in on the British and Greek Consulates, they had to be dispersed with tanks and armed troops. The Turkish Foreign Ministry issued a statement that Turkey had come to 'a full and mature decision' to realise the partition of Cyprus as the only solution to ensure her own security. Kutchuk rammed home the message as the massed crowds, carrying placards bearing anti-British slogans, shouted, 'Cyprus partition or death'. He said Turkish and Greek communities could no longer live together, and another speaker said 26 million Turks were ready to die for Cyprus. Turkish troops were massing on the coast opposite the island. Mob riots, brutal killings and pitched battles between Greek and Turkish Cypriots continued for days. Lloyd told the Cabinet that the Turkish Cypriots 'appeared to be deliberately attempting to create the impression that it was impossible for the two communities in Cyprus to live together harmoniously'. More than 10,000 troops were used to quell the fighting.[5]

In Washington, Eisenhower told Macmillan his priority was to heal the rift in NATO. On 13 June, the British took Macmillan's plan to the North Atlantic Council and told the allies they were 'anxious for the matter to be treated as a North Atlantic problem', as this might be the last chance to reach an agreement. Macmillan was hoping to use collective pressure from NATO to force his plan through.[6]

Greece's response shocked its allies. That day, it pulled its 80-strong staff out of the NATO regional headquarters at Izmir. No warning was given. American protests that this left NATO's southern flank severely weakened were ignored. Averoff insisted that he could not agree to NATO discussing the Cyprus issue, for fear that it might jeopardise Greece's campaign at the UN.

On 15 June, the Turks rejected the plan, insisting on partition as the only means of protecting Turkish Cypriots. They told their NATO allies that partition was already taking place spontaneously, listing seven villages where the Turkish population was moving out *en masse* (in fact they were told they would be killed if they did not go).[7]

Macmillan's representative at the North Atlantic Council warned that Britain could not tolerate any attempt by Greece and Turkey to rewrite the plan: it would allow talks only on how to put the proposals into operation. But the British were no longer in a position to dictate terms. They had taken the issue to a platform which the US dominated, and Washington overruled them. The Americans insisted that it should be 'subject to adjustment', and used their influence to persuade the 12 disinterested NATO countries to welcome the British proposals as a basis for 'constructive discussion', stressing that as an interim plan it did not prejudge the final solution. Greece and Turkey officially reserved their irreconcilable positions to let talks take place.[8]

The details of the Macmillan plan were given to MPs for the first time in the Commons on 19 June. The Prime Minister said the plan was an 'adventure in partnership'. It safeguarded the British military bases and installations on the island, but allowed for internal self-government with separate assemblies and autonomy for each community over its own affairs. Wider administrative affairs would be dealt with by a council presided over by the governor, and including representatives of the Greek and Turkish Governments and six elected ministers drawn from the assemblies, four of them Greek and two Turkish. Citizens could have dual nationality: Greek or Turkish as well as British. External affairs, defence and internal security would rest with the Governor, who would consult the representatives of Greece and Turkey. The international status of the island would remain unchanged for seven years to create an atmosphere of maximum stability. The state of emergency would be dismantled step by step.

Colonial Secretary Lennox-Boyd warned that the situation was 'desperately dangerous'. It had become urgently necessary to announce a policy, and to carry it through, without Greek and Turkish approval in advance. Discussion of the plan would take place at NATO level between the 'three countries directly interested'. No reference was made to the fact that Macmillan had been consulting a fourth power, the Americans, on the issue for some time.

Shadow Colonial Secretary James Callaghan seized on the Government's climb-down from the days when Hopkinson implied Cyprus could never expect to be free and Macmillan, as Foreign Secretary, had said Cyprus was a domestic issue to be decided by Britain alone. Callaghan stressed the importance of self-determination in Commonwealth countries where people were entitled to decide their own destiny. 'Self-determination, when it comes, must come with the consent of the people of the island. It cannot be imposed by force.'[9]

But in a stern warning to the Greeks, the Prime Minister said that if the initiative failed Britain would honour Lennox-Boyd's pledge of December 1957 that if self-determination were ever granted, it would be offered separately to both the Turkish and Greek Cypriots.[10]

Grivas found Macmillan's idea of partnership 'grotesque'. Makarios's personal adviser on foreign affairs, Zenon Rossides, said the British plan, if implemented, would permanently destroy the prospect of a unitary Cyprus because there was no common legislative assembly for both communities. He accused Macmillan of taking a 'temporary phase of artificially fanned strife' and giving it 'permanent form in a divisive constitution'.[11] Averoff thought there could be 'no worse solution', and threatened to pull Greece out of NATO altogether. But Labour's Aneurin Bevan warned the Greeks privately that if the plan did not succeed, Macmillan might wash his hands of the Cyprus problem by pulling back to two bases in the south and 'calling on Turkey to take over the whole area north of the 35th parallel'.[12]

The fate of Cyprus, however, was no longer a matter for Britain alone to decide, for Britain was no longer the real power in the region, as unfolding events in the Middle East showed. To try to counter the spread of Nasser's pan-Arab nationalism, Jordan and Iraq formed a rival federation to the United Arab Republic, but on 14 July 1958, the Baghdad Government was brought down by a coup. King Feisal II and his crown prince were murdered. The body of Prime Minister Nuri Said, was dragged through the streets by a mob. The Lebanese President, Camille Chamoun, feared his administration would be the next to fall. He appealed to America and Britain to intervene to protect the frontier with Syria. Macmillan thought that if the insurrection in Iraq was not reversed, and the Lebanese Government fell, Jordan would be next in line, and the West's influence over the Arab states would collapse, leaving Turkey, Israel and the Gulf sheikhdoms isolated.[13]

In an immediate response, the US Sixth Fleet steamed towards Beirut with 11,000 troops on board. There was no prior consultation with London. It was like Suez in reverse. Britain no longer had the power to act on its own, and Macmillan had to beg Eisenhower and Dulles to agree to a parallel effort in Jordan. Cyprus again became the launch-pad for a major military expedition. But a blunder brought the Government to the brink of disaster. With hundreds of troops already flying to Amman, the British realised to their horror that they had not obtained permission from Tel Aviv to overfly Israel. Macmillan slammed on the brakes. The squadrons were ordered to U-turn lest Israel took action against the unexpected intruders.[14] Trying to hide his 'sickening anxiety', the British Prime Minister once more begged the Americans, on whom the Israeli economy depended, for help. As the Israeli Cabinet went into emergency session, it took personal appeals from Eisenhower to Ben Gurion to obtain permission. Finally, two battalions were sent from Cyprus to Jordan to defend the airfield at Amman and key government buildings. A third was sent to secure a line of communication from Cyprus to Aqaba. American transporters carried supplies from Cyprus to Amman. They also used the Cyprus facilities for their Lebanon operation.[15]

The interventions saved the administrations in Beirut and Amman – and Eisenhower had rescued Macmillan's premiership from disaster. But Britain had lost, through the coup in Iraq, its most important ally in the Middle East other than Turkey, and with it the two airfields which were a key part of Britain's Baghdad Pact strategy. This severely restricted Britain's military influence in the region. America, by contrast, had strengthened its position by taking a lead role in the defence of the Middle East, and Washington signed separate defence agreements with Turkey, Iran and Pakistan, to form CENTO (Central Treaty Organisation), a replacement for the Baghdad Pact.

While these Middle East military operations were being carried out, the internal situation in Cyprus continued to deteriorate. In early July, Grivas ordered a retaliatory onslaught on Turkish Cypriots, particularly those in the police force. In the first three weeks of July, 29 Greek Cypriots, 31 Turkish Cypriots and two Britons died as a result of the fighting. A further 24 Greek

Cypriots and 20 Turkish Cypriots were wounded. Foot ordered two 48-hour periods of standstill on the island, with full curfews in all main towns and a complete ban on traffic. Troops arrested 1500 Greek Cypriots and a large number of Turkish Cypriots. Foot also proscribed the Turkish-Cypriot underground organisation TMT.[16]

Spaak suggested that it was time the Americans brought more influence to bear in Athens and Ankara to break the deadlock. The Greeks could not accept the Turks having a say in the affairs of Cyprus through the proposal for Turkish and Greek Government representatives to work with the island's Governor. The Turks wanted wide powers for their representative and equal footing for Greek and Turkish Cypriots on the governing council.[17]

Privately, British ministers accepted that Turkey's dependence on US aid could help the Americans to get some results in Ankara.[18] Spaak suggested that Washington might discreetly link the question of financial support for Turkey, then under discussion, with a more flexible Turkish attitude over Cyprus.[19] Two days later, Washington signed historic agreements to form CENTO, whose headquarters was being moved to Ankara. The next day, the Turks suddenly told the British privately that they would accept the Cyprus plan in full. Macmillan was dumbfounded. But there was a catch. They insisted that not a word of it be changed. They were willing to abandon all other claims, including partition and a military base.

Menderes also agreed to join Karamanlis, Makarios and Macmillan in appealing to both sides on Cyprus for a halt to the bloodshed. On 4 August, a ceasefire was declared by EOKA and TMT. That day, the Organisation of European Economic Co-operation, the IMF and the US Government announced a large-scale $359 million economic aid programme to Turkey. Two-thirds of it came from America. The United States also postponed the repayment of massive loans granted to Turkey in 1948.

That the Turkish change of heart came as a complete surprise to Macmillan and his diplomats is evidence that the Americans had worked behind the backs of the British. British diplomats noted that Spaak sent his ideas to Washington 'way ahead' of sending them to London, and believed this was further evidence that the Secretary General was under American influence.[20] Dulles was now ready to offer America's public support for the Macmillan plan. It was only a tactical move to extract concessions from the reluctant Greeks – as Britain discovered later.

Macmillan tried to seize back the initiative by setting off on a personal mission to Athens, Ankara and Nicosia in the first week of August. He found Karamanlis was under extreme pressure. The Greek premier, in an emotional outburst, said the Greeks had been fighting the Turks for over 500 years, and that to give Turks a veto over the aspirations of Greeks in Cyprus would be a humiliation.[21] On 15 August, Macmillan responded by downgrading the status of the proposed Greek and Turkish representatives so that neither would actually be part of the Cyprus Government, though their role would stay the same. But Makarios called on Karamanlis to stand firm. When the Greek premier rejected Macmillan's concession, the Turks, despite their demand that not a word could be changed, accepted.

Karamanlis realised the writing was on the wall for enosis when NATO commander General Norstad, on a visit to the Greek capital, told the Greeks that he had consulted the US State Department in advance, and had been told that the US attitude was support for the British plan, period. Karamanlis admitted to Norstad that Greece could never defend Cyprus against a hostile enemy. His objective now was to ensure no steps were taken towards partition. He suggested that the island might be put under a UN or NATO trusteeship. Afterwards, Norstad told British officials he had never felt so disturbed about the Greek situation, which now seriously endangered NATO interests in a vital area.[22]

Macmillan had set 1 October as the date for implementing parts of his plan, whether or not agreement had been reached. As the deadline neared, EOKA stepped up its violence, ambushes, bombings and incidents of arson. The British tried to ease the tension by releasing 100 Greek-Cypriot and 30 Turkish-Cypriot prisoners from the detention camps – but there were still 1900 Greek Cypriots, compared with only 32 Turkish Cypriots, behind barbed wire. Spaak feared that the arrival of the Turkish representative to take up his post on Cyprus on that date would trigger an explosion.[23]

To take the heat out of the situation on Cyprus, the Americans suggested that Ankara could be persuaded to appoint the resident Consul General in Cyprus as their representative. Spaak rushed to Athens, where he found the Karamanlis Government 'turning madly' from one possible solution to another, and even Makarios beginning to support the idea of guaranteed independence.[24]

For the Americans, all the pieces were falling into place. As the Greek Government mulled over how to present their latest appeal to the UN, Makarios told them he now favoured independence for Cyprus under UN auspices after a period of self-government.[25] He had shifted from his goal of self-determination leading to enosis, though his suggestion still left the door open for the UN to give enosis the go-ahead. Makarios later said his decision had been prompted by the Americans.[26]

Grivas was incensed, but the Archbishop told him by letter that the co-operation between Britain and America demanded a bold and realistic approach if a *fait accompli* was to be avoided: 'America has completely aligned its policies with Britain and our only hope of success at the UN is to put the question on the basis of independence'.[27]

Out of the blue, at the North Atlantic Council on 24 September, Spaak called on the British to suspend their plan and put it on the table at talks between the three interested governments. He warned again that the arrival of the official Turkish representative could trigger an explosion. He insisted that it was the task of the Americans to put the proposal to the Turks. But the Turks regarded the proposal as a 'stab in the back' by Spaak.[28]

Lloyd, on a visit to the United States, sought desperately to prevent the Americans undermining Britain's position by backing Spaak's plan for three-way talks. He insisted that talks be based solely on the British plan and how to apply it.[29] This earned him a stinging rebuke at the North Atlantic Council from the Americans, who, casting aside the limits he wished to place on the discussion, insisted that the scope of the conference should be 'liberally interpreted'. They urged all parties not to be tied to prior agreements, but to be willing to put changes into effect 'irrespective of the fact that they might be inconsistent with prior actions'. The 'unqualified' US support for the British plan had proved short-lived. They also strongly defended Spaak's right, as NATO's Secretary General, to put up his alternatives. US NATO representative Burgess offered to go with Spaak to Athens and Ankara to press for conciliation, prompting seething British diplomats to warn London that Spaak and Burgess, after their recent visit to the United States, were now working 'rather more as a team'. The British Embassy in Turkey reported that Washington had suggested talks with a 'rather broader agenda' than the British envisaged. The Foreign Office believed the Americans had 'overstepped the limits of the amount of pressure it was safe to apply in Ankara'.[30] But on 29 September, the Turks, persuaded by US diplomats, announced that they were appointing Burhan Ishin, the Turkish Consul General in Nicosia, as their representative for Cyprus. Ishin had served on Cyprus for most of the previous seven years, and was the least controversial choice they could have made.

Consequently, the 1 October deadline did not spark the conflagration that many had feared. The Greek Cypriots held an island-wide strike. EOKA carried out a spate of bombings and shootings directed at British troops. But there was no inter-ethnic conflict.

~9~

PAX AMERICANA

The Settlement Secures NATO Ties

The Foreign Office was wary of the NATO proposal for talks on Cyprus, because it wanted any conference to bring discussion to a close, not to reopen the whole question. But, bit by bit, the Americans were determinedly steering all sides towards their preferred solution of a system of independence guaranteed by NATO powers, as secretly discussed with the British in September 1957. The Turks further undermined Britain's position by accepting that there should also be a voicing of views on the eventual status of Cyprus. Even Foot advised moving closer to the American stance, suggesting that the long-term aim should be to get both sides to rule out enosis and partition, and that Spaak or the Americans might launch this idea.[1] Finally the Foreign Office relented, and in mid October 1958 came out in favour of Foot's idea. It suggested a 20-year treaty on this with NATO or the UN – which would narrow the debate down to either a tridominium or the US option of guaranteed independence – and accepted Spaak's proposal for talks, as did the Turks. Sensing an historic turning point, Spaak paid tribute to the British, praising the magnanimity of so great a country in submitting matters under its sovereign jurisdiction to discussion at an international conference in a foreign country, probably under foreign chairmanship, and with its own subjects separately represented.[2]

However, to his fury, the Greeks still refused to go to the talks, putting the entire NATO mediation effort in jeopardy. Averoff had wanted to offer 'iron-clad guarantees' against enosis, and to call for independence, but Makarios torpedoed the initiative, and was backed by a knife-edge vote in the Greek Cabinet.[3] Though the Archbishop had previously said Turkey and Greece should renounce forever any claims over Cyprus, he appeared to believe that this did not preclude Cyprus opting for union with Greece after independence – if he could muster enough support from the non-aligned movement and the Eastern Bloc at the UN to push enosis through. Having burned his bridges with NATO, this was the only strategy he had left. For him, everything now rested on the UN debate.

Grivas looked aghast at the events unfolding in Athens, and reacted with a show of force. In October, more than 40 people were killed, including six British civilians and ten servicemen. An RAF Canberra bomber was sabotaged at Akrotiri despite heavy protection. This led to the sacking of all Greek Cypriots employed at the air-bases and in the NAAFI catering units – they were replaced by 8000 British volunteers – and the reintroduction of emergency measures.

Makarios tried to pre-empt US backing for the British at the UN by reminding the Americans in public that the State Department had encouraged him to press for independence. This was strongly denied by the State Department, which claimed it had not taken any position 'as to a specific solution of the Cyprus problem' – a tactical lie, because in fact the US had consistently pressed privately and through NATO for guaranteed independence. Makarios also refused to give assurances that Britain's bases would remain if independence was achieved. 'The Arabs and the USSR don't want those bases there, and we are going to need their help in the UN,' the Archbishop explained.[4] The American statement against backing any particular solution was a blow to the Greek cause at the United Nations, because their motion called specifically for independence. But it was only a tactical device. If Makarios won at the UN, the pressure for an independent Cyprus free of any allegiance to NATO or its traditional defence ties with Britain would become irresistible. That was not the kind of independence the Americans had in mind for this strategically important island.

There was a dramatic curtain-raiser to the debate at the UN Political Committee on 25 November, when Greek Cypriots followed a call from Grivas for a general strike to protest against the British plan. In the debate, Averoff attacked the Macmillan plan as the equivalent of the 'murderous knife of partition'. He claimed the British had exerted 'heavy diplomatic pressure' on the countries that had voted against them in previous UN debates about Cyprus. 'Many governments, we were told, had been given oblique warnings of a possible cooling of political and economic relations, and the hint had been taken to heart, as quite a number of small countries depended on Britain for a large part of their exports,' he said. The Greek motion was backed by Ireland, Czechoslovakia and Romania. It called for a period of self-government leading to an independent Cyprus, with guarantees for the protection of the Turkish Cypriots. But Turkish Foreign Minister Fatin Zorlu accused the Greeks of continuing to seek enosis, and refused to rule out partition as a long-term option. He said any motion that prejudged the final settlement risked creating civil war or 'an even wider conflict'. The United States said that continuing the 'quiet diplomacy' at NATO was the best way to sort out the Cyprus problem, and eleven countries backed a resumption of talks.[5]

On 4 December, US representative Cabot Lodge intervened decisively by making it clear that Washington favoured a revised Iranian draft motion which called for talks between the three governments and the representatives of the Cypriots on the future of the island. These would cover not only an interim arrangement, as Macmillan had wished, but also a final solution, and could be assisted by other governments and personalities if desired. This followed closely the American line at NATO, right down to allowing Spaak and an American representative to attend talks, and Lodge reiterated that Washington did not want to prejudge any decisions on an ultimate solution – because it did not want its option of guaranteed independence ruled out. The motion was passed by the UN's Political Committee by 31 votes to 22, with 28 abstentions.

This was a catastrophe for the Greeks. Having turned down the US-inspired NATO initiative, they had staked everything on winning the vote at the UN – and lost. The defeat broke their resistance to negotiating on a final solution. A secret telegram from British diplomats to the Foreign Office revealed that Lodge's advisers had agreed in advance with the British how to handle the debate. Their common line was that 'if we were to persuade the Greeks to face realities and accept a compromise, we must first convince them that they had no hope of success, and that therefore everything reasonable should be done, including full US support for our position'. The diplomats concluded from American actions that 'the instructions to the US mission at the UN were in the same sense'.[6]

But the debate had also been sobering for the Turks, for it had become clear that partition was as unacceptable to the international community as enosis. Deepening security fears and American pressure impressed on Ankara the urgency of resolving the Cyprus question and making peace with Greece. With timely symmetry, both countries were in the mood for compromise, and the conditions were right for Washington to steer them towards the desired goal. Ankara was being given massive economic inducements by America, which had promised $234 million in aid, and a loan from Britain to help sort out its economic problems. Both were pressing for co-operation on the Cyprus issue.

The increasing tension between East and West concentrated Menderes's mind further. On 3 December 1958, Turkey suddenly felt the threat of Soviet expansion on its own doorstep when Russian officers arrived in neighbouring Iraq to train Baghdad's army, which was now being supplied with Soviet weapons. The formerly British air-base at Habbaniyah was being used by the Soviet-backed Egyptian airforce, operating MiG jets. This was a blow to the West, but was particularly worrying for Ankara, because it gave the Soviets a foothold behind Baghdad Pact lines. It also meant Turkey could ill afford additional hostilities with Greece, its NATO ally to the west.

Thus the moment of Greece's humiliation became the opportunity for securing a workable compromise. Averoff recalled that at the end of the debate Greek morale was at its lowest ebb when Turkish Foreign Minister Zorlu suddenly approached him, accompanied by Ambassadors Sarper and Keural. 'I told my colleagues that I was afraid I might not be able to restrain myself from being extremely rude,' Averoff said. To his surprise, Zorlu quite uncharacteristically announced that he had come to congratulate Averoff on putting up such a good fight. Averoff admitted defeat, but told Zorlu, 'Both our countries are... standing at the same perilous crossroads and we are squabbling in public, whipping up hatred between our peoples, because we are unwilling or unable to agree'. Zorlu replied, 'I thoroughly agree with you. I am more alarmed than I can say by the common dangers facing both our countries'. He then offered to hold private talks to iron out their differences. Averoff, startled, would only agree if the Iranian motion was dropped without being put to the full General Assembly.[7]

The next day an extraordinary change took place, thanks to furious work behind the scenes by the Americans. Averoff asked Lodge to help get the Iranian resolution replaced.[8] The American immediately called together the leading delegates from Greece, Iran, Mexico, Turkey and Britain and thrashed out a new motion, which merely expressed confidence that continued efforts would be made by all parties to reach a 'peaceful, democratic and just solution'. It was adopted unanimously without a vote. The Greeks were spared the embarrassment of a UN vote backing the kind of talks they had already rejected at NATO. But the Americans now had them in a corner. Unless they compromised, the Greeks faced the unchallenged consolidation of the Macmillan plan and the danger that the two communities would increasingly become separated politically, making partition a more attainable objective than a unified independent Cyprus.

Lloyd personally thanked Dulles for the Americans' 'invaluable work behind the scenes' at the UN.[9] The next day, Zorlu and Averoff held their first detailed discussion of the Cyprus question, at which Zorlu offered detailed proposals that came close to Washington's original idea for guaranteed independence, and represented a momentous switch away from insistence on partition. 'Both his manner and the substance of what he said had altered a great deal in the course of the ten-day debate,' recalled Averoff.[10]

Zorlu suggested that to prevent the Turkish-Cypriot community being swamped by the Greek Cypriots, the stronger community should be prepared to share some of its power in a proportion greater than the relative size of the communities, and the head of state should alternate between the two. While he wanted to leave two bases with the British, he also wanted Turkey to be given two coastal bases to protect its southern flank, and offered to agree to Greece having even bigger bases on the island as well. Averoff did not want to hand the Turkish Cypriots political equality, but he was willing to give them communal autonomy in some affairs and a 30 percent share of power and federal government outside the British bases. Zorlu suggested they had a basis for a settlement, and should both report back to their governments and discuss the matter again on the fringes of the next NATO Council meeting in Paris a week later.[11]

Zorlu brought with him to Paris a draft agreement which had been approved by the Americans. Averoff said Zorlu was ready to make concessions and seemed in a hurry to reach a settlement, though he was immovable on the need for a Turkish base on the island.[12]

That night, Zorlu met Selwyn Lloyd at the British Embassy, and recounted his conversations with Averoff. Lloyd displayed alarm at the direction in which Zorlu and Averoff appeared to be heading. He warned that Britain saw independence in some ways as the worst possible outcome, because of the danger of 'letting the Russians in'. But Zorlu assured him that the solution he had discussed with Averoff was 'not really a form of independence'. It would, he said, be necessary to write into the constitution the alliances, and also a right of veto, on both sides in regard to the two communities. The island must be Turkish-Greek, not Greek and not Cypriot. The sovereignty outside the British bases must be shared between Turkey and Greece. It was common ground that British sovereignty should continue over the bases. Zorlu said Averoff had agreed that the way forward was to sort out their differences first and then go to the British. He already knew he would get American backing. Lloyd left it to Zorlu to safeguard Turkish-British interests in his talks with Averoff, a tacit admission that the initiative had been taken out of British hands. When Macmillan heard the news he told Foot, 'Something like a final settlement may be within our grasp... it seems almost too good to be true'.[13]

There was, however, one other obstacle in the way. Two convicted EOKA men were due to be hanged within two days. Ministers from France and Norway put pressure on Britain to quash the sentences. But the strongest representation came from the least likely quarter. Zorlu threatened that if the hangings went ahead the British would have to carry the blame for the inevitable breakdown in talks.[14] The hangings were stopped at the last minute.

When the new plan was put to the British Cabinet, Lloyd said it would involve guaranteed independence for Cyprus, but Britain would retain sovereignty over certain military base areas. He said that while there were risks in seeking to maintain a strategic hold on limited areas in a country not under British control, the interests of Turkey would 'largely coincide with our own and if Turkey guaranteed our strategic facilities in Cyprus by treaty, we should be able to maintain our position'. Moreover, Britain would be relieved of the liability of military occupation of the whole island, though the EOKA threat was likely to remain.[15]

Even at this delicate stage in negotiations, the British launched one last attempt to track down and eliminate Grivas. A joint MI5-MI6 scheme, code-named Operation Sunshine, was devised. According to former MI6 agent Peter Wright in his memoirs, *Spycatcher* (which the British Government tried to suppress), 'It would be too crude to say that Operation Sunshine was an assassination operation. But it amounted to the same thing.' Wright believed he was in a race to find the guerrilla leader before a 'ramshackle deal' was stitched up.[16]

On 17 January, Wright set off on a secret mission to tap Makarios's telephone and plant a bug in Grivas's HQ. With him was John Wyke, MI6's best technical operator. Wyke spent two hours up a telegraph pole outside Makarios's palace in darkness, with Wright handing him tools from below, both sweating with fear every time armed bodyguards patrolled nearby. They implanted an electronic device in the pole and connected it to the telephone cable, before hurriedly making their escape. Next, they tried to track down EOKA's radio aerial, on which they hoped to plant a receiver containing a radio beacon. They believed the guerrillas were monitoring British army communications by radio, and that the beacon would lead them to Grivas himself. They pinpointed two villages, Yerasa and Polodhia, as the centre of Grivas's operations. At one point, Wright spotted what apeared to be an aerial, but was driven away by children throwing stones when he tried to investigate. By February, he and Wyke were closing in on Grivas's position, and kept him under close observation while they planned the final entrapment. However, when Karamanlis and Averoff met their Turkish counterparts, Menderes and Zorlu, in Zurich in the second week of February 1959, to thrash out the details of their joint plan for Cyprus, the hunt was suddenly called off – for fear of damaging the political initiative. Peter Wright recalled, 'Just as we moved into top gear... the entire Sunshine plan was aborted overnight'.[17]

The Greeks and Turks set aside their differences and proposed independence, guaranteed by a treaty between Greece, Turkey, Britain and Cyprus. For the internal structure, they settled on a compromise between power-sharing and majority rule. There would be a Greek-Cypriot president, but a Turkish-Cypriot vice-president; separate communal assemblies, but also a joint national assembly; a joint military headquarters supported by 950 troops from Greece and 650 from Turkey, but a locally maintained Cypriot force of 2500 recruited from both communities. Britain was to keep two sovereign base areas.

Macmillan admitted surprise at the speed at which agreement was reached. When, on 11 February, Menderes and Karamanlis jointly proposed an immediate visit to London, he noted, 'This is getting very interesting. What one fears is that they may join in asking us more than we can concede.' He told Lloyd to ensure that London retained not only sovereignty over the bases, but control over other sites and installations such as radar stations, which were to be 'ours in perpetuity', full facilities such as roads and harbours; and a special arrangement for Nicosia airfield. The Greek and Turkish Foreign Ministers, who negotiated without consulting the Cypriots, told the British they could have what they liked, and that Makarios had agreed to it all. Then, as the Greek and Turkish Prime Ministers flew to London to put the final seal on the agreement, disaster struck the Turks. Their plane crashed, killing 12 of the party, and Menderes was rushed to hospital.[18]

The negotiations carried on, but were thrown into more turmoil on 18 February, when at the last minute Makarios refused to sign. He strongly objected to a clause giving Turkey, along with Britain and Greece, a veto over changes to the constitution. This would stymie any chance of using independence as a stepping-stone to enosis, exactly the point on which he had proved ambiguous in the past. But the three powers told him to 'take it or leave it', and demanded an answer that afternoon. Makarios refused. Lloyd, exasperated, extended the talks for 24 hours. The Archbishop was left to think it over at his luxury suite at Claridges, and in the morning, when he turned up at Lancaster House, surprised everyone by announcing that he was ready to sign.[19]

Intelligence writer Nigel West (pen-name for the former MP Rupert Allason) claimed that Makarios was blackmailed by British security services. He said compromising material on the Archbishop was collected on Cyprus by MI6, which recruited an agent from his entourage. Apparently, part of Operation Sunshine involved a fall-back plan to use the evidence that was accumulated of Makarios's 'rather unusual homosexual proclivities'. West said Makarios was threatened with disclosure of this evidence to force him to sign. 'He was revered by the greater part of the island's population as a political leader and churchman. Any revelation about his homosexuality would have been terribly damaging,' said West.[20] Another account, in a biography of Sir Dick White, then head of MI6, claimed the blackmail was used to secure Makarios's agreement to Britain retaining two sovereign bases.[21] A less colourful theory on why Makarios signed is that Greek diplomats put pressure on members of the Greek-Cypriot 'advisory body' which had come with him to London. On that crucial morning, members voted by 27 to eight for the agreement.

Most accounts of how Cyprus gained independence point to the unexpected meeting of minds between Karamanlis and Menderes at the decisive moment, and credit Macmillan's firmness in keeping to his plan as the prime motivator. In fact, by December 1958 Britain had become a bystander, left out of the negotiations over the future of its own colony. That is why Macmillan was so often surprised as each breakthrough was made on the slow road to conciliation. The final settlement was based on exactly the principle advocated by the Americans in their secret meeting with British officials in September 1957 – an arrangement which the British had insisted would be fraught with difficulties. According to British minutes of the meeting,[22] the Americans looked on guaranteed independence as the ultimate solution. 'The arrangement would be guaranteed by a number of NATO powers and could be altered only by mutual agreement,' the Americans said. The Turks had flatly rejected the idea, yet these proposals found their way into the Zurich agreement in February 1959 as a result of encouragement from Ankara, an astonishing turnaround from their insistence that partition was the biggest concession they could make.

In the event, the agreement was praised by Macmillan for its 'spirit of partnership', by Karamanlis for being a symbol of 'friendship', and by Menderes for opening 'an era of peace… and sincere co-operation between the two communities'. However, there was also a hidden agenda, as the Greek and Turkish leaders came to a secret 'gentlemen's agreement', which was never to be revealed to the Cypriots. The British Cabinet was shown the details, and the Foreign Secretary said they should not be published 'at any stage'. But the document has since surfaced. It shows the Greeks and the Turks wanted to limit self-determination for the Cypriots in the interests of Western defence, even before the new nation was born. In the deal, both Karamanlis and Menderes agreed to press for the new Cypriot state to join NATO and to ban AKEL and all communist activities – despite AKEL's massive popularity among Cypriots.[23]

Turkish agreement on guaranteed independence might never have been possible, but for the behind-the-scenes inducements from Washington – Ankara's conversion came as two years of negotiations with Washington over defence arrangements were coming to a climax.[24] Turkey had been eager to accept nuclear weapons from the United States since late 1956, and was involved in talks with Washington over the positioning of Jupiter missiles in Turkey throughout the crucial stages of the haggling over Cyprus's future. On 19 February, the day Makarios signed the Cyprus agreements, the Soviet news agency, Tass, reported that America and Turkey were locked in talks on an agreement to build new military bases and ballistic missile launching sites in Turkey.[25]

On 5 March, two weeks after Cyprus's fate was sealed, Washington signed a new agreement with Turkey, Pakistan and Iraq, pledging to defend them against aggression. It meant America was formally implementing its promise of a year earlier to take over from Britain as the might behind the Baghdad Pact (which Iraq was on the point of leaving) and defender of the Northern Tier. Turkey was also given two out of the seven squadrons of IRBMs to be stationed in NATO countries outside Britain. These moves may also have reduced Ankara's concern about not having a military base on Cyprus if it gained independence.

Greece, too, had made far-reaching concessions on Cyprus. So what persuaded Karamanlis to bridge the final gap? His snubbing of NATO help over Cyprus, and Greece's failure at the UN left him embattled, facing heavy economic pressure from the three most powerful NATO partners. America was threatening to cut off economic aid to Athens, and Britain and France were demanding the payment of pre-war debt. After the Zurich negotiations, by contrast, the Greeks signed a deal in which the Americans would supply Greece with nuclear weapons, ballistic missiles and training. The warheads would remain under American control. The Soviets protested that the United States was turning Greece into a nuclear *place d'armes*. Later in the year, Eisenhower rewarded Karamanlis personally for his co-operation by visiting Athens for informal talks.[26]

The last details to be worked out before Britain could hand over sovereignty on Cyprus concerned the bases and facilities it would keep. Makarios, bitter about the way the settlement had been forced on him, drove a hard bargain. Britain asked for 160 square miles, the Cypriots suggested 36. At one point, Makarios threatened to launch a civil disobedience campaign if he did not get his way. The Turks feared he would put the entire set of independence agreements at risk. After months of haggling, it was agreed that Britain should retain 99 square miles encompassing two sovereign bases at Akrotiri and Dhekelia and retain the right to use a string of military sites housing vital installations within the territory of the new Cypriot state. The completion of the talks cleared the way for independence.

~10~

A SHAM INDEPENDENCE

The Unsinkable Aircraft-carrier

At midnight on 15 August 1960, the Union Jack above Government House in Nicosia was lowered, and a fanfare of trumpets, followed by a 21-gun salute, marked the birth of the new Cypriot state. Inside, Governor Sir Hugh Foot, in white tie and tails, announced the end of British rule, and representatives of Britain, Greece, Turkey and Greek and Turkish Cypriots signed the formal independence agreement. Menderes and Zorlu were not there: military leaders had seized power in Ankara in May, and they had been taken prionser – later to be hanged. Makarios said it meant the Cypriots had been granted the 'basic right to regulate their own affairs', and stressed that the success of the new state depended on 'mutual appreciation and respect of the national ideals, spirit and traditions of the island's Greek and Turkish inhabitants'. For the Turkish Cypriots, Kutchuk said the state would survive through 'everlasting peace and law and order', which they were determined to create. Critics predicted gloomily that in the new Cyprus, Greek would turn against Turk, right against left, and the island would go down in a sea of blood and hate. But Foot swept aside their pessimism, declaring boldly, 'People who have been at the edge of hell do not want to go back'.

As the Cyprus flag was unfurled for the first time above the Council of Ministers building in Nicosia, and fluttered in the wind, crowds of Greek and Turkish Cypriots cheered as church bells rang out. The flag's design, a gold silhouette of the island on a white background, underscored by a pair of crossed green olive branches, symbolised peace and unity between Greek and Turkish Cypriots. Later that day, Makarios and Kutchuk were invested as the first President and Vice President of the new Republic of Cyprus. Foot, setting sail for home on board HMS *Chichester*, to the strains of the bagpipes of the Black Watch and the screams of Javelin aircraft tearing through the sky in a ceremonial flypast, was convinced that the settlement had prevented a civil war, and that the killing had been stopped.[1]

In the event, Foot left in his wake a set of independence agreements – comprising the Treaty of Establishment, Treaty of Alliance, Treaty of Guarantee and the 1960 constitution – which were fatally flawed. They established a system of government and security that was doomed from the start to promote divisions which eventually led to bloodshed. It had been devised by outside powers, bartering over their own political and defence interests on the island, and not by the people who had to live there, and resulted in neither real independence and unity nor a workable system of government. Under pressure from the NATO allies, the Greek Cypriots had been forced to accept a constitution that denied them government by an elected majority, denied them the freedom to change their own constitution, and guaranteed the NATO powers military influence and facilities on the island. The agreements were not designed to give the Cypriots real freedom. They were meant to safeguard Western defence interests – by preventing Cyprus's political problems causing war between Greece and Turkey, by stopping the communists from gaining control over key areas of the island's government, even if that was what the people wanted, and by keeping the crucial military facilities available for Western use.

The Greek-Cypriot President and Turkish-Cypriot Vice President were to be assisted by a Council of Ministers comprising seven Greek and three Turkish Cypriots, with at least one of the latter given one of the three most important portfolios: foreign affairs, the economy or defence. Though the Council of Ministers could vote by simple majority on most issues, the President or Vice President could veto decisions in those three big areas. There was also a House of Representatives comprising 35 Greek-Cypriot and 15 Turkish-Cypriot members, elected by voters from their own communities. It could pass laws by simple majority, except in the areas of finance, electoral law and local government, which required separate majorities among the members from each community, effectively giving both sides a veto. Debates took place in the two official languages, Greek and Turkish, translated for each side.

There was also an intermediate level of government, two Communal Chambers with complete power over affairs exclusively affecting their community, such as religious matters, education, and local government taxation.

Funds were to be allocated to these chambers on an 80:20 ratio, roughly reflecting the share of population represented by each chamber. In addition, there were to be separate municipal councils for each community in the five biggest towns. Constitutional disputes were to be dealt with by a Supreme Constitutional Court. The most controversial feature of the agreements was the Turkish-Cypriot power of veto. It meant that if both sides did not proceed in a spirit of compromise, the political process could be halted indefinitely on areas as fundamental as the budget and the setting of taxes.

The continuity of this system of government was underwritten by the Treaty of Guarantee, under which Cyprus agreed not to take part in any union with any state, and to ban all activity which might encourage either union or partition of the island. In the event of a breach of the treaty, the guarantor powers – Greece, Turkey and Britain – agreed to consult on the measures needed, and to take action. Failing joint action, each guarantor power had the right to take unilateral action to restore the status quo. Under the Treaty of Alliance, in addition to British troops in the sovereign bases, 950 Greek and 650 Turkish troops were stationed on the island under a tripartite command. The allies thought this would be enough to deter any rebellion against the order they thought they had established.

As the independence agreements were being signed, there were worrying intimations of the trouble that lay ahead. There were frenzied scenes at Nicosia airport when 20 EOKA men, free to return under the independence amnesty, arrived back on Cyprus from Greece in triumph. And crowds in the old quarter of the city celebrated the arrival of the bulk of the 650-strong contingent of Turkish soldiers. The mood reflected the emphasis of the agreements, which was more on handing out military and political prizes to the NATO powers involved than on establishing a unified and independent Cyprus.

The biggest prize went to Britain. The Treaty of Establishment provided that most of the island should become an independent republic, but it also allowed Britain to retain two large sovereign base areas on the southern coast and extensive rights of control over numerous defence sites and installations dotted throughout the territory of the new republic, impinging on the independence of the new state. At the same time it jettisoned the security burden of having to repress a hostile population, so costly throughout the EOKA campaign. So much of the detail of the 1960 agreements is devoted to guaranteeing Britain's continued use of military and intelligence facilities on Cyprus – 56 pages of the 103-page treaty establishing the 'independent' republic, for example – that it is easy to conclude that this was what the 1960 settlement was really about. The imperative was to keep the island as an unsinkable aircraft-carrier and intelligence base in the global battle against the Soviets and to bolster Western military influence in the Eastern Mediterranean and Middle East. The agreements allowed Britain to keep a comprehensive set of intelligence, logistics and strategic facilities, enabling it to use the island as a platform for all levels of military activity, from Cold War spying to fighting regional wars or aiding the defence of the West with nuclear weapons in any new world war. These capabilities were just as important to the Americans as they were to the British, since they ensured Britain could play its role in the strategic defence of Western interests.

Rarely are references made to the facilities Britain employed – and still employs – outside the bases and inside the new republic, yet they helped make Cyprus one of the West's most strategically important spy bases. As a result of the 1960 Treaty of Establishment the island was left bristling with sophisticated electronic listening equipment which fed – and still feeds – a constant flow of top secret information to Britain and America. This 'signals' intelligence played a crucial role in the defence of the West during the Cold War. The spy stations were set up under British colonial rule, and the treaties establishing the new Republic of Cyprus gave Britain sweeping powers to retain and protect them. The information gleaned by them is passed to Washington under the terms of the secret 1947 UKUSA agreement which shared out responsibility for global electronic intelligence collection between the United States, Britain, Australia, Canada and New Zealand. The Americans had also been secretly using their own intelligence facilities in Cyprus during British rule. In addition to the eavesdropping facilities, a number of the sites retained by Britain contained installations which were essential to military operations, such as landing and storage facilities at the ports. The functioning of all these installations required close co-operation with the Cypriot administration, and gave the outside powers an overwhelming reason for interfering in the internal affairs of the new state from the start, whether or not they publicly admitted it.

Signals intelligence, which includes electronic and communications intelligence, provides one of the most secret, yet most important, weapons of modern warfare. It involves the use of radar and electronic receivers to intercept signals that give clues to the enemy's military capability, tactics, plans or activity. It can be used to tap into signals and conversations between tank commanders and their headquarters, fighter planes and their bases, or diplomats and their government. Between them, these facilities can pick up messages in Morse code or voice, or even the heat emissions of missiles or aircraft as they take off. Britain had an entire regiment – 9 Signal – and other units on Cyprus devoted to operating this equipment and thousands of intelligence staff employed to decipher and analyse the encrypted messages and signals at Government Communications Headquarters (GCHQ) in Cheltenham. Up to 20,000 people were employed worldwide in British signals intelligence, and the Cypriot signals staff handled tens of thousands of classified documents each day.[2]

Like many other intelligence installations, those on Cyprus not only intercepted 'traffic', but also monitored the direction from which signals came, the pattern of destinations to which they were being sent, and controlled the movement of transmitters to chart the movement of enemy military units, aircraft or ships. Changes in volume of radio traffic were monitored to warn of the build-up of military preparations for an attack, or of collusion between enemy states.[3]

Transmitters on the island relayed the intercepted material to GCHQ, or Washington, or other sources in the Middle East. They were also used to jam enemy radio broadcasts and transmit broadcasts to counter enemy propaganda in the region.

Today, four times as much intelligence is collected through hi-tech spying than by the old-fashioned secret agent. Masses of detail can be gleaned about the enemy's weapons systems, order of battle, plans and changes in activity. It can make the difference between winning or losing a war, and played a crucial role in both world wars. The cracking of the Enigma code, by which German U-boats disguised their communications, helped Britain win the Battle of the Atlantic and proved a turning-point in the Second World War. As Winston Churchill said, without Britain's mastery of the 'secret war', as he called the intelligence operations, 'all the efforts, all the prowess of the fighting airmen, all the bravery and sacrifices of the people, would have been in vain'.[4]

Cyprus assumed prime importance for British intelligence in the Middle East following the withdrawal from Palestine and Suez. When the 1960 agreements were negotiated, the boundaries of the two British sovereign bases were drawn up to include three of the four most important intelligence sites – indeed the peculiar shape of the Dhekelia base, with its north-eastern boundary stretching out like an antennae, is designed purely to encompass the road out to the intercept station at Ayios Nikolaos. The sovereign bases were deliberately made bigger than needed at the time to leave 'elbow room' for new installations to be constructed, and to bring in installations from other areas on the island.[5] The British Government never has to give up the bases because Britain retains sovereignty over them, but it has the right to use a series of sites and installations outside the bases. Its power over the bases, sites and installations is far greater, for instance, than the United States has over its facilities in Britain, and they severely restricted the new state's sovereignty and independence.

The Episkopi base area contained the strategic airfield at Akrotiri, a major electronic intelligence station at Paramali, and the Middle East Air Force and Middle East Land Force headquarters. The airfield was earmarked to provide the main nuclear capability of the Baghdad Pact, accomodating four squadrons of strategic bombers. The nuclear weapons were to be stored in two 'special weapons sites' near the airfield.[6] This was Britain's only answer in that region to the Soviet Union's nuclear bomber threat and emerging nuclear missile capability. There were plans to provide, on the eastern side of the Akrotiri peninsula, reserve Foreign Office transmitter and receiver sites, RAF operational transmitters and the reserve site for the existing facilities at Heraklis, which were being used to send intercepted intelligence material to GCHQ.[7] The Episkopi base also had a wide stretch of land to the west of Episkopi village set aside for an 'aerial farm development' (a mass of receivers) on the high ground to add to the wireless stations already being used by the signals regiment near Paramali.[8]

The Dhekelia base contained two state-of-the-art intelligence intercept stations: an RAF signals station at Pergamos and a similar army signals station at Ayios Nikolaos. They were manned by 2 Wireless Regiment and 9 Signal Regiment, which had previously been stationed in Iraq and Palestine. The Pergamos station included personnel capable of deciphering and analysing material, as well as intercepting it. Ayios Nikolaos included an RAF transmitting station and message centre, an ordnance depot and a forest of high-frequency direction-finding aerials, used for pinpointing the position of enemy transmitters.[9] Another site near Athna was used for overt and covert Foreign Office radio activities. It was linked to a transmitter near Zyyi. Chiefs of staff said facilities in the bases, and at Troodos, made Cyprus 'an essential focal point in worldwide military telecommunications systems'.[10]

A key concession to Britain in the Treaty of Establishment went largely unnoticed by commentators, yet it called into question the extent to which Britain could ever allow Cyprus to be truly independent, particularly in foreign policy and internal security matters. The treaty lists 20 sites outside the bases which Britain could continue to use 'without restriction or interference', ten of them indefinitely. Britain was also granted the right to use another 11 small sites and installations after consultation with the Cyprus Government. Among the ten permanent sites were the electronic intelligence intercept and transmitting station at Troodos, high in the Troodos mountains, and a powerful RAF radar nearby at Mount Olympus. This was part of a chain of NATO early-warning radars stretching from Iceland to Cyprus, designed to counter the Soviet nuclear threat. The Mount Olympus site also included relaying, receiving and transmitting facilities. Two other radar sites were retained at Cape Kiti and Cape Greco. Another site at Heraklis contained an RAF transmitting station for sending to London the intelligence intercepted at Ayios Nikolaos and Pergamos.

In addition, north of Zyyi a 119-acre site was retained for the Foreign Office medium-wave radio transmitter, to broadcast to the Arabs and for RAF radio purposes. There was another radio relay station at Mount Yaila in the Kyrenia range for Forces Broadcast Service use, and for a planned NATO radio relay station. British planners were keen to ensure the retained sites and bases catered for 'NATO signals sites' as well as their own.[11] The entire airfield at Nicosia, which could take fighters and transporters, and housed a number of military camps, made up another site. Some areas and runways were jointly used with the Cypriots. Britain retained the right to deploy anti-aircraft guns around the airfield, even though it was on Cyprus territory. Britain also kept port facilities at Limassol and Famagusta, and various overt and covert transmitters, fuel depots, camps and firing ranges.

There was no mention in the 1960 agreements of the monitoring and communications stations that the Americans covertly used during British rule. Yet, incredibly, they secretly carried on operating them after independence without raising the issue with the Cypriots.[12] A secret British map, prepared for the

Colonial Office, shows two sites – at Yerolakkos and Mia Milea, to the east and west of Nicosia – marked as American wireless stations.[13] In their embassy in Nicosia, the Americans had a communications intelligence relay centre which handled all diplomatic messages by cable for the Eastern Mediterranean area. In Karavas, they also maintained a large station which monitored broadcasts from all countries behind the Iron Curtain and employed up to 50 language specialists.[14]

In 1959, GCHQ reported that the Americans wanted to bring what they described enigmatically as a 'naval unit' then operating in Nicosia into the British bases. The most likely explanation as to why GCHQ was interested, and why a naval unit needed the 800–1000 acres requested is that the Americans wanted to set up their own 'aerial farm developments' inside the proposed sovereign bases. Naval intelligence was of particular importance to the Americans as the Sixth Fleet made the biggest contribution to their military presence in the area.[15]

The Americans had been able to use the Cyprus bases indirectly for some time through intelligence-sharing arrangements with the British. They seemed to treat the fact that it was the British who held the facilities as a mere formality, and took it for granted that they, NATO and other members of UKUSA would reap the benefits. As early as 1949, the *New York Times* reported that the island had 'extensive' radio broadcasting and monitoring facilities, the latter that it was 'under joint Anglo-American aegis'.[16] According to T.W. Adams and A.J. Cottrell, the US goals for the newly-independent Cyprus were:

> First the Republic of Cyprus should develop political stability and join together with Great Britain, Greece and Turkey to form a solid bulwark against communism. Second, Cyprus should stress economic development, free democratic institutions and a pro-West orientation. Third, the US should enjoy unrestricted use of its existing communications facilities on the island. Fourth, the British Sovereign Base Areas should remain inviolate and available to any Western Nation for any purpose.[17]

The origins of the UKUSA pact go back to the early part of the Second World War, when the British and Americans agreed to swap intelligence information and know-how. In 1944, the benefits of extending this pact to other countries were discovered when Soviet intelligence material picked up in Australia revealed a world-wide network of Soviet spies working to undermine the power of the West and whip up anti-capitalist movements. The spies had access to the high-powered transmitters at each Soviet Embassy, and the messages sent from these masts were intercepted by Britain and America, Australia and Canada. This led to the exposure of a number of top Soviet spies such as Klaus Fuchs and Donald Maclean. By 1949, the United States had 1821 intercept stations worldwide. Britain monitored Soviet Bloc communications from its Cyprus installations and bases in West Germany and Turkey.[18] By the mid 1950s, Western powers had a global electronic listening network able to monitor signals from Soviet ground controllers and air defence commanders. As part of this network, information was sent to America's National Security Agency via a communications intelligence relay centre in Nicosia. The Americans also had permission to use Cyprus to launch U-2 spy planes, which were used to monitor Soviet military developments, including the emerging Soviet ballistic missiles deterrent.[19]

Cyprus had in the 1950s also become important to the United States as an air-base. The 1958 Lebanon and Jordan operations had proved its potential in Middle East conflicts, and the Americans had the right to move bomber groups into Cyprus and Turkey in the event of a global war against the Soviets.

However, there was one potential problem for the Americans with the Cyprus independence agreements, because in the negotiations Foot had made a concession which prevented the bases being handed to Washington at a future date. This meant that their access to the facilities would last only as long as Britain stayed on the island. Foot insisted to Makarios and Kutchuk that the Government had no intention of relinquishing its sovereignty or control over the sovereign base areas, and 'therefore the question of their cession does not arise'. But this did not satisfy them. In 1960, they forced the issue in an exchange of notes clarifying the Treaty which said that if British military requirements changed, and Britain at any time decided to divest itself of sovereignty or effective control over the sovereign base areas, or any part of them, 'such sovereignty or control shall be transferred to the Republic of Cyprus'.[20] The Cabinet had wanted to keep open the option of handing the bases over to NATO at a future date.[21] Foot's concession tied any advantage the United States gained from the bases to a continuing British presence.

A detailed examination of the Treaty of Establishment shows how incomplete was the independence that had been granted. Very little of the treaty and accompanying annexes was about setting up the new state. Most of it was about giving the British control over the territory it was supposed to be making independent, not about giving Cyprus freedom.

The British authorities were given the right to 'exercise complete control within the 31 [British-controlled] sites'. They could guard and defend them and exclude from them anyone they wished, even officials of the new republic. Only the British army had the power to police the sites and arrest anyone within them. Yet outside the sites, the Cypriot authorities had to provide security and prevent any interference with their operation. For instance, if requested, Cyprus had to restrict the movement of aircraft, ships and vehicles, the erection of installations and the operation of radio and electrical equipment near British sites and facilities. The British also had the power to arrest saboteurs or anyone trying to hinder their use.

Britain could use roads and ports in Cyprus freely for the movement of troops to and from the sovereign bases, sites and installations, with the consent of the Cyprus Government. British military aircraft could fly in Cyprus airspace without restriction, British engineers could install communications and electronic systems on Cyprus's territory and lay submarine or other cables between bases or sites.

British troops could train in six areas inside Cyprus territory, and where the training sites were sea areas or airspace, the Cyprus Government had to keep non-British vessels or aircraft out of them during exercises. Britain was also given unlimited use of Nicosia airfield and 'special facilities' in the control tower 'for the operation of UK military aircraft in peace and in war'. It could also commandeer the air traffic control system in an emergency. Cyprus had to keep the taxi-ways and dispersal areas at Tymbou airfield ready for use by the British as a reserve landing-ground for Nicosia.

These were wide-ranging powers for one state to enjoy within another, and limited the independence of Cyprus far more, for instance, than did American rights over bases in Britain. What would British MPs say if the Americans were given the power to take over at will Heathrow airport – Britain's equivalent of Nicosia airfield – for military purposes in peacetime or war, and even if the United Kingdom was not involved in that conflict? What would they say if the entire airfield was designated an American site, and the British authorities were only allowed joint use of certain facilities within it?

However, the 1960 agreements went much further than merely ensuring Britain retained its military facilities: they were also designed to prevent a communist or pro-Soviet government taking the island out of the Western sphere of influence, even if that was what the people voted for. In a briefing note to the Americans before a settlement had been decided, the British emphasised:

> It is of great strategic importance that Cyprus should not come under the control of a government which was favourably disposed towards the USSR. The presence of a Soviet (or potentially Soviet) base in the rear of NATO forces and close to the Turkish mainland would be liable to have a most seriously undermining effect on the stability of the right flank of NATO and upon the Baghdad Pact.[22]

This was prevented by the combination of the military presence of three NATO powers on the island and the veto powers of the Turkish-Cypriot minority, which could be relied upon to side with Turkey in foreign affairs, and could veto economic policy.

When it came to the use of the sovereign bases, the Cypriots were given no say at all, even if their use made the island the subject of a military attack. During the pre-independence negotiations, Menderes, hosting a dinner for the British Defence Minister, raised the question of what position Cyprus would take if Britain used its sovereign bases to launch a war against a Middle East state, risking a retaliatory strike on the sites in Cypriot territory. The minister went home and took legal advice from the Foreign Office. While accepting that Cyprus might be dragged into hostilities as a result of British action, the Foreign Office said it was the Cypriots' own fault for accepting the 1960 treaties. It would be 'an inevitable consequence' of the granting of military rights to the British, and 'it must be assumed that the representatives of the Republic were prepared to run the risk when they accepted the terms of the London agreement'. Had they forgotten that the NATO powers ganged up on Makarios and forced him to sign?[23] Foreign Office officials also told ministers that the freedom of use of the bases for foreign troops 'does preserve to a substantial degree the UK ability, in conjunction with allies, to launch an operation in the Eastern Mediterranean'.[24]

In short, the Cypriots had been granted only a nominal independence in which the will of the majority could be prevented by a minority veto, the constitution could not be changed without permission from NATO allies, and the defensive allegiance could not be changed in any forseeable circumstances. Not only that, but Britain, the power that had supposedly granted independence, could, in collusion with America, continue to use the island at will as an unsinkable aircraft-carrier and strategic electronic spying base from which it could launch any military operation it liked – even a nuclear attack – regardless of whether it put the Cypriots at risk by leaving them vulnerable to retaliation.

However, before so much as a shot was fired by Britain in any conflict, concern mounted in Cyprus that the purposes for which Britain was using the bases was making the island a Soviet nuclear target, without the Cypriots having a say in the matter.[25] During the haggling over the size of the bases, Makarios had sought assurances that nuclear weapons would not be sited in them, but the British refused to discuss the matter.[26] In the first months of independence, rows broke out over reports in a Greek newspaper and in Britain's *Daily Express* that the British had begun stockpiling nuclear weapons in Cyprus without consulting the Cypriots. The *Express* said that underground nuclear arsenals for stocking H-bombs were being built on the island.[27] *Ethniki* in Cyprus said military sources had confirmed that the British were building special stores two miles long at Akrotiri for hydrogen and atomic bombs, and that stockpiling of nuclear weapons had begun some time ago in one of the bases. From Greece, Grivas accused Britain of turning Cyprus into a giant base with its network of sites.[28] Foreign Office officials observed that the nuclear question left Makarios and his Foreign Minister, Spyros Kyprianou, 'in a pickle', but they had agreed to British sovereign bases, and 'can't complain if Britain uses them how they wish'. However, they noted with alarm that 'the inferences Cypriot MPs are drawing is that independence is a sham'.[29]

~11~

CONSTITUTIONAL COLLAPSE

The Bloodbath Begins

The independence treaties left Cypriots – particularly Greek Cypriots – with a political half-life. If the NATO allies thought the contrived constitutional arrangement would enable the two communities to live peacefully together, they were badly mistaken. The complex structure of power-sharing, principally through political vetoes, solidified the divisions between the communities and failed to overcome the antagonism caused by the fears and aspirations of the two peoples. The fact that they needed a veto at all indicated that the two communities were not ready to become one nation. The tension that resulted when Makarios's policies were blocked by the Turkish Cypriots persuaded him to look for support from non-NATO countries which might back attempts to change the Cyprus constitution against the wishes of the NATO powers which guaranteed it.

The Turkish Cypriots were allotted 30 percent of jobs in the civil service, gendarmerie and police, and 40 percent in the army, despite representing only 18 percent of the island's population. At least one of the commanders of these three security forces was to be a Turkish Cypriot. Public service appointments, promotions and transfers were to be decided by a public service commission, endorsed by votes from representatives of each community. A Supreme Constitutional Court was set up to iron out disputes. It was made up of three judges, one Greek Cypriot, one Turkish Cypriot, with a neutral presiding. There was also a Court of Appeal.

But the limits on majority rule did not satisfy the Greek-Cypriot majority, which had fought for one thing – enosis – and had been given another – independence. The line-up of Makarios's first Government reflected the unfulfilled aspirations, and offended the Turkish Cypriots – who had been willing supporters of British rule. Foreign affairs went to Nicos Kranidiotis, who had links with Grivas, and had been put under house arrest by the British during the emergency. Andreas Papadopoulos, a former EOKA gang leader, was given communications and works. Tassos Papadopoulos, a former EOKA propaganda chief, became Minister of Labour. Polykarpos Georghadhis, a former EOKA commander in Nicosia who had escaped incarceration by the British and led one of the mountain guerrilla groups, became Minister for the Interior. The strong EOKA representation failed to impress Grivas, now in voluntary exile in Greece, who denounced the independence treaties as a sell-out. For him, only enosis would do. His followers in Cyprus put out black-edged leaflets denouncing independence as 'treason and national disaster'.

Almost as soon as he became President, Makarios caused an intercommunal row by serving redundancy notices on hundreds of Turkish-Cypriot policemen who had been auxiliaries during the British campaign against EOKA. He said their numbers exceeded the 30 percent quota, but Turkish Cypriots claimed he appointed Greek policemen far in excess of their 70 percent quota. This was followed by a dispute over taxes, which required separate majorities among representatives of each community. The first new tax rate was to be set in December 1960, but as no agreement was reached the deadline was extended to March. The Turkish Cypriots claimed some of the budget was being earmarked to pay for more Greek-Cypriot civil servants than the 70:30 ratio allowed, and for unfair allocations to developments for Greek Cypriots. When they tried to set a deadline for the Greek Cypriots to reach an agreement, Makarios ordered the tax department to ignore it, and keep collecting taxes at the old level. Kutchuk retaliated by calling on Turkish-Cypriot firms not to pay duties or taxes to central government.[1]

In December 1961, the Archbishop finally tried to introduce an income-tax bill. But the Turkish Cypriots said they would only support it if the tax rates were reviewed every year or two. As neither side could agree, Makarios issued demands for Greek Cypriots to make payments in lieu of taxes through their communal chamber. The Turkish Cypriots retaliated with a similar move. The row was taken to the Supreme Constitutional Court, but the chaos continued, as the court merely confirmed the right of both chambers to impose their own tax laws.

The arguments spilled over into the question of who should man the armed forces. The constitution said forces stationed in areas wholly populated by one ethnic group should belong to that community. Kutchuk believed this meant there should be separate armed units at platoon and company level, to guarantee protection from sectarian violence. But on 20 October 1961, Makarios put a motion to the Council of Ministers calling for the integration of the armed forces at every level. Kutchuk used his veto to block the move. Makarios then refused to create a national army at all, and the 2000-strong bicommunal force envisaged by the constitution was never formed. This created a vacuum in which private armies sprang up. By early 1963, the Turkish Cypriots had an estimated 2500 armed men, the Greek Cypriots 5000, which meant that inter-ethnic arguments could escalate into full-blown warfare.

They quarrelled over civil service jobs too. The Greek Cypriots saw the 70:30 ratio as unfair discrimination against them, and held up its enactment any way they could. In the first three years, 2000 job appointments were challenged in the courts. The separate municipalities were also a focus of tension, Greek Cypriots believing them a first step towards partition. The Turkish Cypriots feared they would be dictated to without them. After lengthy wrangles over the municipality boundaries, the Greek Cypriots refused to renew the municipal law and, in early 1962, tried to replace them with unified authorities.[2]

To put the Greek Cypriots' case to the international community, Makarios embarked on a series of state visits. After Cyprus joined the Commonwealth, he attended its Prime Ministers' Conference in London in March 1961, visited Nasser in June, a conference of non-aligned states in Belgrade in September, and President Kennedy in May 1962, among others. He never took his Vice President with him, and Kutchuk's veto powers proved worthless in this sphere. Makarios sought both aid and support for his attempts to change the Cyprus constitution and achieve self-determination for Greek Cypriots. Makarios's pursuit of non-aligned and Soviet support infuriated the Americans, whose policy was to bolster the Archbishop to prevent communist influence rising. Washington's priorities, revealed in State Department papers, were 'continued access to American communications facilities, an economic aid programme to facilitate development and to combat communism, and reliance on the guarantor powers to maintain the constitutional order on the island'.[3]

The communications bases were a constant headache, because they had not been covered by the 1960 agreements. The Americans had retained them on the republic's territory in breach of Cypriot sovereignty. When Makarios visited Washington in May 1962, the State Department decided it would be best not to raise the issue unless the Cypriots brought it up. Kennedy concentrated on pressing Makarios to form his own political party to provide some effective political opposition to the communists, who were achieving 30 percent of the Greek-Cypriot vote. The Americans wanted Makarios to stop stirring up tensions with the Turkish Cypriots, and stop trying to gain support among neutrals at the UN. They reminded him that his basic interests lay with the West, not the non-aligned movement.[4]

But the Greek Cypriots continued to press for enosis, ignored the safeguards provided for the Turkish Cypriots, and withheld portions of the aid due to them. The Archbishop was reported as saying, 'Until this small Turkish community is expelled, the duty of the heroes of EOKA cannot be considered as terminated'.[5] The US Ambassador warned that the failure to establish internal security had led to murders and intimidation, and that communist penetration had become a threat.

By January 1963, the State Department had given up trying to get Makarios to set up a moderate party – he argued that he should not take sides among his flock – and feared that their aid programme 'may not be moving fast enough to help [him] in the 1965 election'. The communists were gaining in the rural areas, but Makarios was in no mood to take a stance against the left, as he was asking the countries backing them to lend him support in the UN.[6] He also ignored calls to leave the constitution alone, and in March 1963 the international jurist and his assistant on the Supreme Constitutional Court decided they could take the wrangles and personal attacks no longer, and resigned.

American fears of communist success in Cyprus came as the Cold War reached its most apocalyptic moment, the Cuban missile crisis, which had an important knock-on effect for Cyprus, because the ensuing acceleration of the arms race made its electronic spying facilities vitally important to the West's nuclear deterrent in the years to come. The spark for the crisis was the installation of Jupiter missiles in Turkey, giving the Americans a launch site on the Soviet border. In response, the Russians tried to install IRBMs on America's doorstep in Cuba. In October 1962, Kennedy organised a naval blockade of Soviet ships carrying the missiles to Cuba, and both superpowers put their forces world-wide on nuclear alert in case the confrontation escalated. As the naval forces steamed towards each other, the world held its breath. One clash could have ignited nuclear war. But both sides backed down. The Soviets agreed to withdraw their missiles from Cuba after the Americans pulled their Jupiters out of Turkey. The lasting effect of the Cuban crisis was a deepening of distrust between the superpowers and the escalation of the nuclear arms race, as the Soviets sought to ensure that they could match the Americans missile for missile, and never be humiliated again.

Throughout 1963, the Greeks on Cyprus grew increasingly confident of their position, thanks in part to the support offered by the Soviet Bloc diplomatically and through the supply of arms. According to Richard Patrick, who undertook one of the most detailed studies of the conflict between the two communities on Cyprus, the Greek Cypriots were pursuing a secret strategy known as the Akritas Plan. Its existence was confirmed by the then President of the House of Representatives, Glafkos Clerides. The aim was to amend the negative parts of the 1960 constitution; abrogate the Treaties of Guarantee and Alliance, which forbade enosis; and achieve enosis through a plebiscite on the right to self-determination. The Greek-Cypriot leaders accepted that an armed struggle would probably be needed to overcome Turkish-Cypriot opposition. They secretly trained and armed an army of several thousand men to be ready to quell any revolt by the Turkish Cypriots at such speed – a few days – that Britain and Turkey would miss the chance to intervene and restore the status quo, as they were entitled to under the Treaty of Guarantee.[7]

The Turkish Cypriots, on the other hand, were building up arms and preparing to counter any attempts to achieve enosis with demands for partition and union with Turkey. Their underground army, the TMT, accepted that a constitutional deadlock was inevitable, and would lead to sectarian killings, kidnappings and riots. They planned to defend themselves from military attacks by sealing off the Turkish quarters in the larger towns and fortifying Turkish villages. Patrick said Turkish-Cypriot leaders, including Denktash, confirmed to him that they aimed to further the case for partition by provoking violent inter-ethnic incidents that would justify a Turkish invasion. They also wanted to create and direct a Turkish-Cypriot refugee movement into the northern part of Cyprus.

On 30 November 1963, while the US Government and its allies were reeling from Kennedy's assassination, Makarios put into action the first stage of the Akritas strategy. He proposed 13 constitutional changes that would have abolished the Turkish Cypriots' power of veto over legislation on defence, security, foreign affairs, elections, municipalities and taxation; and ended the separate Turkish-Cypriot municipalities, the 70:30 ratio in public services and the 60:40 ratio in the armed forces. Overall, these changes would have destroyed the power-sharing principle behind the 1960 agreements.

Makarios argued that these were common-sense measures needed to make government simpler. But the Americans believed they amounted to an extreme revision of the constitution, centralising power in the hands of the Greek Cypriots. Ankara rejected them. The mood was tense. An EOKA monument was bombed. The Greek-Cypriot police, commanded by Georghadhis, were ready for trouble, and the Greek-Cypriot irregular forces in Nicosia knew where to collect their arms. On the Turkish-Cypriot side, machine-guns had been handed out to members of TMT.

In the early hours of 21 December, as self-styled Greek-Cypriot 'special constables' investigated a quarrel over a prostitute in the Turkish-Cypriot quarter of the capital, a hostile crowd gathered. There was an exchange of fire. One policeman was wounded. One Turkish-Cypriot women and one man lay dead. That day, Makarios declared that the Treaty of Guarantee – by which Greece, Britain and Turkey pledged to protect the 1960 constitution – was no longer valid. The burial of the two Turkish-Cypriots was attended by thousands in an atmosphere of anger and fear which spilled over into the streets. Turkish Cypriots mounted machine-guns on their mosques and rooftops. Crowds gathered on the road to Kyrenia and shot at and stoned passing Greek-Cypriot vehicles. Soon a gun-battle raged across Nicosia. Hotels, bars and restaurants closed down. Ambulances raced through the streets. Armed police told journalists, 'There's a war on'.[8]

Six people died in the first two days of fighting. As Greek-Cypriot forces were mobilised and armed, ostensibly to prevent further outbreaks of violence, Turkish Cypriots in the gendarmerie and police forces abandoned their posts. On the third day of fighting, 17 Turkish Cypriots and 11 Greek Cypriots were killed.[9]

The sniping spread to Larnaca, Famagusta, Limassol, Paphos and Kyrenia, and the mobilisation unleashed the private Greek-Cypriot armies which had been organising for some time. The largest was led by Georghadhis, whose men were armed with rifles, automatic weapons, mortars and armoured bulldozers. Makarios's personal physician, Vassos Lyssarides, and newspaper publisher Nicos Sampson headed two other private militia; the latter was a convicted EOKA assassin who boasted that he had killed someone for every year of his life. Sampson led a co-ordinated assault on the suburb of Omorphita, where Turkish Cypriots had tried to seize Greek-Cypriot arms. Other attacks were made on Kumsal, Kaymakli and other Nicosia suburbs and nearby villages. Hundreds of Turkish Cypriots fled. One of the most notorious incidents took place at Kumsal, near Orta Keuy, where 150 inhabitants were taken hostage. Nine people were killed, five of them when Greek Cypriots broke into the house of a Turkish army major and butchered his wife, the woman from next door and his three children. A reporter who visited the scene said, 'In the bathroom, looking like a group of waxworks, were three dead children piled on top of their murdered mother. In a room next to it we glimpsed the body of a woman shot in the head.'[10] The bodies had been left for five days to be shown to journalists. The house, including the bloodstained, bullet-ridden bath, has been preserved in the same state to this day, with a sign outside: 'Museum of Barbarism'. On 24 December, 31 Turkish Cypriots and five Greek Cypriots were killed.

The fighting caused alarm in Ankara. Turkish Prime Minister Ismet Inonu warned Britain and Greece that Turkey would have to intervene unless quick action was taken to protect the Turkish Cypriots. He urged his allies to take joint action to restore peace. On Christmas Day, he sent five jets on warning flights to buzz Nicosia. In London, ministers abandoned their Christmas dinner for an emergency Cabinet meeting. Aviation Minister Julian Amery, who had negotiated the details of the bases and defence rights on Cyprus with Makarios, was called in to the Cabinet meeting to help. He told them, 'You had better put your foot down pretty hard now because if Makarios gets away with this you will not be able to stop him'.[11] Britain's worst fears were being realised. The island was descending into civil war, threatening the viability of the bases and spying facilities. Now Turkey was poised to intervene. As one senior British military source, Field Marshal Lord Carver, recalled, 'This would have led to the risk of war… the disruption of NATO and even wider dangers, possibly involving the intervention of the Soviet Union'.[12]

Prime Minister Sir Alec Douglas-Home pressed both sides to allow a British force from the sovereign bases to separate them while a solution was hammered out. He was trying to prevent further Turkish action, or clashes between the

Greek and Turkish army contingents stationed on the island, which would have escalated the conflict. Reports reaching Nicosia indicated that three Turkish troop-carriers had entered Cyprus's territorial waters. Fortunately, Makarios was also fearful of a Turkish invasion, and agreed to let the British send a tripartite force, known as the joint truce force, to cool the growing anger. He also withdrew his abrogation of the Treaty of Guarantee and agreed to attend a peace conference in London, though he made it clear that he still thought the 1960 treaties must go, along with the Greek and Turkish soldiers stationed under the Treaty of Alliance.[13] The truce force was headed by Major General Peter Young, the Commanding Officer of the British bases. Cyril Pickard, an assistant under secretary at the Foreign Office in London, and Lieutenant Commander Martin Packard, a Greek-speaking fleet intelligence officer from Malta, worked under him. The force comprised 1500 British troops, 1000 Greek soldiers and 800 Turkish soldiers.

The first British troops went on patrol in the capital on 27 December. They immediately supervised a ceasefire and created a barrier between the Greek and Turkish quarters of Nicosia, effectively partitioning the city. Under British supervision, 545 Turkish-Cypriot hostages were exchanged for 26 Greek Cypriots. Turkish troops also moved onto the road between Kyrenia and Nicosia, where Greek-Cypriot forces had overrun Turkish-Cypriot positions. Within days, the first of two tripartite patrols was set up by Packard, with liaison officers from the Greek and Turkish contingents. Packard's unenviable task was to try to bring the warring communities together. It was made harder by the discovery of a mass grave at Ayios Vasilios. On 12 January, the bodies of 21 Turkish Cypriots were exhumed. A number of them seemed to have been tortured and shot with their hands and feet tied.[14] In one of his first jobs, Packard had to investigate – and later reportedly confirm – rumours that Turkish patients in Nicosia General Hospital had had their throats slit by Greek medical staff, and that their bodies had been taken, fed into mechanical choppers and buried.[15]

More than 8000 Turkish Cypriots from 22 towns and villages had fled their homes in the first ten days of fighting. Kutchuk said, 'There is no possibility of the Turkish community living with the Greek community again. There must be partition'.[16]

~12~

AMERICA'S SECRET OPTION

A Limited Invasion

The fighting threatened to burden the British with exactly the kind of security problem they thought they had jettisoned by giving independence to Cyprus. The peace conference in London began on 15 January 1964 in unpromising circumstances, as Turkish warships started manoeuvres in the waters between Cyprus and Turkey, with Greece already amassing ships off Crete. NATO's Supreme Commander in Europe, General Lyman Lemnitzer, flew to Athens to try to defuse the tension. Before long, Makarios was to pay for his wrecking action on the constitution, as Britain and America began colluding to support Turkish attempts to separate the two communities and create the conditions that would make partition a practical military objective. The Americans were privately furious with Makarios for trying to leapfrog the restraints of the 1960 arrangements. A British conference seemed a safer way to control the situation than letting Makarios go to the UN, where the Soviets might use him to drive a wedge between Greece and Turkey and split NATO.

In London, Clerides called for an unfettered independent Cyprus under a simple parliamentary system with only minority rights for the Turkish Cypriots. His Turkish-Cypriot counterpart, Denktash, insisted that the 1960 agreements

should be upheld, and demanded that the two communities be physically separated. Confidential British records passed to the Americans showed that the
Turks wanted a geographically separate administrative and political structure
that would require the compulsory movement of an estimated 35,000 Greek
Cypriots and 45,000 Turkish Cypriots to 'concentrate all or most of the Turkish
Cypriots in one or two large areas', leaving the Greek Cypriots in the rest of the
island. Clerides saw this as a demand for partition, but the Turks said it could be
achieved within a federation.[1]

The British put forward a compromise formula: a presidential system should
be replaced with a parliamentary one, an international peace-keeping force
should be brought in, and 'a scheme to assist the voluntary movement of population should be organised with the objective of eliminating as far as practicable
mixed villages. Greek villages should be grouped together and Turkish villages
should be grouped together for the purpose of local administration and police
duties.' But the talks, hosted by Secretary of State for Commonwealth Relations
Duncan Sandys, collapsed.[2]

When British and American officials met in Washington to discuss the next
steps, the US Acting Secretary of State, George Ball, asked if partition might be
the best solution.[3] With Kruschev offering Makarios support, and news that
the Greek Cypriots were importing arms from the USSR and Czechoslovakia,
they were braced for a dangerous escalation of the violence. Desperate to get the
troubles off their hands, the British pushed unsuccessfully for a permanent
NATO force on Cyprus. At first, neither the Europeans nor the Americans,
already embroiled in Vietnam, Panama, the Congo, Indonesia and the Berlin
question, would get involved.[4]

But on 28 January, the mood suddenly changed. Frustrated by the lack of
action against Makarios, Inonu issued the Americans with a dramatic ultimatum:
agree within a day to take action, or we will invade. The only way to stop a war
within NATO seemed to be for the British and Americans to go in first and
protect the Turkish Cypriots.[5] Ball tentatively agreed a joint US-British plan to
offer a temporary 10,000-strong NATO force, of which up to 2000 would be
American, for three months, provided Greece and Turkey would agree not to
exercise their right to intervene under the Treaty of Guarantee. To prevent
President Johnson backing out, the British leaked the proposal. But the bluff
backfired, because the American Embassy in Nicosia was bombed. Ball flew to
London to sort out an Anglo-American position. He said, 'Viewed from
Washington, the issues were clear enough. Cyprus was a strategically important
piece of real estate at issue between two NATO partners: Greece and Turkey. We
needed to keep it under NATO control'.[6] The British put new pressure on
Makarios to accept a force from NATO countries if not under NATO auspices,
by warning of the grave danger that the Turks would invade and partition the
island. But Makarios proposed instead a UN force, which would also allow the
communist members of the Security Council to meddle in the island's affairs.[7]

The Soviets backed Makarios, and pushed Cyprus to the top of the Cold War agenda by issuing a tough warning to Britain and America against trying to 'put this small neutral state under the military control of NATO'.[8] In Cyprus, the explosion at the US Embassy was followed by the burning of American-owned private cars, and 800 of the 1500 Americans on the island were put on standby for evacuation.

The situation deteriorated in early February, as several Turkish-Cypriot villages were attacked. In Ayios Sozemenos, 15 miles south of Nicosia, a pitched battle began after a jeep carrying six Greek Cypriots was fired on, killing two of them. Six Greek Cypriots and five Turkish Cypriots were killed, and 18 Greek Cypriots and three Turkish Cypriots wounded, in house-to-house battles initiated by the Greek-Cypriot police. British troops in the truce force moved in to establish a tense ceasefire. Frank Kitson, a major in the force, said that the troops had prevented a retaliatory massacre of Turkish Cypriots which could have triggered a full-scale Turkish invasion. 'I have often wondered whether this was in some Turkish mind when the two Greeks were ambushed so close to the village,' he recalled. 'After all, it was not very difficult to forecast the Greek reaction and the villagers had no adequate means of defending themselves'.[9] In fighting at Polis, 800 Turkish Cypriots fled their homes and took refuge in a secondary school.

As the fighting continued, Packard, as one of the two deputies to the truce force commander, travelled back and forth across northern Cyprus, seeking out trouble, pulling the sides apart, and trying to negotiate local agreements. He was praised for his bravery in British newspapers. A vital problem he had to overcome was the lack of established intelligence on the opposing armed factions – the gathering process had been abandoned with independence. Kitson, who was second-in-command of the 3rd Green Jackets, one of the sovereign base garrison brigades, began organising intelligence research in Nicosia and posting soldiers to monitor the comings and goings of key people. Names, phone numbers and car registrations of activists on either side were checked, and the pattern of contact between them monitored, to build up a picture of who was organising the armed action on both sides.[10]

The troubles spread to villages on the edge of the Akrotiri base. But the biggest battles took place in Limassol, where there were heavy exchanges of fire for three days. The British Commander, General Young, reported that the Greeks had launched 'a deliberate attack, supported by a homemade tank, an armoured bulldozer, and assorted weapons such as bazookas and, it is alleged, mortars'. Young flew in by helicopter, accompanied by Cypriot Interior Minister Georghadhis, and secured a ceasefire, after which RAF ambulances were sent in to pull out the wounded. At dawn, Greek-Cypriot fighters stormed Turkish strongholds, firing automatic weapons. During the fighting, 30 British military families were turned onto the streets by Greek Cypriots wanting to use their houses as forward positions. The British army did not intervene because of the risk of casualties.[11]

The CIA warned that the Greek Cypriots believed the Americans wanted to use a NATO force to try to partition the island. This meant any US troops sent to the island would be at risk of being 'singled out for attack'.[12] This left Ball determined to pursue plans for an international force without American troops, while placating the British and Turks.

The Americans were alarmed by the reckless aggression shown on both sides. They knew that the British peace-keeping forces already in place were more bluff than substance, and would dissipate if seriously challenged by further outbreaks of violence. Johnson was told that a new element must be injected to break the *impasse*. To an extent, this was already happening by default. Population movement made it almost inevitable that the solution would have to be federal, involving separate cantons for the Turkish Cypriots, as the Turks had suggested in London. Around 18,000 Turkish Cypriots left their homes between the Christmas fighting and mid-February. Sixty percent crowded into the Turkish-Cypriot quarters of Nicosia and Kyrenia. The Americans suspected some of the movement was the result of coercion by Turkish extremists.[13]

Ball flew to Nicosia for a showdown with Makarios on 12 and 13 February. When he arrived, he was shocked to find that the capital resembled an 'armed camp'.[14] He telegrammed his boss, US Secretary of State Dean Rusk, to say the situation had deteriorated markedly, especially in Limassol, where he was told there were 150 casualties and the Greek-Cypriot police were firing heavy explosives into the Turkish quarter, and had launched an all-out attack. He said the problem the Americans faced was to prevent degeneration into widespread civil war, and to restrain Turkey under mounting provocation.[15]

Flanked by American officials, including Assistant Secretary of State Joseph Sisco, and the British Acting High Commissioner Sir Cyril Pickard, Ball lambasted Makarios for his bloody-mindedness, his 'cruel and reckless conduct' and the outrages inflicted on the Turkish Cypriots.[16] He pressed the Archbishop to accept a revised plan for a peace-keeping force comprised of troops from British Commonwealth countries and one or two neutral countries, instead of from NATO. Ball talked to Makarios alone for over an hour in Nicosia, and held discussions with him accompanied by Cypriot ministers and Clerides. But the Archbishop would not agree to his plan unless the UN backed him with a resolution against aggression and in support of the territorial integrity and political independence of Cyprus. After that, a federal solution which watered down the Turkish Cypriots' right of veto might be possible. This would have been the last straw for the Turks – nullifying Ankara's right to intervene in Cyprus at a time when all attempts at putting in an alternative pro-NATO or pro-Western peace-keeping force had failed.[17]

Ball warned Makarios sharply that if he continued to push too far, the Americans would not lift a finger to stop a Turkish invasion. But Makarios did not budge. He did not want a peace-keeping force whose terms of reference were left in the hands of the Western powers, because he feared they would be used to reinforce the creeping separatism of the Turkish Cypriots, and that would lead to partition. But if the force was answerable to the UN Security Council, the Soviet Union's influence might work in his favour.[18] Exasperated, Ball accused the Cypriot President of turning the island into his 'private abattoir'. He telegrammed Johnson: 'The Greek Cypriots do not want a peace-keeping force; they just want to be left alone to kill Turkish Cypriots'. This was the turning point in Anglo-American policy on Cyprus. From here on, even the British forces on the island were deployed in a way which supported a joint policy favouring separation of the two communities.[19]

Makarios was walking on hot coals. Turkey had begun naval preparations on its south-eastern coast, and the British warned servicemen that their families should always be ready to evacuate at an hour or two's notice, taking only a suitcase with them.[20]

Faced with the dire situation of Turkish action, leading to a war with Greece that might easily spread, disastrously damaging America's strategic interests and weakening NATO, the Americans needed a fall-back plan in case their peace-keeping-force proposals failed. Before Ball left for London on 8 February, he consulted Johnson, and Washington officials drew up an astonishing contingency plan to allow Turkey to invade Cyprus and occupy a large area of the north of the island – and, if necessary, an additional enclave in the west – to protect Turkish Cypriots. The plan had been cleared by the Department of Defence, and most of the relevant officials in the State Department before Ball left for talks with his British counterpart, Duncan Sandys, the Commonwealth Relations Secretary, during which they discussed how this could be put into action. The Americans learned from Sandys that Britain had prepared a similar plan.[21]

Following the secret consultations, a revised draft was sent to Ball on 14 February, during his diplomatic shuttle between Britain, Greece, Turkey and Cyprus. It gave precise details of how the American Ambassadors in Athens, Ankara and Nicosia were to deal with their host governments to make it work. If the Turks were provoked by further trouble on Cyprus, and decided to intervene, the Americans would first try to buy time, before the Turks entered Cypriot air space or territorial waters, for the British to send reinforcements. Next they would try to delineate areas of Cyprus into which the Turks could move their forces, in the hope that the Greeks would see this as a limited intervention and could be persuaded not to go to war with Turkey.[22]

Once the Americans knew that Turkey had decided to take action in Cyprus, the US Ambassador would tell the Turkish premier that, as the geographic and military situation was so overwhelmingly in Turkey's favour, Ankara could proceed with a 'deliberate and carefully controlled movement' rather than an aggressive military assault. The point of this was to avoid Greek military retaliation, and persuade world opinion that Turkey was making a 'disciplined' intervention, as was her right under the Treaty of Guarantee. A delay in Turkish action might sway Greek opinion and allow time for British reinforcements to be sent in and, if it was still on the cards, for pressure to be put on Makarios to accept a US-UK initiative for a peace-keeping force. He would be told he had only hours before a 'Turkish invasion' begins, that the Americans were trying to urge a 'short delay' but could not guarantee results, and pressed to accept 'whatever version of peace-keeping force has US support at the time'.[23]

If, however, the Turks refused to delay, the American Ambassador was under specific orders to act in concert with his British colleague to seek to ensure Turkish troops operated only in the areas agreed under the plan, and did not risk confrontation with Greek forces. They would ask Ankara to treat any forces sent to the island as merely an expansion of their existing 650-strong contingent – established under the Treaty of Alliance – and to put all of them under the command of the senior British officer on the island. The plan stated that 'controlled intervention' was necessary to protect the lives of the Turkish minority as well as to avoid an armed clash with Greece. Turkey should agree to confine its intervention to specific territorial limits, in the hope of preventing fighting elsewhere.[24]

The plan identified exactly which parts of Cyprus should be taken over, suggesting, for example, that the Turkish contingent would 'move out from Kyrenia into a rough triangle including Lefka and having its apex in the northern half of the walled city of Nicosia. The Turks would stay away from the airport and the airport-Nicosia road as long as the airport is not used for hostile purposes.' The Turkish troops should, the plan said, act only in self-defence, but if violence against the Turkish Cypriots continued, they 'might move into another enclave, based on the port of Paphos' in co-ordination with the British commander and the Greek Government. It said that if the US-UK peace plan was still under consideration, the Turks should agree to withdraw their forces when the new peace-keeping forces landed on the island.[25]

The American Ambassador in Athens would tell the Greeks not to rock the boat by starting military action against Turkey, because it would reduce Washington's chances of controlling any Turkish intervention, and that if there was a risk of war with Turkey 'it would seem militarily wiser for them to keep their troops at home to meet the threat to the (Greek) mainland'.[26]

Ball had already begun contingency planning with the British and the ambassadors concerned. In fact, the first steps were taken on 13 February, after American civilians had been evacuated, amid the rumours of massive Turkish-Cypriot casualties. Makarios had refused the proposal for a Commonwealth-led peace-keeping force, and a Turkish military intervention seemed inevitable, unless drastic action was taken. At midnight, the British announced, just as the American contingency plan envisaged, that an army command organisation was to be flown to the island. Publicly, the world was told the job of these officers was to be ready to run an international peace-keeping force, whatever the outcome of negotiations. The headquarters of Britain's 3rd Infantry Division of the Strategic Reserve, commanded by Major General Michael Carver, was flown out to Cyprus within hours. Carver and his 170 officers immediately took over direction of the security forces from General Young, who was relieved of his role and returned to his duties in charge of the sovereign bases.[27] The War Office gave no clues that the move was part of the secret plan agreed with the Americans. A bigger command structure and a tough new commander had to be sent in to ensure that if the Turks invaded, their troops could be channelled into carefully delineated areas.[28]

Even as the British troops headed for the island, Turkish ships put to sea with army units on board, threatening an invasion. Controlling the crisis immediately became an emergency priority in the talks being held between Johnson and Douglas-Home in Washington. It was described as the 'skybolt' of the talks, a comparison with the Nassau conference of 1962, in which the nuclear missile issue wiped virtually everything else off the agenda.[29] Douglas-Home told Johnson that the main worry was that a full Turkish invasion would be followed by 'the near certainty of Soviet intervention'. Dean Rusk warned the US representative at the North Atlantic Council that the situation could become 'catastrophic' if events led to fighting between Greece and Turkey.[30]

In Ankara, Ball set in motion the next stage of the contingency plan. He tried to calm the Turks by reassuring them that the Americans would seek a UN peace-keeping initiative which would not encroach on Turkey's right to intervene. He then flew to London for a meeting with British Foreign Secretary Butler and Sandys. Consequently, Britain surprised the UN with an urgent plea for a meeting of the Security Council to consider a request for a peace-keeping force – which Makarios had so far rejected.[31] As the contingency plan envisaged, this move pre-empted any appeal to the Security Council by Makarios and his allies.[32]

At one point during this frantic diplomatic activity, Turkish warships steamed towards the island. But when they neared Cyprus's waters they suddenly halted, mysteriously echoing the first stage of the Washington plan, in which they were to be asked to delay entering Cypriot territorial waters while British troops were sent to Cyprus. However, the arrival of the British troops and the UN initiative proved enough to persuade the Turks not just to delay but to abandon their invasion for the time being. Troops on those ships reported later that they were told this was the real thing. 'Then just as we approached Cyprus we were told to return to Turkey'.[33]

In the end, the controlled invasion envisaged in the US contingency plan did not happen – and perhaps the Turks never realised that they could have moved into Cyprus ten years earlier than they eventually did, had they forced the issue. But at this time the plan was only a contingency for use as a last resort, if the Turks could not be dissuaded from military action. Ten years later, when there seemed a real danger of losing the military facilities in Cyprus, the Americans were to have stronger motives for encouraging the Turks into Cyprus than they did for keeping them out.

~13~

A CRUDE PARTITION

The British Defend Turkish Enclaves

Despite recalling its ships, Turkey was still massing 10,000 troops on its southern coast. There were reports that on the island the Turkish Cypriots were attempting to concentrate their people in enclaves and set up their own local administrations as a potential stepping stone towards partition.[1] Ball told Johnson that the Cyprus situation remained 'the most dangerous confrontation since the Cuban missile crisis', and that there was a 50 percent chance of war.

Packard, heading the tripartite truce force patrols, worked around the clock, criss-crossing the island to try to prevent clashes and stem the movement of Turkish Cypriots out of mixed villages, which he believed made a political solution more difficult. His reputation for stopping skirmishes and defusing tension between villagers without firing a shot became legendary. While the diplomats and generals in Washington and London plotted large-scale military operations, he used the simple tactic of face-to-face negotiation to persuade them to put down their weapons.[2]

A *Times* reporter accompanied Packard on a truce force patrol, along with two majors, one each from the Greek and Turkish armies, on a routine two-day tour of 20 villages in hotspots near Nicosia. As they passed through one village, Packard stopped the jeep and asked a young boy why he was carrying a sub-machine-gun. The boy, frightened, blurted out that he thought some Greeks were going to burn Turkish homes, and that he was going to protect them. In an instant, the patrol was surrounded by tense and frightened men and children, five or six of them, armed with guns. Packard urged them to go home and put the guns away. 'We are here to save lives and bring peace,' he said. 'You must help us.'³

On the way to the Greek village of Dahli, the patrol came to a crossroads where Turkish Cypriots had set up a gun emplacement manned by a dozen boys and men. They were led by a youth wearing a cap with the insignia of the Turkish army. Packard summoned the boy and asked the Turkish major to convey a warning: 'Tell this boy that it is very dangerous for him to be wearing the insignia of the Government of Turkey. If any shooting starts here, it will imme-diately become a war, a big war.' After an hour's argument, the boy removed the insignia and climbed back into his vehicle, spitting at the major and calling him a traitor.⁴

Everywhere he went, Packard listened to grievances and made extensive notes. Sometimes he was too late. At Potamia, which had until recently been equally divided between Greeks and Turks, he found that most of the 319 Turks who had lived there had gone to Louroujina. When they flew over Potamia the next day by helicopter they discovered that scores of new observation posts and gun emplacements had been erected around the village. 'This is like medieval times, each village armed against the other, each fearing the other will attack,' said Packard. The most menacing place the patrol visited was Louroujina, where Turkish leaders were concentrating large numbers of refugees, many against their will, from smaller villages. It was heavily fortified with gun emplacements and pill boxes, and full of photographers, reporters and police-men, as well as Turkish-Cypriot political leaders and a large contingent of British troops. It was exactly the kind of armed retrenchment Packard was trying to prevent.⁵ He had made it his personal mission to bring the two sides together. Having originally been ordered by Young to create a tripartite mediating operation, he regarded himself as 'answerable wholly to the process of mediation – and no longer... subject to a military working for national aims'.⁶

But Packard's approach was anathema to Ball, and contradicted the tactics of the new British commander, who was following the plans agreed between Ball and Sandys. Their priority was to prevent a conflagration in the Eastern Mediterranean that would destroy NATO's southern wing, and the effect of their policy was to bring the Turks a step closer to being able to make partition a reality by bolstering ethnic separation. According to Peter Murtagh in the *Guardian*, when Packard showed Ball around Cyprus during the February crisis, the American told Packard, 'You've got it wrong son. There's only one solution to this island and that's partition.'⁷ Carver, who took over in Cyprus after Ball and Sandys discussed the US contingency plan for a Turkish invasion, directed the force in a way that made reintegration an unlikely prospect, but made the contingency plan a more practical option. Carver's senior intelligence officer, Frank Kitson, said that most British action strengthened the Turkish-Cypriot positions and reinforced their moves towards separatism. 'We were helping to bring about a crude form of partition under which the Turkish Cypriots occupied and administered certain parts of the island.' He said this was an inevitable consequence of the fact that most attacks were carried out by the Greek Cypriots on the Turkish Cypriots, and confirmed the military's view that if the British had not stepped in there would have been a Turkish invasion and a major war. 'Looked at objectively our activities did favour the Turkish Cypriots,' Kitson said.[8]

At the end of February 1964, Makarios announced that he was expanding his armed police-force from 2000 to 5000, and formed a 12,000-strong Greek-Cypriot home guard. He also set up links with a Soviet airline, prompting his Turkish-Cypriot Vice President to accuse him of turning Cyprus into 'another Cuba'. When the first Soviet airliner, an Illyushin, landed at Nicosia, nearly 4000 Greek Cypriots gathered on the tarmac to welcome the crew and, according to a Turkish-Cypriot news sheet, chanted, 'Long live Kruschev' and 'Down with American gangsters'.[9]

On 4 March, the UN agreed to America's request for a UN peace-keeping force made up of troops from Western and neutral countries, though the allies still had to be persuaded to actually send their troops. Leaders of both communities on the island exchanged hostages – 49 Turkish for four Greek. But the Turkish Cypriots estimated that a further 176 of their people were still missing, and tit-for-tat fighting soon broke out and spread throughout the island. In one incident, Turkish Cypriots seized hundreds of Greek Cypriots in Ktima in the west, allegedly in retaliation for the shooting of a Turkish Cypriot and because of the missing hostages. The Greek Cypriots responded by taking hostage hundreds of Turkish Cypriots in Ktima and Lapithou. Fourteen Turkish Cypriots and 11 Greeks were killed in a struggle for control of Ktima before British troops arranged a ceasefire and patrolled the line between the two forces.[10]

On 12 March, Inonu accused the Greek Cypriots of lining up to massacre Turkish Cypriots, and once more threatened to invade unless a peace-keeping force was brought in within 36 hours and Turkish-Cypriot hostages were freed. The Turkish threat prompted a flurry of diplomatic activity by the Americans and the British, who gave the UN 24 hours to get some troops on their way. The following day, over 1000 Greek Cypriots, some of them manning bulldozers as makeshift tanks, massed on the edge of the Turkish-Cypriot quarter in Nicosia, as if preparing for a pogrom. Turkish ships were ordered to embark troops, and Inonu sent an urgent warning to Makarios to stop the attacks on Turkish Cypriots. The US Sixth Fleet was already on its way to the Cyprus area, and Soviet submarines and two Soviet destroyers lurked nearby. At sea, too, were ships from the Greek and British navies. The Eastern Mediterranean seemed a hair-trigger away from a disastrous war.

A few minutes before Inonu's deadline, Canada, Ireland and Sweden offered to send troops for the UN force, Canada immediately. The brinkmanship had worked. The Turks told the Americans they would hold off.[11] Yet a decision by Turkish MPs to allow Inonu a free hand to send an invasion force to Cyprus as and when he saw fit meant there remained the constant threat of action.

The UN peace-keeping force officially took over from the truce force from the end of March, but the change-over was slow. Initially, it was mainly a matter of the existing British troops putting on UN blue berets as soon as the first trickle of Canadian troops arrived. The force eventually comprised 6500 men, of whom more than half were British. The rest came from Austria, Australia, Canada, Denmark, Finland, Ireland and Sweden. But the Americans covered 35 percent of costs, and the operation was heavily influenced and controlled on the ground in a way that suited the strategic interests of Britain and America from the outset. When the UN troops arrived, for instance, they found a British command structure already in place, headed by Carver, who was made deputy commander of the UN force. He immediately took effective overall control because his commander, General Prem Singh Gyani, took a fortnight's leave in India before taking up his appointment. Carver admitted that Gyani's temporary replacement 'sensibly did not attempt to do anything... while I got on with the job'.[12]

Carver also secretly retained Kitson to run his intelligence operations from the basement of the British High Commission in Nicosia. As UN forces are forbidden from carrying out such work, Kitson was put directly under Carver's command but allowed to pass on selective information in secret to the UN commander.[13]

Packard confirmed that although Carver was nominally deputy commander of the UN force, the support he received from the British military gave him the dominant role at a critical time. Packard believed there were two ways forward: one was towards reconciliation and a unitary state, favoured by international opinion, by moderate Cypriots and by the UN; the other was towards separation and federalism or partition. 'That route was favoured by some Turkish extremists and by American and British strategic planners. The role played by the military under Carver helped move events towards the separatist route, which led in due course to the [1974] Turkish invasion,' said Packard.[14] Carver himself admitted later that the way the peace force was used preserved the 'de facto segregation arising out of the December fighting' between Greek and Turkish Cypriots 'made it appear that they could not live together'. In fact, this was in line with the British proposal at the London conference to eliminate mixed villages, but it inevitably strengthened the enclaves which the Turkish Cypriots were creating as a stage towards partition.[15]

Eventually, between May and August 1964, the Turks exploited the UN-protected stand-off around these strongholds to develop their own civil and military administration. This process was organised by the Turkish army contingent on Cyprus to tighten control over the Turkish Cypriots, simultaneously improving their defences and promoting separation from the rest of Cyprus.

In the Turkish-Cypriot quarter of Nicosia, Kutchuk took charge of a General Committee whose members came from the community's share of the Council of Ministers, the House of Representatives, the judiciary and the executive arm of the Turkish Cypriot Communal Chamber, as set down by the 1960 agreements. District committees were set up in the main towns – Famagusta, Larnaca, Limassol and Paphos – with village and municipal councils below them. This system worked through decrees issued by Kutchuk, and local decisions made by leading fighters who devised the administrative boundaries to suit military priorities – such as the best way to organise the defence of the swollen population centres. The Nicosia district was split into two districts under one officer.[16]

Villages were grouped to take account of the number of inhabitants, roads between them, and transport available. They were organised by police officers and fighters, and defended by part-time fighters. Above these groups were subregions, at whose headquarters were posted full-time fighter units. The sub-regions were grouped into seven full regions commanded by Turkish army colonels, usually in charge of two or more battalions. Above them, a Turkish army general commanded all Turkish-Cypriot military affairs.

The UN peace-keeping force, as Carver admitted, helped protect these administrative units where their boundaries were challenged by force by the Greek Cypriots. According to Richard Patrick, in some cases this meant there were two concentric rings of fortified posts separated by a contested area patrolled by UN troops.[17] This assisted the grouping and organisation of Turkish Cypriots that made the separate Turkish and American contingency plans for Ankara's troops to temporarily occupy a large portion of the island a more practical option.

The military tactics prompted Makarios to warn the British that if they used their forces against Greek Cypriots he would seek changes to the conditions under which they were able to operate their sovereign bases and retained sites.

Makarios wrote to the premiers of Greece and Turkey asking them to withdraw their contingents in Cyprus to their normal stations, and leave the peace-keeping to the UN soldiers. He wanted to end the Turkish troops' control of the strategic positions they would need to hold if they were to help stage an invasion. But the UN force fell considerably short of the 10,000 troops that the British and Americans had demanded, and was overstretched. Inonu warned that any move against Turkish troops would be treated as an act of aggression against Turkey.

At the beginning of April, the Greek Cypriots attacked the Turkish-Cypriot area around Kokkina, the main landing area for shipments of arms from Turkey. Seven Turkish Cypriots and one Greek Cypriot died in a battle at Ghaziveran on the strategically important coastal road. Makarios flew to Athens to consult Greek premier George Papandreou, who issued a statement supporting the Greek Cypriots' struggle for self-determination and their claim that the arrival of the UN force and a UN mediator meant the 1960 agreements were dead. Makarios asked Papandreou for reinforcements for his National Guard, but tried to dissuade his old political rival, Grivas, from offering his services as its head. Grivas threatened to return to the island if a Turkish invasion seemed imminent.[18]

On his return, Makarios outmanoeuvred his enemies by offering to disband all Greek-Cypriot fortifications on Cyprus under UN supervision, grant an amnesty to all Turkish Cypriots, and help resettle Turkish-Cypriot refugees. He even suggested that the Turkish army should replace the British contingent in the UN force. These moves would have reduced the risk of a Turkish invasion by forcing the Turks to leave their strategic positions and drop their focus on defending the Turkish enclaves. His offer exposed the Turks' opposition to making the unitary state work. The Turks were furious at his clever appeal to world opinion. Their army contingent in Cyprus was ordered to seize control of the strategic road running north from Nicosia to Kyrenia, the control of which would be essential to the establishment of a beach-head for any invasion. Inonu said his troops would hold their ground until the Cyprus constitution was restored and the Turkish Cypriots were assured security.

The tactic of the UN force in the ensuing battle for the Kyrenia road was typical of Carver's approach. On 25 April, the Greek Cypriots countered by trying to seize part of the strategic road themselves, with 300 men. They attacked the Castle of St Hilarion, overlooking the road in the mountains near Kyrenia, which Turkish fighters had held for some time. UN troops stopped the battle and set up permanent posts on the Kyrenia pass to prevent a recurrence. But they left the Turks in their strategic position, in control of the castle.

At the same time, NATO pressed Greece to curb Makarios's excesses, and Johnson personally urged Papandreou to be cautious. The message was reinforced when a squadron of three warships from the Sixth Fleet entered Greek waters and docked near Athens, provoking a wave of anti-American demonstrations. Turkey, too, flexed its muscles, gathering 30 warships at Iskenderun, north-east of Cyprus, in its biggest ever combined services exercise, including landing manoeuvres. Kruschev accused the NATO powers of opposing Cyprus's independence, and trying to convert Cyprus into an 'unsinkable aircraft-carrier'. When NATO foreign ministers discussed the Cyprus problem in secret at the Hague on 13 May, Turkey, Britain and the United States rounded on Greece for supporting Makarios's assertion that the 1960 treaties were defunct. The agreements had, after all, been the result of lengthy negotiations through the North Atlantic Council under American leadership.

On 11 May, two Greek army officers and the son of the Greek-Cypriot chief of police were shot dead in a gun-battle in the Turkish-Cypriot quarter of Famagusta, which they had entered by mistake. Within three days, 32 Turkish

Cypriots had gone missing, presumed kidnapped and murdered, in reprisal. The UN immediately sent a political officer, Dr Galo Plaza, a former president of Ecuador and experienced mediator. He was to report directly to the UN Secretary General, and took over emergency negotiations between the two communities. However, though the Famagusta kidnapping was one of the largest incidents in the 1964 troubles, it was a relatively isolated one. It is often described as the trigger for Turkey's most well-known invasion threat. But the threats did not come until three weeks later. In fact the pitched sectarian battles which characterised the December and February fighting had largely petered out by May. What violence there was tended to be battles for strongholds controlling strategic roads in the north-west, where the Turks were most likely to land if they invaded.

This drop in general violence may be explained by the work of Packard, who, in defiance of the policy of encouraging mixed villages to disband and Turkish enclaves to consolidate, had continued the work towards reconciliation that he started when the truce force was in place. He held secret meetings with military leaders from both warring factions about trying to reunite the Greeks and Turks in the battle-scarred towns and villages. He believed the problem of ironing out the differences between opposing sides in mixed villages was less complex than the political problems affecting the island as a whole, which came with the military interests of outside powers attached. His aim was quite simple: to get the Turkish-Cypriot minority back into the Greek-dominated villages from which they had fled, protected by soldiers with the UN force who, for a limited period, would escort people to work. He was surprisingly successful in securing agreement on this. Through private meetings he obtained assent from not only the local village leaders in mixed areas, but also the leaders of the secret armies on both sides, secret military representatives of Greece and Turkey, and Makarios and Kutchuk and their advisers. In public, all sides appeared belligerent and immovable, but in private they were prepared to compromise. 'Because the arrangement was informal and removed from political posturings, everyone was prepared to give it a chance,' Packard said. According to his plan, the Turkish Cypriots were to begin to move back to their abandoned property – which Packard said had in many cases been preserved in excellent order by their former Greek neighbours – on 12 June, accompanied by UN soldiers.[19]

While the Packard talks were going on behind the scenes, Plaza conducted a more public mediation. Both sides were invited to make their position clear. On 14 May, Makarios responded by calling for the establishment of a fully independent, unified sovereign state 'with full powers of self-determination', unhampered by treaties with other countries. In Nicosia, Plaza persuaded Makarios and Kutchuk to move their forces 100 yards back from the ceasefire line dividing the warring factions, creating a 'no-man's-land' controlled by UN troops. But Makarios saw this as a way of putting his control of that part of his capital further out of reach.

When Turkish Foreign Minister Kemal Erkin arrived back in Ankara from the NATO meeting on 19 May, he emphasised that he had not ruled out a Turkish invasion: it depended on whether the attacks on the Turkish-Cypriot population continued. But in Ankara, where campaigning had begun for senate elections, he faced taunts by the opposition that he had 'missed the bus' in not launching an invasion after the Famagusta abductions. The next day, Turkey began more naval and military exercises off the port of Iskenderun.

On 1 June, Makarios raised the stakes by putting all Greek Cypriots between the ages of eighteen and fifty on standby for conscription in order to create a new National Guard. Turkey retaliated by landing 'volunteers' at the Turkish-Cypriot enclave of Kokkina and prepared for a full-scale invasion. In the early hours of 3 June, Ball, acting Secretary of State while Rusk was attending the funeral of Indian Prime Minister Jawaharlal Nehru, was told by the US Ambassador in Ankara that the Turkish Security Council had decided on an invasion of Cyprus. He said 'volunteers' who had already landed were to form part of a beachhead on the island, and that Turkish forces were already deployed in the Iskenderun area, in southern Turkey, with the mission of establishing a 'political and military beachhead' on Cyprus. The real purpose of Turkish military action was to stop the Packard plan dead in its tracks, and prevent any UN mediation which might force Turkey to give up the progress it had made towards Turkish-Cypriot separatism. Inonu admitted that was his prime motive to the Americans the next day.[20]

The following day, Rusk returned and, aided by Assistant Secretary of State Harlan Cleveland and Sisco, his deputy, prepared a note for Johnson to send to Inonu to deter him. Ball described it as 'the most brutal diplomatic note I have ever seen'. As they scripted it, Makarios announced the call-up of his first batch of conscripts for active service in the National Guard: all eighteen- to twenty-one-year-old Greek-Cypriot males. Turkish Cypriots were exempted. Erkin warned: 'If it continues like this, our going to Cyprus will be predestined'.[21]

The American reaction was swift. Washington demanded that Ankara take no military action before full consultation with the United States. This was not the time to resort to the contingency plan. With a UN force in place, a UN mediator working for peace, and no widespread communal violence, it would not be possible to carry world opinion on a Turkish invasion. Inonu told the US Ambassador, Raymond Hare, that he was surprised that Washington was ruling out action that the Americans had always said they might have to take. He said when Ball was in Ankara that he had made clear the necessity of being prepared to intervene at any time. And Johnson assured him that intervention remained possible as a last resort. In his telegram, Hare repeated an extraordinary plea made by Inonu: 'All the government of Turkey has in mind is [to] occupy part of [the] island and stop there. Greeks could occupy part [of the island] and [the] peace force could remain between them. From that position one could get down to meaningful discussion. [Inonu] hopes Greeks would not interfere but if they do then [there] will be war.'[22]

Hare stressed that precipitate action would shock world opinion. But Inonu said he had no other option and was unable to delay. This time the Americans really believed the Turks were going in, and a war with Greece, or even the Soviets, could result. NATO's Supreme Commander in Europe, General Lemnitzer, rushed to Ankara to urge caution. As war-fever reached boiling point, President Johnson sent the 'brutal' note to the Turkish premier on the night of 5 June. It said that if Turkey invaded Cyprus unilaterally, it could not depend on NATO to defend it against Soviet retaliation. The American President told Inonu, 'I hope you will understand that your NATO allies have not had a chance to consider whether they have an obligation to protect Turkey against the Soviet Union if Turkey takes a step which results in Soviet intervention, without the full consent and understanding of its NATO allies'.[23] To underline his warning, in the early hours of 5 June, before the letter was sent, an American naval task-force including one carrier, one cruiser and four destroyers moved into position within reach of Cyprus.[24]

Ball thought the letter was the 'diplomatic equivalent of an atom bomb', and would trigger an explosive reaction from Ankara.[25] It contrasted starkly with the weak pressure Sisco applied in Ankara ten years later, when the Turks did invade. When Inonu was handed the note by Hare, he read it intently. His Foreign Minister, alongside him, was furious. He said the assumption that Turkey wanted to partition the island was just not true: the occupation would only be temporary, and they had prepared a proclamation to emphasise this.[26] The Turks were now, it seems, ready to take action on the lines of the American contingency plan. If they had insisted on this in February, the Americans would have let them. But with the UN force in place it was too late.

About to face his Cabinet, Inonu almost snapped. He challenged the Americans to support a Turkish intervention, yes or no. But Hare insisted that Johnson would regard such a move with grave misgivings. He urged a delay in Turkish military action to allow for consultations with Washington. The Turks asked how long he wanted. When he suggested just 24 hours, Inonu's anger subsided, and he acquiesced.[27]

Despite their veto of an invasion, the Americans did not want to see the island reunited, or the 1960 agreements upheld any more than the Turks. The bloody intercommunal battles had shown that the 'guaranteed independence' they had secured for Cyprus had become too dangerous. Civil war could seriously restrict the use of the island's military facilities or ignite a disastrous war between NATO allies. The Americans shared Inonu's view that Makarios had become a dangerous threat to their interests. His flirtations with communist countries, and his failure to undermine support for AKEL meant that a truly independent Cyprus would now be a strategic liability to the West. It would leave Makarios free to pursue the type of independent policies which the 1960 constitution had been elaborately designed to avoid, such as alignment with the Eastern Bloc.

The following evening, Rusk telegrammed Athens with a dramatic warning for Papandreou to do something about Makarios. He told his Ambassador in Athens that the Turks had agreed to delay intervention, but Greece must offer Turkey some other way to redress its grievances over Cyprus if military action was to be averted. Rusk said, 'The sword of Damocles is still hanging by a thread, now one fibre weaker'. He warned that Makarios had to be curbed. '[The] Turks now believe the government of Greece is [a] puppet of Makarios and he pulls their strings. They act on this assumption... Some visible evidence to disabuse them of this idea seems needed.' He also said the Greek Cypriots would have to explain why they had introduced conscription and bought heavy military equipment and helicopters which seemed to justify the claim that they intended to exterminate the Turkish Cypriots.[28] The case against the Greek Cypriots hardened with the disappearance that same day of a British UN liaison officer in Cyprus, Major Macey, who was investigating the Famagusta kidnappings.

The first casualty of the Americans' move against Makarios was the Packard plan to reintegrate the Turkish-Cypriot refugees into ethnically mixed villages. Packard, against all the odds, had privately secured agreement from all sides to resettle the refugees in their old homes under UN protection. But on 11 June, 12 hours before the first Turkish Cypriots were due to be escorted back into their mixed villages by UN troops under his plan, he was ordered off the island and sent back to England on a transporter plane with only one seat bolted to its fuselage.[29] The UN commanding officer on the island, Gyani, immediately offered his resignation in protest. At first, Packard was told he had to go because his life was in danger. This was an attempt to use Macey's disappearance, along with his driver — Macey's dismembered body was found later — as an excuse to get Packard out of the way. The military waited five days after Macey disappeared before deciding that Packard had to be removed. Newspapers were told that Packard was sent back because relations between the Greeks and British were as bad as they had ever been — but, even if this was true generally, it was not so in Packard's case, as he enjoyed the confidence of the leaders of both communities. Macey, by contrast, was the senior UN officer liaising with the Turkish-Cypriot leadership, and the Greek Cypriots, no doubt because of his role in investigating the mass kidnappings, believed he was spying for the Turks. When Packard got back to London, he was given yet another, but spurious, reason why he had been forced to go — an allegation of womanising.

Packard was outraged. He thought the plan was the best hope for reuniting the island and bringing peace. But he claimed his British commander — who believed Makarios's campaign for self-determination was communist-inspired[30] — would not listen. 'Because the arrangement was informal and removed from political posturings, everyone was prepared to give it a chance. Everyone, it appears, except General Carver,' said Packard.[31] He and another UN liaison officer were immediately replaced with Canadians who could speak neither Greek nor Turkish. The same day, Ball flew to Athens and Ankara to persuade Papandreou and Inonu to discuss a new deal on Cyprus which would exclude Makarios.

Ball warned Papandreou that unless he was more co-operative, Johnson might not stop the Turks next time. Papandreou insisted that a solution had to be based on enosis. But Ball, employing the same argument suggested in the draft contingency plan, said Turkey would never accept enosis, was militarily stronger than Greece, and had a major logistical advantage in any conflict over Cyprus.[32] In Washington, Johnson reiterated the American warning. He told Greek Ambassador Alexander Matsas, 'If I can't get you to talk, I can't keep the Turks from moving'. He added that Greece must avoid at all costs humiliating its ally, Turkey. 'Even in the Cuban missile crisis, we always left the enemy a way out. With an ally it is even more important,' he said. Matsas agreed that there were two dangers: Graeco-Turkish tension and the risk of Makarios drifting to 'the other side' in the Cold War. Johnson said negotiations with the Archbishop were impossible because he wasn't interested in the security of the West, but Greece, Turkey and the United States were. Though Makarios would have to be consulted 'at some point', agreement between Greece and Turkey was the important thing. 'Let's see what you can do for us and will see what we can do for you,' he told the Greek.[33] In Athens Papandreou suggested leaving the Archbishop out of any negotiations. Ball said this was exactly what he had in mind.[34]

Ball worked on the same theme in Ankara. He told Inonu that the Americans totally mistrusted Makarios, and that even the Greeks were beginning to see him as an enemy of their interests. Though stung by Johnson's strong warning against invading Cyprus, the Turks were confident that the United States shared their objectives, and the Greek willingness to abandon Makarios gave them hope. Ball reported back immediately to Johnson, and on 11 June – the same day that Packard was taken off Cyprus – they invited Inonu and Papandreou to Washington for talks to reach an understanding over Makarios's head. Ball believed that if the President 'worked them over' separately a deal could be achieved.[35]

A few days later, a clandestine meeting took place in a mountain retreat in Cyprus between General Carver and Georghadhis. Georghadhis told Carver that Grivas was about to return to Cyprus, and made an extraordinary appeal to the UN Deputy Commander to persuade the British not to object. Carver did not believe Georghadhis's claim that Makarios knew all about their meeting, but he passed on the Cypriot minister's request to both the UN and the British Government. Neither raised any objections, even though the British had spent four years trying to eliminate Grivas.[36] Georghadhis was later implicated in trying to assassinate Makarios with the help of the CIA. Ball, in his memoirs, revealed that the return of Grivas held attractions for the Americans, because

they thought he would be easier to work with than Makarios, and they established an underground contact with Socrates Iliades, Grivas's lieutenant and
director of Cyprus's defences.[37]

The Grivas initiative was prompted by Papandreou, who on 15 June admitted
to Johnson his fear that Makarios would take Cyprus into the Soviet camp.
Papandreou suggested that 'Natification' of Cyprus through a form of enosis
offered a way forward, since by placing the whole island under the North
Atlantic Alliance, the influence of international communism on the island,
which had reached dangerous levels, would diminish. NATO control would also
remove Cyprus as a bone of contention between Greece and Turkey, he argued,
because it would prevent the Soviets getting a foothold, and would therefore
safeguard the security of Turkey and the entire Middle East. Without
Natification the island would 'inevitably be transformed into another Cuba'.[38]

Grivas arrived in Cyprus on 18 June. A day earlier, the British announced
the withdrawal of their 3rd Division headquarters staff, including Carver.
Ostensibly, Grivas's role was to co-ordinate the rag-tag Greek-Cypriot armed
forces – most of the irregulars regarded him as their hero because of his leadership of the anti-British guerrilla campaign. But he had a secret agenda – to get
rid of Makarios – which was covertly backed by the State Department. Ball himself admitted in his memoirs, 'The fact that the Grivas plan also called for the
ouster [sic] of Makarios enhanced its attractiveness'.[39] No doubt Grivas, now
sixty-six, also appealed to the Americans because of his history of violent
anti-communism. He was also the only potential rival to Makarios who could
command widespread support, and therefore weaken the Archbishop's leadership. Washington's acceptance of his return to Cyprus was the first of many
supportive gestures towards elements from Greece that conspired to eliminate
Makarios from the political equation.

Back in London, Packard was commissioned, along with a military intelligence colleague from Cyprus, to write a report on their attempts to achieve
permanent reintegration of Cyprus. But as the 400-page account was completed,
it was seized, along with all the supporting documents, and disappeared. The
Whitehall official who ordered the report, Cyril Pickard, never saw it. Packard
was posted back to Malta, despite calls from Cypriot leaders on both sides for his
return to Cyprus.[40]

Packard, who had kept a secret copy of the report, concluded that the British
played 'a key role in the division of the two Cypriot communities'. He said the
route to a negotiated reconciliation was blocked because of a British decision,
based on a narrow concept of Anglo-American strategic interests. He said, 'The
maintenance of the Sovereign Base Areas and other military facilities was
deemed of paramount importance by the British and American governments,
and their advisers certainly thought that this aim would more easily be achieved
in a divided Cyprus than in a cohesive, unitary state'.[41]

~14~

THE NATO PLOT

Plans to Split Cyprus

Following separate talks in Washington in June 1964, Inonu and Papandreou agreed to formal negotiations at Geneva which Dean Acheson, the distinguished former US Secretary of State, would attend. The talks were to be the first concrete attempt by the Americans to carve up the island between Greeks and Turks. The plan was to build on the creeping separatism of the Turkish Cypriots, and reflected American military thinking. If the Cyprus Republic was dismantled, and the island split between Greece and Turkey, there would be no 'Cassocked Castro' left in power to woo the Soviets, no more appeals to non-aligned leaders like Nasser, and an end to the Cypriot communists' hopes of gaining power on the island. There was an important military advantage in this. Under 'double enosis', all of Cyprus would be controlled by NATO countries, once more making the whole island available for Western defence purposes, as it had been under British rule.[1]

Before the talks began, Acheson and Ball canvassed a wide range of proposals for Cyprus, including partition and resettlement, federal, confederal and cantonal schemes, and even 'double enosis', whereby all the Greek Cypriots would resettle in one part of Cyprus, which would become part of Greece, and all the Turkish Cypriots in the other part, which would become part of Turkey.

In the meantime, fighting broke out in the north-west of Cyprus. Mortars, grenades and automatic weapons were used. Sampson, the notorious EOKA killer, was reported to be lining up his private army in the area.[2] The Turks sent in fighters by boat under the cloak of darkness between Lefka and Polis, and the Greeks shipped in troops through Limassol. The UN said 5000 were sent during June and July to serve under Grivas.

Within weeks of arriving on Cyprus, Grivas had overstepped his position as commander of the 950-strong Greek army contingent. He took effective command of all the Greek and Greek-Cypriot forces on the island, the biggest being the National Guard, now estimated to number 24,000. Grivas did not regard himself as answerable to Makarios. He talked directly to Papandreou over the Archbishop's head. Athens and Washington thought his arrival might help bring the disparate Greek-Cypriot armed groups under tighter control and reduce the risk of provoking the Turks. In his first public speech since going back, Grivas was uncharacteristically conciliatory towards the Turkish Cypriots. On Cyprus Radio and at a 10,000-strong rally, he demanded a referendum so that the Cypriot people could decide for themselves the fate of their country. But he also said he had returned to encourage co-existence with the Turkish community and help find a 'just solution' to the Cyprus problem. It sounded more like an agenda set by British or American diplomats than the fanatical calls to arms of his firebrand past. The call for peaceful coexistence drew laughter from the Nicosia crowd. But he insisted, 'I am not joking. That is what I feel and really believe.'[3]

The talks at Geneva began on 4 July. Acheson brought with him an American plan to split the island between Greece and Turkey. In return for Turkey agreeing to the union of most of the island with Greece, Athens would give Turkey a sovereign base. The purpose of the base would be to prevent the island being used by hostile forces to mount operations against Turkey, and to keep open the approaches to the Turkish ports of Mersin and Iskenderun. Acheson suggested it should cover at least the entire Karpas Peninsula – the long panhandle that protrudes from the north-east of the island – which was ideally located for the defence of Turkey's southern ports, and easily separable from the main body of the island. This was the minimum area the Turks would accept.[4]

While the Turkish Cypriots outside the proposed base area would become Greek citizens if enosis took place, Acheson proposed giving most of them a degree of local autonomy through the establishment of up to three Turkish-Cypriot dominated cantons with local self-administration. One of these would cover the Turkish quarter of Nicosia and the area stretching north of it to the Kyrenia range. He said that in these areas the Turkish Cypriots might control taxes, the police, the justice system and local services, while still being accountable to the main government of the island. Affairs concerning the Turkish Cypriots in the rest of the island might be controlled by a central Turkish- Cypriot administration based in Nicosia. An international watchdog, perhaps appointed by NATO, would ensure minority rights were upheld.[5] However, Papandreou would concede only a NATO base, not a Turkish one, and opposed the Acheson plan.

The Soviet Union was naturally alarmed by NATO's active intervention in the Cyprus question, and the continuing threat from Turkey. Kruschev also likened the situation to the Cuban crisis, and warned that the Soviet superpower was committed to helping liberation wars against colonisers and imperialists. He called on Britain and all other countries to pull their troops off the island and let the Cypriots sort out their own problems. He said that if Ankara attempted to move in, it could start a dangerous chain reaction and trigger a world war.[6] Kruschev's backing gave Makarios renewed hope for his quest to achieve self-determination through the UN. After three days of talks with the Athens Government, he said he would ask the General Assembly to back Cyprus's right to 'unrestricted independence', and to let its people determine the country's future.[7]

The Cypriots were not represented at the Geneva talks, but Makarios had made it known that he wanted a unitary state with government by a simple elected majority and communal rights protected by the constitution. The Turkish Cypriots sought a bizonal federal system of government, with the island split into two regions, the Turkish one covering an area north of a line from Kokkina in the north-west to Famagusta in the south-east. Grivas, by contrast, favoured something close to the Acheson plan, and wanted to offer Turkey one of the British bases instead of the Karpas peninsula. Ball told Johnson on 4 August that 'the Greeks may be ready to get Makarios out of the picture by instant enosis, which would be agreed upon secretly by Greece and Turkey'.[8]

While the negotiations were taking place, Greek-Cypriot forces began grouping around Kokkina. The UN commander sought assurances from Makarios that they would not attack. The Archbishop maintained that they would only block supplies to the Turkish-Cypriot rebels, but he refused to let UN troops check on the military build-up. Grivas flew to Athens on 5 August as guest of Papandreou to discuss Acheson's proposals, which were still being mulled over.[9]

On 6 August, the Greek-Cypriot National Guard mounted a full-scale assault on Turkish-Cypriot positions in north-west Cyprus, inflicting heavy losses. For three days, the Greek Cypriots had pushed forward with an offensive against Turkish-Cypriot areas in an attempt to seize a stretch of coastline that the Turkish Cypriots had been using to bring in reinforcements and arms supplies from Turkey. Ball accused Makarios of deliberately trying to provoke a conflict with Turkey and sabotage the American initiatives.[10] It succeeded in doing just that.

On the morning of 8 August, when the villages around Kokkina had fallen, and the fall of Kokkina itself seemed imminent, Ambassador Hare sent a 'CRITIC' telegram to the State Department. It said Erkin had left a cabinet meeting to tell him they were going to take air action to save Kokkina. Erkin reminded the American of the lengths to which the Ankara Government had gone to achieve a peaceful climb-down. Only after every option had been exhausted did they now feel there was no alternative but the use of force. 'Even so [they] will restrict action to minimum, of police type, and will make this clear,' reported Hare.[11]

Shortly afterwards, as Turkish Cypriots fled their villages under fire, 30 Turkish jets swooped over the area, attacking Greek-Cypriot positions. The next day, 64 jets were sent in, this time bombing and strafing Greek-Cypriot villages. The UN said the Turkish jets fired rockets, canon and incendiary bombs on to the Greek Cypriots. The Cyprus Government said there was shelling by destroyers, and claimed napalm was used to wipe out villages. One doctor brought out the body of a boy, burnt and blackened, which he said was the result of napalm. He said 40 patients had been admitted the previous day with fatal burns, and that 300 wounded had passed through his hands. A hospital was hit when a 500lb bomb was dropped on a Greek-Cypriot armoured car. Official figures later put the Greek-Cypriot death toll at 55, with 125 injuries.[12]

On the second day of air strikes, Makarios warned Ankara that if they were not halted immediately all the Turkish-Cypriot villages on the island would become potential targets of a Greek-Cypriot attack. He appealed to the Soviets and the Egyptians for arms and support. Kruschev wrote to Inonu, demanding an end to all military operations against Cyprus. In Washington, Ball set up a 24-hour command post in case the fighting escalated into a much bigger war. In Nicosia, the US Ambassador, Taylor Belcher, pleaded with Makarios to order a ceasefire. As Makarios replied, 'Do you think that the Turks would stop if I did so?' an aide rushed in to announce further air strikes by first four, then seven, Turkish planes on the villages of Pomos and Kato Fyrgos to either side of Kokkina, setting the village centres ablaze. Makarios turned to the Ambassador and shrugged. 'What can I do?' The American said he should reconsider his 'terrible decision' which was 'so fraught with dangers for his people'. On his way out, Belcher asked Makarios by what deadline the Turks would have to stop their air attacks to prevent an offensive against the Turkish Cypriots. Markarios said 3.30pm. The Ambassador anxiously telegrammed the State Department, warning that the Turkish bombings had to stop to avert 'a holocaust on this island with all its ultimate consequences for our alliances, not only in this area but elsewhere'. Makarios obliged the Americans by extending the deadline to 6pm, and offered to issue a ceasefire to allow negotiations to take place if the Turks responded.[13]

Many Turkish Cypriots, however, had already fled their villages and were hiding in the hills, praying for a Turkish invasion. Ankara pulled its aircraft and bases out of the NATO command system so that it could use them for action over Cyprus if needed. Throughout the day, Ankara Radio played martial music. There were reports in Athens that Turkish warships had entered Cyprus's territorial waters and rumours that Turkish troops were actually landing in the north-west of the island. Newspapers in Ankara announced that the invasion fleet was on its way. Huge military convoys were on the move in north-eastern Turkey to reinforce the border against attack from the Soviet Union.[14] Ball warned that any fighting between Greece and Turkey could escalate into a confrontation between East and West.

Throughout 9 August, diplomats worked feverishly at the United Nations to ensure an Anglo-American resolution calling for an immediate ceasefire was adopted in the Security Council. Nine voted in favour, none against. Communist Czechoslovakia and the Soviet Union abstained. The Greek representative said that if Turkey's attacks continued, Greek fighters would come to the aid of Cyprus. A squadron of Greek airforce jet fighters flew over southern Cyprus and Nicosia at low level in a show of force. The US delegate to the UN, Adlai Stevenson, gave a chill warning: 'Until all hostilities stop, no one will stop. Perhaps within a matter of hours we will be over the brink and into the abyss and no one can see the bottom.'[15]

Late in the afternoon, both Ankara and Makarios complied with the UN ceasefire call. Ball said the return of Grivas was crucial to defusing this crisis, because it weakened Makarios's position.[16]

At Geneva, Acheson put forward a second version of his proposals, in an attempt to win over the Greeks. The new plan compromised on a number of key issues: the Turkish base would not become sovereign Turkish territory, but would merely be leased for a number of years, perhaps 50; the base area would be much smaller than first proposed; there would be no central Turkish-Cypriot administration in Nicosia; and the Turkish Cypriots would not be allowed to set up separate administrative units in special areas where they contained a majority. Instead, two of the eparchies into which Cyprus was to be divided – and which had a large Turkish-Cypriot population – would always be headed by a Turkish Cypriot and a set ratio of its officials and police force would have to be Turkish Cypriots. A high official in the central government of Cyprus would take up complaints of discrimination or failure to honour minority rights.[17]

While the Turks would accept the first plans as a basis for talks, they rejected the second. The Greeks, having rejected the first, almost, but not quite, accepted the second. In Cyprus, Clerides, the Greek-Cypriot Speaker of the House of Representatives, dismissed the Acheson plan as 'absolutely unacceptable'. On 18 August, Acheson telegrammed Ball with the news that little progress could be made.[18]

Frustrated that both sides could come so close to agreement and yet remain obdurate, even at the risk of world war, Ball and Acheson turned their minds towards more drastic measures. They devised an astonishing plot to use NATO to force Greece and Turkey to split their differences over the Acheson proposals and accept the result. This is revealed in a note from senior White House officials Robert Komer and McGeorge Bundy briefing Johnson for a National Security Council meeting on Cyprus on 19 August. Komer and Bundy said the Turkish air attacks, and now Soviet threats, had brought the issue to the boil. Makarios was playing with fire, and the mood on the island had become violently anti-US and pro-Soviet, which made the Acheson plan harder to achieve *by agreement* (authors' italics). Speed seemed imperative if they were to push through a settlement before the 'Makarios-Moscow axis' was firmed up. Ball and Acheson – who were 'carrying the main load' as far as policy over Cyprus was concerned – were therefore thinking of a NATO pressure ploy to force a solution. Komer and Bundy reported, 'Acheson himself would split the remaining differences between the Greeks and Turks. We would then ask all NATO powers to join in telling the Greeks and Turks to buy; calling on Greece on behalf of the guarantor powers to restrain Makarios; and if this fails to maintain order, declaring that whatever violence may occur must be confined to the island.' To achieve the latter, NATO would declare that no NATO-supplied arms could be used by Greece and Turkey against each other. Otherwise an attempt would be made to take back the arms and punish the offender by denying him any more military aid. The NATO powers would act to prevent Turkish action against Greece or vice versa, and if the Soviets intervened, the alliance would move. The high-risk plan would involve putting the US Sixth Fleet between the Greeks and the Turks 'since we [the United States] have the only power in the Eastern Mediterranean'.[19]

Komer and Bundy described it as an 'ingenious and complex' plan, but acknowledged that it might be difficult to secure widespread support within NATO for such action. An alternative was to use it to back up a scheme put forward by Papandreou for instant enosis. Papandreou pleaded that the only way to short-circuit Nicosia's burgeoning alliance with Moscow was to impose enosis straight away, and leave the Greeks to make a deal with the Turks. Komer commented, 'We feel that the Turks would never buy unless the terms are worked out beforehand. But if they can be, Papandreou's plan may be simpler and more direct than the NATO scheme – or perhaps the two could be combined to reinforce each other. If the Greeks turned to NATO (knowing already what they would get) we would be home.' The potential spanner in the works was Makarios, who had outmanoeuvred the Greeks and Turks every time so far, and believed he had Soviet backing. Komer and Bundy said the ultimate question was whether a Greek-Turkish deal, if they could get one, could be imposed on the Cypriots. Komer told the President, 'Whatever road we take, we have all the ingredients for a major crisis shortly. Makarios will try every trick he has and the Soviets are now committed to make at least some trouble.'[20]

On 8 September, Acheson and Ball told Johnson over lunch, which was attended by Bundy, Rusk and Secretary of Defence Robert McNamara, that they believed the only solution now was a *fait accompli* in which the Turks would move to occupy the Karpas peninsula, triggering instant enosis by the Greeks 'with the consequent supersession of Makarios'. The Turkish action could be triggered by almost anything, the most immediate possibility being the refusal to let Ankara rotate the troops in its 650-strong Cyprus contingent with fresh troops from Turkey. Acheson had discussed the plan with Turkish military leaders, and they had shown great interest. Acheson's plan assumed that a resort to action was expected one way or another. According to Bundy, the President said the choice was 'whether it should be messy and destructive or controlled and eventually productive, in accordance with a plan'.[21]

Due to concern over the dangerous turn of events in Vietnam, Washington took no action on the plans to divide the island, and Acheson gave up trying to bridge the gap between Greece and Turkey by diplomacy. He had broken new ground by persuading Papandreou to be ready to let Turkey have a base on Cyprus, and even Grivas concurred. But no permanent solution had been secured. Ball, in his memoirs, reflected wistfully on times past when 'the great powers of the day were quite ready to use their combined strength ruthlessly, without concern for the rights of sovereignty, the integrity of territory, or the abstract principle of self-determination' to impose a solution. The Americans had travelled a long way down the road of self-interest since they had cited the UN Charter as a reason why Britain should end their colonial rule over Cyprus. They had already begun to consider a conspiracy to divide the island – and remove the possibility of Makarios delivering it into the Soviet sphere of influence. Key elements from the 1964 plans were echoed in the crisis of 1974.

On Cyprus, the nine months of fighting, the Greek-Cypriot attacks, the Turkish-Cypriot agitation for autonomy, and the policies of the Americans and the British left the 1960 independence project in tatters. The island was now bitterly disunited and the communities physically separated, the Turks massed in armed ghettos, a kind of half-way stage between an integrated Cyprus and partition. For the time being, the use of Turkish air power appeared to have deterred further Greek-Cypriot offensives. The fighting left 103 Turkish-Cypriot villages in ruins, and around 25,000 Turkish Cypriots had become refugees – whether as a result of the violence or agitation by their own political leaders. Between December 1963 and August 1964, there were at least five occasions when the Americans had to stave off major threats of Turkish military intervention in Cyprus and a Greek-Turkish war. These were the crises in December, February, March, June and August.[22] But in Washington, the secret plans to divide Cyprus between Greece and Turkey, if necessary by force, were left on the shelf – for now.

~15~

FALLEN ALLIES

Grivas Risks War

The Americans paid a heavy price for their failure to sort out the Cyprus troubles. Unable to secure at the negotiating table in August 1964 what they had threatened to take by force, the Turks began to pursue a more ambivalent foreign policy. While pressing Washington to declare itself in favour of their federated state solution, the Turks developed closer relations with Moscow. The Soviets, keen to exploit the differences between the allies on NATO's southern flank, sent senior officials on a series of visits to Ankara between October 1964 and September 1967. The Americans believed the Cyprus situation was 'still potentially explosive', and the Soviet overtures further complicated the problem. Turkey became 'the most serious casualty' of the whole Cyprus tangle of 1964 as far as Washington was concerned. The American veto of a Turkish invasion severely dented Turkish trust in the alliance with Washington. Ball even suggested that Ankara later pulled out of the American plans for a multilateral nuclear force in Europe in return for Soviet support over Cyprus, which it gave at the UN in December 1965.[1] Relations with Turkey were strategically crucial to the United States because of its key position as a bridge between Europe and Asia, and as a barrier between the Soviet Union and both the Mediterranean and the Middle East. It was a vital link in CENTO, the central link in the West's circle of containment around the Eastern Bloc, and maintained one of the largest armed forces in NATO. But between 1964 and 1967, relations between Washington and all three NATO allies interested in Cyprus were thrown into turmoil, and trouble continued to brew on the island.

In January 1965, the Soviet Foreign Minister, Andrei Gromyko, condemned the Acheson proposals that 'NATO circles' were 'trying to impose on the Cypriots in order to make the island their military base'. He called for the withdrawal of all foreign troops and the abolition of all foreign bases. Makarios, meanwhile, had triumphantly persuaded a conference of 47 non-aligned countries at Cairo to endorse his view that the island should be free to determine its future without outside intervention. He pledged that Cyprus would stay in the non-aligned camp, expelled a Greek government spokesman in Cyprus for calling for a 'NATO solution', and cultivated relations with Nasser, who also wanted to rid Cyprus of its British bases.

At the end of March, Greek ships carrying missiles to Cyprus from Nasser's United Arab Republic turned back after American diplomatic intervention. In October, news that Soviet anti-aircraft missiles were being sent to Cyprus provoked another political crisis, and Turkey put its forces on alert. Other arms, including 30 Soviet-built tanks, were said to have arrived on the island. Clerides admitted later that the Egyptians trained the Cypriots in the use of Eastern Bloc arms, including ground-to-air missiles, tanks and artillery, which the Soviets had been supplying since before the Suez crisis. Clerides said, 'The reason we bought these from the East was because the Western countries refused to sell. They didn't want to strengthen us against Turkey and they didn't want us to have an army or weapons. They thought that by starving us of weapons we would be more susceptible to solutions they might recommend.'[2]

Bolstered by the support of communist and non-aligned countries, Makarios removed most Turkish-Cypriot rights, by abolishing the separate Greek and Turkish electoral rolls, which enabled Turkish Cypriots to vote for Turkish-Cypriot representatives and Greek Cypriots for Greek-Cypriot representatives. He then tried to break the will of the Turkish Cypriots in their self-imposed internal exile by restricting goods reaching them. The measures included a heavy tax on grain sold to Turkish Cypriots. In September 1965, the UN commander, General Thimayya, visited Kokkina, and reported that conditions would deteriorate rapidly if supplies were not increased, and that 600 refugees were living in caves. The UN persuaded Makarios to relax the blockade, but a year later the UN estimated that a third of the Turkish-Cypriot population still needed some form of relief.[3]

The UN Security Council noted with alarm that the situation on Cyprus had grown tense. But Makarios's Foreign Minister, Kyprianou, told the British and Americans that if the Security Council passed a resolution hostile to Cyprus, his government would immediately raise the issue of the British sovereign bases and

American spying stations. Some Cypriot ministers had already called for the withdrawal of all foreign troops and the closure of the British bases as a first step to a settlement.

Instability in Greece added to the problems in Cyprus. Grivas had been stirring up trouble in Athens by trying to implicate the Prime Minister's son, Andreas Papandreou, in a conspiracy to purge the army of right-wing elements. When the King blocked attempts to make changes in the army's higher echelons, George Papandreou resigned in an attempt to force a general election. But many MPs in his party betrayed him, and struck a deal with the King to stay in power under a new leader, Stephanos Stephanopoulos. Makarios became alarmed when an enquiry into the conspiracy allegations threw up a letter in which Grivas, who since then had returned to Cyprus with the tacit approval of the British and Americans, suggested he would try to oust the Cypriot President. Grivas claimed this was a fake.[4] But Makarios sacked government officials who supported the former EOKA leader and asked Stephanopoulos to relieve Grivas of his command of the Cypriot National Guard. This would have left Grivas in charge of only the Greek army contingent on the island. Stephanopoulos refused. He needed to have one officer in command of all armed forces on Cyprus if war broke out.

Makarios tried to weaken the National Guard, and switched funds to the Greek-Cypriot police, whose loyalties were less divided – by 1967 there were 2200 regular policemen, and his paramilitary police-force reached battalion strength. He bought 1000 rifles, 1000 sub-machine-guns, 20 rocket launchers, 20 mortars and 20 light tanks from Prague to arm them. But Grivas told Greek ministers he could not take responsibility for security on Cyprus unless the bearing of arms was confined to men under his command. After pressure from Greece and Turkey, Makarios was forced to lock away the Czech arms, subject to UN inspection. In the midst of this turmoil, an Athens newspaper revealed that the Archbishop had initiated the Akritas Plan in 1963, under which the Greek Cypriots aimed to use overwhelming armed force to make the Turkish Cypriots accept widespread constitutional changes.[5] But Makarios remained defiant, and embarked on a tour of African and South American countries to whip up support for the Greek-Cypriots' position in the UN.

During this period, the Americans faced a threat to their military interests from an unlikely quarter: Britain. Harold Wilson's Government, elected in October 1964, lurched from one balance-of-payments crisis to the next, and an international rescue package failed. The Americans feared disastrous consequences if they let the United Kingdom 'go to the wall': Wilson would have to dramatically devalue the pound and slash Britain's defence commitments around the world. Ball said this would be 'disastrous politically', since it would leave Washington more than ever the lone world policeman – and 'require us to assume permanently additional overseas commitments'.[6] Though they had been ambivalent towards the British empire in the past, the Americans believed that in many areas, such as the Middle East, the British performed important security functions that no other nation could take over.[7] Cyprus fell into this category, as Britain had secured for itself an extraordinary array of military facilities and rights on the island which, under the terms of the Treaty of Establishment, the British could not hand over to Washington if they pulled out.[8]

To solve its economic problems, the Labour Government was, according to David Leigh, attempting to retreat from Empire, with a corresponding reduction in the number of intelligence bases it had available.[9] Consequently, the Americans reached a series of secret agreements with Wilson and Callaghan to bale out the pound with massive economic assistance, in return for Britain upholding its worldwide defence role. Before any defence reviews were finalised, Wilson consulted the Americans to make sure any decision met their conditions for supporting the pound. A Treasury representative in Washington said Johnson 'made it clear to Wilson that the pound was not to be devalued and no drastic action east of Suez was to be taken until after the US elections [in November 1968]. In return the pound would be supported to any extent necessary.'[10]

Wilson went to the polls for a second time in March 1966 and was returned with a substantial majority of 94 MPs. But the economic crisis deepened, and to secure American help he agreed to demands by Johnson's officials that he implement an incomes policy, rather than cut overseas defence commitments.[11] Consequently, Britain maintained more than 100,000 military personnel east of Suez and 30,000 in the Middle East, mainly in Aden. Deputy Labour leader George Brown observed that Wilson was 'bound personally and irrevocably to Johnson and had ceased to be a free agent'.[12]

Nevertheless, in February 1966, the Government announced it would pull out of Aden in 1968, reduce its forces in Cyprus, Malta, Guyana and eventually in south-east Asia, drop military aircraft development projects and phase out aircraft-carriers altogether. Privately, the Americans recognised that Wilson had been forced to take 'the most severe deflationary measures of any post-war British government', and Wilson had withstood considerable pressure from his own MPs to send home all British troops east of Suez.[13]

To offload some responsibilities, Wilson handed Diego Garcia, a British island in the Indian Ocean, to the Americans on a 50-year lease for use as a naval intelligence and nuclear air-base, and colluded in clearing the 2000 inhabitants off the island.[14]

But Britain's declining economy, world events, and the increasing American demands put a great strain on the 'special relationship' between the two countries. They rowed over Washington's attempt to set up a European nuclear defence force, because this posed a threat to Britain's 'independent' deterrent, and over Wilson's repeated refusal to send British troops to Vietnam – not even a token platoon of bagpipers – to ease American isolation on the issue.[15] In February 1967, according to Clive Ponting, Washington offered an astonishing 25-year multi-billion dollar loan to stabilise the economy in return for a pledge that

Britain would keep a major strategic presence in the Far East. Politically, Wilson could not accept a deal that would make Britain subservient to the United States and might force him into a commitment in Vietnam. But without the loan he had to slash public spending – especially on defence.[16]

When Wilson visited Washington in June, Rusk warned the President that the British had made up their minds 'to liquidate most of their overseas commitments remaining from the empire and to become an integral part of the European movement'. He observed, though, that there were a number of tiny possessions scattered throughout the world – such as Cyprus – which the British 'simply cannot cast adrift'.[17] In July, the British Cabinet decided to pull out of Singapore and Malaya by 1975, and agreed to work towards a full withdrawal from the Middle East as soon as they could shed treaty obligations.[18] This marked the beginning of the end of Britain's role as a worldwide military power, and alerted the Americans to the prospect that one day they might lose the use of the Cyprus facilities.

Wilson's hand was forced by a new Middle East crisis. Since early 1966, tension had been increasing between Israel and its Arab neighbours, particularly on the Israeli-Syrian border. Nasser, whose forces had been greatly reinforced with help from the Soviet Union, decided in May 1967 to move his troops up to the Israeli border, and demanded the withdrawal of UN troops patrolling the Gaza strip, right along the Sinai frontier between the UAR and Israel, and the straits of Tiran, which provided Israel's access to the Gulf of Aqaba and the Indian Ocean. He then moved forces into a position overlooking the straits, and announced that he was going to close it to Israeli shipping. At this point, King Faisal of Saudi Arabia was in London pleading with Wilson not to pull British forces out of Aden and Southern Arabia. Faisal was worried that Nasser would subvert the Gulf and eventually attack his and other independent Middle East countries. Ten Soviet warships were sent to the Mediterranean. On 5 June, war broke out. Arab radio stations broadcast allegations that British aircraft had joined in the Israeli attack on the UAR, and that the communications system on Cyprus had been used to help the attacks. Wilson called this the 'big lie'. But Nasser closed the Suez Canal and Iraq, Kuwait, Algeria, Syria and the Lebanon cut off oil supplies, in some cases only those to Britain and the United States. The war ended after six days, after Israel seized control of UAR territory in Gaza, Sinai, the Golan Heights and on the west bank of the river Jordan.[19]

The closure of the Suez Canal and the loss of Middle East oil pushed the British economy deeper into crisis, and on 18 November Wilson was forced to devalue the pound. To make devaluation work required massive spending cuts, and he made half of them in defence. It was decided to pull out of the Far East (apart from Hong Kong) and the Gulf by 1971. The number of aircraft based in Cyprus was also to be reduced. Overall, more than 150,000 military and civilian personnel were cut. The aircraft-carriers would go too.[20]

The Americans were furious. Rusk accused Britain of 'opting out' and described it as 'the end of an era'. A senior State Department official put it more bluntly: 'You are not going to be in the Far East. You are not going to be in the Middle East. You are not even going to be in Europe in strength. Where are you going to be?'[21]

Only in the inescapable commitment to sharing electronic intelligence with the United States did Wilson increase spending. Britain was paying £100 million – as much as its Far Eastern commitments – towards activities carried out under the secret UKUSA agreement for gathering and sharing intelligence, and this rose to more than £600 million a year by the 1980s. Thus, to the relief of the Americans, Britain hung on to its Cyprus spying facilities. But the seeds of doubt over Britain's commitment to staying on Cyprus had been sown, and would influence American policy in 1974. To receive its share of intelligence from America's network, Britain had to keep up the flow of material from British stations to the National Security Agency. But Wilson vetoed any move to keep up with the next major development in intelligence, the race to develop spy satellites, which America was left to dominate. This made Britain's network of ground stations, including its most important overseas facilities on Cyprus, one of Britain's key contributions to the defence of the West. Eventually stations like those on Cyprus at Troodos, Ayios Nikolaos and Pergamos even had an advantage over spy satellites in a global war in one respect, because the Soviets developed the technology to blind satellites in space. The significance of these facilities is often overlooked because they are kept so secret. But the intelligence partnership with the United States was just as crucial to Britain's defence as the co-operation on nuclear weapons. Without intelligence on the enemy's capability, intentions, readiness for war, and the imminence of attack, it is impossible to prevent and counter an attack, nuclear or otherwise. Without intelligence on that enemy's weapons development it is impossible to maintain a credible deterrent.

Since the Cuban missile crisis, the Soviets had begun a massive build-up of conventional and nuclear weapons, and strove for superiority in its space programme in an effort to achieve military parity with the United States. The number of ICBMs (intercontinemtal ballistic missiles) the Soviet Union possessed rose from an estimated 75 in 1962 to 570 in 1967, compared with the United States's 1054, and the facilities on Cyprus helped Britain and America keep tabs on how the Soviets' nuclear development programme was progressing. They did this by monitoring Soviet nuclear missile tests to see how advanced the weapons were. The facilities also provided early warning of any preparations for conventional or nuclear war. This intelligence capability grew more important in the years ahead as the missile gap narrowed and the Soviets tried to overtake the technological advances in nuclear weaponry that gave the West the edge in the arms race.

During this rocky period for America's relations with Britain and Turkey, a military coup in Greece in April 1967 sent relations with Athens into confusion too. The coup was the final stage in a series of political crises sparked by Grivas's allegations about Andreas Papandreou. The CIA in Athens feared the general election due by May would produce a popular backlash against King Constantine's interference, giving George Papandreou a massive majority. They were worried that this would leave Andreas, whom they blamed for Greece's rejection of the Acheson proposals, and who was becoming increasingly anti-American, a dominant figure in the Government. A senior CIA official warned that Andreas would close down the US bases and communications facilities in Greece and pull the country out of NATO. The CIA in Athens believed a Papandreou victory would 'seriously damage American interests' and exacerbate tensions between Greece and Turkey. They recommended a covert programme to support pro-Western, anti-Papandreou candidates in marginal seats. The proposal went to the highest level, at the National Security Council, before Johnson vetoed it. When King Constantine sought Washington's view of 'extra parliamentary' action to prevent a Papandreou victory, the Americans planned to tell him that their response to a coup would 'depend on the circumstances'. But before they got back in contact, a military junta seized power in Athens in a bloodless coup.[22]

The coup, on 21 April, was not led by generals or loyalists to the King. A rival right-wing faction – made up of colonels and senior officers from the Greek intelligence service, KYP, and the military police – had beaten them to it. George Papandreou was placed under house arrest. Andreas and other left-wing leaders were imprisoned and charged with plotting a communist takeover. However, the Americans proved remarkably relaxed about the usurping of democracy in Greece. There was no show of force by the Sixth Fleet in the Mediterranean or Aegean, no breaking off of diplomatic contacts with the new, military, government. The American Ambassador did secure a suspension of heavy arms shipments to Greece, but the US military constantly argued for it to be lifted. This may have been because the leader of the junta, Colonel Papadopoulos, had been on the payroll of the CIA since 1952, and had acted as the senior liaison officer between the Greek secret service and the CIA. A former confidant of Johnson, Eliot Janeway, disclosed that when he visited Greece in late 1966 he was surprised to discover that 'our visit coincided with the preliminaries for the Greek military putsch, sponsored by the CIA and the undercover Defense Intelligence Agency'.[23] According to Christopher Woodhouse, a former British agent in Greece, the Greek military attaché in Washington was told by the Americans that, though the White House did not support Papadopoulos's coup, the junta would be tolerated as a means to undermine communist support in Greece.[24] In the absence of any decisive policy against it, the Papadopoulos Government strengthened its grip on power, though it left the monarchy in place.

The junta in Athens took an aggressive stance on the Cyprus situation, seeking to secure a settlement based on a favourable version of the Acheson proposals. Since 1965, up to 10,000 Greek troops had been smuggled onto the island, initially with the agreement of Makarios. But Papadopoulos, a former head of counter-intelligence in the KYP, held views closer to Grivas's than Makarios's on the Cyprus question. And the heavy influence of the Greek army in the Cypriot forces gave the military Government in Athens an undue power over events on the island.

In July 1967, the British were warned that the colonels might be close to staging a coup in Cyprus to get rid of the Archbishop and achieve enosis. Foreign Office officials advised the Cabinet that if the coup went ahead, the Government should publicly oppose it but not let British troops get involved. The suggestion was made in a huge paper on Cyprus recommending that Britain should make its presence in Cyprus 'virtually permanent'. The motive appeared to be to pre-empt any move by Makarios to use communist support in the UN to demilitarise the island. According to the diaries of Cabinet minister Richard Crossman, the Foreign Secretary, Brown, explained after the Cabinet meeting, 'After all, the Cypriots have got a very bad record of voting with the Russians in all UN matters'. However, Crossman and Defence Secretary Denis Healey thought the idea of 15,000 British troops standing by while the junta seized control of Cyprus was 'totally intolerable', and they refused to discuss it.[25]

The coup did not happen, as the junta tried instead to forge a deal above the Cypriots' heads. After re-opening private contacts with the Turks on the Cyprus question at a NATO meeting in June, they held talks with the Turkish Government at the Evros frontier in September. The Turks thought the military-minded colonels would recognise the need to divide Cyprus to keep the communists at bay and prevent the island being turned into a Soviet satellite. The Greeks offered the Turks a military base if they accepted enosis for the rest of the island. But Turkish premier Demirel demanded two bases and 10 percent of the island's territory. The Americans would have settled for this, but not the Greeks. All that could be agreed at Evros was a face-saving statement calling for greater co-operation and more effort to find a solution.

Frustrated by the *impasse*, Grivas took matters into his own hands. For several months, Turkish Cypriots in the southern village of Kophinou, which overlooks the strategic meeting point of the roads to Nicosia, Larnaca and Limassol, had been setting up road blocks and preventing the Greek-Cypriot police from passing through the town. Grivas devised a plan to break the Turkish-Cypriot resistance. His troops, backed up by heavy weaponry, surrounded the area, and on 15 November he sent the first patrol into the neighbouring village of Ayios Theodoros. That afternoon, he even turned up in the village himself with photographers to announce his success to the world. The next day, when the patrols continued, the Turkish Cypriots opened fire as Grivas's men tried to pull down a road block. The surrounding Greek-Cypriot forces immediately launched an all-out attack, bombarding the Turkish-Cypriot positions in both Ayios Theodoros and Kophinou with artillery shells and automatic weapons fire. UN positions containing British troops were overrun and disarmed. Twenty-four Turkish Cypriots and two Greek Cypriots died in the attack.

Grivas had made a dangerous error of judgment. Turkey threatened to bomb his forces if the action did not stop, and warned the UN that if its troops did not drive the Greek and Greek-Cypriot troops out of the area immediately 'a crisis which will go beyond the borders of the island will be unavoidable'. The violence ceased within hours. But when press photographs the next morning revealed the extent of the action against the Turkish Cypriots, the Turkish Grand National Assembly authorised the Government to take military action as the need arose. Twenty-five Turkish bombers were loaded for action at the Incirlik base shared with the Americans.[26] All the main airports were closed to traffic, and six frigates and two other naval vessels were sent to the Aegean. The Turks massed troops and artillery on the border with Greece, and prepared invasion forces for a landing on Cyprus. Demirel vowed his Government would do 'everything possible and necessary' to stop aggression against the Turkish Cypriots. There were demonstrations throughout Turkey calling for war with Greece, and Turkish jets flew through Cyprus airspace. Anticipating grave danger, British forces began to move the 2400 Britons on Cyprus into the Dhekelia sovereign base, and 600 Americans were flown to Beirut, though around 100 remained in the Embassy and at US spying and communications stations.

The Greek colonels recoiled at the risk of all-out war with a stronger military power, and summoned Grivas back to Athens. The Turkish-Cypriot areas at the eye of the storm were cleared of National Guard troops. But the Turks continued to build up their forces opposite Cyprus, and armed their aircraft with bombs, some of them napalm, ready for an onslaught. At the same time, the Americans discovered that the Greek airforce was preparing to strike Turkish troop ships.[27] On 24 November, Turkey announced it was determined to settle the problem once and for all. Greece and Turkey were on the brink of war. As severe storms delayed any Turkish plans to land on the island, Johnson's special envoy, Cyrus Vance, Canadian Prime Minister Lester Pearson, and the NATO and UN Secretary Generals engaged in frenetic diplomatic activity to prevent an escalation that would tear NATO apart. The Americans pressed Ankara not to force Greece into a corner from which it had no option but to fight back. As a result, Ankara made some quite reasonable demands: the withdrawal of all Greek troops above the limits set down in the 1960 Treaty of Alliance, the collection by UN forces of all arms held by unauthorised civilians and militias, the strengthening of the UN force's mandate to keep the peace, the reconstitution of the Cypriot police into a mixed-community force, compensation for the victims of the violence, and security measures to protect the Turkish Cypriots.

Makarios quibbled over the points he considered an internal matter, but the colonels had no stomach for a war. When Taylor Belcher, the US Ambassador to Cyprus, warned the Archbishop that the Turks were ready to put 50,000 men ashore, supported by heavy artillery and unhindered air attacks, he backed down.[28]

The withdrawal of 10,000 surplus Greek troops from Cyprus represented a humiliating climb-down for the Greeks, but was a source of relief for Makarios.

It dramatically reduced the internal threat to his position, especially as Grivas was forced to stay in Athens and surrender his Cyprus command.

The Soviets avoided taking sides in the dispute because their objective was to preserve an independent Cyprus that one day might elect a government led by the popular communist movement AKEL, close the British bases and hand base rights to Moscow. Parker T. Hart, US Ambassador in Ankara, said, 'While one might have assumed that a fratricidal struggle within the south-east wing of the NATO alliance could have been very much in its interest... the Soviet Union and its Warsaw Pact satellites were making it clear to me that what they feared most was either a partition of Cyprus between Greece and Turkey or an outright conquest of the island by Turkey. In either case, Cyprus would become the potential site for NATO bases and the strongest communist party in the Middle East, AKEL, would go down the drain.'[29]

At the turn of the year, the Turkish Cypriots rubbed salt into Greek wounds by setting up a rival government to the Greek Cypriots for the towns and villages inhabited by their own community. It was described as a 'transitional adminis-tration', to exist until the 1960 constitution was fully back in operation. Kutchuk was made President of the administration and the exiled Denktash became Vice President. The Greek Cypriots regarded this as an extreme act of provocation, another step on the road to partition.

After the November crisis, Johnson did not risk any bold new initiatives on the Cyprus question. He was due for re-election in November 1968, and had his hands full with Vietnam – the issue which made him so unpopular that he even-tually decided not to run for a second term. A request from King Constantine for US support for a counter-coup in Greece was turned down, and the Americans told the British that they wanted London to support the colonels' regime in Athens because 'the only alternative would be a communist coup which would weaken NATO's flank'.[30] Concerning Cyprus, Johnson put on hold the attempts to force a solution above the Cypriots' heads, and left the UN to get on with a process of talks between the leaders of the two communities. The Greeks had burned their fingers, but the crisis had also exposed Makarios's vulnerability with a hostile military government controlling his armed forces. He was more ready to co-operate with the Johnson administration, but only where it suited his purposes. For instance, in the aftermath of the Vance mission, the status of the secret American intelligence and communications facilities on Cyprus was recognised officially, through an exchange of letters on 22 January.[31] According to Laurence Stern, the Archbishop agreed to permit the operation of CIA U-2 reconnaissance flights from the British base at Akrotiri; to the setting up of CIA radio monitors to eavesdrop on Middle East and Communist Bloc traffic; and to the fixing of secret antennae linked to the US electronic intelligence network. Stern said the CIA paid Makarios an annual sum of around $1 million through a secret fund to use as he wished.[32] In fact, the Americans had been operating wireless and communications facilities on the island for years, some of them since the late 1940s, and some of them jointly with the British, but had not negotiated their status after independence – until now.[33]

Makarios, standing for re-election, also softened his position on enosis. He appealed to Greek Cypriots to make a 'courageous' compromise and be willing to accept a 'feasible' solution that might not fulfil all their desires. He had little enthusiasm for seeking political union with a military dictatorship. He won the election, in February 1968, with 95.45 percent of the vote against a representative of the newly formed Enosis Front, with a turnout of over 90 percent. As a sign of goodwill, he ordered Greek-Cypriot forces to pull down their fortifications and abandon their roadblocks around the Turkish-Cypriot quarter of Nicosia. Exploratory talks between Clerides and Denktash, were held throughout the summer and autumn. The gulf between Athens and Nicosia became unbridgeable in October 1968 when a foiled plot to blow up junta leader Colonel Papadopoulos was attributed to, among others, Makarios's Interior and Defence Minister, Georghadhis. For several months, Makarios refused to bow to pressure from Athens to sack him.

Johnson's decision to stand down was more ominous for the Cypriot administration than Makarios could ever have realised, as Johnson had been the crucial restraining influence on both the Turks and his own senior officials who wanted NATO to force an Acheson-style solution on Cyprus. Nevertheless, during his presidency the United States abandoned its commitment to the concept of a guaranteed independence for a united Cyprus, the 1960 settlement which Eisenhower had worked so hard behind the scenes to secure. The search was still on for an insurance policy against a communist takeover, a way of splitting the island between Greece and Turkey that would leave the facilities in NATO hands if the British ever withdrew.

But the Americans had already accepted that Turkey could one day be allowed to occupy part of Cyprus, and had begun to think of ways of imposing a solution that divided Cyprus between Greeks and Turks. The next President, Richard Nixon, had fewer qualms about the kind of covert action needed to get rid of Makarios, and during his tenure the strategic motives for doing so weighed ever heavier.

~16~

THE 'RED PRIEST'

Assassination Target

Makarios's flirtations with the Eastern Bloc struck a raw nerve with the new US President, Nixon. He first made his name by campaigning to expose Alger Hiss, a State Department official linked to a Soviet spy network. He cut his teeth in politics by painting his rivals in his 1946 Congress and 1950 Senate campaigns as communists – even though they were liberal democrats. He was hand-picked by Eisenhower as vice-presidential candidate to escalate these attacks. The targets included Acheson, the man who wanted to split Cyprus to prevent communism taking over, whom Nixon described as a man with a colour blindness – 'a form of pink eye towards the Communist threat to the United States'. Nixon's biographer, Theodore White, observed that, from the Alger Hiss case on, 'the real or fancied menace of conspiracy always interlocked, as a paranoia, with his genuine sense of patriotism'.[1]

During the Nixon years, American agencies around the world stopped at nothing to keep pro-Western regimes in power – from backing the right-wing junta in Greece to plotting against Salvador Allende in Chile – and they were never likely to balk at overthrowing Makarios if it meant keeping the Cyprus facilities in Western hands. Makarios's history of arms deals with communist states and his courting of non-aligned leaders such as Nasser made him suspect. An early incident in Nixon's presidency tainted him further. In September 1969, when Nixon and his National Security Adviser, Henry Kissinger, were trying to force North Vietnam to the negotiating table to settle the war, they urged friendly nations to apply pressure on the Hanoi Government. But they were furious to discover that Cyprus was one of four non-communist countries still shipping to North Vietnam. When Makarios refused to sever the trading link, Nixon cut off American aid.[2] Throughout his presidency, Nixon backed a military regime in Athens which repeatedly tried to eliminate Makarios by force (see Appendix).

In fact, Makarios was not a communist. He had begun his political career by trying to build up the political influence of the Church at the expense of the island's popular communist movement. After the junta seized power in Athens, he relied increasingly on the support of the parties of the left – but only because right-wing elements sympathetic to the Greek Colonels moved against him. However, it was how the Americans perceived Makarios, accurately or not, that governed their policy on Cyprus, and his antagonism towards the junta in Athens gave them a common interest in removing him from office.

Within months of taking over at the Oval office, Nixon showed an extraordinary warmth towards the junta, offering private approval and public tolerance of their regime. At Eisenhower's funeral in Washington, he refused to meet the exiled King Constantine, but did meet Brigadier Pattakos, one of the three leaders of the military government, and reportedly got on well with him.[3] It put the seal on the relations that had developed between the junta and his campaign team during his battle for the presidency. According to Seymour Hersh, in 1976 Henry Tasca, who served as US Ambassador to Greece between 1970 and 1974, testified off the record to the House Intelligence Committee that in 1968 the junta funnelled funds to Nixon's election campaign via a supporter of theirs, Thomas Pappas, a wealthy Greek-American businessman who ran a $200 million industrial complex in Greece and whose enterprises had expanded thanks to the junta easing restrictions on them. Pappas had links with Greek and US intelligence agencies, and he had Nixon's ear. One report said the CIA used his enterprises as a cover for its operations in Greece.[4] Nixon's vice-presidential candidate, Spiro Agnew, having refused to give the junta his backing before joining the campaign, suddenly became enthusiastic. Two days before a referendum on the undemocratic regime in Greece, he publicly said the junta was not power-hungry, but only wanted to create the right conditions for free elections to take place, and accused Andreas Papandreou, who had become a focus of democratic opposition to the junta, of being a communist. The United States' suspension of heavy arms shipments to the junta was soon allowed to become ineffectual, with more arms sold to Greece than before. When Tasca took over as ambassador in Athens, Nixon told him that restoring military aid was the goal: on the question of persuading the Greeks to take steps towards restoring the constitution, he told him, 'Make it look as good as you can – but the priority is military assistance'.[5] Nixon and Kissinger wanted some promises of a movement towards democracy from the junta, including a pledge to hold elections by the end of 1970, if it helped introduce a climate in which the arms ban could be ended, and Tasca was ordered to spell this out to the Greeks. Nixon was prepared to accept the junta's assurances 'at face value' and 'without reservation'.[6] In September 1970, Nixon formally ended the suspension. Two years later, Pappas became a key fundraiser in Nixon's re-election battle, and vice-president of the campaign's finance committee. His name came up in the Watergate trials when, on secret tapes from the White House, Nixon revealed that Pappas was the first man they asked for cash to pay off the Watergate burglars.[7]

Like Nixon, the colonels did not trust Makarios. They too feared he might turn the island over to communist rule or, worse, provide a base from which democratic opponents of their regime could operate. With every act of defiance by Makarios, they came to regard him not just as a danger to Greece's defence interests but also a popular threat to their regime. Over the next few years, Papadopoulos's intelligence and military officers made repeated attempts to solve the Makarios 'problem' by trying to assassinate him or oust him by force. In several instances the Americans had advanced knowledge of Papadopoulos's plans for Makarios; in one, the CIA station in Athens seemed deeply involved. But, paradoxically, every time a plot looked liked being made public, American diplomats applied pressure to have it stopped. There seemed to be a clear dichotomy between covert and public American foreign policy on this issue during Papadopoulos's leadership. Behind the scenes, US officials admitted they would get no satisfaction on Cyprus until Makarios was eliminated from the equation. In 1969, former Acting Secretary of State Ball was quoted by State Department officials as saying, 'That son of a bitch [Makarios] will have to be killed before anything happens in Cyprus'.[8]

There were numerous potential agents of Makarios's demise. In Cyprus, his refusal to contemplate any form of enosis, Acheson-style or otherwise, while the American-backed junta remained in power in Athens left him facing some dangerous enemies. Ultra-right-wing supporters of enosis, many of them former members of EOKA, backed the colonels. They began demonstrating their opposition with bombings, attacks on police stations and the assassination of left-wingers. In January 1970, Makarios, while visiting Kenya, was warned by a US diplomat in Nairobi of a plan to assassinate him on his return to Cyprus. At the end of February, the US Ambassador in Nicosia, David Popper, told him to expect an attempt on his life in the next 15 days.[9] On 8 March, as Makarios's helicopter took off from the courtyard of the President's Palace to take him to a memorial service at a monastery, it was raked with bullets fired from the roof of a school. The pilot was hit and critically wounded, but managed to crash-land on an open space nearby. Makarios survived unscathed. Police found a Sten gun and two rifles abandoned by the snipers on the school roof.

Investigations began immediately, and suspicion fell on Georghadhis – though the evidence does not establish whether he was abetting the assassination attempt or in fact trying to prevent it (he was previously accused of plotting to kill Papadopoulos). The enquiry was conducted by police and Greek officers of the National Guard. On 13 March, Georghadhis was prevented from leaving the country when he tried to board a plane to Beirut. Two days later, after receiving a phone call, he drove to a secret rendezvous with two Greek army officers – one of them a National Guard assault unit commander, Colonel Papapostolou – on a lonely road outside Nicosia. Georghadhis was accompanied by a policeman friend, Patatakos. The car was ambushed and fired on from behind. Georghadhis was shot in the head. Patatakos escaped unhurt, and later handed the Government a document which appeared to implicate Colonel Papapostolou in the plans to kill Makarios. Patatakos said Georghadhis had asked that if anything should happen to him, he should give the document to Makarios. The plan, dated 27 January, outlined a plot to take over Nicosia on 28 May.[10] Georghadhis's successor as Defence and Interior Minister, T.K. Anastasiou, later claimed Georghadhis had warned him, too, of a plot against Makarios, but implied that Georghadhis and the Americans were mixed up in it. According to Stern,[11] the CIA station in Athens fiercely opposed a request by their own diplomats in Athens for a CIA investigation into Georghadhis's execution. The following year, Makarios asked the CIA station chief in Nicosia, Eric Neff, to pack his bags. Apparently, Neff shared Ball's sentiment that Makarios should go, and had also worked closely with Georghadhis, when he was in power, against communist targets.[12] In Nicosia, four men were later sentenced to 14 years in jail for conspiring with Georghadhis to attempt to assassinate Makarios. They all pleaded not guilty.

Makarios held elections in July, hoping to capitalise on public sympathy following the assassination attempt. But the results offered little comfort to him or the Americans. Clerides's pro-Makarios Unified Party won only 15 out of 35 Greek-Cypriot seats. The pro-enosis faction secured only 7 seats, while the Communists (AKEL) took 9 and the Socialists won 2 seats. The strength of the Communist vote – at around 30 percent – underlined NATO's fear that AKEL might go on to win a future election, and deliver the island into Moscow's hands.

The NATO countries involved in Cyprus opened secret talks on the future of the island at NATO meetings in Lisbon in May 1971, and later in Paris. This followed the precedent set in 1958, when the United States pressured Greece and Turkey at the North Atlantic Council to accept a form of guaranteed independence for Cyprus. American intelligence analysts believed Greece and Turkey were ready to accept 'double enosis'. But it was thought that only Greece could take action against Makarios, because interference by Turkey might provoke Soviet intervention. The colonels, on the other hand, could pass off any clashes with Makarios as an internal affair between Greeks. These were the same arguments that had been outlined to Johnson on behalf of Ball and Acheson in

1964, when the Americans considered letting Greece declare enosis and then split the island with Turkey on lines previously agreed by NATO. One senior Turkish diplomat reported that at the talks the Turks demanded a break-up of the unitary Cypriot state, and the Greeks seemed willing to offer Turkey some territory for a large military base. The population would not be moved. All these discussions were held without the participation of representatives of the country whose fate they were attempting to decide.

Shortly after the May NATO meeting, a Greek Cypriot wrote to Grivas telling him that a British intelligence officer had asked him to find out if he would accept an Acheson-style solution. The Cypriot told the agent that if Ankara, Athens and Grivas could agree on a plan, there would be no need to worry about Makarios, as all that had to be done was to send Grivas to Cyprus.[13]

But in June 1971, Makarios outwitted the gathering coalition of Western powers plotting against him by making an eight-day state visit to Moscow to appeal for help. The Soviets issued a communique restating Soviet support for maintaining Cyprus as an independent, unitary state; voicing satisfaction with Cyprus's policy of not aligning itself with NATO and stressing its opposition to foreign intervention or threats of military force. Most worrying for the West, the Soviets reaffirmed their call for the removal of all foreign troops from the island and the abolition of all foreign bases – and Makarios backed their position. Like Nasser before him, Makarios had learned that when a strategically-placed country, however small, becomes the subject of interest of two opposing super-powers it can play one off against the other to its own advantage.

Following the NATO meetings, Papadopoulos ordered Makarios to offer some concessions to the Turkish Cypriots, but he refused, and the intercommunal talks broke down. At this point, Grivas was suddenly allowed to 'escape' from house arrest in Athens, and returned to Cyprus to stir up opposition to Makarios. Was this the plan referred to in the letter about the British agent? Had such an arrangement been sanctioned at the secret NATO talks by the Americans or even the Turks as part of a plot to get rid of Makarios and achieve double enosis? Curiously, Turkish-Cypriot leader Denktash reportedly was told by the Greeks that 'as long as Grivas is in Cyprus, no Turk will get a bloody nose',[14] which may be further evidence of collusion between the NATO allies. And high-level con-tacts between Greece and Turkey continued throughout 1972 and 1973, despite Grivas's presence in Cyprus.

Grivas landed secretly by night, allegedly disguised as a priest, and began organising armed groups into a new version of EOKA called EOKA-B, with the aim of overthrowing Makarios. His recruits started by raiding police stations for arms and distributing leaflets calling on his former EOKA comrades to join him once more in the battle for enosis. They denounced Makarios for seeking a 'feasible' settlement rather than full union with Greece. Leslie Finer, the BBC correspondent in Athens, who had collaborated with Grivas on his memoirs, warned that the EOKA-B leader was ideally placed to start a conflict that would allow the junta to intervene to 'restore order' and tighten its grip on the island. 'It is impossible to grasp what is happening in Cyprus now, except on the basis that the Athens regime is paying for its keep by serving long-term American design: the removal of Makarios,' he said.[15] In January 1972, though the democratic elections promised by the Greek colonels had failed to materialise, the United States secured agreement to home-port a carrier task-force at Piraeus. This made it easier for the United States to project its naval power throughout the Eastern Mediterranean. The US airforce was given base rights at Suda Bay on Crete.

In the same month, the fears over Cyprus's drift towards the Soviet Union reached crisis proportions when Makarios, convinced that his enemies were moving in on him, secretly landed a considerable quantity of Czech arms. They were to be used by his loyal police force. But Grivas's agents uncovered the landing and informed Papadopoulos. Furious at the defiance of the 'Red Priest', the junta leader issued an impossible ultimatum: he ordered Makarios to hand over the arms to the UN, throw all left-wingers out of his Government and sack ministers hostile to the junta, including Foreign Minister Kyprianou. Further, he demanded that Makarios form a government of national unity on the centre and right – even though AKEL and EDEK (the Communist and Socialist parties) had the backing of close to one in two Greek Cypriots – and include moderate representatives of Grivas. Assuming Makarios would not comply, Papadopoulos had already secretly put junta and EOKA-B units on standby to stage a coup in Cyprus.

The arms landing caused alarm in Ankara and Washington too. The Turks feared they might be used against Turkish Cypriots, or to arm the police in the south of the island so that the National Guard would be free to mass in the north as a deterrent to a Turkish invasion. Following talks with Nixon, the Turkish Prime Minister, Dr Nihat Erim, also demanded that the weapons be handed over to the UN, and sent troops to the southern coast opposite Cyprus, in a clear warning that Turkey would invade if either Makarios or the junta took matters into their own hands.

On 14 February, three days after Papadopoulos's ultimatum, Makarios's police unearthed preparations for a military takeover. Clerides hurried with the news to US Ambassador David Popper. As the Archbishop and his head of secret services were busily burning documents, Popper wired Washington and Athens, where US Ambassador Tasca 'warned Papadopoulos against any heavy stuff'.[16] The coup plan was put on hold. Clerides recalled Makarios and his intelligence chief telling him they had irrefutable evidence that a coup was going to take place that night.

> Makarios asked me to see the American Ambassador. He was out at lunch and I left
> him an urgent message that we must meet. He left the lunch and came to the
> embassy. I explained that we were aware a coup was imminent, that we had issued
> arms, that there would be bloodshed, and I asked him to ask the president of the

United States to intervene. He sent a message using the wartime emergency proce-
dure, which goes in a matter of moments. Within an hour I was called back to the
embassy and told that the American government had made strong representations to
Papadopoulos and the Greek government gave assurances that they would not move.
They did not deny that they were going to have a coup.[17]

The Turks seemed to know of the coup threat long before Makarios. The Greek
Cypriots first suspected something was afoot when their secret service decoded
a message from Turkey to the Turkish Cypriots telling them to store food in their
homes and to be on alert. 'That's why the service began investigating the Greek
officers here (in Cyprus) and they discovered there was going to be a coup,' said
Clerides. He was then dispatched to the US Embassy to urge the Americans to
take action. 'Next morning our secret service, which was following the directions
sent to the Turkish side by radio, decoded a message that Ankara had ordered
Turkish forces to stand down.'[18]

There was no respite for Makarios, however, as he soon faced opposition
from yet another quarter, within his own church. Three pro-enosis Bishops,
whose support had been enlisted by Grivas, met as the Holy Synod of the Cyprus
church and called for Makarios's resignation. Grivas immediately put them
under his protection. Despite a 50,000-strong demonstration in his favour, the
Archbishop agreed to store the Czech arms in a UN-inspected area. But he used
the opportunity to call for a reduction of armed forces on all sides in Cyprus,
leading ultimately to demilitarisation. Then in May, Kyprianou, whose resignation the junta had sought, quit the Government and, in line with the junta's
demands for a change of government, Makarios made sweeping changes to his
Cabinet. He appointed seven new ministers, and changed the portfolio of an
eighth, in his ten-strong top team. Kyprianou had been one of his closest
supporters. It was a characteristically pragmatic concession, designed to prevent
the array of forces lined up against him becoming irresistible.

But Papadopoulos's men were already working on a third plan to topple
Makarios. This was foiled by Cypriot intelligence in July 1972.[19] The plot was to
include tank, mortar and artillery attacks – a use of heavy arms which implied
that the junta's officers in the National Guard were behind it rather than
Grivas's EOKA-B movement.

In September, six US destroyers dropped anchor in Phaliron Bay outside
Athens. Home-porting began with no concern that this amounted to a very
public vote of confidence in a military regime which had overthrown democracy
in Greece and replaced it with repression and torture.

Shaken by the plots against him, Makarios sought to strengthen his domestic
position by submitting himself once more for re-election in January 1973. Newspapers supporting his office boldly challenged the authority of the junta in Athens
by demanding the expulsion of Greek army officers from the island's forces and
calling on former Greek premier Karamanlis to set up a Greek Government in
exile in Nicosia. But before nomination day, pro-enosis supporters demanded a

plebiscite on union with Greece instead of the presidential vote, and carried out raids on police stations, stealing arms, ammunition and uniforms. The operations culminated on the day before nomination day with attacks on 18 police stations by 150 gunmen, some with dynamite.[20] Makarios was elected unopposed for a third term. But a spokesman for Grivas warned that he would face the same terror experienced by Britain in Cyprus if he 'betrayed' enosis.

The EOKA-B attacks continued throughout March and April, mainly against police stations, whose arms and ammunition were seized, and several of which were blown up. The most daring EOKA-B operation was a bomb attack on the house of the Interior Minister, George Ioannides. On 8 April, there were 32 explosions in Paphos, Limassol and Larnaca. To counter EOKA-B, Makarios set up a new auxiliary police force, called the Tactical Police Reserve, under the command of an army officer. He hoped this would be free of the influence of Georghadhis's allies, Grivas, or pro-enosis extremists in a violent underground movement called the National Front, and he repeatedly warned that Grivas's bomb attacks and armed raids created the prerequisites for partition. But Makarios's reluctance to formally write off enosis as a legitimate goal also undermined the attempts to negotiate with the Turkish Cypriots and relieve pressure from that quarter. In April the rebel bishops reconvened as a Holy Synod and decided to strip Makarios of his archbishophric, because he had refused to give in to their demand that he should give up the presidency.

Makarios was embattled. Ranged against him were the United States, Turkey, Greece, Grivas, the National Front, elements in the National Guard, his own police force, two out of three private armies on the island, the Turkish Cypriots and senior members of his own church. But he still had a few tricks up his sleeve. He outmanoeuvred the bishops by calling a Supreme Synod, attended by Orthododox Patriarchs from Middle-Eastern countries, which accused them of causing a schism and had them defrocked. Thus ended one source of finance for EOKA-B, because the rebel bishops had been funnelling funds from the diocese of Kitium and Kyrenia to Grivas's men. He also sent his new Tactical Police Reserve on search-and-destroy missions against EOKA-B. In one raid at the end of June, they captured more than 40 Grivas supporters and charged them with conspiracy to overthrow the Government. On 25 July, they captured large supplies of ammunition in a raid on the Limassol area, which involved gun battles against machine-gun posts.

But Grivas retaliated. On 27 July, half the central police station in Limassol was destroyed by a bomb and the Justice Minister, Christos Vakis, was kidnapped. Leaflets bearing Grivas's name were distributed. They demanded the resignation of President Makarios if he continued as Archbishop and the freedom of Greek Cypriots to decide their future rather than face a settlement imposed by Makarios.

Meanwhile, Makarios's forces captured Grivas's deputy, 20 or so of the senior EOKA-B members, and evidence of a fourth plot to assassinate the President.

Documents and numerous photographs revealed plans to post snipers along the route of his daily two-mile drive from the archbishopric to the presidential palace. The assassination attempt was to be followed up by an attack on the palace itself. When these details were made public on 10 August, Papadopoulos was forced to distance himself from Grivas's activities. He ordered the general to back down, and the kidnapped minister was released.

The fourth plot may have been the result of Turkish pressure. Disillusioned with the junta's attempts to work out a Greek-Turkish solution to the Cyprus problem over Makarios's head, at talks in Vienna in May, they told the Greeks to sort out the problem in a way that handed territory to the Turks or face the consequences. They would wait a few months and no more. According to Polyvios Polyviou, following the ultimatum the Greek regime decided that the only way to settle the Cyprus problem was to overthrow Makarios and replace him with someone more amenable to their 'suggestions'. This decision was apparently communicated to the American Government, which 'approved' of Papadopoulos's conciliatory attitude towards the Turkish Government but 'discouraged' any incidents that might lead to bloodshed and possibly a Graeco-Turkish confrontation.[21]

On 7 October, there was yet another attempt to kill Makarios. The method was similar to that outlined in the exposed August plot, but it was botched. Four mines were detonated on a road minutes before the Archbishop was scheduled to pass by in his car, on his way to conduct a service in a village near Famagusta.

Ultimately, Papadopoulos never got his man. In November, it was he, not Makarios, who was thrown out of power, amid growing civil unrest in Athens and calls for the return of Karamanlis. Brigadier Dimitrios Ioannides, head of the Greek military police, decided to prevent the fall of the junta by seizing control of the military government for himself. Ioannides was a far more sinister figure than Papadopoulos – in 1964, he and Sampson had approached Makarios with a plan to 'eliminate' all the Turkish Cypriots, and was angry when the Archbishop dismissed it.[22] Unlike Papadopoulos, he was not a long-time client of the CIA and, from the American point of view, his seizure of power injected an unstable, unpredictable ingredient into the simmering Cyprus situation.

~17~

CRISIS OF TRUST

Spying Bases at Risk

The instability in Cyprus and Greece came at one of the most dangerous periods in the Cold War, when the nuclear arms race between the Soviet Union and the United States reached a critical phase, and when war in the Middle East threatened to escalate into a global nuclear war. Yet in the midst of this turmoil, serious doubts grew over Britain's commitment to keep the spying and strategic air-bases on Cyprus available for Western defence purposes. At the same time, the unpredictable new junta leader in Athens, Ioannides, seemed increasingly hell-bent on provoking war with Turkey. These factors heavily influenced American policy on Cyprus, and in so doing sealed its fate as a divided state.

In 1970, the Soviets overtook the Americans in numbers of ICBMs, and by 1974 they had 50 percent more. Crucially, they outstripped the Americans in heavy ICBMs – missiles with three-and-a-half times more destructive power than light ICBMs – by nine to one. In the same year they took the lead in submarine-launched ballistic missiles (SLBMs). If fired from close to the American coast, these could reach their targets within six to ten minutes. The ICBMs launched from the Soviet homeland could extinguish US cities in half an hour.

This made early-warning systems absolutely critical to nuclear defence. ICBMs were far more potent than SLBMs because their greater accuracy and size made them capable of breaking the US's hardened missile silos. Overall, the Soviets overtook the Americans in total numbers of nuclear bombers and missiles in 1973, and continued to widen the gap in 1974.[1]

However, the Americans still maintained a huge advantage over the Soviets in the number of nuclear warheads they could deliver in any attack. For though they had fewer missiles, they no longer needed a missile for every warhead. They had developed a way of sending up a number of warheads on one missile, which, before re-entering the earth's atmosphere, would split off and independently home in on separate targets. The new missiles were called MIRVs (multiple independently targetable re-entry vehicles).

This revolutionary technology enabled the Americans to raise their lead in nuclear warheads and bombs from 2144 in 1970 to 5254 in 1974. But even in this advanced field, the Soviets had started to make inroads. The first Soviet MIRV system was tested in August 1973 on the SS-18. Having cracked its secrets, the Soviets inevitably tried to close the gap. In the year to March 1974, they tested 285 ICBMs, SLBMs and military missiles, and launched 86 space missions, compared with 86 ICBM tests by the Americans. The race to develop the deadliest missiles affected Cyprus because the only way the Americans could keep ahead in nuclear capability was by monitoring changes in Soviet technology. To do this, they had to keep a close eye on all nuclear testing, particularly of ICBMs and MIRVs, by using facilities in Cyprus, Turkey and Iran in this region. Information picked up by British spy stations was shared with the Americans under the UKUSA agreement. The Cyprus facilities were part of a panoply of electronic intelligence and radar installations developed by the West over decades to monitor every level of Soviet nuclear missile activity.

Originally, they had been set up to provide an early-warning system backed by fighters which would intercept Soviet nuclear bombers. Now they had to help guarantee America's ability to launch its own ICBMs within minutes of Soviet missiles taking off, if the US deterrent was to remain credible. But their role now also included gleaning intricate details of Soviet missile test launches. For this, the range of intelligence tasks included using communications facilities to home in on military units and listen into their orders as they prepared for a missile launch, radars to monitor the heat emissions from missiles at launch and in flight, and electronic intelligence facilities to analyse the missiles' guidance systems or data which the warhead or missile sends back to earth about its performance during a test flight.[2] This kind of information can provide intelligence on such questions as the number of warheads carried by the missile, its range, payload and throw-weight, the probable size of its warheads, and their level of accuracy.[3] Satellites and spy planes could contribute, but ground stations were said to be more effective at this time because they could detect a greater set of signals, and could monitor a fixed location around the clock.[4]

Turkey housed 26 US intelligence sites for monitoring Soviet military and nuclear activity and other military threats. This, the scale of the country's armed forces and its geographical location as a bridge between Europe and the Middle East and a buffer between the Soviet Union and the Mediterranean made it a strategically indispensable ally, a factor which heavily influenced US handling of the Cyprus problem. But Cyprus also housed some of the most sophisticated equipment needed to monitor the Soviet nuclear missile tests at Kapustin Yar, near Volgograd (formerly Stalingrad) in southern Russia, and Tyuratam, east of the Aral Sea in Kazakhstan. These were the two main sites where Soviet land-based cruise missiles and ICBMs were tested. The Cyprus facilities included over-the-horizon (OTH) radar installations. They were built by the British, but because of the intelligence-sharing relationship with Washington they played a key role in keeping the Americans abreast of Soviet missile and MIRV capability as they tried to limit the arms race through the SALT II talks in 1973 and early 1974. Some reports said they were operated by the Americans. The equipment was so advanced and so important to nuclear defence that the Americans considered landing troops to defend them when fighting broke out on Cyprus in 1974. Orders were given to destroy them if protection was not possible, and during the crisis a heavy guard was placed on the RAF radar on Mount Olympus.[5]

The OTH radar used a very powerful signal and worked by bouncing a beam off the earth's ionosphere so as to see round the corner of the earth's curvature, giving it a longer range than other types of radar. There were other OTH sites in Japan, ideally placed to monitor Soviets ICBMs and SLBMs as they landed on the Kamchatka Peninsula during missile tests. According to the Stockholm International Peace Research Institute (SIPRI), Cyprus was the ideal site for the most advanced type of OTH radar, because the sensor needed an over-water propagation path and had to be between 1500km and 3000km from the test activity. Experts dispute whether this advanced system, called OTH back-scatter, was brought in before 1974 or afterwards. Before back-scatter, there was a system of forward-scatter OTH which involved a network of four transmitters in the Far East bouncing signals between the ionosphere and the earth's surface to five receivers in Europe, including one in Cyprus. SIPRI said this system lasted until 1975. Other reports suggest its role may have been superseded by 1974, but if it was still in use, it would have been an important component, possibly a very important component, of the early warning stystem of the West, and would have had great strategic importance.[6]

OTH radars were more effective than other radar, because they could detect a missile test-launch from its earliest stage. US sites in Iran could monitor missiles from Tyuratam once they were 100kms up. The sensors in Turkey could normally begin monitoring at 400kms' height. But only an OTH back-scatter radar in Cyprus could monitor consistently from blast-off. Similarly, the Cyprus radar was within the ideal range for detecting Cruise missile test flights from Kapustin Yar,

1. In the 1950s Britain tried to crush the Cypriot uprising in order to keep the island for use in military campaigns such as the Suez operation.

2. ABOVE. Archbishop Makarios (left) in 1959 with EOKA leader George Grivas (right), who later consented to US plans to split the island between Greece and Turkey, and Nicos Sampson (centre) who replaced Makarios in the 1974 coup.

3. BELOW. Greek attempts to change the constitution in 1963 led to inter-ethnic atrocities. The Museum of Barbarism in Kumsal District, Nicosia, preserves this blood stained bath in which these children of a Turkish officer were shot by Greek-Cypriot gunmen.

4. George Ball, US Acting Secretary of State, who in 1964 discussed plans with the British to allow a limited Turkish invasion and later proposed forcing Greece and Turkey to agree to a division of Cyprus.

5. A Turkish soldier (left) during the invasion of 1974 and (below left) a Greek-Cypriot girl with a picture of a lost loved one. There are 1,600 Greek Cypriots still missing after the invasion and 200,000 refugees unable to return home.

6. Secretary of State and National Security Adviser Henry Kissinger, when the US role in the Cyprus crisis was investigated by Congressmen, fought hard to prevent the release of documents showing dissent by junior officials against State Department policy.

7. British Foreign Secretary James Callaghan sought US support, first to reverse the Junta's coup on Cyprus and then for joint military action to deter the Turkish occupation, but Kissinger opposed him.

8. Glafkos Clerides, President of the Republic of Cyprus today, and acting president in 1974, did not believe that Turkey would invade Cyprus without warning the United States, for fear of having to face the US Sixth Fleet.

9. Rauf Denktash, Turkish–Cypriot leader in 1974 and president of the unilaterally declared Turkish Republic of Northern Cyprus today, said documents captured from Greek soldiers showed that, but for the Turkish landings, the Turkish Cypriots would have been massacred.

10. Henry Kissinger (left), with Brendan O'Malley in 1999, denied that the Americans had any grand design to remove Makarios, but said he was worried about maintaining the stability of NATO's southern flank.

and these could not be picked up by line-of-sight sensors in Turkey, because of their low flight altitude.[7]

Through intelligence monitoring, the Americans discovered in 1973 that the Soviets had developed four new missiles which bent the rules of SALT I. These included two new MIRV ICBMs, one of which, the SS-18, could carry eight warheads. Both missiles had a revolutionary launch technique which allowed them to carry more warheads, and permitted rapid re-use of the silo to fire another missile. In the autumn, the Soviets conducted a rapid testing programme for land-based MIRVs. They then unveiled the SS-19, the most potent of the lot. At least two of the new missiles – the SS-18 and the SS-19 – were test-launched at Tyuratam, and were monitored from Cyprus and Turkey. Monitoring a development programme for an ICBM involved tracking 20–30 tests over several years. One range used for testing medium- and intermediate-range missiles began at Kapustin Yar, and ended either at Sary Shagen or near Lake Baikal. The more important launching site was Tyuratam, which had 80 operational launch-pads. It was used for ICBM tests, with missiles hitting the Kamchatka Peninsula, north of Japan, and later, in the longest-range tests, landing in the South Pacific near Fiji.[8]

In February and March 1974, the Soviets test-launched four new ICBMs from Tyuratam – the SSX-16, SSX-17, SSX-18 and SSX-19. All had greater accuracy and potential for use against US silos. Three of the four featured MIRVs. The SSX-18 could carry up to six MIRV warheads. Experts at *Aviation Week and Space Technology* magazine said it meant Moscow was 'fast closing' the technology and deployment advantage that the United States enjoyed when it agreed to maintain fewer missiles than the Soviets in the SALT arms limitation agreement in 1972.[9]

In April 1974, US Secretary of Defence James Schlesinger said the Americans had monitored the Soviet tests since SALT I, and discovered Soviet research and development in ICBMs 'of astonishing depth and breadth'. He told Congress, 'One of the most important developments in the strategic threat during the past year has been the Soviet Union's demonstration of a MIRV technology… the scope of the Soviet programme… is far more comprehensive than estimated even a year ago'. Washington saw this as a highly dangerous twist in the arms race, because it gave Moscow a massive first-strike capability – at a time when the United States was publicly committed to a 'no first strike' policy. Soon, strategists predicted, the Soviets would have the firepower to wipe out virtually the entire American ICBM deterrent in a surprise attack.[10] The Federation of American Scientists warned that the ICBMs would look 'more and more vulnerable to attack if MIRV and increases in accuracy cannot be prevented'.[11] Congress was told that launch on warning could save US ICBMs only if adequate information was accessible to the President and Secretary of Defence.

Henry Kissinger believed Moscow would eventually be able to use the advantage of its heavier missiles, combined with a MIRV capability, to carry a greater number of individual warheads than the American missiles could. The

Soviets' new 'cold-launch' technique enabled them to replace their 1000 single-warhead SS-11 missiles with SSX-19s, which had between four and six MIRV warheads each, without breaching SALT I. According to defence experts, the development gave the Soviets the ability to expand the numerical advantage in ICBMs conceded in SALT 1 into a huge and significant superiority, and at the same time wipe out all of the advantages the United States thought it would enjoy throughout the 1970s in numbers of warheads and accuracy.[12] Kissinger, who was now Secretary of State as well as National Security Adviser, believed this would make the United States's ICBMs, which were the heart of the West's deterrent, 'vulnerable to a Soviet first strike' by the mid-1980s at the latest (see Appendix).

Alarmed by these dangerous advances, he tried to secure a US advantage in MIRVs against a Soviet advantage in missile delivery systems in the SALT II negotiations. But the talks ended inconclusively in April 1974, and the Soviets raced ahead with MIRV production, making thousands more warheads.[13]

During this period, when the intelligence gathered by the British bases and installations in Cyprus was at a premium, a serious rift opened up between the United States and Britain which made Washington question the value of leaving the facilities in British hands. The disagreements occurred during the Yom Kippur War in October 1973, in which the Arabs, armed by the Soviets, attacked Israel, and the White House at one point faced the most dangerous nuclear incident since the Cuban missile crisis. It dramatically illustrated how conflict in the Middle East, because of the strategic importance of oil, could put at risk the security of the whole world. It emphasised the importance of the network of Western intelligence and logistical bases in the region, particularly those on Cyprus, to the United States and Europe. It also showed how closely Henry Kissinger was able to control foreign and security policy during a world crisis, even as the Nixon presidency became embroiled in the Watergate scandal.

On 6 October 1973, the Arabs launched an attack on Israeli-occupied territory, the Egyptians using Soviet arms to launch an offensive across the Suez Canal and, to the north, the Syrians pushing the Israelis out of the Golan Heights with 1400 tanks, many of them Soviet-built, and using Soviet missiles. These offensives were supported by forces from Jordan, Iraq, Saudi Arabia and Morocco. The aim was to recover the territory lost to Israel in 1967. In heavy tank battles, the Israelis drove the Syrians back to within 18 miles of their capital, Damascus. The Israelis carried out air strikes against the ports of Latakia and Tartus, the main entry points for Soviet arms supplies for the Syrians. But they suffered severe losses to the south in the Sinai desert, where a 100,000-strong Egyptian force pushed forward. After four days, a fifth of the Israeli airforce – 100 of 500 planes – had been destroyed, along with a third of their 2000-strong tank force.

With the Soviets giving the Egyptians massive resupplies of weaponry, the Israelis knew they could survive only if the United States came to their rescue. Egypt and Syria could muster more than a million men, 3300 tanks and 950 aircraft to Israel's 300,000 men, 1700 tanks and 500 aircraft. In Washington, Nixon was preoccupied with a political scandal in which Vice President Agnew had been forced to resign for accepting bribes. Nevertheless, he agreed to send fresh arms to the Israelis. The Americans began a massive airlift of weaponry and armour, including helicopters, howitzers and tanks. To prevent the Arabs gaining the upper hand and seizing control of the whole of the Middle East, Kissinger wanted all the NATO allies to contribute to the airlift. At the very least, he wanted them to make available staging-posts and refuelling facilities for the American transporters and give permission to fly over allied territory.

But one by one, Britain, France, Turkey, Spain and Greece denied the Americans the use of their bases, or made it clear that they should not ask for such a favour. Yet the Soviets were airlifting 700 tons a day to the Egyptians over secure air routes. Kissinger said the allies' veto meant that US planes from Germany had to make their way out over the Atlantic and around into the Mediterranean, avoiding French and Spanish airspace. This route doubled the journey to Israel to 2000 miles. The Europeans feared that if they helped Israel, the Arab states would retaliate by cutting oil supplies or raising oil prices. Kissinger was livid at this short-term view, when NATO's real interest lay in preventing the Soviets or the anti-Western Arab states achieving domination of the Middle East. He was particularly angry with British Prime Minister Edward Heath, who refused the Americans use of the Cyprus bases for either the airlift or intelligence, despite the special relationship between their two countries in defence and intelligence matters. Reconnaissance planes had to begin their journey from the United States, more than 6000 miles away, instead of Akrotiri, 70 miles from Israel, even though Cyprus had previously been used to launch American U-2s to photograph deployment of Soviet missiles along the Suez Canal.

A second factor dividing Britain and America emerged when the conflict threatened to trigger a full-scale nuclear war between the superpowers. After massive tank battles in the Sinai Desert, the Israelis pushed forward across the Suez Canal, cutting off the 20,000-strong Egyptian Third Army. Rounding on them from behind, the Israelis threatened President Sadat's crack troops with annihilation. But the Soviets felt they could not stand by. The allegiance of their client states in the Middle East depended on a symbolic recovery of at least part of the Egyptian territory in the Sinai. They had amassed more than 80 warships in the Eastern Mediterranean, and 40,000 Soviet troops were on standby to be airlifted into the battle zone. At 9.35pm on 24 October the Soviet Ambassador delivered a dramatic message to Kissinger from Brezhnev. It urged joint US-Soviet action to enforce the ceasefire, or else the Soviet Union would act alone.

Tension had been mounting at the Pentagon all day as US listening posts tracked signals from the Soviet military to its Southern Command. These revealed that seven airborne divisions in the Ukraine and Caucasus were on alert, naval deployments were being made in the Mediterranean, and several large troop and cargo transports were being flown to Cairo. Soviet warships were also moving into position. It was the job of the electronic eavesdropping facilities on Cyprus to pick up intelligence on exactly this kind of information in the area.[14] Kissinger recognised the danger: the Soviets were backing up their demands with military muscle, and if the Americans tried to stop them, it might mean war between the superpowers unless the Soviets could be warned off. He called Nixon at the White House, and recommended they challenge Moscow to back down by threatening a nuclear war.[15]

It was 10pm. Nixon, upstairs in the family quarters, was distracted by the repercussions of firing Special Prosecutor Archibald Cox, a Watergate investigator who had demanded that the President hand over incriminating tape recordings. He gave Kissinger full authority to deal with the crisis. At 11pm, a National Security Council committee, the Washington Special Action Group, held a meeting at the White House. Kissinger was there in his dual role as Secretary of State and National Security Adviser. He was joined by Defence Secretary Schlesinger, CIA Director William Colby, Kissinger's deputy, Brent Scowcroft, Presidential Chief of Staff Alexander Haig, and Chairman of the Joint Chiefs of Staff Thomas Moorer. But neither Nixon or Gerald Ford, who had yet to be confirmed as Vice President by the Senate, attended. Schlesinger agreed with Kissinger's decision to reject Moscow's plan and escalate the crisis by issuing a worldwide strategic nuclear alert. Kissinger was tense (see Appendix). It was a dangerous gamble. At 11.41pm, Moorer placed troops on standby worldwide, awaiting orders to attack. The Strategic Air Command and one fleet of Polaris nuclear missile submarines were deployed one stage short of readiness for war. Aircraft-carriers off Italy and Crete were sent to the Eastern Mediterranean, and a task-force headed by the attack carrier *John F. Kennedy* was ordered to link up with them. Fifteen thousand airforcemen were alerted at Fort Bragg, North Carolina, as the 82nd Airborne Division was ordered to move out. Up to 60 B-52 strategic bombers based in Guam, in the Pacific, were ordered back to the United States as further preparation for mounting a nuclear attack.[16] The message to Moscow, relayed by Russia's own electronic intelligence, was stark. They would have to threaten a nuclear counter-attack – or back down. Fortunately, they stepped back from the precipice. The next day the crisis dissipated, as the Egyptians and Soviets accepted a UN peace-keeping force and the Israelis remained where they were.

The nuclear threat had worked, but it caused consternation among the NATO allies, because they had not been told of it in advance. The first many of their leaders learned of it was the stories splashed across the American newspapers early that morning, reporting that troops and Minuteman ICBM missile bases were being mobilised for a nuclear war. According to Duncan Campbell, some forces at American bases in Britain were ordered to the highest level of alert, poised to launch a nuclear attack, without prior consultation with the British Government.[17] Edward Heath was outraged, and publicly refused to endorse the American action. He was joined by leaders of West Germany, Spain,

Italy and France in a chorus of disassociation from the American alert and Washington's role in arming Israel. This, and the refusal to let the Americans use their facilities, sparked a crisis of trust within the North Atlantic alliance.

Kissinger could not forgive this betrayal. If the Europeans could not be trusted to back the United States on an issue which threatened to provoke a serious East-West confrontation, what was the value of the alliance, he wondered.[18] At a press conference on 21 November, he lashed out at the British in particular for their failure to co-operate. British defence officials claimed that to underline his fury at being denied the use of the Cyprus bases, he shut down all American intelligence links with Britain, including nuclear early-warning and GCHQ links – the most prized element of the special relationship – for a week.[19] Kissinger denied this (see Appendix). It was an astonishing claim, given the interdependence of both countries on sharing intelligence, and that the two superpowers had just come to the brink of nuclear war. The Yom Kippur rift was the most serious breach in defence relations between the two countries since the Suez Crisis. As far as Cyprus was concerned, Kissinger could not avoid seriously questioning the value of the British air and intelligence bases there if their use might be denied the Americans at the most critical moments.

Fears about Britain's reliability grew as Heath lost control of the political situation at home. With inflation soaring, partly as a result of oil price hikes following the Yom Kippur War, he tried to tackle it by holding down pay. But this triggered a wave of strikes, and brought the economy to the edge of collapse. Industry was forced into a three-day week to conserve fast-dwindling fuel stocks. Unable to resolve the crisis, Heath called a general election. It was Heath versus Wilson again. Both had damaged American military interests while in government, but there were now fears in some circles that Wilson was not just unreliable, but a traitor to the West.

Rumours had long circulated in British and American intelligence about Wilson's and other MPs' links with the Soviets. Wilson was tainted by his attempts as a minister in Attlee's Government to set up major trade deals with Moscow. Military chiefs claimed that a deal to supply jets in return for key imports would have delivered the Soviets military secrets on a plate.[20]

In 1961, a high-ranking KGB defector, Anatoli Golitsin, told the CIA that a 'ring of five' spies was recruited by the Soviets in Britain in the 1930s, but he could not name them. MI5 believed they included Guy Burgess, Donald Maclean, Kim Philby and Anthony Blunt, all of whom had been exposed as traitors, though Blunt's treachery had not yet been made public. But the identity of the fifth was a mystery. In 1963, Labour leader Hugh Gaitskell, a right-winger who fought attempts by the left to take over the party, died suddenly of a mysterious illness. Gaitskell's doctor suggested his death had been caused by lupus disseminata, a rare disease in temperate climates. Some in British intelligence suspected he had been assassinated by the Soviets. Golitsin claimed that just before he defected he learned that the KGB was planning a high-level political assassination – the murder of the leader of an opposition party in Europe – to get their man into the top place. He was convinced that Gaitskell had been eliminated to enable their agent to take over the party and run the country.[21] Wilson won the Labour leadership contest and became Prime Minister the following year.

Golitsin's allegations caused a stir when he repeated them to the Americans. CIA director John McCone demanded an explanation from his British counterparts, and warned Kennedy of the allegations that Wilson was a communist mole. But Kennedy refused to act without hard evidence. In Britain, a joint MI5-MI6 body called the Fluency Committee was set up, with Peter Wright as its chairman, to investigate the claims. Fearing that Gaitskell might secretly have been poisoned or infected on a visit to the Soviet consulate, Wright alerted James Angleton, the CIA's head of counter-intelligence, who searched Russian scientific papers and found that seven years earlier the Soviets had been developing a chemical that would induce lupus-type effects in rats after repeated doses. He could not establish whether they had since found a way to infect a human with a one-shot dose. Nevertheless, after the 1964 general election Angleton came to England to tell his MI5 counterpart, Sir Martin Furnival-Jones, that secret sources alleged Wilson was a Soviet spy.[22]

Until 1967, the Americans had little reason to believe the claims against Wilson, because he proved such a good friend, maintaining worldwide defence commitments and holding out on devaluation as the Americans requested, in return for their support for the pound. But the 1967 devaluation and ensuing rescinding of military commitments changed all that.

In 1968, the paranoia about Wilson was fed by new American fears over the security of intelligence-sharing arrangements with Britain, after an RAF signals intelligence specialist working at Pergamos in Cyprus was found guilty of spying for the Soviets for five years. He had been monitoring Soviet airforce units' radio signals, and was jailed for 21 years. His case was highly sensitive because of the important role the Cyprus facilities played in collecting technical data on enemy nuclear missile developments. Then another defector, Josef Frolik, who had spied for Czechoslovakia in London, told the CIA that the Labour Party was infiltrated by Eastern Bloc agents, including three MPs and a minister. Two MPs admitted being paid by Czech intelligence. Most damaging for Wilson were the claims of a Soviet agent, Oleg Lyalin, who defected to Britain in 1971. His information led to the expulsion from Britain of 105 Soviet agents. Lyalin told MI5 that Joseph Kagan, a friend and political benefactor of Wilson, was in contact with an undercover KGB officer, Vaygaukas, in London. Kagan admitted only to meeting Vaygaukas for games of chess, and denied any suggestion of spying.[23]

According to Colin Wallace, a former army intelligence officer who took part in an MI5-orchestrated campaign to discredit Wilson, after the Lyalin disclosures the CIA feared GCHQ was compromised and 'wanted to take over the [British] security service full stop'. They did not like the fact that Britain had direct access to the information from the facilities the Americans had built in British bases.

'The Americans distrusted British intelligence enormously,' said Wallace. 'Angleton was paranoid that the whole of intelligence had been subverted.'[24]

Wallace said that at the time he believed Wilson was a spy because he was being fed that information by people at the highest level of British intelligence. He explained, 'If you lived in that paranoid period – during the three-day week – it was all too easy for the security community to believe there was a grand communist strategy funded by the Soviet Union'. He said it was a time when terrorist groups were active all over the world, many of them supported by the Soviet Union or its satellites in the Eastern Bloc, and the IRA was trying to get illegal weapons from Czechoslovakia. Northern Ireland was being torn apart by spiralling intercommunal violence and paramilitary attacks on the security forces. His job was to wage psychological warfare against the IRA. It was easy for someone in his position, fed on the fears of his superiors, to assume that if the Soviets did arm the IRA and if Wilson was a 'Soviet agent', he must also be backing the IRA. Thus Wilson became a target of black propaganda campaigns in which Wallace was involved.[25]

There was another factor which made the Americans suspect Wilson, and made him seem a bigger threat to their security interests than Heath: his commitment to slash defence spending and pursue multilateral nuclear disarmament with a view to removing American Polaris missiles from Britain. He also eventually pledged that Britain would not take up the next generation of nuclear weapons.

The run-up to the general election in February 1974 was one of the most unstable periods in British politics since 1926. A number of leading right-wing military and intelligence men feared Britain was on the point of collapse, and had to be saved from takeover by socialists. After Labour won the February election in 1974, the press reported that 'private armies' of volunteers were being organised to keep industry running in the event of the power dispute turning into a general strike. By mid-1974, one of them claimed 100,000 members, and support from MI5.[26]

During this period, MI5 spread black propaganda about Wilson to damage his chances of staying in power after the second general election, which, due to his government's lack of a majority, would have to be held in a matter of months. Peter Wright, pressed by Angleton to do something about Wilson, said that up to 30 MI5 officers backed a plan to leak selective details about leading Labour politicians, especially Wilson, from MI5 files.[27] Wallace admitted putting out anti-Wilson material in an operation known as Clockwork Orange. This included the suggestion that Wilson, Lady Falkender, and other Labour ministers had created a communist cell at 10 Downing Street. The black propaganda took its toll on Wilson. When security at Heathrow Airport was taken over by the military and police four times between January 1974, during the state of emergency and the miners' strike, and the October 1974 general election, Wilson began to fear that the security services were using the excuse of a Palestinian threat to prepare for a coup.

The Americans were still bitter about Wilson's 'betrayal' of the special relationship when he devalued the pound in 1967 and ended Britain's worldwide
defence role. When he returned to power in 1974, he immediately announced
plans for sweeping defence cuts. All undertakings outside NATO were to be
looked at case by case, which immediately posed questions over the future of the
crucial strategic air-base and electronic intelligence facilities on Cyprus. In May,
the Government stressed that the cuts would not be piecemeal: they would involve a major overhaul, saving several hundred million pounds. Reports reaching
Cyprus that Britain was preparing to withdraw from the island were taken so
seriously that banks refused mortgage loans to Cypriots offering as security the
prospect of rent from British servicemen.[28]

Tom McNally, then political adviser to Foreign Secretary James Callaghan,
has confirmed that the British had long tried to shed the expense of the Cyprus
bases from the Defence White Paper commitments, but every time they tried,
the Americans threw up their hands and insisted that they keep them. Field
Marshal Sir Michael Carver, Britain's Chief of Defence Staff at the time, has
revealed that in the light of Labour's commitment to reducing defence spending
to 4.5 percent of GNP, the chiefs of staff considered making reductions in the
forces in Cyprus, and had begun to discuss whether forces should be kept in
Cyprus at all when Ioannides staged the coup in Nicosia.[29] Not only could the
Americans no longer be sure that Britain would let them use the Cyprus facilities
when they most needed them, but now they could not be sure there would be
any facilities left to use at all.

This would threaten the future of the intelligence and missile-monitoring
facilities on the island and deal a serious blow to the CENTO alliance designed
to keep the Soviets out of the Middle East, as the nuclear strike capability from
Cyprus would be lost. It left the Americans scouting around for an insurance
policy against British withdrawal. A month after Wilson announced his plans to
review defence spending, the Americans, as though testing Makarios's willingness to allow them to operate in the bases in place of the British, landed marines
at one of the SBAs.[30] This caused a political outcry on Cyprus, even though the
Cyprus Government confirmed that the troops had arrived, with its knowledge,
to help clear the Suez Canal. The Americans then knew they would face considerable opposition if they sought a presence on the island, and the treaties that
set up the Cyprus constitution specifically forbade the transfer of the bases and
facilities under British control to anyone other than the Cyprus Government. If,
on the other hand, an Acheson-style arrangement, in which Turkey was given
control over a slice of Cyprus, was put in place, this problem could be by-passed.

~18~

THE INVISIBLE HAND

The Greek Colonels Oust Makarios

But the question of the future of the Cyprus facilities was just one of a series of factors that made the idea of a Turkish foothold on Cyprus more attractive to the Americans. Ioannides, once he seized power in Athens, threw relations with the United States into turmoil. He openly questioned the value of the defence ties and demanded an aid programme for letting the Americans keep their facilities in Greece. Ambassador Tasca warned him it would be foolish to start totting up America's account with Athens – as he might find on balance the Greeks owed Washington money. The Greeks, after all, were sheltering under the defence shield provided by the nuclear umbrella, the nuclear tactical force, the Sixth Fleet, the reserve forces earmarked and based in the United States, and the commitment to defend Greece against any Warsaw Pact attack. 'It was not a good relationship. He'd gotten in a very weak government, very inefficient and incompetent on foreign policy; he seemed to be very naive in taking the kinds of positions that could only lead to disaster,' said the Ambassador.[1]

Another blow to American policy was the death of Grivas in January 1974. It left a power vacuum which some of his more extreme lieutenants were only too keen to fill. The funeral ceremony, for instance, was hijacked by Sampson, the newspaper publisher and former leader of an EOKA execution squad. Now the leader of his own private army, he draped himself in the Greek flag, and in a highly-charged speech he banged on the side of the coffin and called on the tens of thousands of mourners to continue the fight for enosis and avenge the death of their leader.[2] Both the Greek junta and the Americans had regarded Grivas as a useful instrument for undermining Makarios's hold over Cyprus and bringing about some form of union with Greece. Grivas's chosen successor, Colonel George Karousas, concerned about provoking a Turkish invasion, was less in favour of using military force to fight Makarios, preferring instead to mount a political campaign for enosis. But Ioannides had other plans. His forces abducted Karousas, and he took over the direction of EOKA-B himself and intensified its campaign of violence against Makarios. 'Grivas turned out to be more of a steadying element than a destructive one,' recalled Tasca. 'EOKA-B became divided, more violent.'[3]

Early in 1974, the Cypriots told the Americans they had intelligence warnings of an attempt to assassinate Makarios before Greek Easter. But US diplomats dismissed these concerns, even though their own intelligence agents had picked up similar information. British diplomats admitted to hearing of such a plan, but played it down. The feast day passed without event, but in the spring Makarios's intelligence service uncovered EOKA-B records showing it had spent $6000 a day on arms smuggling and other operations since mid-1972.[4]

A number of claims have been made that much of the funding came from the Americans via Ioannides. The Socialist leader on Cyprus, Dr Vassos Lyssarides, said, 'We have a lot of evidence that money was transferred to EOKA-B by the CIA. That's where the real money came for them to continue their activities in Cyprus.'[5] Belcher, US Ambassador to Cyprus 1957–60 and 1964–9, said Greek-Cypriot officials suspected that plots were being hatched, and that there would be further attempts to depose Makarios, organised by EOKA-B and by the Greek intelligence service, KYP. 'While we were there, very senior officials in the Greek-Cypriot Government spoke of possible coups and alleged that there was considerable involvement on the part of the US Government,' said Belcher. 'I was told in very strong terms that there was documentary evidence available to the Government of Cyprus that the CIA was financing the EOKA-B organisation through money passed through Ioannides in Athens, who then passed it on to the Greek National Guard officers who were working with the EOKA-B in Cyprus.' In April, some American officials demanded that Washington put pressure on the colonels to warn them off taking action against Makarios, but the State Department did nothing. Tasca confirmed that there were 'some contacts between EOKA-B and our own intelligence people in Cyprus'. As a result, his staff received irregular reports about what EOKA-B was doing in Cyprus.[6]

The EOKA-B groups grew increasingly bold in their activities, forcing families to fly the Greek flag, daubing walls with slogans against Makarios and

Clerides, and attacking government supporters. The beleaguered Cypriot President responded by outlawing EOKA-B in April and ordering his forces to seize illegal weapons and round up suspected EOKA-B members.

At the same time as Ioannides was destabilising Makarios, relations between Greece and Turkey rapidly broke down over a row about oil rights. Oil had become a burning issue, due to worldwide price-hikes after the Yom Kippur War. Greece began exploratory drilling for oil in the northern Aegean in 1973, but in November Ankara awarded oil exploration rights in areas of the Aegean which the Greeks regarded as their own. It stirred up an unresolved controversy about sovereignty over the Aegean continental shelf and territorial sea limits. The Turks disputed whether Greece should be allowed to claim territorial rights around its 3000-plus islands in the Aegean, which would drastically reduce the area apportionable to Turkey. But in February 1974, when the Greek Government announced that large deposits of gas had been found near Thasos, Athens claimed all mineral rights in Greek waters and on the continental shelf.

Tension mounted at the end of March, when Greek fighters intercepted Turkish bombers, which Athens claimed were invading Greek air-space, and NATO manoeuvres were broken off. Turkish Foreign Minister Turan Gunesh said Turkey would never allow the Aegean to become a Greek lake. Turkey sent a survey ship supported by 32 warships into the disputed area to study the feasibility of oil drilling. The issue was discussed at a NATO meeting in Ottawa on 20 June and in Brussels five days later. The Americans backed a Turkish proposal for a joint ministeral committee to go over all the problems between the two countries and try to settle them, but Ioannides thought it outrageous even to sit down with the Turks. At the end of June, Ankara raised the stakes by announcing it would extend the exploration programme into other areas. On 14 July, the Turks announced that they had granted four oil exploration permits covering 174,000 hectares of disputed waters. Three days later, Ankara claimed sovereignty of the entire continental shelf east of the median line between the Greek and Turkish mainlands, regardless of the location of Greek islands. Throughout the Aegean crisis, Turkish and Greek armed forces were repeatedly put on alert, and their naval forces carried out provocative manoeuvres.

Ioannides later said that the hard point of the crisis was reached at the beginning of June 1974 at the NATO conference in Brussels. The Turks issued an ultimatum regarding differences in Thrace, where there is a Turkish minority, the Aegean and Cyprus. 'Otherwise [the Turks] threatened that they would intervene independently. At the same time the Turks strengthened their striking forces and began mobilising troops on the coast opposite the Greek islands,' he said.[7]

Washington thought Ioannides irrationally anti-Turk, to an extreme degree, and was spoiling for a fight. Tasca recalled, 'Ioannides had a complex about 400 years of Turkish occupation that "they did us in and some day we must get even with them"'.[8] Compared to his predecessor, he was dangerously volatile and unpredictable. He had also interfered with the US home-porting arrangements.

In April, a former junta member who visited Washington was under the impression that Nixon, the Pentagon and the CIA favoured restoring democracy in Greece under Karamanlis, but Kissinger 'was in no hurry' to get rid of the junta.[9] In May and June, Ioannides's irrational behaviour made war with Turkey increasingly likely. The Americans had to find some way to prevent him igniting a disastrous conflict, even if it put at risk their relations with Greece in the short term.

An opportunity came in Cyprus because, recognising his armed forces were not ready to challenge Turkey in Thrace or the Aegean, Ioannides decided to concentrate on cutting Makarios down to size. At home, his reckless handling of Turkey, after months of arrests and allegations of torture, emboldened opponents to demand a return to democracy. In Cyprus, Makarios dared to outlaw EOKA-B, and his resistance to Athens's plots against him gave heart to democrats in Greece. Ioannides needed a diversion that would stave off Turkish action in the Aegean and restore the prestige of his regime. But any Greek action in Cyprus also risked triggering a military response from Turkey that might escalate into all-out war.

For on at least seven occasions previously, many of them when the Greeks had taken the law into their own hands on Cyprus, Ankara had mobilised for war only to be held back by pressure from Washington. The Americans had judged that to let Greece and Turkey fight it out would be disastrous for Western interests, destroy NATO's southern wing and leave the entire Eastern Mediterranean area vulnerable to a Soviet take-over. But now they faced a complex set of problems that could be solved by tipping the scales of foreign policy in favour of Turkey, specifically on Cyprus. On the island itself, the Americans badly needed an insurance policy against the risk of Britain giving up its bases and intelligence facilities, so vital to keeping the West ahead in the nuclear arms race, to providing early warning of a nuclear attack, and to protecting Western interests in the Middle East. They also needed to prevent the increasingly left-leaning Makarios from allying the island with the Eastern Bloc. And to rid themselves of the danger of war between Greece and Turkey, they needed to find a way to jettison the rash Greek dictator too.

Despite his direction of EOKA-B activities, Ioannides's main weapon of influence in Cyprus was the National Guard, which was controlled by officers from Greece. His staff began hand-picking officers with pro-junta sympathies for the force, ready for a concerted plot to remove Makarios and replace him with a puppet regime obedient to Athens. When they stacked a list of proposed new recruits with men loyal to Ioannides, the Cypriot President rejected 57 of the names. When the National Guard commander ignored the Archbishop and began training the listed recruits, Makarios threatened to purge the force. He believed many of the Greek officers had been working with EOKA-B to try to bring down his Government. Senior Cypriot officials told Belcher in June 1974 that they 'knew' the CIA was paying Ioannides to subsidise EOKA-B in order to get rid of 'the Castro of the Mediterranean'. They said the bag-man was a CIA man from Cyprus.[10] Shortly afterwards, Makarios's police captured some of the EOKA-B leaders and a large cache of documents, which led to around 200 arrests.

On 1 July, Makarios cut the length of military service for Greek Cypriots in the National Guard to reduce the size of the force. Desperate to stave off military retaliation from Ioannides, he resorted to the tactic that had worked on several occasions before – making public his belief that Athens was preparing a new coup against his Government. In February 1972, this had been enough to enlist American pressure on the junta to hold off. On 2 July 1974, the Archbishop fired off a defiant open letter to Ioannides, directly challenging the junta leader's conduct over Cyprus. Its contents were broadcast around the world. In it, he dramatically accused the Greek colonels of conspiring to undermine his authority and constantly hatching plots to overthrow him. He charged the junta with plotting with Grivas, EOKA-B and the National Guard to carry out political murders and liquidate the state. He said documents found in the possession of high-ranking EOKA-B members showed that large sums of money had been supplied to the organisation from the Athens Government, and enclosed a copy of one of them. He warned that the way Athens had divided and driven Greek Cypriots to mutual destruction would lead to catastrophe. 'More than once I have sensed, and on one occasion almost felt, the invisible hand stretched out from Athens seeking to destroy my human existence,' he said.

Now he demanded that Athens immediately recall all its officers in the National Guard, and send instead 100 instructors and military advisers to help restructure the forces in Cyprus. He ended with a defiant assertion of his independence: 'I am not a district governor appointed by the Greek government, but the elected leader of a great section of Hellenism, and as such I demand appropriate treatment from the mother country'. Thirteen days later the colonels replied with gunfire.

At 8.30am on 15 July, Makarios was greeting a party of schoolchildren from Cairo at his Nicosia palace when shots were heard. Armoured cars and 14 tanks burst through the gates, and shells pounded the walls. Machine-gun fire, loud explosions and sirens were heard across the capital. Black smoke billowed from burning buildings. The Presidential Guards held out for three hours. Then the assailants searched for the Archbishop and set fire to the palace. Cyprus Radio broadcast the shock announcement, over martial music, that Makarios was dead and the National Guard had taken control. 'Anyone who puts up resistance will be executed at once,' said the announcer. Fighting quickly spread to other parts of the island as forces loyal to Makarios tried to resist.

~19~
SEARCHING QUESTIONS

Kissinger and Callaghan are Cross-examined

Within five days of the coup, Turkish jets swooped over the northern port of Kyrenia, bombing and strafing Greek-Cypriot strongholds, as Turkey landed thousands of troops. In two days of heavy fighting, they seized control of a corridor from Kyrenia to the Turkish quarter of Nicosia and agreed a ceasefire. But they continued to funnel 30,000 troops onto the island, and on 14 August burst out of their bridgehead and advanced east, south and west. Turkish premier Bulent Ecevit announced that the new military operation would be short, and was intended to save Cyprus and preserve her independence. But the Turks continued until they had occupied over a third of the island, displacing 200,000 people, a third of the population. Around 4000 Greek Cypriots were dead, 2000 were missing and 12,000 had been wounded during the coup and invasion. More than 900 Turkish Cypriots were believed dead or missing. The Greek junta collapsed, and Athens, stung by the way Turkey had been allowed to move into Cyprus, pulled out of NATO's military command structure and eventually cancelled the home-porting arrangements of the US Sixth Fleet.

As MPs and congressmen on either side of the Atlantic surveyed the damage, they demanded to know why the United States and Britain appeared to have done nothing to prevent the crisis erupting at each of the critical points. They opened enquiries into their respective governments' conduct, to find out why they had not tried to prevent or reverse the coup in Nicosia, obviating the need for the first Turkish intervention, or stop the Turks from expanding their bridge-head into a widespread occupation. Had they really been powerless to act at these pivotal moments, as their leaders claimed?

Benjamin Rosenthal, who led a House of Representatives examination of US foreign policy during these events, said Washington must share the blame for the crisis because of the encouragement it gave the Greek junta that sponsored the coup in Cyprus. He said the seizure of power by the colonels in 1967 was the only case in 25 years of NATO's history where a functioning democracy had been turned into a military dictatorship. But Washington had established normal relations with the junta, rescinded its arms ban, claiming disingenuously that a 'trend towards constitutional rule' had been established, and made Greece the Eastern Mediterranean base for the Sixth Fleet. When Ioannides seized power from Papadopoulos, and an even more oppressive dictatorship followed, the United States did not flinch. There were crucial questions to be asked about American conduct. 'Why did the United States persist in its tacit support for the dictatorial government in Greece? Why, in the crucial week of 15 July, 1974... did not the United States publicly demand a reversal of acts by the Greek dictatorship which clearly produced a disaster bound to involve our country?' America had betrayed the people of Greece by ignoring the fate of democracy as long as the colonels provided the United States with air and naval bases, Rosenthal said. And when the junta provoked a coup on Cyprus, Washington again ignored the affront, hoping that the world would accept another dictatorship without protest. This bore serious implications for any unstable country relying on relations with the United States, for it signalled that America was prepared to put its military interests above those of democracy.[1]

Greek-American Senator Paul Sarbanes said Americans should be deeply concerned by the State Department's failure, despite repeated warnings from many sources, to take action to avert the subversion and effective partition of Cyprus. He damned the administration for failing to support Makarios, which would have preserved stability and peace; for failing to prevent the first Turkish military intervention by denouncing the coup and pressing Ankara to hold back – as Johnson had; and for failing to limit and restrict Turkey's military action once it had begun.

Summing up, the chairman of the investigation said the United States, as the main supplier of arms to Greece and Turkey – $100–300 million a year to both countries – bore a moral responsibility, and was in a key position, to influence the Cyprus situation. Yet military aid had been used to support the Greek dictatorship whose policies culminated in the violent attack on the legitimate President of Cyprus; and American arms, supplied to Turkey for defensive purposes, had been used to invade and occupy over a third of the island.

Leading statesmen in the drama have consistently argued that the United States was powerless to act decisively because the White House was embroiled in the Watergate crisis. Both Wilson and his Foreign Secretary, James Callaghan, said Watergate had distracted not only Nixon, but also Kissinger, who was caught up in the supervision of the resignation procedures. 'It was a tragedy at this time that the United States were diplomatically in baulk,' said Wilson. They were repeating the sentiments of Kissinger himself, who, in his lengthy memoirs, *Years of Upheaval*, uncharacteristically declined to go into detail on the Cyprus crisis, saying mysteriously that he would have to leave the full story to a later date (see Appendix). His brief account was devoted to rationalising about how fragile the foreign-policy-making process had become with the US Government 'on the verge of collapse', and the President in no position to impose coherence.[2]

But his arguments were full of contradictions. He said that the administration was consumed by Watergate, yet admitted that the Cyprus crisis 'claimed our energies even as we were steeling ourselves for the final act of Nixon's tragedy'. He argued that they knew the next communal crisis in Cyprus would provoke a Turkish intervention, and that a Greek-sponsored coup would 'free Turkey of previous restraints'. Yet he ignored calls to condemn the coup because, he said, this would have made a Turkish intervention more likely. He said forcing a Greek retreat by threatening to pull out American nuclear weapons or end home-porting would damage American interests, because Washington would be seen as the agent of Greece's humiliation. Yet he admitted that it was a dominant view even inside the State Department that the colonels were 'hated' by the Greek people, and that failure on Cyprus would lead to their overthrow.

Kissinger conceded that Turkey's demand for the return to power of Makarios, whose removal they had been working towards for years, left 'little doubt' that Ankara was 'counting on using the Greek refusal as a pretext to move Turkey's army into Cyprus'. He said stopping them would have required military action, and the administration, in the last days of the Watergate crisis, was 'in no position to make credible threats'. Yet he later said Washington forced the ceasefire during the first invasion by threatening Ankara that it would remove nuclear weapons from forward positions.

He also tried to prevent secret evidence of what went on being handed over to members of the Select Committee on Intelligence, which investigated American intelligence performance during the crisis. Kissinger admitted his policy decisions had provoked vigorous dissent. But when questioned about two officials who correctly predicted the crisis, he refused to allow a key dissent memo to be shown to the investigation or to let the author, Cyprus desk officer Thomas Boyatt, answer questions on its details (see Appendix). The battle went all the way to the President, but Gerald Ford invoked executive privilege to counter the subpoenas. Exasperated, one committee member accused the State Department of a cover-up. He said, 'If this committee could ever unravel the mess, many heads would roll and with regard to the State Department, if we could ever get into the Cyprus question… many shocking revelations would occur'.[3]

Like their American counterparts, British MPs were anxious to know why the Cypriot people had been so badly let down by the three powers who were supposed to be guaranteeing the independence, territorial integrity and security of Cyprus and its constitution under the Treaty of Guarantee. Greece had backed an armed takeover of the legitimate government by right-wing extremists; Turkey invaded and seized over a third of the territory; and the most powerful guarantor, Britain, took no military action to stop either of these fundamental violations of the treaty.

In 1975, a committee of MPs was set up to investigate Britain's role during the crisis. Mysteriously, the Government tried to limit its scope from the beginning. The normal powers of a select committee, such as the ability to send for people, papers or records, were initially blocked, then conceded only after considerable pressure. The committee was not empowered to travel outside the UK, and had to resort to interviewing Cypriot refugees living in London. And when the MPs cross-examined the key witnesses, Callaghan and Roy Hattersley, his junior minister, their answers were evasive and contradictory.[4]

The main concern of the MPs was to find out why Britain appeared to have abandoned its responsibilities as a guarantor power. They tried to establish whether Britain had a duty under the Treaty of Guarantee to intervene militarily to prevent the coup and invasions, and restore the status quo ante; and whether it had the military capability and advance knowledge necessary to take pre-emptive action at each stage.

When they pressed Callaghan to confirm that Britain did have a duty to take action, he admitted, 'I dare say legally we had'. But he insisted that there was no moral obligation, because the power-sharing 1960 constitution had in practice become a dead letter. On whether Britain had the military capacity to intervene, Callaghan said, 'It would have been impossible for us to have assembled the forces and imposed on the Greek Cypriots and the Turkish Cypriots the working of the constitution that they had singularly failed to operate after 1960'. Yet while Hattersley agreed that Britain did not have the forces on the island to intervene to stop the coup or invasion, Callaghan admitted that if the British forces under UN auspices had been given authority to take action, it would have been a different situation. When the MPs said he was implying that by donning a new beret the forces were suddenly capable of intervening, Callaghan back-tracked, arguing that he personally had not denied that the troops had the capacity to intervene.

Asked point-blank whether Britain had made preparations for a Turkish invasion, Callaghan claimed he did not know what they were referring to. Told that the assault carrier *Hermes* and 3000 troops had been diverted to Cyprus and asked if that was in case of an invasion, Callaghan avoided a denial, saying, 'Not necessarily, no'. Asked if *Hermes* could have been positioned to prevent the second invasion, he could only say, 'I suppose so, I do not know'. And when pursued on this point, with the argument that there were plenty of British forces in the area which could have prevented a northern invasion of Cyprus, he again evaded the answer, saying, 'I'm not able to comment on that because I just do not know at this stage'. In fact, according to a memorandum submitted by the Ministry of Defence, extensive military preparations were made: following the coup, the garrison of 3000 troops in the sovereign bases was increased to 5500, the naval and airforce support in the Eastern Mediterranean was strengthened by the sending of additional warships, including *Hermes*, and fighters. Before the second invasion, a further reinforcement took place, including the deployment of Gurkha troops and Phantom aircraft.[5] Moreover, Callaghan's own political adviser, Tom McNally, has admitted that Britain actively considered placing *Hermes* and other warships between Cyprus and Turkey to deter the Turks, but the Americans vetoed military action.[6]

The MPs were astonished when Callaghan denied that Britain had any advance knowledge – a prerequisite for preventative action on the coup and either phase of the invasion. They found this difficult to accept, given that Makarios himself had publicly accused the Greek National Guard of plotting with EOKA-B. With regard to the initial invasion, the former Greek Foreign Minister, George Mavros, had told the MPs that the French, who had far less representation and interests in the area than the British, knew that Turkey was going to invade (and Wilson and Callaghan were in Paris the two days before the invasion). Furthermore, the sort of military preparations necessary to support any invasion, involving the shipment of tanks and armour, could not have been invisible to the most casual reconnaissance. 'If it is true that the three stages of the Cyprus crisis came as a surprise to the British Government, this argues deficiencies in Government intelligence which ought to be remedied,' the MPs said.[7]

The Committee decided that Britain had a legal right, a moral obligation and the military capacity to intervene, but did not do so. Britain had considerable forces at hand, and could have intervened with or without Turkey, to reverse the coup and had 'little doubt that either alone or as part of a UN force, Britain could have forestalled the first Turkish invasion'. The chairman declared that the Cyprus crisis had been a true test of Britain's standing in the world, which should be measured not by its military might or economic wealth, but by its standards of justice, integrity and humanity, and by the way it protects the weak. On all these counts Britain had failed over Cyprus – for reasons which the Government refused to give.

~20~

WARNINGS OF
A COUP

The CIA Knew in Advance

W hen Kissinger later tried to persuade Clerides that Watergate prevented him from doing much about Cyprus, the Cypriot leader laughed in his face. 'I remember the scene. I was in America and Kissinger started explaining to me that he had been wrongly accused, that he wanted to help Cyprus, that he knew nothing about it because he was absorbed with the Watergate scandal. I looked up and behind his desk was a huge photograph of a gorilla beating its chest and the caption underneath was: "If you don't tell me the truth, I'll beat it out of you". [So] I told him if he kept telling me he knew nothing he would force me to do what the gorilla was saying. And he laughed. I mean, the secret services of the United States were not paralysed because of the Nixon scandal. Reports were sent in, [there were] daily briefings to the Cypriot Foreign Secretary that Turkey was about to invade Cyprus. Turkey would not be foolish enough to do it without telling the United States. What would happen if the United States intervened and sent in the Sixth Fleet? Nonsense.'[1]

In fact, Kissinger was in a uniquely powerful position to mastermind American foreign policy over Cyprus even as the Nixon Presidency was disintegrating. He had retained his post as National Security Adviser when he took over as Secretary of State in 1973. This meant he was the only Secretary of State to also hold the chairmanship of the top secret 40 Committee, which approved covert operations by the CIA. And as chairman of the National Security Council every major intelligence plan passed through him. The dual role gave him unprecedented control over both foreign policy and covert intelligence operations. One member of the Select Committee on Intelligence investigation accused him of amassing power over intelligence operations and diplomatic initiatives while keeping his staff in the dark. Representative Dellums said, 'We have testimony that you have participated in directing operations which were not fully discussed, analysed or evaluated by those authorised to do so. In fact sometimes they were purposefully hidden.' He wondered aloud if this meant that Kissinger had an arm-lock on the intelligence community, and that at this particular moment in history it was all down to Henry Kissinger and his enormous individual power.[2] One former NSC aide, Roger Morris, said that with Nixon's presidency in political and psychological ruin, Kissinger's authority made him, at critical moments, 'no less than acting chief of state for national security', and his grip on government continued under Nixon's successor, Gerald Ford[3] (see Appendix).

Kissinger believed it was easier to change policy by circumventing the normal channels and excluding from the decision-making process many of those who were theoretically charged with carrying it out. According to Ray Cline, director of intelligence and research in the State Department between 1969 and 1973, Kissinger perfected this 'secrecy principle' during his White House days, keeping only a few of his closest senior officials informed about key decisions. 'The bulk of the staffs in State – and elsewhere – have in general continued to be ignored,' said Cline. In fact, a number of them were wire-tapped as the atmosphere of suspicion and fear of leaks enveloped Nixon's administration.[4] Kissinger did not like to leave anything to chance. According to the reporters Bernard and Mervin Kalb, who wrote a study of Kissinger, when they asked him what was the key to his success, the Secretary of State quoted Metternich: 'Because I know what I want and what the others are capable of, I am completely prepared'.[5]

This style of operation enabled Kissinger and Nixon to use two-track diplomacy, presenting one line on policy in public while secretly pursuing another. It meant they could hold off pressure both from public opinion and from within the administration as they explored new initiatives with other countries and manipulated the White House policy-making process to produce the required result. Thus, as we will show, during the Cyprus crisis, publicly Kissinger called for stability in NATO's south-eastern front, but privately the United States tacitly encouraged the Greeks to lead a coup on the island and gave an implicit green light to the ensuing Turkish invasion (see Appendix).

Cyprus was by no means the first example of this under Nixon. Morris cites West Pakistan's attempts to crush support for independence in East Pakistan in 1971 by sending tanks on to the streets of Dhaka, killing thousands. The US

State Department, despite dissent from junior officials, offered no rebuke to Pakistan for its 'genocide', and lied in denying that the United States was supplying it with arms clandestinely. Nixon and Kissinger were negotiating a rapprochement with China, and wanted to show that they could stand by China's ally, Pakistan, in the face of hostile world opinion. When India entered the war on behalf of East Pakistan, Kissinger told officials to 'tilt' towards Pakistan, in contrast with public statements of neutrality. Nixon ordered a military show of force to deter India, but the warships arrived too late, and Pakistan gave up the fight. In Chile in 1970, Kissinger tried to prevent the first democratic election of a communist-socialist government in the West by covertly funding the opponents of Allende before the vote and in the run-up to congressional confirmation. 'I don't see why we have to let a country go Marxist just because its people are irresponsible,' he told the 40 Committee.[6] When this failed, the United States had to quickly pull down a major intelligence station it had set up on Easter Island,[7] and Nixon ordered the CIA to stage a coup without the knowledge of the US Ambassador, whom they kept in the dark by using separate channels of communication. The plot failed, though Allende later died in a home-grown coup encouraged by the CIA.

The Select Committee on Intelligence investigation was told that during the Nixon years the United States had undertaken 'cynical, hypocritical and evil acts' to compete for power with the Soviet Union and hid the cost of the multi-million dollar operations. The chairman said, 'In some cases, the Ambassadors would be cognisant. In some cases, the Ambassador would not be cognisant. In some cases, the CIA had approved operations; and in some cases, it had opposed operations. In one case, both the State Department and the CIA opposed an operation, and the operation proceeded. In no case that has come to our attention has the Special Assistant to the President for National Security Affairs [Kissinger] opposed any of these operations which went ahead.'[8]

The style of the Pakistan and Chile operations – neutral public statements contrasting with the tilt of busy diplomatic activity and covert intelligence action behind the scenes – continued during the Cyprus crisis. A few close officials, such as Sisco, Assistant Secretary for the Near East and South Asia since 1969, were given an important role. An insider with 18 years' service, he had carried out Kissinger's orders during the Pakistan crisis to dampen dissent over America's role in backing the aggressor. He had also worked closely with Nixon and Kissinger on the Middle East, an area of foreign policy which had a great deal of autonomy from normal procedures, but was kept under a tight rein by the President and his National Security Advisor.[9]

By contrast, strong suspicions were raised over the way Kissinger cut himself off from most of the State Department's expertise in this strategic area during the crisis – by removing Ambassador Tasca; the chief of the Cyprus desk, Tom Boyatt; the chief of the Greek Desk, George Churchill; and the chief of the Turkish Desk. Both Churchill and Boyatt were considered by Tasca to be first-rate officers.

He said, 'George knew Greece and it was a big mistake to take him off Greece'. On 12 August, Tasca himself was relieved of his post, even though Karamanlis's Government sent an official message to the US Government asking that he stay on.[10]

While in post, Tasca and other key figures found themselves mysteriously sidelined. Tasca, who as Ambassador in Athens should have been at the heart of any bid to halt Ioannides's attempts to usurp democracy in Cyprus, found himself excluded from vital information, and was allowed to go on holiday at what turned out to be a crucial point in the build-up to the crisis. Boyatt, the one official who tried to avert the disaster by impressing on the Ambassador the need to warn off Ioannides, was overruled by Sisco. And intelligence officers who passed on warnings of Ioannides's intentions were ignored.

For some time, Kissinger and Nixon had been excluding even the key foreign policy bodies from decision-making, so it was not a big step to keep particular officials in the field in the dark as well. For instance, the National Security Council, whose policy formulation Kissinger closely controlled, met increasingly infrequently once he added the post of Secretary of State to his portfolio. It existed to screen and co-ordinate all viewpoints on foreign and defence policy decisions. Later in the Nixon administration it sometimes went several months without meeting. Similarly, the 40 Committee did not meet formally between 1972 and 1974. Yet during that period, its chairman, Kissinger, authorised 40 covert actions. James Gardner, a former liaison man between the State Department and the 40 Committee, confirmed that some covert operations were not put before the NSC or even the 40 Committee, though Kissinger said every covert operation was personally approved by the President.[11]

Former senior NSC staff member William Watts said that when matters were discussed at the NSC there was an extraordinary emphasis on security, secrecy and on limiting the number of people brought in to consider highly sensitive matters. This applied not only to covert operations, but to general policy. There was even greater secrecy over the work of the 40 Committee. In the 20–25 meetings of the National Security Council which Watts attended, no 40 Committee business was ever discussed in front of a full meeting of the NSC.[12]

During the Cyprus crisis, Kissinger restricted the distribution of intelligence in a dramatic way by insisting that higher grade classifications were put on information. Before he became Secretary of State, the top secret classifications such as NODIS, EYES ONLY were rarely used. But in the crisis a 'very large proportion' of the messages were NODIS, which meant that the distribution was strictly controlled by the Secretary of State's close officials. Tasca was frozen out. For instance, intelligence reports in late June warning that a coup might be imminent were not passed to him or widely disseminated throughout the intelligence community[13] (see Appendix).

The unusual political structure in Greece enabled Washington to employ two channels of communication with Athens. Even though he was not in the official military Government, the real power in Greece was Ioannides, with whom the CIA, with 60 agents in the country, had long-term contacts. Only the CIA was used to communicate with the junta leader, making it the main agent of US foreign policy towards Greece. Tasca only knew about Ioannides what the CIA chose to tell him. The CIA had a separate channel of communication with Washington, and he had no way of knowing if he had been kept informed of the CIA's dealings with Ioannides, even though CIA agents followed orders approved at the highest level in Washington.[14] Tasca was left to deal with officials of the puppet Government. But they knew nothing of Ioannides's plots on Cyprus because the junta leader dealt directly with EOKA-B, by-passing his own Government.[15]

Throughout the weeks in the run-up to the coup, the CIA in Athens repeatedly warned Washington of the danger of subversion in Cyprus by Ioannides's men, but Tasca did not get the message. On 3 June, only days after the Turks had tested the junta's nerve on oil rights in the Aegean by sending a survey ship into Greek waters, there was a warning that Ioannides was considering action against Makarios. This was reported on 7 June in the *National Intelligence Daily*, widely read by State Department, Pentagon and National Security officials:

> Ioannides claimed that Greece is capable of removing Makarios and his key supporters from power in 24 hours, with little if any blood being shed and without EOKA assistance. The Turks would quietly acquiesce [in] the removal of Makarios, a key enemy... Ioannides stated that if Makarios decided on some type of extreme provocation against Greece to obtain a tactical advantage, he is not sure whether he should merely pull the Greek troops out of Cyprus and let Makarios fend for himself, or remove Makarios once and for all and have Greece deal directly with Turkey over Cyprus' future.[16]

This last argument is the same as the scenario urged on the Americans when they considered forcing Greece and Turkey to split the island between them in 1964.[17] According to the *New York Times*, Ioannides himself told a CIA man in Athens – an unconfirmed report said it was the station chief – on about 20 June that he was contemplating military action against Makarios. Then, on 27 June, the State Department first got word that the coup was definitely on. But Tasca was not told, and the State Department did nothing.

According to Belcher, junior State Department officials had been trying for weeks to persuade Kissinger 'to instruct Ambassador Tasca to warn Ioannides not to be so foolish as to create a fait accompli which would force the Turks to move to protect their Cypriot brothers'.[18] It was not until 29 June, three and a half weeks after the first warning of Ioannides's plans, that Tasca was first ordered to warn Ioannides against toppling Makarios. Kissinger, who as National Security Adviser and Secretary of State made sure he had supreme access to the whole network of intelligence reports, left on 25 June for meetings in Brussels and Moscow without taking any action on Cyprus (see Appendix). While he was away, it was left to a junior official, Boyatt, to pass the order to Tasca. Boyatt ruled out the use of explicit pressures,[19] and the order was not backed up with specific details of the risk of a coup. As a result, the Ambassador, who unlike the CIA had no access to the junta and was frozen out of communications between Ioannides and Washington, did not see the urgency of the situation. He therefore questioned the order, wiring the State Department, to urge them to review it in case it upset Ioannides. He admitted it was unthinkable that the Greeks would try to stage a coup in Cyprus without first seeking the US view on such a move. But the CIA in Athens did not give him any firm warnings of a coup: if they had, he would have 'turned the place upside down'. When he had received similar coup warnings in 1972, Tasca had restrained the Papadopoulos Government.[20]

Boyatt sent the order back to 'go ahead anyhow', but Tasca had left Athens for a family engagement in Switzerland. Concerned that a crisis was about to break, Boyatt took the matter to his boss, Sisco, Kissinger's most senior official responsible for the region. Sisco rang Tasca's deputy in Nicosia, Elizabeth Brown. She repeated the Ambassador's ill-informed opinion that there was no need to warn off Ioannides. Sisco chose to ignore Boyatt's concerns. Instead of insisting that the matter was urgent, and she should pull out all the stops, he said, 'All right, fine, we won't send any message to Ioannides'.[21] So the final decision rested with the official closest to Kissinger. Later in the crisis, Boyatt was taken out of his Cyprus job after writing a memo strongly disagreeing with the wisdom of US policy during this period. He had consistently warned of the likelihood of a coup, and correctly predicted that the Turks would respond by landing troops on the island, and that the Greeks would not be able to stop them.[22]

After the crisis, the top echelons of the CIA tried to pin on intelligence analysts the blame for the fact that Ioannides had not been properly warned off staging a coup against Makarios. The CIA's post-mortem on the affair recorded, 'There were some noticeable shortcomings… On the basis of a single CIA report from Athens, the analysts in early July, notwithstanding their earlier concern, conveyed the impression to the policy makers that the world had been granted a reprieve: Ioannides, they suggested, had now decided not to move against Makarios, at least for the time being.' They also said they had been denied details of conversations between 'US policy makers and their representatives on the scene and between these policy makers and certain principals in the dispute', which contributed to the analysts' failure to predict events.[23]

Tasca, of course, had no useful information to give, because he was not privy to the contacts with Ioannides. But the analysts disputed the focus on the one report saying the coup was off. In a dissenting memo, they said they had been reporting the breakdown in relations between the junta and Makarios since November 1973; and that from the beginning of July (after Sisco had overruled Boyatt's plea for action) intelligence reporting consistently stressed that there remained an unresolved conflict between the Greek-Cypriot President and

Ioannides. Even a 3 July report which passed on Ioannides's personal reassurance that he was not about to take action was prefaced with the warning that events had moved closer to a showdown. On 11 July, two days after Kissinger returned from Moscow, the analysts repeated Ioannides's latest assertion, but reported, 'The Junta is almost certainly reluctant to lose its influence over the National Guard, and an attempt to remove Makarios in one way or another cannot be ruled out'.[24]

Not that these warnings were necessary for Kissinger to know there was a threat to the Cypriot presidency, for Makarios had sent his provocative open letter to Ioannides, demanding the withdrawal of Greek officers from Cyprus, on 2 July. It was flashed around the world by the US's Foreign Broadcast Information Service (FBIS), which operated monitoring stations on Cyprus. Shortly afterwards, three Greek Foreign Ministry officials known to be against a coup in Cyprus resigned. And on 11 July, Makarios rejected Ioannides's counter-demands, leaving the junta leader no option but to confront the Archbishop or lose face. The next day, Makarios told the US Ambassador in Nicosia about Ioannides's plots against him. This was repeated by analysts on 13 July. Summing up, the analysts said, 'More and clearer warning of the coup against Makarios was given in this case than is usual. We did not predict the timing of the coup, but we made it clear that there was a coup in the making.'[25] The obvious question is, with so much evidence on hand of Ioannides's plans for Makarios, why did Kissinger not ensure that firm action was taken to deter the junta leader? (see Appendix).

Tasca pointed out that the Turks must have been convinced about the plans for a coup, because they must have started preparing their July 20 invasion before the fall of Makarios. And this mobilisation would have been picked up by the numerous American monitoring facilities in Turkey and Cyprus. Said Tasca, 'Makarios fell on July 15... don't tell me you can launch 25,000 men, aeroplanes, ships and tanks in three or four days... you can't do that'.[26]

But the State Department chose to act on the basis of a single report which contradicted the continuous and mounting evidence that Ioannides was on the verge of overthrowing Makarios. According to the Select Committee on Intelligence the full, unsanitised post-mortem report indicated that the reassurance came from an untested source. However, the analysts said that the evidence that the coup had been postponed actually came from 'the instigator Ioannides himself', implying that Washington chose not to act against a coup because the man behind it had said it would not go ahead.[27] An unconfirmed report in the *Cyprus Mail*[28] said that the CIA reported plans to assassinate Makarios several days before the coup, and that Kissinger treated these warnings with 'excessive apathy' (see Appendix). The Soviets, who also had intelligence warnings, approached the State Department to suggest joint action with Britain and the United States to prevent a possible coup, but were 'cold-shouldered'. Ioannides himself later insisted that the United States, far from dissuading him, had actually encouraged him to go ahead with the coup.[29] Tasca saw a CIA report that Ioannides had told a colleague that 'everything was alright as far as the US and he were concerned'.[30] The CIA agent said to be closest to Ioannides, Peter Koromilas, was sent to Athens to confer with him just before the 15 July coup.[31]

According to the Greek-Cypriot Socialist leader, Vassos Lyssarides, a big wire station was set up in Nicosia Airport to enable the rebels in Cyprus to maintain contact with headquarters in Greece.[32] The British, who share their intelligence with the Americans, should have picked up the signals through one of their many electronic intelligence listening stations on the island. The Ayios Nikolaos facilities monitored Greek and Turkish communications. Whether from Cyprus or from Greece, the Americans had been monitoring the same link. *Newsweek* reported that US intelligence had intercepted a message from Cyprus to Athens an hour after the Nicosia coup began which said, 'Operation President is underway and on schedule'. The night before the coup more than 100 Greek army officers in civilian clothes were seen boarding a Boeing 727 for an unscheduled flight to Nicosia.[33]

Clerides said that at the time most Greek Cypriots, including Makarios, believed Athens would not dare stage a coup because it would inevitably trigger a Turkish invasion. But the junta had other ideas. Clerides believed they felt that if they ousted Makarios, the Americans would not allow Turkey to intervene. He suggested that the junta got this idea because their contacts were mainly with the CIA. 'Probably the CIA created this impression and it was not the correct picture. Maybe they deliberately created that impression in order to help the coup and to help the Turkish invasion.' The CIA, he said, may have thought they could kill two sparrows with one shot. 'First, they would get Makarios, whom they did not look on favourably because of his relations with the Eastern Bloc countries, out of the way. Then, also in this way, part of Cyprus will be occupied by Turkey and the other would go to Greece. Partition. Finito, the Cyprus problem.' This would mean the end of the running sore in Graeco-Turkish relations, the problem which negotiation after negotiation had failed to settle between 1963 and 1974.[34]

~21~

WASHINGTON STALLS

Britain Sends a Task-force

On 15 July 1974, the news of the coup and the shock announcement of Makarios's death were flashed around the world, but unbeknown to the coupists, the Archbishop was still alive. As the Palace Guard fought the intruders, he and two bodyguards escaped through a back window and scrambled across a dried-up river bed onto a deserted road. They flagged down a passing car and, with Makarios crouched on the floor, fled to the mountains. The National Guardsmen had blundered. They had picked the tank crews from men loyal to the junta and given pro-Makarios soldiers leave. But instead of ambushing Makarios earlier in the morning as he returned to Nicosia from his summer retreat with only a light escort, they had waited until he had reached the comparative safety of his palace. When the tanks thundered on to the streets of Nicosia, some of them got stuck in the rush-hour traffic. Twenty-five tanks and commandos were meant to attack from several sides simultaneously, but they failed to completely encircle their target, and Makarios slipped the net.

Vassos Lyssarides, the Socialist leader – and physician to Makarios – whose house was next door to the presidential palace, recalled hearing the first artillery blasts. 'I had some policemen with me so we took each one of us a gun, being sure that we were surrounded – at least to die a little bit more honourably.' But he too broke through the gap in the ring of tanks, and fled to the Syrian Embassy. From there he and his bodyguards made for the mountains, to organise resistance.[1]

Clerides, constitutionally the next in line to the presidency after Makarios, was lying on a stretching machine in the Nicosia hospital, receiving treatment for back trouble, when his bodyguards burst in with news of the coup. He hurried to the House of Representatives, of which he was President, to remove his confidential files and dispatch them to a safe hiding-place. When National Guard soldiers reached him, they placed him under house arrest.[2]

Although the coup was codenamed Operation President, the junta did not seem to have put much thought into who would take over. Perhaps Makarios's escape spoiled their plans. If he had been killed, Clerides would have taken over automatically, despite his total opposition to the coup and the junta. The junta's men spent most of the morning knocking on doors trying to find someone willing to be President. 'They went to a judge of the High Court, who refused them,' said Clerides. 'They went to the house of the President of the Supreme Court, but he was abroad. In desperation, when they couldn't find anybody, they went and picked up Nicos Sampson.'[3]

When the soldiers came for him, Sampson thought he was being arrested, but he was taken to a police headquarters and told he was going to be President. At 2.50pm he was sworn in. He sought to assuage international fears by declaring that Cyprus would remain independent and non-aligned. But as a former leader of an EOKA execution squad, a friend of Ioannides, and leader of an armed band against the Turkish Cypriots in the 1963 troubles, he was a provocative choice. Though he said there would be no union with Greece, few believed him, because he was a well-known pro-enosis fanatic.

Widespread fighting followed, between pro-Makarios and pro-junta forces across the island. In Nicosia, four heavy trucks were used to transport the dead to the city's cemetery. There were mass graves at Lakatamia, Limassol and Paphos. In the capital, Soviet-built National Guard tanks blocked road junctions and surrounded the central Post Office, Nicosia airport, the radio station and other strategic points. Troops enforced a curfew, and flights to Cyprus were suspended.

The coup caused alarm and consternation among the Turkish Cypriots. Denktash recalled, 'In the morning I was in my office as usual at 7.30 and at 8.30 shots started to be fired from the Greek quarter and particles of bombs started falling on my roof. Then we heard that there was a coup and Makarios was dead. We contacted the Turkish government immediately [saying] that this was a takeover by Greece and all our safety, the lives of our people, were endangered and Turkey should honour her treaty obligations. Our concern was to bring Turkey to our aid, otherwise we were finished.'[4]

The Turks needed no prompting. In Ankara, Ecevit held an emergency meeting of his National Security Council, and told his military chiefs that action must be taken. The only question was whether it should be immediate retaliatory action or an extended two-stage intervention. He warned his generals that the coup made it all too easy for the Greeks to declare enosis and gain a base which would give them the potential to attack Turkey from two fronts, the east and the south. He was worried, too, that the guns might soon be turned on the Turkish Cypriots. When told his forces could land troops by Saturday, he penned instructions for them to secure a bridgehead on Cyprus.[5]

The situation was at least as dangerous as the worst of 1964 and 1967, and it was obvious to the British and Americans that it would take immense pressure to prevent Turkey fighting back, as Ankara had threatened to invade many times before and the coup was the most dramatic breach of the 1960 agreements to date.

The British believed Makarios was dead – though they had no proof – and regarded it as their duty to take the lead in dealing with Greece and Turkey to stave off a disaster. At an emergency meeting on the morning of the coup, Foreign Office ministers and senior officials agreed that Turkish military action had to be avoided to prevent a regional war. Turkey was convoying troops in full battle-dress to ports opposite Cyprus. Turkish, Soviet, American and British naval ships were either on alert or unusually active.

In a separate meeting in the War Room in Whitehall, Harold Wilson, senior ministers and military chiefs gathered to consider the military action Britain could take to hold off Turkey and defend the facilities if they were attacked. The options included a proposal to place warships between Cyprus and Turkey to deter an invasion. As a minimum, it was necessary to send forces to help defend the British bases and facilities on the island, and be ready to evacuate British holidaymakers and workers on the island in the event of war.[6]

Wilson therefore ordered military chiefs to send a task-force to Cyprus. The assault carrier, *Hermes*, heading for Malta with 700 commandos on board, was ordered to change course for Cyprus, and be ready to land its commandos on the island at 24 hours' notice. The guided-missile destroyer, *Devonshire*, was put on a war footing and, along with the frigates, *Rhyl* and *Andromeda*, set sail for Cyprus. The commandos were to supplement the 3000 British troops stationed in the SBAs. They were supported by Lightning fighters, surface-to-air missiles and air defence artillery. There were also two squadrons of Vulcan nuclear bombers, transporters and helicopters.

Other NATO allies joined Britain in urging Turkey to show restraint, and waited anxiously for Washington's reaction. Only massive pressure on the colonels to pull the coupists out of Cyprus and a show of force against Turkey would prevent Ankara exercising its legal right to take action to restore the con-stitutional status quo. It would have required action as strong as Johnson's in 1964, when he threatened to abandon NATO's commitment to defend Turkey against a Soviet attack and sent a naval task-force to deter a Turkish invasion.

But Kissinger's response was bafflingly neutral. He convened an emergency meeting of the Washington Special Action Group – comprising top officials from the State Department, the Defence Department and the CIA – then authorised an official statement saying, 'The United States has long been on record as opposed to any resort to violence on the island. Our policy remains that of supporting the independence and the territorial integrity of Cyprus and its constitutional arrangements, and we urge all other states to support a similar policy.' It directed no rebuke against the perpetrators of the coup, and demanded no specific steps be taken to restore the constitutional arrangements. American officials believed it amounted to a coded warning for the coupists in Cyprus not to go one step further and try to declare enosis. But it put no pressure on them to back down, and no military signals were sent either – the Defence Department publicly conceded that no change had been ordered in the alert status of the US Sixth Fleet, the main American military force in the region.

This did not help Makarios. He had resurfaced at Kykko monastery, with a hundred armed policemen, and broadcast a declaration from a clandestine station: 'I am alive, and, as long as I live, the clique that has rebelled will not rule Cyprus'. He appealed to the world not to allow Cyprus to be turned into a dictatorship. The monastery then became a prime target of National Guard forces, though Makarios left with bodyguards for Paphos. It was bombarded as troops fanned out across the hillsides and closed in on the stronghold. Sampson also moved heavy armour towards Paphos, and gunboats shelled loyalist positions. Makarios's men had only machine-guns and light weapons.

But Makarios was able to contact a British field officer in the UN force and ask for British help in getting him off the island. The reaction was swift and decisive. In the midst of the fighting, Callaghan ordered the RAF to send in a helicopter to rescue him. It was fired on but not hit, and took Makarios to the British base at Akrotiri, putting the SBA at risk from a rebel attack. The RAF flew him in a transporter to Malta, and on to London. After fighting all day on 16 July, Paphos and Limassol fell to the coupists.

Callaghan told the House of Commons that he was demanding from Athens a withdrawal of the Greek officers in the Cypriot National Guard as soon as possible, even though the junta claimed the Cyprus coup was an internal affair. In Athens the British Ambassador, Sir Robin Hooper, pressed the Government to replace all 650 Greek officers commanding the National Guard. This strong stance was not matched by the Americans. Tasca's message from Kissinger for acting Foreign Minister Constantine Kypraios was merely that Greece should exercise the 'utmost restraint'.

Similarly at the UN, the Americans were curiously non-committal. When Cyprus's UN representative, Zenon Rossides, urged the Security Council to order a ceasefire and prevent outside force being used in Cyprus, the Americans, this time with British support, persuaded the Council to adjourn without acting, on the grounds that more details were needed to make a judgement. Rossides protested, but the British would not move on this without Kissinger's prior agreement, and the Americans were stalling efforts to stoke up international pressure against Greece.[7]

By contrast, Ecevit told the Secretary General that the armed coup had created a grave situation, and urged the United Nations to take immediate steps to prevent more illegal weapons and troops entering the island. Recognition of the Sampson administration was not possible, he said. The British spokesman warned that the situation was highly explosive, not only for Cyprus, but for the entire Mediterranean region.

Kissinger held a second Washington Special Action Group meeting and reported back to Nixon. American officials believed the Turks saw the Greek action as 'a kind of de facto enosis' warranting the landing of Turkish troops on Cyprus. But the State Department spokesman insisted that 'the question of recognition as of the moment does not arise', which negated the declared support for the island's constitutional arrangements in their first official statement. Washington took no steps to end the coup (see Appendix).

As the Americans sat on their hands, Ankara turned to the British Government and demanded firm action within 24 hours to reverse the coup, or face unilateral Turkish action. An extraordinary session of the Turkish parliament was called for the next day to debate a motion giving the Government authorisation to declare war 'if the necessity arises'. Ecevit lodged a formal request for consultations with the British Government to seek joint action under the Treaty of Guarantee. The Pentagon reported that units of Turkey's Second Army were being moved hurriedly from inland bases into Mersin and Iskenderun on the Turkish coast, 50 miles north of Cyprus. A NATO meeting in Brussels, called to discuss the Cyprus situation, was told that the armed forces of both Greece and Turkey had been put on precautionary alert.

Makarios arrived in London on 17 July with none of the trappings of his office, not even a change of clothes. Officials were sent into the West End to buy a bishop's crook and clerical garments. The Archbishop presented himself at Downing Street composed, dignified and impeccably dressed. But he was stung by the lack of support shown by the Americans. Callaghan recalled, 'He said bitterly that it had only been necessary for the Colonels to declare themselves anti-communists to win a measure of understanding'.[8] At the very time that Britain was playing host to the ousted Cypriot President, American officials began talks with the new regime on Cyprus, and publicly suggested that the Nixon administration, though it had not yet officially recognised Sampson, was leaning that way. Sampson's Foreign Minister had been received by the US Ambassador in Nicosia, Roger Davies. Kissinger dismissed calls from his own specialists in Greek, Turkish and Cypriot affairs for the administration to back Makarios and charge the Athens junta with illegal intervention in the island's affairs. Instead, the State Department continued to maintain that there had been no outside intervention in Cyprus. This was despite reports that two Greek aeroplanes had flown middle-ranking Greek officers from Athens into Nicosia, implying direct links between the junta and the coupists on Cyprus. Kissinger later admitted that US officials were convinced that Ioannides instigated the coup (see Appendix). Kissinger's aides said they believed Makarios was 'finished politically',[9] and he told Callaghan privately that he did not want Makarios to return to the island.

In Britain, Callaghan told MPs that the junta bore a heavy responsibility for the situation in Cyprus, and outlined a six-point diplomatic plan of action to help the deposed Cypriot President. These included consultations with Kissinger, support for Cyprus's request for a meeting of the UN Security Council, a joint statement by the EC powers, a French initiative to put pressure on Greece, and a NATO statement. But the British efforts were hampered by conflict with Washington. The Americans dragged their heels as the British tried to win backing in New York for a UN motion affirming the legitimacy of the Makarios Government. Callaghan admitted later that at this point Britain and America were unable to 'march together'.[10]

Tension continued to mount on all sides. The Soviets accused the NATO powers of being behind the coup. And Bulgaria and Yugoslavia moved troops to their borders with Greece. A Soviet flotilla of cruisers and destroyers was detected in Cypriot waters. The Turks put their navy on a war footing, and at least two warships put out to sea. The Americans spotted Soviet warships, sent from the Black Sea, manoeuvring in the Mediterranean, and their own ships in the Sixth Fleet did not return to port.

The strategic fear in NATO was that, if Greece and Turkey went to war over Cyprus, the Soviet Union would be able to seize the military advantage in the Eastern Mediterranean. The defence of the area, which included the sea approaches to the Suez Canal, Israel and the Arab countries of the Middle East, relied on the Greek and Turkish navies, the US Sixth Fleet, five squadrons of the RAF – including the two squadrons of Vulcan bombers with a nuclear capability based at Akrotiri – and the British and American electronic monitoring facilities on Cyprus.[11]

During Wednesday 17 July, Ecevit consulted US Ambassador William Macomber, who had returned to Ankara from talks with his bosses in Washington, before flying to London with his top generals, arriving in the evening. Accompanied by ministers and two generals, he attended a working dinner with Wilson, Callaghan and Defence Minister Roy Mason at Downing Street. Wilson sought in vain to persuade Ecevit to agree to tripartite talks with Greece. At one point during the meal Callaghan and Wilson left the room for a short period to contact Kissinger. But Ecevit asked Wilson to take joint action in Cyprus and let the Turks use the Akrotiri base to launch the operation. The idea was to land a token force and, if the Sampson Government did not capitulate, Turkish and British troops were to proceed inwards from Limassol.[12] Wilson later recalled, 'He asked us to allow him to use the Sovereign Base at Akrotiri for the purpose. He received a courteous, but declaratory "no".'[13]

During his telephone call, Callaghan asked the Americans to put pressure on their clients in Athens to get rid of Sampson. Kissinger sent Sisco to London to consult with the Turkish and British leaders. Ecevit was adamant that if Sampson did not go, military action would have to be taken. He did not believe the Greeks could defend Cyprus against a Turkish landing, and he calculated that he could afford to leave 70 percent of his forces on the Aegean front to deter Greek retaliation.[14] Callaghan warned him that Turkish military action would mean war with Greece, and would be very damaging for NATO.

When Turkish officials informed the Turkish Cypriots that there had been no progress in the London talks, Denktash sent a stern message back, warning that they were losing time because the Americans appeared to be saying that the issue had been settled. The reply was, 'Don't worry, Turkey is making the necessary contacts'. The next day, 19 July, the Turkish Cypriots were told, 'Tomorrow morning at dawn we are coming'.[15]

Meanwhile in London, on 18 July, Ecevit agreed to delay his return to Ankara so that he could consult with Sisco, but would only do so privately at the Turkish Embassy. When Wilson pressed Ecevit to say whether Turkey would take military action, all Ecevit would say was that the Turks would do all they could to 'restore the equilibrium' on the island, and that they would safeguard the security of Turkey and the Turkish Cypriots. American papers reported that the Turkish navy had moved into the waters between Turkey and Cyprus, that landing craft were being moved to Mersin and Iskenderun, that an armoured division was making its way towards the ports from its base in Adana, and that around 90,000 troops were on the move.[16]

~22~

AMERICA'S VETO

Kissinger Blocks Military Deterrent

W hen Ecevit met Sisco, he told him that Sampson must go, the Greek officers must be recalled, and Turkey must have a military footing on Cyprus with access to the sea. Sisco, an experienced Middle East negotiator, had come armed with nothing capable of dissuading the Turks from sending in their forces – nothing to match Johnson's 1964 letter, which he himself had helped pen, or the 1967 promise to force Greece to remove all forces in excess of its treaty quota. Just as Kissinger did nothing to reverse the coup, which he accepted would inevitably provoke a Turkish military intervention, neither did his right-hand man in the region put any credible pressure on Ecevit not to go ahead with an invasion. Sisco merely pleaded with Ecevit not to take action before he returned from Athens, where he was offering to put Turkey's demands for a stake in Cyprus to the Greeks, in case the junta might concede without Ankara having to fight the war. Ecevit told Sisco he had to have an answer by the next day.[1]

When Sisco left for Greece, Callaghan and Wilson warned Ecevit that Britain expected Turkey not to resort to arms. But Ecevit made no promises. Wilson recalled, 'He and his team returned home, but we were sure that we had not heard the last of him'.[2]

On Cyprus, Sampson's troops, having already arrested more than 1000 opponents, began a massive hunt for left-wing and pro-Makarios politicians. They seemed oblivious to the Turkish threat – enough troops and landing craft were assembled on Turkey's southern coast to be able to crush Sampson's forces with ease. Turkey's Aegean fleet had entered the Mediterranean, where British, American and Soviet ships were converging on Cyprus. At military airports in Turkey, fighter aircraft and parachute units were standing by. At Mersin, opposite Cyprus, thousands of troops moved into the coastal forests and encamped. In one bay, 15 transport ships were being loaded with equipment.[3] In a show of political strength, the Turkish Government announced that it was extending its claim of sovereignty over the continental shelf in the Aegean to take in an extra 2.5 million acres in areas claimed by Greece.

During 18 and 19 July, Wilson and Callaghan were in Paris for talks with Giscard D'Estaing, but Ecevit's threats weighed on their minds. A British submarine, *Onslaught*, was sent from Malta to join the Cyprus task-force. The Turkish military build-up made the Greek colonels jittery. Late on 18 July, they made their first concession. At the NATO meeting in Brussels, they announced that the 650 Greek officers commanding the Cypriot National Guard would be replaced, starting within days, though they still denied any responsibility for the coup. In Britain, MPs accused the Government and other NATO countries of going soft on the junta in not insisting on the withdrawal rather than the replacement of the Greek officers. 'This country appears to be siding with the line alleged now to be taken by Dr Kissinger,' said Liberal MP Emlyn Hooson, referring to reports that Kissinger said Makarios was a 'spent political force'.

The Soviets suspected that the the coup had been masterminded by NATO because it did not like the island's non-alignment and independence, and accused NATO members of preventing the UN Security Council from taking any decisive action over Cyprus. Since the coup, the Security Council had failed to respond to Cypriot calls for an immediate resolution demanding a ceasefire and condemnation of Greek intervention. Britain initially led demands for unequivocal support for Makarios as Cyprus's legitimate head of government, but gave way to US pressure to stall any decision on recognising the new Government in Nicosia and prevent any resolution being passed which blamed Greece for the coup. The Security Council meeting was postponed for five days.

The Secretary General of the Commonwealth, Arnold Smith, who demanded British action at the UN, recalled, 'The British told me they would not act in the Security Council unless Kissinger agreed in advance… Instead, they hesitated while Kissinger sent his envoy to talk with the Greek Colonels and the Turkish Government. The opportunity was lost'[4] (see Appendix).

Kissinger's delaying tactics were fiercely criticised by junior Washington officials, who believed his decision to seek a postponement, ostensibly to wait until all the facts were in, gave Sampson's forces a critical breathing-space in which to secure their control of the island. They suggested that had the Security

Council ordered an immediate ceasefire, Archbishop Makarios might have succeeded in holding a part of the island. But with the Sampson regime now in full control, the question was whether the United States had given the new Government *de facto* recognition.[5]

In fact, the Americans seemed to be doing everything they could to help the Turks make up their mind that intervention was the only way they could get satisfaction. On 19 July, the State Department conceded for the first time that there had been 'outside intervention on Cyprus, after officials revealed that their embassy in Athens had 'recently' sent Kissinger details of the junta's involvement in the Nicosia coup.[6] Ecevit also revealed that Sisco assured him in London that American aid, which had been cut back, would be resumed – despite Turkey's military preparations.[7]

However, when the UN Security Council finally met on 19 July, it embarrassed Washington by agreeing to receive Makarios in his capacity of President of Cyprus. Addressing the Security Council, Makarios said Greece's military junta had extended its dictatorship to Cyprus without a trace of respect for the independence and sovereignty of the republic. The coup was clearly not an internal matter, but an invasion from outside, which would prove catastrophic for Cyprus. He urged the Security Council to use all the means at its disposal so that the democratic rights of the Cypriot people could be reinstated without delay.

The Turkish representative said Turkey considered it its duty to make use of the rights conferred on it by international treaties. As Britain had already spurned Ankara's request for joint action, this was a clear indication that Turkey wanted to intervene unilaterally. When the British Ambassador in Ankara demanded an assurance that Ecevit was not about to land troops on Cyprus, he was told that no order to attack had been given. The British read this ambiguous answer as an admission of intent.[8] During the night of 19 July, British forces in the Eastern Mediterranean prepared to defend the sovereign bases against a possible Turkish invasion, and Admiral Cassidy was flown from *Hermes* into Akrotiri to direct the operation.

Harold Wilson was woken up at 3am in Durham, where he was due to address the annual Miners' Gala, with an urgent warning that the Turks were on the verge of invading Cyprus. As a precaution, he asked the Ministry of Defence to prepare a schedule of the position of all ships and RAF units near Cyprus, and asked for RAF transport to be ready to take him to London at short notice if the need arose. He then went back to bed. In the small hours, a large Turkish amphibious force headed for Cyprus.[9]

As news of Turkish paratroop landings on Cyprus spread, the focus of criticism of America's handling of the crisis switched from its failure to reverse the coup to its failure to avert Turkish military intervention. Why had the Americans allowed events to develop to the point where one NATO ally was able to invade a neutral state in which two other NATO members had a significant political or military stake? Did they not know of the risk of Turkish action? Were they unable to do anything about it? Or did they encourage it to happen?

When congressmen set out to investigate these questions, they started from the belief that there must have been a serious failure of the US intelligence services in the run-up to the invasion. It would have been serious indeed if they were right, because the Americans and the British had an entire network of sophisticated intelligence-gathering facilities in the region, including on Cyprus, which was specifically designed to detect military threats. In fact, the CIA's own post-mortem on the crisis said electronic intelligence was widely used after the overthrow of Makarios, and played a 'major role' in monitoring the build-up of Turkish military forces for the Cyprus landing. The Americans had their own Foreign Broadcast Information Service monitoring stations on Cyprus, which were part of the CIA's monitoring network, and the post-mortem reported that 'FBIS... offered timely (and necessary) coverage throughout the period'.[10] Also situated on the island were the British spying stations and tracking facilities whose function was to eavesdrop on military communications and spot the movement of aircraft. The information they provided was shared with the Americans. The Americans could not have missed the movement of 90,000 Turkish troops and an armada of landing craft to the coast opposite Cyprus. Such a failure would have raised serious questions about the strategic value of the intelligence investment in the island.

Just as there was no shortage of electronic intelligence reports of Turkish troop movements, there was no lack of CIA warnings of the impending invasion, nor of similar reports from US diplomats in Nicosia and Ankara. There were also numerous media reports and eye-witness accounts of the build-up of invasion forces on Turkey's southern coast. The mounting evidence prompted calls from within the State Department for US action to deter the Turks. This was confirmed by the director of the State Department's Bureau of Intelligence and Research, William Hyland, who said, 'The initial landing – the warning that it might occur – was well known to the State Department'.[11]

The congressmen discovered, however, that the problem had not been whether the United States had sufficient foreknowledge of the Turkish threat, but who was told about it. The CIA in Turkey and Cyprus saw clear evidence of preparations for an amphibious landing, and warnings were passed to the State Department. But key National Security Council and State Department officials complained that they had not been alerted. The State Department's Cyprus Desk was not told. Neither was Tasca. As Ambassador to Greece, he ought to have been the main line of communication between Washington and Athens, with the task of convincing the colonels that they must back down from the coup to avoid a Turkish military backlash. Similarly, Tasca was not kept fully informed of talks Kissinger and Sisco had with Ecevit, and the latter's determination to achieve a military foothold on Cyprus. Tasca found out some details second-hand, but no-one told him what the policy was. Neither was he told the content of crucial telephone conversations between Kissinger and Callaghan in the days after the coup.

Tasca blamed this withholding of information on 'the manner in which the State Department operates under Kissinger and the approach that Kissinger has in the flow of information and intelligence to various official levels of the department, and other departments'. He added, 'I do not think it is a healthy way to operate'.[12]

Members of the US Select Committee on Intelligence could not understand why, though Tasca had not been told of the danger of a coup, the Turks went ahead and massed troops for an invasion; why, when American officials were given assurances that the coup was off, the Turks carried on their military build-up; why, though the administration was given intelligence reports of the gathering of Turkish troops and ships, these were kept from Tasca and other key officials; and why, unlike on previous occasions, no effective steps were taken to deter the Turks from invading. They said the suggestion was that the Turks knew about the coup in advance, wanted to use the moment to secure a military foothold, and knew they were not going to be stopped by the Americans or the British.[13]

This conclusion was reinforced by Tasca's account of what happened when he began to fear the worst about Ankara's intentions. He went directly to Kissinger and urged him to interpose the Sixth Fleet between Cyprus and Turkey to prevent an invasion. But Kissinger accused him of getting hysterical, and slapped him down[14] (see Appendix). Representative Murphy concluded that 'with the invasion plans taking place in Turkey, with the CIA talking to the chief conspirator behind the coup on Cyprus, and our Ambassador left out of it entirely, our intelligence knew the invasion was coming and we deliberately denied the Ambassador this information. One might conclude further that we favoured the invasion.'[15]

Once it was clear that the Turks were preparing to invade, there were two courses of action that Washington could have taken to put a lid on the crisis. They could have moved decisively to compel Ioannides to remove the coup leaders in Nicosia and restore constitutional order, and they could have sent in a powerful naval force to deter a Turkish landing in the meantime. So how did the principal agent of Kissinger's will in the region, Sisco, deal with Greece and Turkey in the days before the invasion? According to press reports of his visit to Athens, Sisco did not even discuss the question of restoring Makarios. He merely warned of the dangers of not making concessions.[16] If the reports are true, Sisco did not even put Turkey's full demands to the Greeks. Despite the intelligence reports of Turkish military movements, Sisco did not convince Ioannides that he should take Turkey's sabre-rattling seriously. Tasca only met Ioannides on 19 July and, because he too had been kept in the dark, did not warn the junta leader that drastic action was needed to hold off the Turks.[17] Before then, all American contact with the Greek dictator had been made by the CIA station chief in Athens. The night before the Turkish invasion, Ioannides's acting Foreign

Minister still believed the Turks would accept that Sampson's seizure of power was an internal struggle between the Greeks on the island, and would not invade.[18]

Consequently, members of the Greek Government were shocked to hear a report from a BBC correspondent in Athens that five Turkish destroyers and 31 landing craft had put to sea. Later press reports said 20 medium-sized landing-craft, carrying more than 30 tanks, five small landing craft, five warships and two large troop transports filled with soldiers were heading for Cyprus.[19] But Ioannides, when plotting the coup on Cyprus, appeared to have made no contingency arrangements to prevent a Turkish invasion in response.

The Greek dictator was not the only party misinformed about the seriousness of the Turkish threat: the British and even the Pentagon had been misled by assurances from the State Department. Pentagon officials complained that they had been persuaded to discount an imminent landing by diplomats. They had been assured that Sisco could talk Turkey out of it.[20] Sisco had also persuaded the British that the Turks would hold off, at least until 21 July.

Furthermore, there were suspicions that the Americans had actually encouraged the Turks to invade – not least because when Sisco returned to Ankara he again made no threats of punitive action. His tactics were, first, to plead that an invasion would be disastrous for NATO, which Turkey relied on for its defence; then, when this did not work, to offer to come up with an American plan, an offer which lacked credibility because a similar move had failed in 1964.[21] The effect was to convince the Turks at the very moment of opportunity that the Americans were not going to do anything concrete to stop them going in. They lost no time, and Sisco was forced to hurry to the airport lest he be caught in the country when the invasion began.

Ball, who rated Johnson's 1964 note as a diplomatic 'atom bomb', dismissed Sisco's shuttle mission as worthless. He said, 'He wasn't armed with enough in the way of American leverage to be able to accomplish anything with the Ankara government and they went ahead'.[22] He must have wondered if the Americans were trying to achieve by manipulation what he had secretly proposed to force Greece and Turkey to do in 1964, to divide Cyprus between them and safeguard the use of its military facilities for the West. Strong evidence that Washington wanted the invasion came in the intelligence post-mortem. It found that in five out of six developments before and during the crisis, State Department initiatives – or the lack of them – were consistent with intelligence reports, the one exception being over the first Turkish invasion. 'The intelligence warning of that event appears to have been explicit, but the State Department apparently did not act on it,' the post-mortem said.[23]

The one other power that had a legal right, under the Treaty of Guarantee, to sort out the problems on the island was Britain. The treaty had been set up in the first place to prevent precisely the threat of attempted union with Greece or partition by Ankara and had been accepted because Britain – as the third, but most powerful, guarantor power – provided the necessary safeguard against either scenario. During the 1974 crisis, the British Government therefore came under heavy criticism for its failure to act decisively, in particular for its failure to deploy military forces to deter the Turkish invasion. When challenged on this question, Callaghan insisted that he had no advance knowledge of the two stages of Turkey's invasion.

Clerides has accused him of lying on this issue. He recalled that the Greek Cypriots obtained regular reports from several sources that the Turks were building up their forces, that Turkish troops had embarked on ships, and even that the commander of the force had been sighted, wearing binoculars. 'We noticed the concentration of ships in the Turkish harbours near Cyprus and we noticed the movement of troops towards the same area. Then the information came that the troops were loading. They had actually gone on board. All that, we knew,' said Clerides.[24] British intelligence had all the information they needed on the build-up from their intelligence facilities, the BBC monitoring station on the island and reports in *The Times*, *Guardian* and *Daily Telegraph*. The build-up would have been easily spotted by reconnaissance planes operating from Akrotiri or elsewhere in the Mediterranean. The select committee of British MPs investigating the crisis said it would have been obvious even to the most casual observer that tanks and armour were being amassed and loaded onto warships. They did not mention that the island housed some of the most sophisticated electronic spying facilities for just such detection work.

The MPs then focused on what action Britain could have taken to prevent the invasion. They suggested to Callaghan that it would have been a perfectly easy solution to station *Hermes* off the north coast of the island to block the Turkish ships and stop them landing tanks and troops on Cyprus. But he dodged the question: 'I am not here to comment on military matters'. Dissatisfied, the MPs pressed him further. MP William Rees-Davies insisted, 'Had you in fact stationed *Hermes* to the north, there with the cover that you then had, both air and other logistic support, it would effectively have prevented the Turks from their second invasion'. But Callaghan stonewalled. The MP pressed him once more: 'Surely that must be a matter you considered at the time?' Callaghan suggested the MP might be a better judge than he of military capabilities. 'Whether the *Hermes* or the Turks would have succeeded, I do not know. It would, of course, have meant war between Turkey and Britain.'[25]

According to Clerides, the action suggested by the MPs had been proposed by Britain on a previous occasion. He recalled being present in 1964 when the British warned the Cyprus Government that a number of destroyers had been spotted by the RAF steaming towards Cyprus. 'I remember the incident very well,' he said. 'I was asleep in Makarios's office – I was on night duty – when I received a call from the British military attache, who said he had to speak to Makarios, it was very urgent. I said if I knew the nature of the conversation I'd wake him up. He told me he wanted to give some information about the movement of Turkish warships and I immediately woke up Makarios. A proposal was made to us that we should withdraw our forces from the coast and allow British forces to be deployed to the north of Kyrenia, so they would be interposed between us and the Turks to avoid a direct clash.'[26]

The MPs accused the Government, and Callaghan in particular, of lightly casting aside Britain's duty to intervene as a guarantor power. But evidence has emerged that in fact the Government looked long and hard at taking military action, but was unable to do so for lack of American support. Tom McNally, political adviser to Callaghan at this crucial time, said the Foreign Secretary did feel there was a treaty obligation that Britain should try to carry out.[27] But ministers were divided on whether to go ahead: the one thing they agreed on was that Britain did not have the firepower in the area to deter the Turks on its own. Callaghan later conceded as much when asked whether Britain had reinforced the area at that time. He told MPs, 'Reinforced is a word one uses in connection with potential military operations. We were not thinking of potential military operations by ourselves.' He avoided mentioning whether they were thinking of military operations with someone else. This is because behind the scenes Callaghan repeatedly urged the Americans to take joint military action, but Washington vetoed any such move.

The British had in fact made rapid contingency plans to cover three main objectives. These were to help deter Greek or Turkish military action that might exacerbate the crisis and trigger a wider war; to defend the sovereign base areas and the strategically crucial intelligence and radar facilities on the island; and to protect British troops and citizens. For these purposes, British ships had been sailing eastwards through the Mediterranean since the day after the coup. By 18 July, a British task-force comprising *Hermes*, the guided-missile destroyer *Devonshire*, one frigate and an auxiliary support, had reached the island and were patrolling off its coast. The submarine *Onslaught* and another frigate joined them over the next two days. Between them they carried tanks, helicopters and more than 3300 troops, including crack marine commandos, which could double the number of troops at the sovereign bases and defend the intelligence facilities and strategic bomber base on Cyprus. At military briefings in Whitehall, the Navy was asked if it could interpose ships between northern Cyprus and Turkey to deter an invasion. Tom McNally recalled, 'The Navy made it clear that they could, if necessary, put the task-force in between northern Cyprus and Turkey. A small, but significant force could have been deployed. The task-force could have been ordered to move into a threatening position.'[28] It would have meant firing on Turkish ships and planes if necessary, but the Navy agreed it could be done.

However, there was considerable concern that the British force might not be an adequate deterrent on its own. Callaghan accepted that it could also have meant war between Turkey and Britain, because if the deterrent did not work the only way to stop the Turks invading would be to sink their ships. It was accepted, however, that the British task-force could contribute to a credible deterrent if there was a joint effort with the Sixth Fleet. Therefore, throughout the crisis, Britain sought US support for joint military action, having sent a task-force to prepare for it, and believing the Americans had enough military capability in the vicinity to carry out such an operation. The Sixth Fleet, which operated out of the home port in Greece, and normally included two carrier groups of about a dozen warships each. On 18 July, as the British warships steamed towards Cyprus, they detected large-scale ship and aircraft movement on their way, indicating that a group of American warships, led by the 60,000-ton aircraft-carrier *Forrestal*, and a group of US amphibious craft, was on hand in the Eastern Mediterranean, ready for action.

The British demands for joint military action have been kept secret ever since, apart from oblique references in Callaghan's memoirs. Callaghan admitted that he was afraid that if Britain acted alone in the face of US opposition it could lead to a repeat of the humiliation at Suez. Then US destroyers had moved themselves alongside Egyptian ships to stop the British firing at them. US radars had also deliberately disrupted the signals of British and French ships. 'I was determined that if military force had to be used in Cyprus there must be a clear understanding with the United States, with their support fully guaranteed,' he said. Otherwise, he believed, Britain would be courting military disaster.[29]

On 19 July, with the task-force patrolling off the coast of Cyprus, *Onslaught* was sent to the north-west of Cyprus to monitor any moves by a Turkish invasion force or other warships. With most of the ships in place, and another frigate on its way, Callaghan sent a detailed message to Kissinger calling once more for joint British-US action. His plan included the return of Makarios. But Kissinger opposed it.[30]

Publicly, Britain defended its failure to prevent an invasion on the grounds that the Turks, as guarantors, had a right to intervene. But the real reason was that Kissinger would not agree to a joint military deterrent – and no action could be effective without American support. McNally said, 'I think in the last analysis, if there is a villain of the piece – well, a real old politician – it's Henry Kissinger, with whom Jim was in close contact. The Americans were not very keen on two senior NATO partners coming to blows in the eastern Mediterranean.' McNally said the Turks had threatened that if there was any military intervention against them, they would leave NATO, but the Americans were not interested in sending anything to stop them going in at that time. McNally added, 'Kissinger made it quite clear that he was not going to see that whole eastern flank thrown into disarray and possibly into Russian hands over some rather piddling difficulty, which didn't really have an overriding sign of right on either side'[31] (see Appendix).

Callaghan's political adviser stressed that a major concern of the Americans was the safety of the eavesdropping facilities on the island, which they had always considered available for their use. 'It was made abundantly clear to us that the American priority was for full Turkish involvement in NATO and the security of the [intelligence] establishments on Cyprus, which they saw as being safe.' He said the Americans had always treated Britain's retained sites as their own, and wanted to ensure their protection. But they also felt that the Turks had come to the point where they had decided to invade, and it would not help to try to stop them. Callaghan had been ready to fly to Ankara at one point, but he was persuaded not to go by his own Foreign Office officials.[32] Julian Amery, a member of the British Government during the 1963 Cyprus troubles, said that when it came to enforcing the 1960 guarantee by military action, the Foreign Office was always 'very much guided by the United States'.[33] McNally said it was made 'quite clear that Henry Kissinger was not going to get the Americans involved and didn't think it was a good idea for Britain to get involved either'.[34]

The US refusal was devastating: it left Britain impotent. As one defence expert explained, positioning too few warships in the path of the Turks, merely as a gesture, would have been futile, since warships cannot afford to wait to re-taliate when facing a hostile force: they have to shoot first. A token force could have been embroiled in a sea battle, and lost. The task-force would have required reinforcements that would have taken a week to assemble. The alternative was to go in with the Americans in a joint operation. Their flagships alone each carried 80–90 combat aircraft,

'The only thing that would have worked is deterrence,' said McNally. 'The actual idea of a sea battle somewhere between northern Cyprus and the coast of Turkey – this only stands up if you have this indomitable British fleet turning back the marauding Turks without a shot being fired. We could have had a war in the eastern Mediterranean which we could have lost.' He remembers Mason walking down the corridor to the office carrying great bundles of files, and a civil servant observing dryly, 'There's Roy going with two hundred reasons why we can't fight'.[35]

The British were left trying to bluff Turkey into thinking they would inter-vene. Strenuous efforts were made diplomatically at the UN and around the world to persuade Ankara that British forces were moving into position. McNally said warships and planes were moved in menacing ways, but as far as he was aware there was never any note delivered to Turkey saying, 'If you do this under the Treaty of Guarantee, we'll be bound to intervene'. Instead, the tactic was simply to let Ankara know that *Hermes* was 20 miles off Cyprus. 'But the attempt at bluff was dismissed by the Turks because they were clear the Americans were not involved at all in the exercise,' he said. 'Undoubtedly with American support we could have intervened. We moved ships around and pre-tended, but whether the Americans were telling the Turks I don't know – they never looked very frightened'. He believed that once they had a clear idea that the Americans were not going to do anything to stop them this time round they decided to go ahead.[36]

The rationale Kissinger gave Callaghan for avoiding joint military action was not that it was not possible, but that he feared the result would be the loss of Turkey from NATO. This was a reasonable assumption in the light of the dis-trust of the West generated in Ankara by Johnson's 1964 letter. But this begs the question why did Kissinger allow the crisis to reach the point where a Turkish invasion was inevitable? Why did he fail to deter the junta from staging a coup in Cyprus, and then resist international efforts to force Sampson to stand down? Why did he issue no credible threats to deter Turkey from the intervention this would provoke? Kissinger's action ensured the Turks knew their only hope of keeping the Greeks off Cyprus was to intervene militarily themselves, as was their right under the Treaty of Guarantee. Despite the culminating crisis over Watergate in Washington, Kissinger chose to act against the advice of experts[37] in his own department, and in a way that ran the greatest risk of provoking a legally justifiable Turkish military intervention in Cyprus. If the Greeks had been in a position to counter-attack, the confrontation would have spelled disaster for NATO. It would have deprived the alliance of crucial military facilities in Greece and Turkey and dramatically loosened its grip on the eastern Mediterranean, a strategically crucial oil route for the West that was under constant threat from the potentially explosive situation in the Middle East. NATO had already been weakened by Wilson's decision to look for heavy cuts in defence spending. But war between Greece and Turkey would render NATO's entire south-eastern wing inoperable and create a political vacuum in the eastern Mediterranean which Moscow would be only too willing to exploit. Such a crisis would dramatically shift the strategic balance between East and West.

The most logical explanation of why Kissinger pulled his punches with the Turks is that he believed the threat of Greece going to war over such a move could be contained (see Appendix). According to Clerides, the Turks later insisted that they had even given NATO a plan for dividing the island before the first invasion.[37] And the Americans knew that Greece, presiding over a disorganised, badly-supplied army, and with its airforce out of range of Cyprus, was in no position to prevent an invasion. It was as if the secret US plans of 1964 had been played out – in Turkey's favour.

~23~

THE TURKISH LANDING

Britain on the Brink of War

At 4.20am on 20 July 1974, Kissinger rang to tell Callaghan that the Turks were invading Cyprus. Callaghan hurriedly dressed and rushed to Downing Street. Wilson was flown straight to London. Callaghan's first task was to contact the Greek, Turkish and Soviet Ambassadors to try to prevent the crisis escalating into an explosive regional conflict. When Wilson arrived, he consulted Mason and Callaghan, and later a wider group of ministers along with the Chief of the Defence Staff, Field Marshal Michael Carver, who had been deputy UN Commander in Cyprus in 1964. They ordered the reinforcement of the British bases with more fighter aircraft. Wilson said in his memoirs that he now directed ships from the Atlantic and elsewhere in the Mediterranean to move towards Cyprus, but in fact most of the British task-force had already reached the island, and other vessels were already on their way. British commandos were flown into Akrotiri to secure the bases and spy sites, and to help get Britons off the island. The task-force was not used for the intention Callaghan had hoped it would – joint action with the Americans to deter the Turks. This left British troops powerless to intervene in the conflict, but they still had the perilous task of defending Britain's strategic facilities, and a key role

187

in the UN peace-keeping force – and within days they faced a threat that was to bring Britain to the brink of war with its NATO ally.

From dawn on 20 July, as Turkish aircraft bombed Greek-Cypriot forces, more than 30 Turkish troopships and landing craft, protected by destroyers, off-loaded 6000 troops, along with tanks and trucks, at Kyrenia. Hundreds of para-troops were dropped around Nicosia and in the mountains between the capital and Kyrenia. Ecevit announced that he had sent the troops into Cyprus for peace not war, that the aim was not to invade Cyprus but to end an invasion. In Cyprus, Denktash said the landing was a limited action, directed against the Greek junta, not Greek Cypriots.

Sampson had made scant military preparations to repel the Turks. It was as if he didn't expect them to come in. The Cyprus Broadcasting Corporation, con-trolled by his regime, had told the public that the rumours of an invasion were irresponsible, and that they need not worry. The Cyprus Secret Service was in disarray, since many of its members, including its leader, had gone into hiding to avoid being captured by the coupists. National Guard camps in the area had all been moved to Nicosia, Limassol and Paphos, for operations against pro-Makarios forces. Only on 19 July did Sampson begin to move tanks and troops north to face the Turks. Then, in a desperate attempt to muster defences, he freed 10,000 loyalists arrested by his men.

After bitter fighting with Greek-Cypriot forces, the Turkish paratroops joined up with Turkish-Cypriot fighters guarding the fortress of St Hilarion and the 650-man Turkish contingent based just north of the capital, in an attempt to secure the Kyrenia-Nicosia road. AKEL, the communist movement, claimed that Greek Cypriots had been betrayed by the Greek National Guard, because when radar screens showed the Turks approaching, some officers called for defence plans to be put into action, but no measures were taken.

The Greek junta was also taken by surprise, and was hopelessly unprepared. Only four of its 12 divisions were at war strength, and these were based in northern Greece or near Athens. The colonels immediately announced a general mobilisation, but it took two days to complete. According to one report, when the Greeks unpacked their stores of rifles bought from America they found the containers held only stones.[1]

Clerides believed the junta was duped by the CIA into thinking the Turks would not go in. He said that Ioannides, and Papadopoulos before him, had dealt throughout their career with the CIA in Athens, and made the mistake of iden-tifying American policy with the CIA. 'They relied much more on what the CIA told them, because they were the people they knew. The State Department was some distance from them,' said Clerides. 'I think probably the CIA gave them the impression that if they ousted Makarios, they would not allow Turkey to invade. Why do I come to that conclusion? The junta was panic-stricken once the Turkish army invaded and they could not co-ordinate their efforts. They ordered an army and submarines to Cyprus. But when the four submarines arrived outside Kyrenia they were recalled. The army ignored its orders and prepared to march on Athens to oust Ioannides. They were completely disordered. They did not know what sort of action to take, because they had obviously relied on some assurance that if they ousted Makarios, then America would hold Turkey at bay.'[2]

Their naivete contrasted with Karamanlis's appraisal of the Greek defensive capability in 1958, when he admitted to NATO allies that Greece could never defend Cyprus militarily.[3] Athens could only have brought all or part of Cyprus under its direct control if the Turks agreed to it – in the kind of deal that Ball and Acheson proposed in 1964.

As the Turkish paratroops advanced on Nicosia airport, heavy street fighting broke out in the Turkish sector of the city. Turkish jets bombed Greek-Cypriot areas in the capital and wiped out two National Guard armoured columns, heading north to reinforce Greek Cypriots at Kyrenia. One source said 68 Turkish soldiers were killed in the first three hours after the invasion.[4]

At the first sign of military intervention, the Americans and Soviets rushed warships into the area. The Americans ordered *Forrestal* and six destroyers to form a task-force and proceed to Cypriot waters. The Sixth Fleet's flagship, the cruiser *Little Rock*, and the amphibious warship *Inchon*, carrying 1300 marines, steamed towards the island. The Soviets put seven airborne divisions on alert, and sent ships from the Black Sea into the Mediterranean. Henry Kissinger hastily contacted Moscow to ward off a superpower conflict. He announced that neither power would intervene militarily in the Cyprus dispute, and neither Greece nor Turkey would get fresh American arms. He had urged both sides not to go to war, but said, 'So far there is nothing to bet money on'.[5]

Neighbouring states, such as Syria and Egypt, warned their armed forces to be vigilant in case the conflict spread. The British moved warships into position. As the frigate *Andromeda* joined the task-force, *Hermes* and the frigate *Rhyl* began patrolling near the Dhekelia base, while *Andromeda* guarded the Akrotiri base approaches, to protect Britain's expensive intelligence and military facilities. RAF personnel and families were ferried by road convoy to Dhekelia.

The US State Department issued a statement: 'We regret this military action by Turkey just as we deplore the previous action by Greece that precipitated the crisis'. It was the first time they had publicly blamed Greece for the coup, but it was too little too late, and hardly likely to put Ankara off its action. Indeed American diplomats now worked frantically with the British, not to reverse the military intervention, but to put pressure on the Greeks to stop them going to war with Turkey, and the result of their efforts was to encourage Turkey to occupy a limited area of Cyprus. Sisco embarked once more on a shuttle mission between Greece and Turkey. In Athens, he faced the wrath of Ioannides, who is said to have shouted at him, 'You have betrayed us: I am going to attack Turkey'. Sisco retorted that America was the only friend Greece had left, and warned him against any military retaliation, especially across the border with Turkey. He insisted that Turkish troops should be allowed to establish lines of communication with Turkish-Cypriot enclaves and remain there until a settlement was worked out. The aim was to let the Turks establish their bridgehead without the violence spiralling into a wider conflict.[6]

By the end of the first day, the Turks had captured a strategic point overlooking the port of Kyrenia. And the original landing force had been reinforced by further waves of troops. The paratroops had seized control of a strategic pass through the mountains, establishing themselves at a number of points on the road linking Kyrenia and Nicosia. Though it was all going according to plan, the Turks were worried about rumours that a group of Greek warships had left Rhodes, which could mean Athens was about to enter the battle.[7] They sent a reconnaissance plane to check on the nationality of the mystery convoy, without success.

The fighting continued during the night and into the next morning. In Paphos, on the west coast, and Limassol, in the south, the Turkish-Cypriot garrisons surrendered. The fiercest fighting was at Nicosia airport. Greek-Cypriot forces, reinforced during the night when 200 Greek commandos were flown in, were trying to fight off advancing Turkish paratroops. The Turks wanted to stop the Greeks using the airfield to provide air cover for the landing force which was believed to be heading towards Cyprus escorted by seven destroyers. In the south, the British bases commander warned the Turks that if their fighters strayed over British sovereign territory British aircraft would intervene. He feared the Turks would attack the convoys of British families, mistaking them for Greek-Cypriot military movements. If so, the British would have to fight back.[8]

In Nicosia, the British secured a temporary ceasefire to evacuate 4000 foreigners. They left in a thousand trucks, buses and cars draped in Union Jacks and escorted by British armoured cars. But fighting left 380 civilians trapped for 30 hours inside the Ledra Palace Hotel, close to the Turkish Cypriot quarter of the capital, without food, power or water in the baking heat.

Terrible atrocities reported on each side exacerbated the situation. The Turks said the National Guard was forcing Turkish Cypriots out of some villages, and their quarters in Larnaca, Paphos and Famagusta. Turkish-Cypriot refugees fleeing the island said the Greek Cypriots took thousands of hostages, raped Turkish-Cypriot women and shot children. The Turkish Embassy in Nicosia was told of mass murders in their enclaves. The Greeks alleged indiscriminate Turkish bombardment of National Guard targets in populous areas with napalm bombs and rockets. Throughout the day, Turkish jets had targeted the Greek contingent's camp and National Guard bases. The European Commission for Human Rights was told that in one village 12 civilian men fleeing the Turkish bombing were shot in front of their wives, some while holding their children. In another incident, 17 members of two neighbouring families, including ten women and five children aged between two and nine, were killed. Their bodies were found in a yard. There were numerous other cases.[9]

Newspapers reported that Turkey was trying to seize the northern half of Cyprus, including Kyrenia, and parts of Nicosia and Famagusta. Having over-run Kyrenia, its forces bombed Greek-Cypriot positions in the mountains above the port. The seizure of the road to the capital enabled them to link up with their paratroops on the plain north of Nicosia, opening up a supply route to the city's Turkish-Cypriot enclave and troops attacking the airport. Their tactics bore a remarkable resemblance to those in the contingency plan drawn up by the Americans in 1964, in which the Kyrenia-Nicosia road marked the eastern boundary of the area earmarked for Turkish occupation. This area, extending from Nicosia to the north and west of the capital, contained more than half the island's 120,000 Turkish-Cypriot population. The degree to which the Turkish-Cypriot fighters were armed seemed to imply careful co-ordination between them and Ankara before the invasion. The Turkish Cypriots had Sten guns, Thomson sub-machine-guns, mortars, BREN guns, heavy machine-guns and Lee Enfield 303s – and large supplies of ammunition.[10]

The fighting brought Greece and Turkey to the brink of war, both massing troops and tanks along their common border in Thrace. Greece was funnelling troops onto the islands opposite Turkey, and the Turks were concentrating forces opposite Cyprus. Following the announcement of mobilisation in Greece, civilians in Athens rushed to the shops to stock up on food, fearing the worst. The UN Security Council tried to calm the situation by calling for an immediate ceasefire and immediate withdrawal of all foreign troops above the limits set by the independence treaties. It urged the three guarantor powers to start immediate talks to restore peace and constitutional government in Cyprus.

The British continued to strengthen their task-force. Two auxiliary tankers joined the force on 21 July, and the following day another British frigate, Brighton, was sent from Gibraltar to join Hermes off Cyprus. In the meantime, the crack troops of 41 Commando battalion landed with 14 four-ton trucks to bolster the sovereign bases' defences. The task-force also brought an infantry battalion, an armoured reconnaissance regiment, a squadron of Dragoon guards and a squadron of Royal Horse Guards. Some units were redeployed to the UN force, leaving the strength of the reinforced base garrisons at 5553.[11]

But it was the Americans who took the lead in the frantic behind-the-scenes diplomacy to stave off war. In Athens, Sisco pressed the Greeks to remove Sampson in favour of Clerides, and offer more guarantees for the safety of the Turkish Cypriots.[12] In Ankara, Sisco told the Turks there were two conditions for the Greeks choosing talks in London instead of war: an immediate ceasefire, and agreement to confine the invasion force to specific areas.[13] These conditions also closely echoed the Americans' own 1964 contingency plan. However, the Turks insisted that Greece should recall its convoy, pull its troops out of Turkish-Cypriot enclaves, and order the Greek and Greek-Cypriot forces to cease offensive operations. The Greeks had threatened to leave NATO and declare war on Turkey if it did not end its action in Cyprus within 48 hours. The threat gained credibility because the Turks believed the mystery convoy heading for Cyprus comprised up to nine ships, some of them destroyers.[14]

The convoy threw Kissinger's efforts to control the situation into confusion. Sisco hurried back to Athens to discover whether the Greeks really were set on a course for war. When he arrived, Sisco found the junta fragmenting on the issue. Though Ioannides told him Greece would declare war unless the Turks accepted his terms for a ceasefire, leading Greek commanders recognised their lack of readiness to take on the second-largest army in NATO. One said it would be madness to go to war in the face of US opposition. Crucially, the head of the Third Army Corps, General Ioannis Davos, would not agree to it, and blocked a purge of officers who favoured an unconditional ceasefire.[15] As the night wore on, Sisco found it increasingly difficult to contact members of the Greek Government to negotiate a ceasefire. Athens was rife with rumours that some of the leaders were about to be ousted by a coup. Tanks rumbled through the streets. At a Washington Special Action Group meeting, Kissinger told policy-makers he did not think the junta would survive. Sisco contacted four or five Greek leaders before he was satisfied that they had agreed to halt military action.

As the colonels dealt with loyal junior officers, by-passing the traditional military elite, the generals had not even been told in advance about the Cyprus coup. But when the Turks invaded, they regained their authority with the new military imperatives. Dismayed by the recklessness with which Ioannides had moved on Cyprus – without regard to the parlous state into which he had let his armed forces fall – they found willing agents of his demise in the American administration. He had served his usefulness to Washington in getting rid of Makarios and giving the Turks a legitimate excuse to seize a military foothold in Cyprus, but he had to be removed before he wreaked havoc in NATO. Nixon had drafted a letter as threatening to the Greeks as Johnson's famous letter to the Turks in 1964 to warn Ioannides off war with Turkey. But by the second day of the invasion, Ioannides was no longer taking part in the Greek-American meetings. On the third day, Kissinger told the press he thought Ioannides's days were over, which some believed convinced the Greek generals that the United States would back them if they tried to force a change in leadership. Davos presented a petition in which 40 of his officers supported a call for a return to civilian rule.[16]

The Turks knew the Greeks were split, but feared the hawks would go off and declare war on their own. Radio reports from Athens continued to warn that Greece would declare war if the Turkish intervention was not stopped. This accentuated the apparent threat from the mystery convoy. The Turks rushed three destroyers towards the north-western tip of Cyprus, where they expected to find the Greek warships. On their way they fought with three Greek gun-boats, but found no convoy and carried on southwards towards Paphos. Kissinger at this point was worried that the whole Cyprus situation could blow up in his face. He sent an urgent message through Tasca to the Greek Prime Minister pressing for a ceasefire. The Americans had several warships off the south-east coast to ward off trouble. But their own intelligence could not confirm the presence of a Greek convoy. When Turkish warplanes were sent by the dozen to attack the ships, they hit three of their own destroyers, fatally damaging one of them. The convoy was never found, and the destroyers were attacked because they did not give the right answer when challenged by the Turkish pilots. It was hard to distinguish a Greek destroyer from a Turkish one visually, because both countries had the same supplier – the United States. Turkish commanders were devastated by the self-inflicted disaster, but realised that matters could have been much worse if their pilots had mistakenly attacked the British or American ships positioned nearby.[17]

The mystery naval threat made Kissinger anxious to secure a ceasefire, to kill any possibility of the junta going to war. But he encouraged the Turks to treat it as only an interim step (see Appendix). The Americans' long-term interest was to keep Cyprus and its military facilities available for American use. But the immediate imperative was to prevent the junta rallying the Greeks behind them in a war against Turkey. That would have been disastrous for NATO's southern wing. He told Callaghan that if necessary he would use the nuclear stick to beat Ecevit into line. In his memoirs he said that during the night of 21–22 July he forced a ceasefire by threatening Turkey that the Americans would move nuclear weapons from forward positions – especially where they might be involved in a war with Greece.[18] He claimed it stopped Turkish military operations while they occupied only a small part of the island. Yet the operations did not stop that night. And Turkish accounts give a very different story.

Callaghan recalled that at 4.25pm (British time) on 21 July, the Greek Foreign Minister rang in an agitated state, alarmed by Turkish bombings of Greek-Cypriot positions, and warned that Greece would have to attack Turkey if a ceasefire was not agreed immediately. Callaghan said Kissinger responded at once to the Greek ultimatum and at 4.50 told the British Foreign Secretary that he had issued his threat to Ecevit, specifying that the United States would remove nuclear weapons from Thrace and Anatolia if there was no ceasefire. But Callaghan could not understand why the Turkish premier, who came on the line the moment Kissinger had put the phone down, seemed unaffected by the threat, and even said he wanted to postpone the ceasefire. Ecevit claimed he was worried that a pro-Soviet administration might be in power in Athens by the next day, a concern that he was fed to him by Kissinger, with whom he was in constant contact.[19]

In fact, the Turks felt a ceasefire, once they had established a secure foothold, would not only defuse the threat from Greece but give themselves time to reinforce their bridgehead ready for the second part of their planned two-stage operation. And they were convinced that Kissinger was encouraging them to view it this way. According to Turkish writer Mehmet Ali Birand, Kissinger said, 'It was essential for you to seize a bridgehead and this you have done. Now, you will have to await reinforcements before you can advance further.' He offered to talk to the Greeks to get the guarantees the Turks said they needed for the safety of their troops on Cyprus before they would agree to a ceasefire.[20] The implication was that Kissinger approved of the Turkish landing, and accepted that any cease-fire would only be temporary, to allow the Turks to prepare to take more territory (see Appendix). The Americans were channelling the occupation along similar lines to the 1964 US contingency plan, which proposed limiting such an invasion to a triangular area between Kyrenia on the north coast, the Turkish-Cypriot quarter of Nicosia and Lefka in the north-west.[21]

The Turks were astonished by Kissinger's detailed knowledge of events on the ground in Cyprus and Athens. This does not accord with Kissinger's claim that he was out of the picture on Cyprus because of the distraction of Watergate (see Appendix). Kissinger himself admitted later that he had secured special priority for cables about the Cyprus crisis so that he could be kept informed. The Turks said Kissinger seemed to know exactly what land the Turkish troops had taken and, according to a high-ranking officer, he suggested more than once that more reinforcements could be sent to Cyprus after the ceasefire, and small terri-torial changes could be made to strengthen their position. Kissinger told Ecevit on the telephone, 'Your bridgehead is strengthened, your reinforcements are about to land on the island, and can continue to do so after the ceasefire. In short you have time to take all measures necessary for your security' (see Appendix). So assiduously had Kissinger organised international pressure that as soon as he rang off, first Wilson, followed by the NATO Secretary General then other NATO leaders, called to demand a ceasefire. Before midnight, Kissinger called Callaghan with the news that Ecevit had agreed to a ceasefire at 2pm the next day.[22]

The Turks had held out for five hours longer than the Greeks. During that time, Kissinger's aides thought there was still a 50-50 chance of war breaking out, and Kissinger spoke to Nixon three times on the issue. When the ceasefire was announced, Kissinger had been negotiating non-stop for about 48 hours, starting in San Clemente, Nixon's West Coast White House, and continuing in Washington. Throughout, he had been in constant touch by telephone with Ecevit, the junta's 'premier', Adamantios Androutsopoulos, Callaghan and Sisco. Kissinger's aides said he talked to the Greek and Turkish premiers ten times or more each during the 23 hours before the announcement. He also spoke repeatedly to British leaders and to the French and German Foreign Ministers. The British Foreign Office confirmed that Callaghan had spoken to Kissinger five times. Callaghan himself noted nine or ten such conversations. Callaghan had also conferred with Ecevit and the Greek Foreign Minister, Constantine Kypraios.[23]

Having agreed to a ceasefire deadline, the Turks tried to secure the fall of Kyrenia as quickly as they could, and bring in reinforcements. Warships shelled Greek positions on the mountains above the town, and waves of helicopters and transport planes dropped paratroops on the slopes to secure the rear of the port. Fighting continued at either end of the Kyrenia-Nicosia road. At 1pm, Kyrenia fell to the Turks. At 4pm, with Nicosia airport still under Greek-Cypriot control, Cyprus Radio broadcast that the National Guard had ordered the Cyprus armed forces to cease fire. Artillery, naval and air attacks on Nicosia airport and Greek units at various villages continued for up to one and a half hours. Kissinger was confident that the Soviets would not get involved, and expected the junta to fall. Shortly before 5.30pm, Ankara Radio and other Turkish radio stations announced that a third coup had taken place in Greece, led by Davos. Ioannides's regime had been toppled.

By the time of the ceasefire, the Turkish army had captured Kyrenia; it had established itself in the Turkish-Cypriot quarter of Nicosia, and it controlled a 20-mile-wide corridor between there and the landing zone on the north coast. More than 30,000 Turkish troops had landed in Cyprus, and the casualties were heavy. By 23 July, not counting those lost when the Turks attacked their own ships, 57 Turkish soldiers had died, 242 were missing, and 184 wounded.[24] Ecevit declared that the Turkish presence on the island had been established 'irrevocably'. On television, he said Kyrenia was forever Turkish and that the corridor secured by his troops from the beach-head at Kyrenia to the Turkish quarter of Nicosia 'will be a permanent base of strength for the Turkish people on the island'.

The Turks had agreed to hold their fire, but not to end their intervention. Their self-assured defiance astounded the British in particular. Ecevit even threatened to use force to stall efforts to evacuate British civilians from the arena of conflict. The 17,000 Britons on Cyprus – holidaymakers, expatriates and families of servicemen – were told to seek refuge in the sovereign bases. Across the island there was pandemonium as Greek Cypriots beat a hasty retreat from the advancing Turkish forces, while at the same time Turkish Cypriots ran for their lives to avoid retribution by Greek-Cypriot troops. At Famagusta, 50 people, including some tourists, were killed when the Turkish airforce attacked a train shortly before the ceasefire. Turkish jets also strafed a road convoy of 20 vehicles taking tourists from Famagusta to the British base at Dhekelia, wounding two British soldiers.

Some British and foreign nationals found it easier to head north through Turkish-held territory in the hope of being evacuated from Kyrenia. During 22 and 23 July, the bulk of Britain's naval task-force steamed westward around Cape Andreas for this purpose. This presented Wilson and Callaghan with a problem, because the Turkish navy tried to disrupt the Royal Navy's attempts to move its warships close to the beaches to pick up the evacuees. When Callaghan protested to Ecevit, he confessed that his navy had been ordered to keep the British warships 10kms from the coastline. Callaghan then warned him that he was sending the ships in, and if there was any more trouble Ankara would have to answer for it. 'Fortunately for the Turkish ships, they did not attempt to enforce their orders,' recalled the former Foreign Secretary. *Hermes* and *Devonshire* were ordered to head for the north coast to back up *Andromeda* and *Rhyl*, which rescued the 500 evacuees in full view of the Turkish warships. Harold Wilson said the ships were used to rescue people 'threatened with a campaign of murder and pillage by the advancing Turkish forces, who sought to occupy areas of Cyprus which could not, by any stretch of the imagination, be regarded as Turkish-Cypriot territory'. In total, the RAF airlifted 9000 people out of Cyprus.

While the evacuees were being landed at Akrotiri, two Sea King heli-copters recovered 72 men, survivors of the Turkish destroyer mistakenly sunk by Turkish jets.

At 4am on Tuesday 23 July, Sampson resigned. Holed up in a hideaway in the Troodos foothills, he told his war cabinet that with the country divided, and no material support from Athens, he could not carry on. He later recalled, 'I was expecting help from Greece but we didn't get it – we got nothing. We were not covered in the air; we fought with old weapons, we had no warships.'[25] On radio, he claimed to have achieved his primary objective, the overthrow of Makarios. He was temporarily replaced by Clerides, who was constitutionally next in line to the presidency.

The fifty-four-year-old Clerides was a lawyer who had studied at the University of London. He took part in RAF bombing raids over Germany during the Second World War, and escaped from German prison camps three times. He was linked with EOKA in the days of British rule in Cyprus, but had earned the respect of many Turkish Cypriots through his role as a negotiator in the talks between the island's two communities on the future constitution. A Kissinger aide said he was well-known and popular with US officials. State Department spokesman Robert Anderson said his elevation spelled the end of the constitutional crisis that began with the Greek-inspired coup. 'The constitution is being lived up to,' he said. He would not comment on the American view of the status of Makarios, who had met Kissinger two days earlier. Makarios, at a news conference, stressed that be expected Clerides to hand back power when he returned to the island in a matter of weeks. But the Americans were suggesting behind the scenes that Makarios would have to get the agreement of Turkey and the Turkish Cypriots before he could return as President.[26]

The same day, the Greek military Government announced it was handing power back to civilian politicians. Karamanlis returned from exile in Paris to be sworn in as premier. A Macedonian-born lawyer, he served as Prime Minister between 1955 and 1963. He worked closely with the Americans during the 1950s, when Greece and Turkey, in lengthy and delicate negotiations, consented to the American idea of guaranteed independence for Cyprus which led to the 1960 agreements ending British rule. During discussions held privately at NATO meetings, he had suggested putting Cyprus under NATO trusteeship.[27] In Washington, Kissinger told the press he looked forward to close relations with the new Greek Government. Karamanlis was a conservative, but his new Government drew on political support from the right to the left of centre. The

Foreign Secretary was George Mavros, leader of the Centre Union, who, under the junta's programme of political repression, had been internally deported and forced to live on a Greek island. Averoff took over as Defence Minister. He had been Karamanlis's Foreign Minister when the 1960 agreements were signed. At one point, the junta had threatened him with five years' imprisonment for hosting a cocktail party – 'a meeting of more than five persons without police authority'. In Athens, 100,000 people flooded Constitution Square to celebrate Karamanlis's homecoming.

Their optimism soon seemed misplaced. There were ominous signs that the Turks would continue to pursue their military objectives on Cyprus. Turkish Foreign Minister Gunesh claimed the UN resolution calling for the withdrawal of all forces from Cyprus did not apply to Turkish troops. He said they were not outside forces, and would stay until legal order was established in accordance with the 1960 constitution. Ecevit said the Turkish presence was irrevocable, and deputy premier Necmettin Erbakan proposed partitioning the island on a north-west to south-east axis running from West of Kyrenia through Nicosia to Larnaca, with a neutral corridor between the two sides.[28]

Despite the ceasefire agreement, Nicosia continued to rattle with gunfire as skirmishes took place across the 'green line' dividing the two communities. A furious UN Security Council demanded that both sides observe the ceasefire, and UN troops took over Nicosia airport. They soon faced a serious threat, as Turkish tanks and troops massed around the city and closed in on the airport. It was being defended by 500 British and Canadian soldiers in the UN force. The Greeks believed if the Turks seized the airport they would take the entire capital. The UN commander in Cyprus reported that 400–500 Turkish troops, supported by tanks, had taken up positions within a few hundred yards of the airport and were threatening to overwhelm it. The UN soldiers steeled themselves for an attack. According to Clerides, the British persuaded the UN force commanders, whose soldiers were mostly British, to deploy themselves in battle order facing the area from which the Turks would approach, making it clear that they would defend it. Clerides said this was to defend an area in which the British had treaty rights connected with their defence facilities.[29]

News of the confrontation caused consternation in London, where Wilson was waiting for a crucial Commons vote on his minority government's mini-budget. Callaghan ordered British soldiers serving in the UN force to stand their ground. In an angry exchange, he told Ecevit by telephone that force would be met with force. British troops stood ready to open fire if the Turkish soldiers advanced further. He also issued orders for 1300 troops to be sent to reinforce the UN contingent, and for a detachment of between 12 and 14 Phantom fighter-bombers to be sent to RAF Akrotiri to provide air cover for them. All British forces on Cyprus were put on alert. Meanwhile, UN Secretary General Kurt Waldheim made a series of emergency calls to put pressure on Ecevit to back down. An emergency session of the UN Security Council was convened, and

Waldheim tried to round up support from the NATO Secretary General and Kissinger. But Kissinger was reluctant to get involved. Behind the scenes, the State Department was working furiously towards its own agenda, with its Cyprus 'task-force' operating round the clock. It was headed by Arthur Hartman, Assistant Secretary of State for European Affairs, who stressed in the strongest terms to ministers in the incoming Karamanlis Government that it was essential for the future settlement of Cyprus that Makarios should not return to the island.[30] Kissinger tried to calm Greek nerves by promising that Washington would do all it could to prevent further fighting. He told them that he had approached the Turks to seek assurances that there would be no more advances.

Yet, despite Kissinger's promise, the situation suddenly took a dangerous turn. Harold Wilson, nervously waiting for the budget votes to be counted, was given the devastating news that the Turks were now threatening to bomb Nicosia airport. A NATO ally was poised to wipe out British and Canadian soldiers in the UN peace-keeping force. Wilson hurried to Downing Street to telephone Ecevit and demand that he call off his troops. He told the Turkish premier that he was leading his country into a highly dangerous crisis, and ordered him to drop his plan immediately. Ecevit refused point-blank. Suddenly there was a real danger that Britain might go to war with Turkey. It was the first sharp departure from the 1964 contingency plan for a controlled Turkish invasion, which said the Turks would stay away from the airport and the airport-Nicosia road as long as the airport was not used for hostile purposes.[31]

After a tense interval, Ecevit phoned back with a chilling proposal. He said he would go ahead with the bombing, but avoid targeting the area where British troops were positioned. This meant the Canadians would come under fire but not the British. Wilson was furious. He would not allow the lives of British troops to be bartered for those of other UN soldiers. He told Ecevit that if he carried out his threat, British Phantoms would be scrambled, with orders to shoot down the Turkish bombers. When Ecevit persisted, Wilson ordered a red alert, and emergency arrangements were made to reinforce Akrotiri and get the fighters into position. Britain was on the brink of war. Callaghan remembers it as the most frightening moment of his career. A tense 90 minutes later the Turkish premier backed down. Wilson recalled, 'Had he not done so we would undoubtedly have been involved in hostilities which might well have escalated. Apart from the lunacy at Suez, that was probably the nearest that Britain came to war with another nation since 1945.'[32]

~24~

A CREEPING INVASION

Talks at Geneva

Despite Wilson's robust stance on defending the airport, doubts remained about Britain's commitment to retaining its military bases and intelligence facilities on Cyprus. In the House of Commons, on the very day that Ecevit threatened to bomb British troops, Rear-Admiral Morgan-Giles demanded to know what the Government's policy was on the future of the bases. He said Greek and Turkish decisions would be affected by the answer. Morgan-Giles said, 'All that [we know] is that the Government have for nearly five months been undertaking a defence review which throws doubt on their resolve to retain bases in the Eastern Mediterranean, particularly Cyprus and Malta, and which threatens to make cuts in defence expenditure which would make such operations impossible.' Salford MP Frank Allaun asked if the crisis would hasten the winding up of British bases on the island to save manpower and money. Mason would only confirm that deployment of British forces in Cyprus was being examined in the review of worldwide defence commitments. But McNally revealed that the British found the Cyprus bases costly, and had long wanted to wash their hands of them, but the Americans 'would not let them'. He said, 'If you look at a few of the defence reviews... if we could get out of Cyprus, the

Americans would probably have stayed there. I mean the Cyprus bases now are actually great big camouflage things for American spying.'[1]

The MPs had no knowledge of American concerns that the British might abandon the facilities – at a time when some of them were crucial to monitoring developments in Soviet missile technology as well as security problems in the region. They must have found it strange, therefore, when after the airport incident American officials claimed the Cyprus crisis had brought valuable benefits to NATO. For the Americans the successful channelling of the Turkish invasion and the continued expansion of the Turkish bridgehead – in line with Kissinger's advice to Ecevit (see Appendix) – offered the possibility that part of the island would be permanently occupied by a close NATO ally other than Britain, and available for military use if Britain pulled out.

On 25 July, Turkey publicly withdrew its threat to take the airport by force. But the troops surrounding the airport did not pull back. They held their ground to prevent it being used by the Greeks, whose troops were stationed only 500 yards away. It remained a tense, potentially explosive situation. Britain brought in more amoured cars and Phantoms to ensure the airport could not be taken.

Waldheim told the Security Council that elsewhere Turkish forces had begun to advance in several directions from the area under their control in Nicosia and Kyrenia. At the same time, National Guard forces in outlying areas had surrounded a number of Turkish-Cypriot villages, and demanded their surrender. With both sides breaking through the ceasefire lines, the UN forces were at full stretch, and desperately in need of the British reinforcements, which arrived that day. One of the UN force's first tasks was to protect Greek Cypriots stranded in areas under Turkish occupation.[2]

Kissinger refused to criticise the Turks for ignoring the ceasefire. Privately, he told his close officials he would not oppose their territorial objectives.[3] He rated Turkey's value to American security interests higher than that of the Karamanlis Government. Turkey housed vital US bases and sophisticated electronic listening-posts along the Soviet border, installations which made possible, for example, intelligence on Russian military moves of the kind that spurred the October nuclear alert during the Yom Kippur war the year before, and monitoring of Soviet missile activity. But other officials, such as Tasca, were not told what the policy was. As a result, he could see no good reason why Kissinger did not hit the roof when the Turks ignored the ceasefire agreement he had brokered. He said the apparent acquiescence made it very difficult for him to restrain the Greek leaders from an all-out war with Turkey.[4]

The talks at Geneva opened on 25 July, and were attended by the foreign ministers of Greece, Turkey and Britain, but there were no Cypriot representatives. According to a UN Security Council resolution, their purpose was to prevent further fighting and restore constitutional government. The Greeks were incensed by the continuing reinforcement of the Turkish bridgehead, and reports that up to 40 Turkish ships were heading for the island, carrying more troops. Callaghan, who chaired the talks, demanded an immediate assurance that the ceasefire violations would stop. But Gunesh would promise nothing without agreement on a political settlement that took into account the 'new realities' on the island. With Kissinger's encouragement (see Appendix), the Turks treated the ceasefire as a temporary hiatus, and Ecevit privately ordered the armed forces to prepare for the next phase of the Cyprus operation.[5]

On the second day at Geneva, the Greeks threatened to walk out, and there was talk of Greek military intervention if Turkish troops did not halt their advances. Behind the scenes, Callaghan and Kissinger's personal representative, the US Assistant Secretary of State for International Organisation Affairs, William Buffum, worked furiously to stop the talks folding. Buffum played a key role as a mediator, despite officially attending only as an observer. Eventually, the Turks offered a set of proposals which included Greek acceptance of the latest expansion of Turkish control, a UN-controlled buffer zone, international control of Nicosia airport with a British base there, talks on a new constitution, and two autonomous administrations on Cyprus. The Greeks thought the Turkish demands amounted to blackmail, and charged Turkey with 53 ceasefire violations, 12 of them since the talks had begun. Karamanlis felt he could not avoid a military confrontation for much longer.

There was a marked difference between the way Buffum handled the Turks behind the scenes and the way Callaghan dealt with them in public. Buffum held early meetings with Gunesh and his Greek counterpart, Mavros. Turkish accounts of Buffum's meetings with Gunesh reveal an extraordinary failure to criticise Turkish action in breaking the ceasefire negotiated by Kissinger, even after the illegal Sampson regime had been replaced by Clerides, whom Washington favoured. According to Birand, Buffum told Gunesh that the United States was taking a 'realistic approach', and pleaded with the Turkish Foreign Minister to let the Americans know how far they intended to go. Gunesh told Buffum the conflict would not end until two separate zones with autonomous administrations were set up, forming a federal system within one state. They did not want Makarios back. Neither would they let UN or Greek forces use Nicosia airport.[6]

By contrast, Callaghan was adamant that the Turks must not be allowed to reinforce their troops on Cyprus, and that they must halt their territorial expansion. But Gunesh refused to contemplate any limits on Turkish military action. Callaghan tried to break the deadlock by holding his own separate talks with the two Foreign Ministers. Mavros said only putting Kyrenia under UN control, ringing Turkish units with UN troops, and restoring Makarios would save the talks. Gunesh was surprised to find that Callaghan had British and American maps detailing the exact Turkish positions. Callaghan demanded to know when the Turks would stop massing their troops in Cyprus and what Gunesh thought of Mavros's demands. Gunesh rejected any return to the 22 July lines, and called for wide security zones around Turkish military positions and villages – without any UN forces.[7] Callaghan angrily warned him against causing another intractable problem like Northern Ireland. But Gunesh retorted that if Britain made another move to bring in military reinforcements, as it had with the Phantoms, it would pay for it dearly. Callaghan urged Buffum and Kissinger to apply some pressure. With Gunesh and Callaghan barely on speaking terms, the fate of the conference rested on Kissinger's long-distance phone calls with the Greek and Turkish leaders. He secured promises that both sides would hold their ground, and the talks were saved. But there was still the larger problem of trying to achieve some kind of agreement at Geneva that would secure peace. The Greeks insisted that Turkey must pull back its forces, but Ecevit would have no mention of withdrawal, and continued to reinforce the Turkish military position on Cyprus.[8]

When the Security Council raised the question of putting UN troops between the Turkish forces and the Cyprus National Guard, the Soviet representative accused the NATO powers of trying to abolish the independence of Cyprus, first by means of direct military action, and now by means of back-stage plotting. The Turks had an estimated 15,000–20,000 men, supported by 200 American-built tanks and heavy artillery, on Cyprus. In the four days since the ceasefire, they had occupied the port of Kyrenia, the northern village of Bellapais, four suburbs of Nicosia and two villages nearby. They had also closed in on Mia Milea, a hamlet on the Nicosia-Famagusta highway where an American monitoring station was situated. Turkish tanks were advancing westwards from Kyrenia to take control of the road between Nicosia and the coastal town of Lapithos.[9]

On 29 July, faced with mounting evidence that the Turks were landing fresh troops, and were poised to snatch more territory, Callaghan told Gunesh he must change his position by the next morning or he would mobilise NATO, and the UN and would blame Turkey for the breakdown of the talks. But, in the early hours of the next morning, Gunesh said he could not give an answer because the Cabinet in Ankara had gone into emergency session.[10] The situation was saved only by a cynical proposition from Kissinger. That night, during lengthy telephone calls, Kissinger said to Ecevit, 'Do you have to comply with that section of the agreement which calls for the withdrawal of troops? Your soldiers, I seem to remember, continued to advance although you had accepted the ceasefire' (see Appendix). But Ecevit would accept a formula calling for the removal of Turkish troops only after a settlement on Cyprus's future had been agreed. The US Secretary of State secured backing for this from Callaghan and Karamanlis. The Greeks, who earlier had been prepared to face war and almost certain defeat rather than give in on the issue of Turkish advances, agreed to a standstill, and to allow a UN-patrolled buffer zone to be established between the two sides.[11]

The agreement was formalised in a declaration signed by all sides. Callaghan said the parties agreed that the areas controlled by opposing forces would not be extended, all hostile activity should end, and a security zone should be set up at the limits of the Turkish-held territory. All prisoners were to be exchanged or released, policing in mixed villages would be carried out by the UN force, and plans were to be made for a timely and phased reduction of arms and armed forces on the island, within the framework of a lasting solution. Negotiations to restore peace and re-establish constitutional government in Cyprus would begin on 8 August. In the meantime, it was agreed that National Guard forces should pull out of any Turkish enclaves they occupied. Callaghan believed he had brought Greece and Turkey back from the brink of a catastrophic war. But he warned, 'Cyprus will not flourish as long as it remains an armed camp'.[12]

The British diplomatic team was jubilant. They could hardly believe that they had managed to keep the talks going. McNally recalled, 'The Greeks would have to understand it was never going to be the same again, that they would have to give up considerable power, but we came away from Geneva fairly euphoric'. The British believed the next set of talks could produce a new constitution which would maintain the unitary state of Cyprus and get the Turkish army off the island. On the journey home, everyone was on a high, and when they got to the airport, they sat on their suitcases and sang a patriotic song: 'It wasn't Rule Britannia but it was something daft,' recalled McNally. 'Everybody felt that we'd cracked it.'[13]

But the Turks had the most reason to be happy. Since the 'ceasefire' on 22 July, they had almost doubled the territory they held, and the Geneva Declaration consolidated their gains. Ecevit heaped praise on Kissinger for his help, through rolling negotiations across the transatlantic telephone lines, in drafting a new formula acceptable to the Greeks. He said, 'During the last stages of the Geneva meetings Mr Kissinger played a very constructive and helpful role. I think he evaluated the situation and the problem very objectively.'[14] By this stage, the Turks had occupied a corridor from the Kyrenia area to their Nicosia enclave, had seized control of the approach roads from east and west to the northern coast, had cut supply routes from Nicosia, and surrounded the airport.

The British Government pledged an immediate increase in UN troops, 'especially around Nicosia airport'. Callaghan believed the British reinforcements played a steadying role in what could have been a 'most critical' situation. However, though the UN force of 2400 was increased to 4328 by 4 August, its main effect was, arguably, to strengthen Turkish gains by providing a buffer zone around the occupied enclaves.[15] And the Turks were already moving forward to the east. Even on the day of the declaration, UN observers reported that more Turkish troops were landing.

The continuing fighting had taken its toll on civilians. Greek-Cypriot villages had suffered strafing, shelling and tank attacks, and Turkish quarters had been bombarded with artillery fire. The term 'ethnic cleansing' had not been invented yet, but that is what it amounted to. In Limassol, 1750 Turkish-Cypriot men were held in the open in the city soccer stadium. In Larnaca, 873 Turkish-Cypriot men, aged between twelve and ninety, were confined in a school building designed for 100 students, and had to sleep on bare concrete floors, with only two toilets. Meanwhile, 793 Greek-Cypriot prisoners were being held in Turkey. An estimated 10,000 Greek Cypriots had fled the Kyrenia area for Nicosia.

Nevertheless, the British believed the danger had subsided, and the flagship of the task-force, *Hermes*, left for Malta, taking its commandos with it. On her way, she passed the American carrier *Inchon* and her task-group in the area south of Crete. During the first week of August, the Turks built up their forces on the island to 240 tanks, 400 armoured vehicles and 30,000 troops, and there was growing concern that Ankara's motives went much further than the protection of the occupied strip. Having so many forces in place meant that the Turks were working to a short timetable, needing a decision on whether to widen their military operation in a matter of days, because an invasion force, once mustered, could not be put on hold for long. The Greeks asked the British if they would provide air cover for their own reinforcements to counter these Turkish forces, but Callaghan gave them short shrift.

In advance of the new talks, the Americans sent Assistant Secretary of State Arthur Hartman on another whistle-stop tour of the Greek, Turkish and Cypriot capitals to assess the views of the political leaders. It was clear that Washington already accepted that Turkish troops would stay on the island. An official in the Nixon administration said a compromise solution would involve giving the Turkish Cypriots more autonomy in return for lowering the number of Turkish troops on the island.[16] The Greek Cypriots for years had opposed Turkish-Cypriot calls for a federal solution, with the two communities running their own affairs, because they feared it would result in partition. Now the Turks had seized an area which they were running themselves anyway, and the signals coming from the Americans implied that nothing was going to be done to stop this happening.

In the meantime, the Turks pressed home their military advantage by stirring up the Aegean issue again. They sent a ship into an area where the Turks had earlier conducted surveys in connection with their claim for oil exploration rights, which put Greek forces on a state of readiness. At the same time, there were reports that 1000 Greek-Cypriot men from the village of Bellapais, over-looking Kyrenia, had been taken prisoner by Turkish troops.[17] As haggling over the ceasefire line continued, the Turks attacked and occupied the villages of Lapithos and Karavas, site of another US intelligence facility. They drove the Greek-Cypriot forces out by bombarding them with mortar shells. The defenders, with 150 men, had no armour and no anti-tank guns. After this latest conquest, the Turks said about half of their 110,000 people were now within the sector occupied by the Turkish army. But they claimed that outside this area more than 35,000 Turks in 80 villages were being held hostage by the Greeks. These were villages which the Greeks had agreed to pull out of, but had failed to do so. Both sides claimed more than 20,000 civilians from their own community had been forced to leave their homes, and that their houses and businesses had been looted. About 5300 Turkish Cypriots sought refuge in the British Sovereign Base Areas. But there was no doubt who held the upper hand.

As Greece and Turkey prepared for the new talks at Geneva, Gunesh warned ominously that the conference must be concluded swiftly. In desperation, on 7 August Mavros said that Greece would withdraw all its forces – its officers in the Cypriot National Guard and the entire Greek national contingent – if the Turks would do the same. But he was gloomy about the prospects since, he said, the Turks had broken the ceasefire 80 times and had expanded their territory by 40 square miles since the 22 July ceasefire.[18] When Hartman arrived in Athens after visiting Ankara and Nicosia, and called for flexibility in the forthcoming Geneva talks, the Greeks and Greek Cypriots interpreted it as a warning that they could not expect to win back everything that the Turks had taken by force.[19]

The Soviets were rumoured to be offering to provide the Greeks with assurances of protection against Turkish aggression. Moscow's aim was to prevent the Turks annexing a slice of Cyprus, thus giving NATO a permanent foothold on the island at a time when the British appeared to be on the verge of pulling out. However, Mavros dismissed a Soviet official requesting representation for Moscow at Geneva. This may have been because there were also rumours that the Soviets were offering to guarantee Turkey's eastern frontier, to strengthen Turkey's hand in the event of a war with Greece. At the same time, a NATO report indicated movements of Soviet military aircraft and personnel into the Balkans.[20] When Mavros was asked at a press conference whether war between Greece and Turkey was still possible, he replied, 'Nobody wants war, but if a country is confronted with the dilemma of humiliation or war, then there is no choice'.

~25~

THE ROAD TO WAR

Kissinger Over-rules Callaghan

By the time the second Geneva talks began on 8 August 1974, a mood of bitter recrimination had set in. Mavros and Gunesh accused each other of failing to keep promises made at the first conference, while in London Makarios claimed the Turks were hell-bent on partition, and warned he would not sign any agreement he could not support. The Turks insisted that splitting the two communities under a federal state was the minimum demand the talks had to meet. Otherwise a new military operation would begin.[1] The Soviets launched a spy satellite from their space and missile test-base at Tyuratam to monitor the build-up of Turkish troops on Cyprus, now rumoured to number 40,000.[2] From the start, Callaghan, chairing the talks, struggled to stave off their collapse. Over the course of the talks he became increasingly frustrated with Kissinger as the State Department refused to take a strong stance against the Turks, and repeatedly encouraged them to expect significant territorial gains beyond the areas they already held by force (see Appendix).

When Clerides and Denktash arrived at Geneva – the first time the two Cypriot communities were represented in any negotiations during the crisis – Clerides refused to back even the 30 July Geneva declaration, because, he later explained, it 'called on us to hand back to the Turks all the Turkish areas in the south, which we had cleared, whereas in the north the Turkish forces were to remain on whatever territory they had taken'.[3] He wanted Turkey's troops off the island and a return to full political participation by the Turkish Cypriots.

But Denktash said that documents discovered in Greek fortifications, and statements made by captured Greek army officers, showed that but for the Turkish landings the Turkish Cypriots would have been massacred.[4] With Ecevit's backing, he called for a 30 percent slice of Cyprus to be made into a Turkish-Cypriot zone with its own military force, so that it could be protected and economically viable.[5] Gunesh said the sector should have regional autonomy, but responsibility for external defence and finance could rest with a central government.

Callaghan held separate discussions with the representatives of each side to try to narrow the gap. But the British Embassy in Ankara reported that the Turks were already gearing up for a second military operation, and he very quickly became exasperated by Gunesh's tendency to avoid making any commitments without first telephoning Ecevit. At one point, Callaghan exclaimed, 'What kind of a Foreign Minister are you: every five minutes you have to go and ring your government for instructions?'[6]

As Callaghan struggled in Geneva, all eyes turned to Washington, where Nixon was finally forced from office on 9 August to avoid impeachment over the Watergate scandal. His presidency had collapsed in a mire of political dirty tricks, corruption and cover-ups. His mantle passed to Gerald Ford, the one-time minority Republican leader who had risen to Vice President only because his predecessor, Agnew, had been forced to resign over financial irregularities. Ford pledged to continue the Nixon foreign policy and kept Kissinger on as Secretary of State and National Security Adviser. Ford called for cool heads over Cyprus, warning that the crisis threatened the stability of the whole area. That day, Kissinger sent Hartman to the Geneva conference as an observer.

One of Hartman's first tasks was to call on Gunesh and tell him that Clerides was ready to accept a cantonal solution. But Gunesh was unimpressed. That was something the Turks had seen rejected before the current crisis, and now that they had taken military action they wanted a bigger prize.

On 10 August, the talks broke up without Denktash or Clerides even taking their seat in the Palais des Nations. Denktash would not sit alongside Clerides at a table labelled 'The Cyprus Republic'. He wanted labels referring to both men simply as the representatives of their communities, in line with the Turkish view that since 1963 there had been no valid Cyprus Republic. But the Greeks believed this would mean accepting that the Turkish Cypriots were entitled to an autonomous state. Gunesh stormed out of the Palais in support of Denktash. Callaghan, frustrated and angry, set up a press conference to issue a blunt warning to the Turks. He said Britain had decided to reverse its decision to pull out the 12 extra Phantoms it had sent to Cyprus, had scrapped the planned withdrawal of British troops from the sovereign bases, and was sending more troops – Gurkha units – to the island. He was considering putting more British soldiers into the UN peace-keeping force, and asked the UN to position its troops to block further Turkish advances. He warned that Turkey seemed poised to seize by force what it could not attain by negotiation, and that if any British or UN soldiers were fired on, British troops and planes would be sent into action to protect British lives. It appeared to be a threat of war[7] (see Appendix). Ford, Kissinger and 14 NATO ambassadors sent urgent personal messages to Gunesh, urging him to continue with the conference, and stating their opposition to a second military operation in Cyprus. The talks resumed at 5pm.

But Gunesh warned that the crisis would blow up again unless a definitive solution, bringing in dramatic constitutional changes, was produced quickly. Clerides argued that if the Turkish army had intervened in accordance with the Treaty of Guarantee it should be satisfied with the re-establishment of the 1960 constitution. He feared separate zones would make partition inevitable, and that annexation of the Turkish-Cypriot area by Turkey would follow. Callaghan warned that Denktash and Gunesh's plans would split Cyprus into two states and turn the island into a massive refugee camp.[8] But Gunesh said the Greek Cypriots had betrayed the trust of the Turkish Cypriots for years, and demanded that a radically new agreement be thrashed out within a day.

That evening, while dining with Mavros and two of his own advisers, Clerides was interrupted by a dramatic telephone call from Cyprus. 'I remember it very clearly,' he said. 'I was told that a Turkish major was captured with his tank and on him they found the plans for the second invasion: the breaking out from the bridgehead and the lines to which they were to advance. The whole map showing the second operation. I asked for the plans to be forwarded to me immediately... I informed Callaghan.' Callaghan, however, did not seem at all surprised. He was sure that the Turks wanted to break out of their bridgehead. Clerides recalled, 'He [said] they were congested in the bridgehead, and naturally they would want to expand. And he stressed that that was why it was absolutely necessary to reach some kind of agreement, to prevent the second Turkish operation. He called it an "operation", not an invasion. I marked the words.'[9]

Callaghan reminded the Greek Cypriots that Britain was no longer a superpower, and could only take decisive action as part of a UN initiative, or in support of the Americans. Polyvios Polyviou, a member of the Greek-Cypriot delegation, said Callaghan emphasised this over and over again. He said he was in constant touch with Kissinger, who was dealing personally with Ecevit – a former student of his – and that together Britain and America would exert all the pressure they could to save the conference.[10]

The capture of the Turkish military plans was followed by a BBC report which said that if agreement could not be reached at Geneva, Turkey intended to partition Cyprus by force. It quoted a high-ranking Turkish official, who said if it was not agreed to divide the island into two autonomous administrations the Turkish army would overrun the whole of northern Cyprus. The island would be split along a notional line dubbed the Attila Line – after Attila the Hun, the fifth-century conquerer of most of eastern Europe and the Balkans. The line ran from Morphou in the west to Famagusta in the east, taking in the northern sector of Nicosia. This would allow the Turkish Cypriots to occupy 25 percent of the island.[11]

At about the same time, an anonymous plan was handed to Clerides and Denktash in Geneva which called for a substantial part of the north of the island to be made a Turkish area, and would involve an exchange of population. Clerides recalled, 'The paper had no headline, except "Plan For the Solution Of The Cyprus Problem", but it did not say whose plan it was. Certainly it was not mine, it wasn't Denktash's and the Greeks had not submitted it. The Turks had not submitted it and the British denied that it was their plan, so I called it the Illegitimate Proposal, because nobody would accept paternity for it... It must have been some ideas of Kissinger.' Later in the talks, when he spoke to Kissinger by telephone, the Secretary of State said if the Greek Cypriots accepted a Turkish area in the north, administered by Turkish Cypriots and occupied by Turkish forces, they need not accept that the extent of the area should be 33 per-cent of the island, as the Turks wanted. Kissinger would undertake that the Turks would not advance, and that the area was kept below 30 percent.[12]

The Turks by now were boasting about having pushed the Greek Cypriots out of 30 towns and villages, and continued to build installations in their bridge-head. Reports reached Athens that they were also reinforcing their border with Greece. There was a renewed risk of direct war between the two NATO allies, and Greek forces remained on full alert. Kissinger's envoy, Hartman, had offered Athens no promises that serious pressure would be put on the Turks to stop them partitioning Cyprus.[13]

In Turkey, Ecevit held a seven-hour meeting with the commanders of his armed forces. According to McNally, an intelligence report of this meeting spread alarm in the British party at Geneva. They were convinced that a nego-tiated settlement could be reached, until the Americans revealed that the Turkish generals had gathered in Ankara for a pre-invasion planning meeting. The report came from a CIA agent watching the comings and goings at the Ministry of Defence from across the street. By noting down the registration numbers of the official cars as they arrived, he was able to work out which admirals and generals were there, and that an invasion must be on the cards.[14] During this meeting, there were frantic phone calls from Kissinger and frequent representations from the US Ambassador, pressing for a compromise involving the establishment of a number of Turkish-Cypriot cantons rather than a single, separate Turkish state. But Ecevit was in no mood to let the Geneva talks drag on.[15] McNally remembered very clearly that the Turks did not hide their intention that once the negotiations had failed 'they were going to clear it up and clean it up and they wanted it done in a way that was going to be permanent. And that was going to be the end of the story.'[16]

Hartman tried to persuade Callaghan that fears of a new Turkish offensive were groundless. But Callaghan sent a message to Kissinger, urging him to consider the new threat so that Britain and America could agree a joint line of action. He was prepared to restate his earlier warning to Ecevit that British troops in the UN force would resist Turkish advances on Nicosia airport. But as the Turks had since greatly strengthened their forces, he needed assurance of American support if he was to do so. Kissinger's response, delivered by Hartman, was humiliating. He made it clear that the United States was content with Ecevit's reassurances of military restraint, and warned that he would come down hard on the British if they made any more threats. When Callaghan asked how the Americans would respond if the Turks seized more territory, he was told that Kissinger 'would not get himself boxed in on this question'. Callaghan was furious. He was convinced that the Turks would strike again, and telegrammed Kissinger with a warning that the crisis of US inaction was threatening the trust between Britain and America. The special relationship between the two countries was at stake. He told Kissinger the softly-softly approach was not enough; the correct policy was to 'convince them [the Turks] that we were in earnest on both the diplomatic and military level'. But Kissinger insisted that British military threats would sabotage his tactics and escalate the crisis.[17] McNally summed up the situation: 'Kissinger was the key to not giving Britain any military support, or even supporting British military action. He was quite happy for Jim to go through the motions in Geneva. But this was the British guarantee, which Britain could honour as best it could.' As a result, the British were left bluffing. 'There was a concerted attempt to give the impression to the Turks diplomatically at the UN, and around the world that we were moving into position,' said McNally. 'But nobody believed us. Certainly the Turks didn't'[18] (see Appendix).

Kissinger did, however, contact Ecevit in Ankara and suggest a compromise, offering Turkey more territory in exchange for agreement to a system of cantons. Ecevit said these would be much more costly and difficult to defend than a single separate area. Reluctantly, he drew up a plan for six cantons, each one accessible by sea, but he told his negotiators in Geneva that one of the two Turkish plans must be conceded within 24 hours for military action to be avoided.[19] Since Clerides insisted that he had no authority to sanction changes to the constitution of Cyprus – because Makarios would never give it his backing – it appeared that the fate of the talks was sealed.

On the morning of 12 August, a grim sense of foreboding hung over the conference room. Callaghan told Clerides privately that opinion would turn against the Greek Cypriots if they did not put forward a concrete constitutional proposal of their own.[20] That evening, Gunesh submitted the new Turkish plan. The cantons would comprise one main region, taking up 17 percent of the island's territory, and five smaller areas, bringing the total area to 34 percent of the island's territory. Each canton would be fully controlled by the Turkish Cypriots within a confederation, keeping their own administration, language and police force. He said that only the boundaries of the main region had to be detailed straight away. He argued that it represented a compromise on partition. But he demanded that the Greek side accept it before the plenary session, which he had called for 10pm that night. He had been ordered to return to Ankara the next day with the issue settled one way or the other.

Gunesh wanted the largest canton to include the zone which the Turks already occupied around Kyrenia, but to extend far to the south, to take in the Turkish quarter of Nicosia, and eastwards to take in the port of Famagusta. Each of the five other cantons would open onto the coast to give Turkey access by sea. He suggested these should centre on Paphos, Lefka, Polis, Larnaca and part of the Karpas peninsula. Of these towns, only Lefka had a majority Turkish-Cypriot population.[21] However, the British delegation soon became convinced that the Turks did not want to make this compromise. McNally said the British team tried very hard to sell the idea of cantonisation – because it would make eventual reunification easier – but the Turks were not really interested. 'I got the distinct impression early on that the Turks had a very clear idea of what they were going to do and they weren't going to be stopped.'[22]

The Greek Cypriots and Greeks would not even consider such a deal, let alone accept it, because it amounted to giving consent for a Turkish occupation. Callaghan pleaded with Clerides to accept a compromise, and called Kissinger to ask for help. Callaghan and Kissinger both spoke by telephone to Ecevit. Reluctantly, the Turks agreed to allow Clerides 24 hours to put together some counter-proposals. Working through the night, the Greek side drew up an offer to create semi-autonomous Greek- and Turkish-Cypriot administrations within a single integral state. Neither Clerides nor Mavros held out much hope that the Turks would warm to their plan. The captured Turkish military plans had indicated that Turkish troops would be ordered to advance and seize more territory 'when' the conference failed, not 'if'. The Turks had already mobilised their forces in preparation for a new offensive in Cyprus.[23] They deployed 50 tanks across the central plain to within ten miles of Nicosia, moved armoured units into new positions just outside the capital, and ferried reinforcements southwards along the Kyrenia-Nicosia road.

The British airlifted 600 extra troops onto the island and put 300 marine commandos on standby to join them. Another frigate was set to join the naval task-force stationed off Cyprus. The extra soldiers brought the number of British troops on the island to 11,000. The Phantoms were made ready to defend British military facilities. Radio reports said British forces were preparing for combat with Turkish troops. Turkish radio, reflecting the views of the Ankara Government, accused Britain of creating a 'war atmosphere'.[24] The Greeks feared Ankara might even open up a war on two fronts by turning its guns on Greece itself. As a precaution, Karamanlis's generals massed their tanks along the border with Turkey in northern Greece and on Greek islands close to the Turkish coast. On Cyprus, some Greek-Cypriot forces started to pull out of the

Turkish enclaves.[25] That morning, Kissinger ordered Tasca to deliver an urgent message to Karamanlis, pressing him to hold his nerve and consider the Turkish proposals for dividing Cyprus.[26] Karamanlis was said to be deeply distressed by Kissinger's request. Later that day, the messenger was sacrificed. It was announced that Tasca was to be relieved of his post in favour of Jack Kubisch, who had no experience of the area. It was a curious way to try to steady nerves.

By contrast, when Ecevit warned Kissinger that Turkey would use force if a settlement could not be concluded quickly, Kissinger repeatedly acknowledged that the Turkish forces could not remain crammed inside the bridgehead for much longer (see Appendix). His view set him on collision course with Callaghan.[27] The Turkish attitude was echoed by Denktash, who told the British party that the Turkish Cypriots did not trust the Greeks, that this was their chance, and that they were going to take it. He pointed out that he had been Vice President of Cyprus for 18 years, and that in that time he had only spoken to his President once, and he had never seen his state's flag fly over the presidential palace – it had always been the Greek flag.[28]

On the morning of 13 August, Clerides gave Callaghan the official Greek-Cypriot proposals. But Callaghan warned him that while Britain was ready to offer troops to stop the Turks seizing more territory in a UN operation, or in joint action with the Americans, the United States and the UN had vetoed such action. Kissinger would not even halt US military aid to Turkey. Without a military deterrent, Callaghan believed the only way to prevent bloodshed was for the Greek Cypriots to offer to accept a deal based on geographical separation. Though Denktash and Gunesh had demanded that 34 percent of the island's territory be set aside for Turkish-Cypriot rule, Callaghan said they could be beaten down. Kissinger had told him he would do all he could to get it down to between 20 and 22 percent.[29]

But according to Clerides, the American emphasis was more on getting the Greek Cypriots to concede territory than reducing the proposed zone in size. He recalled, 'I was present at a telephone conversation between Kissinger and Callaghan. Kissinger spoke to me also. He said the only thing he could do to prevent the Turks from another military operation was for us to accept the principle that in the north there could be an area which would be administered by Turkish Cypriots. But this area must immediately be placed under the control of the Turkish forces. The extent of the area need not be agreed – he would undertake that it would be below 30 percent. The status of the area in the context of federation would be discussed at subsequent talks.' But Clerides had no intention of sanctioning Turkish sovereignty of a slice of Cyprus, no matter what the size, while a solution was being sought. 'The anxiety there of Kissinger was first that there would be a bi-regional, bi-zonal federation,' said Clerides. 'Second, if I accepted that there will be an area in the north occupied by the Turks, it would prevent us from internationalising the Cyprus problem – by running to the UN – on the basis that there was an invasion and an occupation.'[30]

He and Mavros instead demanded an adjournment of 36–48 hours to enable them to consult with Greek and Greek-Cypriot leaders in Athens and Nicosia, and with Makarios in London. Callaghan tried to persuade Gunesh that Clerides had to go back to Cyprus to win over the doubters. But the proposal sent Gunesh into a rage. He thought it was a ruse to buy time to shore up Cypriot defences before the Turkish attack began. He insisted that if Clerides did not first agree to the principle of allotting the Turkish Cypriots a single geographical zone, the Turks would walk out. Clerides has since admitted it was only a delaying tactic. 'Of course it was,' he said. 'I wasn't going to sign, and if I said I wasn't going to sign they would have invaded Cyprus before I came back. It was a question of whether I would even be able to return to Cyprus. Makarios was in London, I was in Geneva and nobody was holding the helm of whatever ship was left here [in Cyprus].'[31]

Kissinger pressed Ecevit on the issue. But Ecevit insisted that he could not keep his army waiting any longer. It would only be possible if the Greeks first accepted the principle of either a cantonal or bi-regional system, and allowed a no-man's-land to be created around the Turkish-held territory. Kissinger liked the idea, and held talks with all sides to try to secure this plan, which amounted to a clear tilt towards Turkey's objectives. On this issue he clashed with Callaghan. Birand alleged that the Americans blamed Callaghan's refusal to support Kissinger's tilt for the eventual failure of his diplomatic effort and the launch of a new invasion.[32] But Clerides said the Kissinger formula could never have worked, because it meant capitulation for the Greek Cypriots.[33]

Convinced that diplomacy had now failed, he sought out the Soviet observer at the conference, Victor Menin, and asked if Moscow would help defend Cyprus against a further Turkish attack. But less than a year after Kissinger threatened them with a worldwide nuclear alert, the Soviets did not seem willing to risk unilateral military action without tacit agreement from the United States.[34]

By the time the formal talks restarted at 6.45pm, the Turkish generals in Ankara had already decided to launch a new military operation at 3am the next morning.[35] To meet this deadline, the Turks wanted the talks finished and out of the way by 1am. The evening session began, therefore, with a stale reiteration of the positions of both sides. Gunesh insisted that Clerides and Mavros must immediately agree to set up within a few days a Turkish region in the north. This would take in 34 percent of the island's territory, including the Turkish sectors of Famagusta and Nicosia. Otherwise the talks would be terminated.[36]

Callaghan warned the Turks that under the Treaty of Guarantee the only legitimate objective of Turkey's military intervention could be to re-establish the 1960 constitution: Ankara had no right to try to impose a new constitutional settlement. Gunesh disagreed. He said his proposals should not have come as a surprise, as they had already been outlined to NATO and EEC countries. Denktash argued that a new settlement must be made, so that the Turkish Cypriots no longer had to live in fear of intercommunal violence. But the Greek

Cypriots believed they were being forced to split up the country and sanction a transfer of population.

At this point, Kissinger broke days of public silence to offer backing for the aspirations of the Turkish Cypriots. Though warning Greece and Turkey against resorting to military action, the State Department said the United States recognised that 'the position of the Turkish community on Cyprus requires considerable improvement and protection. We have supported a greater degree of autonomy for them.' The statement was a calculated gesture made on the basis of detailed knowledge of the views of all sides at Geneva. The Americans had played an active role behind the scenes in the negotiations, and Kissinger had kept Ford in constant touch with developments. Kissinger himself had been kept informed by his observer in Geneva, Hartman. He had also spoken a number of times on the phone to the Turkish and British Prime Ministers, even though this meant repeatedly interrupting important talks he was holding in Washington about the situation in the Middle East. Kissinger's right-hand-man on Middle East and Mediterranean affairs, Sisco, had also been called away from these discussions frequently, to take calls about the Geneva negotiations. Kissinger had spoken to Ecevit four times in 24 hours, and several times to Callaghan, and he had sent a letter to Karamanlis. He had also been in contact with Clerides and Denktash.[37]

Kissinger was reported to believe that because the Greek junta had backed the overthrow of Makarios, the Turks were justified in securing more guarantees for the Turkish Cypriots than the 1960 constitution offered, including one or two autonomous zones. This would imply that the coup, which the CIA knew about in advance and which Washington failed to warn Ioannides adequately against pursuing, gave the Turks the right to seize control of one or more slices of Cyprus. Certainly, the Turks believed the Americans backed acceptance of their plan[38] (see Appendix).

Clerides was furious at the American stance, and the claim that as even NATO members had had time to view the proposals, the Greek Cypriots had no need of time to consult. He said, 'We are neither a colony of NATO nor of America'.[39]

In Greece, the Government's war council held its second meeting in 24 hours, and there were reports that they might even send troops to Cyprus on the grounds that Turkey's continuing military presence breached the terms of the Treaty of Guarantee. All Greek forces were put on a war footing. After the war council meeting, a large armoured force left Athens for Thrace on the Turkish border. The intended message to Ankara and other NATO governments was that the Greeks would not stand by if Turkey pressed its demands with military force.[40] The rattling of sabres unnerved Callaghan. It seemed that no amount of wheeler-dealing by him could prevent the talks ending in bloodshed. He warned the Turks that any attempt to impose a settlement by force would end in disaster. The British had already learned that lesson to their cost in the 1950s, when attempts to deny Cypriot self-determination collapsed because of the enormous cost and number of troops involved in imposing British rule against the will of the Greek Cypriots. He warned, 'Today the Republic of Cyprus is the prisoner of the Turkish army: tomorrow the Turkish army will find itself the prisoner of the Republic of Cyprus'. He asked that it be put on record that the British stood ready to allow the Greeks the adjournment they sought. If the Turks still refused this request, it would be on their heads if the talks broke up. Tired and frustrated, he called another short break at 1am.

The Turks were puzzled by the Greeks' tough stance. They thought the State Department's announcement made it clear that the Americans expected Clerides to make concessions, and could not understand why he had not taken it seriously. During a break, Gunesh sent a colleague to point out to the Greek delegate to the UN that Kissinger had talked about more rights and autonomy for the Turkish Cypriots. He warned the Greek that Ankara interpreted this to mean that the Turkish Cypriots must be granted more rights and wider autonomy – otherwise Turkey would achieve its objective by force.[41]

The threat was confirmed by British intelligence: Turkish forces were poised to attack. At 1.45am, with Kissinger's backing, Callaghan tried one last throw of the dice. He asked Clerides to sign a pledge that he would return to Cyprus with the aim of 'favourably considering' a solution based on geographical separation. But Clerides refused. He would only offer to consider the plans 'carefully and with an open mind'. Callaghan regarded this as a positive response, and asked Gunesh if he would come back on the morning of 15 August. But nothing short of acceptance there and then of one of his plans would satisfy Gunesh. Sensing catastrophe, Clerides asked Callaghan what action Britain would take if the Turks launched a new military operation. Hamstrung by America's veto of joint military action, Callaghan could only say that he had offered to put more forces at the disposal of the UN. But he stressed that Kissinger and the European allies did not believe diplomatic methods had been exhausted, and if Turkey resorted to military action at this stage the responsibility would rest with Ankara. At 2.20am Callaghan pressed Gunesh once more to come back to the conference table the next morning. Mavros and Clerides said they would attend, but Gunesh walked out and told waiting reporters, 'Diplomacy is silent; the guns are now talking'.[42]

~26~

TO THE ATTILA LINE

US Pressure Contains the Advances

From dawn on 14 August 1974, Turkish Phantoms swept over Cyprus, attacking Nicosia and Famagusta. Three hundred Turkish tanks headed south from Kyrenia, capturing Mia Milea, Kythrea and Chatos, north-east of the capital. Other ground forces grouped around Nicosia, and there were skirmishes between Turkish-Cypriot fighters and National Guard units in the north-west. Under the cover of ceaseless air attacks, artillery bombardments and shelling by warships, the Turks moved their forces east and west in an attempt to cut off the northern third of the island.

Turkish air strikes targeted Nicosia, and their artillery shelled Mia Milea. Near Kyrenia, three Turkish warships shelled pockets of Greek resistance either side of the occupied zone. Before midday, the Greek forces began to fall back on the capital and eastwards to Famagusta. In Nicosia, Turkish tanks blasted holes in the Greek-Cypriot defences, and at one point destroyed a UN armoured personnel carrier. UN observation posts had to be hurriedly evacuated as soldiers were hit. There was heavy fighting around Nicosia airport. Turkish jets bombed its perimeter all day. As armoured units massed on the eastern side of the capital, ready to push on to Famagusta, the island's main port, Turkish jets bombed

Greek-Cypriot strongholds in the city and blew up a series of industrial complexes on the road out of Nicosia, setting fire to homes and factories over a stretch of four or five miles. Then Turkish ground troops began to force the Greek Cypriots southwards.[1]

In Famagusta, National Guard soldiers and Turkish-Cypriot fighters fought each other with mortars, artillery and machine-guns. Throughout the morning bombing raids left buildings ablaze, and huge plumes of black smoke billowed into the sky.[2] Greek Cypriots fleeing the fighting poured out of the city using any means of transport they could find. The safest direction to run was into the British base at Dhekelia, but many took to the Nicosia road, unaware that Turkish tanks were heading towards them from the capital. Cars packed with refugees and laden with mattresses and suitcases strapped to their roofs streamed out of the city. Some had tried to camouflage their vehicles by caking them in mud, to avoid being targeted by Turkish planes.

While Turkey seized large tracts of Cyprus, the State Department repeated its statement backing Turkish and Turkish-Cypriot calls for more autonomy. Karamanlis and Makarios turned their anger on the Americans. Four hours after the new invasion began, Karamanlis announced that he was pulling his country's troops out of NATO's command structure. Greek officers at NATO headquarters in Brussels and Naples were ordered to pack their bags. He blamed NATO for failing to prevent the Turkish invasion. If the Americans had refused to support the junta, or warned Ioannides off a coup in Cyprus, or condemned the coup, or pressed the Turks to compromise at Geneva, or provided a military deterrent against an invasion, the Turks would not now be bombing and shelling their way to partition, the Greeks thought. Distrust boiled over into angry protests across Greece, Britain and America; and the decision to pull Greece's 160,000-strong armed forces out of NATO put the future of the American facilities in Greece in jeopardy. It also left a gaping hole in NATO's southern flank.

Makarios, after a demonstration by thousands of supporters at the American Embassy in London, said, 'The United States is the only country which could have exerted pressure on Turkey and have prevented the invasion. It will be an ominous precedent for the security of other small countries.' Radical Greek feeling was summed up by Andreas Papandreou, who said he was overcome by anger at 'the treatment that the US and NATO have handed to Cyprus'. He complained about the 'spectacular con job' perpetrated over Cyprus by Kissinger and the NATO allies. 'This was blueprinted long ago in the Pentagon and the CIA,' he said.[3] He had argued back in 1967 that the Americans wanted partition of Cyprus, and would use the junta to make this happen.[4]

The State Department denied that their statements could be read as approval for partition. Yet on 15 August, Ecevit, after a meeting with US Ambassador Macomber, told reporters that the two countries' views on the Cyprus question coincided. Both, he said, were in favour of a separate, geographically autonomous administration, though he said the United States felt this should be achieved through talks and not by military means. 'The United States has had a very clearly defined policy as far as Cyprus is concerned and we are grateful to them for this.'[5] Once again, the priority for Kissinger and his Washington Special Action Group was not to reverse the Turkish invasion, but to prevent war between Greece and Turkey and limit the damage to US relations with Athens and Ankara. They even dismissed calls to cut military aid to Turkey, saying it would only have encouraged Greece to go to war.[6] At the North Atlantic Council, NATO Secretary General Josef Luns said this was the 'most serious internal crisis' in the alliance's 25-year history.

At one point on 14 August, Karamanlis had threatened to 'take all the appropriate measures to confront an attack which was mounted not only against the independent state of Cyprus, but also to undermine the institutions and order of the whole world'. Ultimately, he did not have enough firepower to confront Turkey on Greece's border, and he could not mount any defence of Cyprus unless Britain provided air cover – and without American support this was impossible. At an emergency meeting of his military council, Karamanlis was told that after seven years of neglect under the junta, the Greek armed forces were not capable of even limited action against Turkey, let alone a full-scale war.[7] In a nationwide television broadcast he told his people that his country's defences were too weak to risk going to war with Turkey.[8]

Meanwhile, the Turks ploughed on. Following air strikes and mortar attacks on Greek-Cypriot positions around Nicosia, they tried to encircle the city. Jets also bombed National Guard troops at Limnitis, in the north-west, and Turkish warships shelled them throughout the night. To the east, as Turkish forces closed in on Famagusta, the Turkish Cypriots, holed up in the old walled city, blasted the Greek Cypriots with mortar and rocket fire. From the skies, Turkish aircraft dropped 500lb bombs on buildings near the port, wounding dozens of National Guardsmen in strafing attacks.[9]

British forces anxiously eyed the situation, standing ready to defend the strategic bases and installations. On 15 August, the RAF evacuated 3000 Britons in 12 hours, with Hercules transporters taking off every 30 minutes for England. RAF Strike Command diverted most of its 13 VC-10s and 22 Britannias to Cyprus from all over the world to support the airlift. Armed with Sparrow, Martel and Sidewinder missiles, the Phantoms were kept on alert, ready to defend the transporters filled with evacuees from Turkish attack. Around 24,000 Greek- and Turkish-Cypriot refugees swelled the two sovereign bases, especially at Dhekelia, where the queue of vehicles entering the base stretched six miles.

Then, suddenly, the British faced exactly the kind of threat to the bases that Callaghan had feared. During the fighting around Famagusta, a Turkish armoured column, consisting of 30 tanks and 12 armoured personnel carriers, drove up to the perimeter of the Dhekelia base and fired three shells inside its boundaries. As the tanks lined up in battle formation, threatening the base and its strategic intelligence facilities, British Scorpion tanks rumbled out to confront them.

Phantoms from Akrotiri swept the skies, ready to strike at the Turkish armour below. With the two NATO powers only moments away from an explosive incident, Lieutenant-Colonel Ian Cartwright, Commander of the 3rd Battalion of the Royal Regiment of Fusiliers, drove to the fringes of the base to demand a Turkish explanation. The tense confrontation lasted three hours, but ended after the matter was referred to the overall Turkish commander in Nicosia, who sent an emissary by helicopter. The Turkish tanks pulled back and headed for Famagusta, but the incident left British base commanders nervous about Turkish intentions.

Shortly afterwards, hundreds of Greek-Cypriot soldiers were allowed to retreat through the base to Larnaca as Turkish air-raids emptied Famagusta. Since the only route out of the town left open was the one in the south-west, thousands more refugees fled towards the base and camped inside its perimeter. Turkey announced that it would not cease operations until it controlled all of northern Cyprus, from Morphou Bay in the north-west to Famagusta on the south-east coast. In the east, Turkish troops advanced on the Karpas Peninsula. In the north west they captured Myrtou and battled to control Morphou.

When the UN Security Council demanded an immediate ceasefire, Kissinger belatedly took over the public mantle of mediator from Callaghan, though he had been dealing directly with the major players behind the scenes for some time (see Appendix). However, while he tried to persuade Mavros to enter talks, the Turks rooted out the last pockets of resistance in Famagusta in house-to-house searches, occupied part of Nicosia, and tried to cut off the road south to Larnaca, using infantry, armoured cars and tanks. In the north-west they continued their general attack, supported by aircraft, artillery and other heavy weapons, and moved down from the Pentadactylos mountains to occupy the lowland plain around Morphou.

Early on the evening of 16 August, Ankara declared a ceasefire. Clerides, whose Government had moved to Limassol to escape the fighting in Nicosia, accepted it. By the end of the day, 60,000 refugees packed the Dhekelia sovereign base. These included most of the Greek-Cypriot inhabitants of Larnaca, which was feared to be the Turks' next target. The Turks had divided the island along a line from Lefka in the north-west through Nicosia to Famagusta in the south-east.

Once the Turks had achieved their objectives, Kissinger's spokesman now said the United States would not 'understand' any resumption of fighting by Turkey in Cyprus – which comes rather lower on the scale of diplomatic threats than the 1964 warning that it would put at risk NATO's guarantee to defend Turkey against a Soviet attack. There was no suggestion that the Turks ought to pull out of the areas they had occupied. Kissinger was prepared to meet both sides to iron out their differences before the talks began. But Karamanlis refused to negotiate under the pressure of a *fait accompli*.

The Turks were pleased that Kissinger had taken the mediating role out of Callaghan's hands. They said Callaghan's military threats had encouraged the Greeks to hold out when the Turks insisted on dividing the island into Greek and Turkish-Cypriot administrations. By contrast, the United States had approached the situation 'with objectivity in a constructive way'.[10] Ominously, one Turkish paper, *Yeni Ortam*, said Ankara was planning to change the status of Britain's sovereign bases in Cyprus, and would raise the matter if talks were resumed.[11] American officials also criticised Callaghan's tactics, saying he had been wrong to ask both sides to put up their proposals at the start of the talks instead of first putting out feelers to see where compromises could be made and arriving at a jointly agreed proposal.[12] This analysis ignored the crucial point that Callaghan's task was made nigh impossible by the encouragement the Americans gave to the Turks to hold out for their objectives, both by refusing to support deterrent action with Britain, and by giving vocal backing to Turkey's aims. American diplomats agreed that nothing short of interposing the Sixth Fleet between Cyprus and Turkey would have prevented the invasion. One said, 'It is our information that Washington pulled its punches in Ankara. It was a hard-headed decision taken by hard-headed people. America had to lose one friend or the other and they chose to lose Greece.'[13]

For the Turks, Ecevit said his country was now ready to return to Geneva to negotiate a final settlement. The Attila Line was as far as he intended his troops to go, and he wanted to see an autonomous Turkish administration set up in northern Cyprus to co-exist with a Greek administration in a federated republic. The boundaries were negotiable, but he wanted the Turkish share to correspond to about a third of the island.

Nevertheless, the Turks kept advancing, as they had ever since the first cease-fire of 22 July. Backed up by tanks and artillery, Turkish troops surged forward towards the Turkish-Cypriot stronghold in Louroujina, creating a long corridor of Turkish-occupied territory that threatened the security of the main Nicosia-Larnaca road.[14] If that road and the adjacent one to the other southern city, Limassol, fell, the capital would be surrounded on three sides and the Greek Cypriots would be driven into the hills. The whole island might then fall into Turkish hands.

The Americans now openly criticised Turkey's continuing operations. James Schlesinger, US Secretary for Defence, said, 'Turkey's moves at this point have gone beyond what any of its friends or sympathisers would have anticipated and what they are, I think, prepared to accept'. He indicated that America might now cut off Turkish military aid and force it to give up some of the territory it had seized, though State Department officials questioned whether Kissinger knew of his statement in advance. Schlesinger said, 'The spill-over of Turkish forces into areas that no one had expected them to move into is a new element to the problem and we will have to take cognisance of it'. It was further evidence that the Americans had been ready all along to accept a Turkish occupation of a limited area of the island, as their 1964 contingency plan envisaged. Over the weekend of 17–18 August, the aircraft-carrier *Forrestal* left Naples and joined the carrier *Independence* and the helicopter-carrier *Inchon* in the eastern

Mediterranean. The warning from Washington, backed with a show of strength, had an instant effect. The Turks halted their advance. But by this stage they had taken Louroujina, and had built up mortar positions near the British sovereign base at Dhekelia.[15]

The American action came too late to placate the Greeks. Demonstrators marched on the American Embassy in Athens, shouting 'Kissinger murderer' and 'Out with the bases'. There were placards daubed with 'Shame to NATO and the USA'. At the same time, as protestors gathered in Nicosia, Clerides told a press conference that he believed that America could have exerted greater pressure to prevent the Turkish invasion in the first place. The demonstration there turned into a riot. A group of young men wearing berets, khaki shorts and army boots and carrying automatic rifles joined in. When one of them let off a burst from his AK47 rifle, others took up firing positions and opened fire on the Embassy. American marines in the Embassy fired tear-gas bombs into the crowd and warning shots. But two bullets sped through the office into a corridor to which officials had retreated, and hit the Ambassador, Roger Davies, and a Greek-Cypriot secretary. Clerides rushed to the Embassy, where he put on a gas mask to get through the tear gas and helped to carry out the Ambassador. 'This is terrible. This is terrible,' he cried. Davies and the secretary died. Davies had only been in the post six weeks. Previously, he worked under Sisco as Deputy Assistant Secretary for Near Eastern and South Asian Affairs. There were bitter protests in America too, including one at the White House at which an effigy of Kissinger was hanged.

The fighting left the island with a massive refugee problem. Out of a population of 600,000, an estimated 200,000 Greek Cypriots had been uprooted and forced to flee south of Turkish lines, while an estimated 60,000 Turkish Cypriots remained south of the Attila Line, uncertain of their fate. Bitter accusations were exchanged over the treatment of ordinary civilians in both communities. Clerides accused the Turkish troops of raping seven girls at Mia Milea and murdering in cold blood seven Greek Cypriots tending their livestock in their village on the Famagusta road. At the UN, the Turkish representative accused Greek-Cypriot forces of burning and desecrating mosques, murdering and deporting civilians, abusing women and children, and incarcerating Turkish Cypriots in concentration camps.[16] The Greek Cypriots were still holding hostage several thousand Turkish Cypriots, and many Turkish enclaves were ringed by armed irregulars or National Guardsmen. In village after village along the northern coast, houses had been destroyed or emptied, their belongings scattered over the floors as a result of Turkish weapons searches. The economic life of these areas had been brought to a standstill.[17]

The Cyprus Government reported 16,000 Greek-Cypriot casualties, including 4000 people killed and 12,000 people wounded since the crisis began five weeks before. Nearly 1000 Turkish Cypriots were dead or missing. More than 1600 Greek Cypriots are still missing today.

~27~

SABOTAGED
BY CONGRESS

The Bitter Legacy Lives On

The one factor which Kissinger hopelessly underestimated in his handling of the 1974 Cyprus crisis was the backlash among congressmen over his failure to deter Turkey's military action. American politicians looked in horror at the results of US foreign policy over Cyprus. More than a third of the island was occupied, NATO faced the most serious internal threat in its history, and Greece and Turkey were on the verge of war. When Hartman, speaking on behalf of the State Department on 18 August, denied that the United States had tilted towards Turkey, they tore into him for defending a policy which had brought 'nearly catastrophic' results.

Representative Lee Hamilton from Indiana said, 'We have supported the independence of Cyprus, but today its independence is deeply jeopardised and it looks as if partition may be the result. Our relations with the Greek government have seriously deteriorated, we have [anti-American] demonstrations all over Greece. We have had a distinguished American Ambassador murdered... Two of our great friends, Greece and Turkey, are very close to going to war with each other over this whole matter. Yet you are not critical of American foreign policy.

You don't see any mistakes in it. It is very hard for this committee to accept the kinds of results we see so far.'[1]

Though Kissinger vehemently opposed them, representatives and senators pushed on with a campaign, that began during the Cyprus crisis, for an embargo on arms to Turkey which, once implemented, disastrously upset the trust between Washington and Ankara.

Senator Paul Sarbanes summed up the case against Kissinger and his officials:

> Despite repeated warnings from many sources, including members of of the Congress... and many other concerned groups, the State Department at every critical juncture failed to take action to avert the tragedy now confronting us. It refused to support Archbishop Makarios, the democratically elected president of Cyprus, when such support could have preserved stability and peace in Cyprus. It failed to prevent Turkish military intervention by denouncing the attempted coup in Cyprus. It refused to bring pressure to bear on Turkey to prevent the invasion of Cyprus and to limit and restrict Turkish military action once such an invasion occurred. Contrast, if you will, the actions of the late President Johnson, who warned a Turkey preparing to go to war in no uncertain terms of the American Government's position and thereby preserved peace in the area.[2]

The comparison with Johnson, however, overlooks the crucial facts – which weren't available then – that Johnson and his closest officials repeatedly considered, and discussed with Greek and Turkish leaders and Turkish generals, different variations of a plot to divide the island between the two NATO powers. Either the Greeks would attempt to secure enosis and hand parts of the island to Turkey or Turkey would take part of the island and prompt the Greeks to declare enosis in the rest of it. In either scenario, the United States would concur and apply pressure on Turkey to ensure their action was, as Johnson put it, 'controlled and eventually productive', using the methods laid out in the February 1964 contingency plan for a limited invasion.

The plot reflected the belief of British and American strategic planners in 1964 that the military facilities would be better protected in a divided Cyprus than a unitary independent state. By 1974, the quickening pace of the nuclear arms race, the need to monitor Soviet nuclear missile tests, and provide early warning of nuclear attack from a growing Soviet arsenal, and Britain's wavering commitment to stay on Cyprus, had raised the stakes further.

As a result of the Turkish occupation, the British lost 12 of the 31 military and intelligence sites and installations in Cypriot territory over which they had special rights under the Treaty of Guarantee, but not the most important ones. By contrast, three separate sites used by the Americans in the occupied area continued to operate after the invasion, at Yerolakkos, Mia Milea and Karavas, according to two of the foremost experts on electronic intelligence, Jeffrey Richelson and Desmond Ball.[3]

Clerides cited a bizarre incident in Kissinger's office which shows how closely Kissinger was working with the Turks in this period. Clerides said Kissinger was talking to him about the return of refugees, and someone reminded the Secretary of State that he should be careful because of his image in Turkey, and the trust they had in him. 'He looked at me and said that by a strange coincidence the Ambassador in Turkey was here. He said he would like to consult him on this, on what the reaction in Turkey would be. He pressed a button and a panel on the wall which was not visible, opened. Immediately the Ambassador appeared from behind the panel and sat down,' said Clerides. Kissinger told the Ambassador that he and Clerides were discussing what could be done, and asked him what he thought the effect would be on the Turkish Government. And instead of assessing it, the Ambassador instantly and exactly repeated that it would harm the trust the Turks had in the Secretary of State. Clerides was flabbergasted. 'This preoccupation, which his subordinates had sensed, was that he was guarding very jealously the trust the Turkish government had in him. It shook me to the core.'[4]

The main difference between the events of 1974 and the carve-up envisaged by Acheson and Ball was that Greece did not get part of the island, and felt utterly betrayed by the Americans, because they had let the Turks seize a third of it. It was a calculated risk. The Americans gambled that the fall-out in relations with Athens would not be as irreversible as critics imagined, that Greece would feel dangerously exposed to the threat from the Eastern Bloc without NATO support, and in the long term would have to return to the fold. The Greeks were unlikely to woo the Soviet Union as an ally, since the Athens establishment had fought a long and bitter civil war against the communists at the end of the Second World War.[5] Indeed, though Karamanlis ended the home-porting arrangements for the US Navy at Piraeus shortly afterwards, he allowed most of the military functions carried out by the United States in Greece to continue in existing US bases or Greek airforce bases – and Greece eventually returned to play a full part in NATO six years later.

The British, though Callaghan was frustrated by his failure to negotiate a settlement, could not help but applaud the way Kissinger had deftly managed to protect British and American defence interests throughout. McNally said, 'In the end the essential military interests of the West remained intact – the intelligence [facilities] and the Turkish membership of the Alliance – and any other scenario put those in jeopardy'. He believed Kissinger's overriding priority throughout the crisis was to maintain Turkey's commitment to the eastern flank of NATO. If America had not placated the Turks (after the Nicosia coup) and a full-scale conflict with Greece had broken out, Turkey might well have declared its neutrality – and in those circumstances it was doubtful that the Russians would have stood idly by. 'When all the dust settled it looked a damn sight more stable for the Americans than some fool British military expedition, knocking the Turks about,' he said.[6]

Kissinger rewarded Callaghan's stoicism at Geneva by flying over to Cardiff to be there in person at a ceremony giving Callaghan the honour of the freedom of the city. The visit attracted many demonstrators with placards, including one which read, 'Callaghan, Murderer of Cyprus'. But nothing could shake Callaghan's admiration for the American Secretary of State. Callaghan recalled, 'At the end [of the meeting] he said with a charm and warmth I could not resist, "Jim, you and I have a trusting relationship, and I shall always open my mind to you knowing you will understand, even when we have differences".'[7]

The anger Kissinger felt towards Britain's betrayal of US interests during the Yom Kippur War had finally been forgotten. MPs in Britain, however, displayed no such satisfaction with Callaghan's handling of the Cyprus crisis. Some had already suspected that the division of Cyprus represented a *fait accompli* on behalf of NATO, to insure against the day when Britain pulled out. Even Labour's Andrew Faulds, who was pro-Turkish Cypriot, said many MPs would not be happy if part of the settlement of the Cyprus situation or part of the defence review were to include 'the abandonment of our base facilities simply for them to be taken over by the United States'.[8]

The following month these fears were heightened – and American justification for their strategy was reinforced – when Roy Mason announced cuts in defence spending across the board, including important military commitments relating to its Cyprus bases. He said the proportion of GNP allocated to defence would be reduced from 5.5 percent to 4.5 percent over ten years. It was indeed decided to pull out of Cyprus and Malta. Once more, the State Department swung into action. After strong representations by the Americans, the decision to abandon Cyprus was reversed.[9] When the review was finalised in March 1975, the government announced wide-ranging cuts in commitments outside NATO, but also within it. But there was to be no wholesale withdrawal from Cyprus. By contrast, British forces were to be wound down and withdrawn from Malta by 1979. Cyprus did suffer some cuts. Crucially, the Vulcan bombers that provided a nuclear strike capability to CENTO were no longer to be permanently stationed on the island, and the squadrons of Lightning fighters and Hercules transporters were to be withdrawn and replaced by smaller detachments. But the spying facilities were spared.

Kissinger had less success with his own congressmen. In September 1974, the campaign for a ban on arms to Turkey was given further legitimacy by the findings of Benjamin Rosenthal, chairman of the Committee on Foreign Affairs investigation into America's role in the Cyprus crisis. He accused Ford and Kissinger of applying to Turkey the same quiet diplomacy that had been so unsuccessful in dealing with the Greek junta, and called for an urgent suspension of military aid to Ankara. He said the United States, as the main supplier of arms to both Greece and Turkey, had a moral responsibility, and was in a key position to influence the Cyprus situation. Ninety percent of the arms used by the Turks to seize 34 percent of the island's territory were US-supplied, but US arms had also been used for seven years to support the Greek military dictatorship, culminating in the coup against the constitutional Government in Nicosia. The situation was balanced on a knife-edge, he concluded: either Greece or Turkey might resort to unilateral action out of frustration, posing considerable danger to world peace and US interests. He said a suspension of arms supplies was 'urgently needed before the Turkish government is tempted to embark on a Phase III military action to aid the Turkish Cypriots'.[10]

That month, the House and Senate cut off military aid to Turkey until substantial progress had been made towards a Cyprus settlement, but Ford vetoed the measures, and a protracted political battle followed, resulting in the arms cut-off being suspended until 10 December. In the meantime, Washington secretly stepped up deliveries to Turkey of jet fighters, bombs, missiles, ammunition and trucks to double the previous year's level between September and November.[11]

Kissinger staged a meeting with Greek and Turkish Foreign Ministers in Brussels on 11 December, and declared that Turkey had been willing to make concessions several months earlier but had not done so because of the embargo campaign. This helped delay the arms cut-off until 5 February 1975. Then, in the last week of January, Turkey made the surprise announcement that it was pulling 1000 troops off Cyprus, after pressure from Kissinger. But congressmen refused to stop the ban coming into force. Ford was furious. He said the ban would impede the negotiation of a settlement on Cyprus and 'affect adversely not only Western security but the strategic situation in the Middle East', jeopardising 'the system on which our relations in the Eastern Mediterranean have been based for 28 years'.[12]

The Turks immediately demanded negotiations on the future of the 26 US bases and installations in their country. These included one nuclear bomber base, strategically crucial telemetry stations and other important intelligence-gathering facilities for monitoring Soviet military communications. The administration battled feverishly to repeal the embargo. Ford met 140 legislators at a White House breakfast – part of one of the most intensive lobbying efforts ever attempted on any foreign policy issue. Opponents said this would mean capitulating to Turkish 'blackmail'. Defence Secretary Schlesinger, who had earlier criticised the Turks, now testified that the loss of intelligence stations in Turkey would be a disaster. They had provided crucial information on the alert of Soviet airborne divisions during the Yom Kippur War, and were now needed to monitor Soviet compliance with strategic arms limitation deals. However, attempts to persuade the House of Representatives to suspend the ban were defeated in July, humiliating the President.[13]

The next day, the Turkish Government retaliated by announcing that the activities of US bases – including electronic monitoring stations that tracked the movement of Soviet troops and missile launches within the USSR were to be suspended. Turkish forces would take control of all but one of the US military installations, and use of the biggest NATO air-base, Incirlik, was restricted to NATO purposes. Operations were halted at 26 bases and installations, including four key intelligence-collecting centres at Karamursel, Sinop, Diyarbakir (and Pirinclik) and Belbasi.[14]

America's allies in Europe were aghast at this disastrous turn of events. They had forgiven Washington's *realpolitik* on the Cyprus question only because it seemed to have provided the best result for Western security interests, but now the whole strategy had been undermined – and there was no knowing what other future policies might be torn up by congress. Even Kissinger, according to Nixon biographer A.L. Sulzberger, claimed he could have settled the 'Aegean mess' but for the congress-imposed arms ban. Instead, the rift over Cyprus had become the biggest failure of his career as a statesman.[15] Nixon himself believed Turkey was now dangerously close to cutting itself loose from its allies, imperilling vital military and intelligence facilities, and dramatically undermining the West's strategic position in the Middle East.

Piece by piece, relations with Turkey had to be put back together again. According to Anthony Sampson, the State Department began by secretly approving a circumvention of the arms ban, enabling Turkey to buy two squadrons of Starfighters produced in Italy.[16] By October enough heads had been knocked together for a new bill, partially lifting the arms embargo, to be passed by the House and Senate and signed by Ford. It allowed Turkey to receive $52 million of arms paid for before the embargo came in, and $133 million more. The President had to report every 60 days on progress on Cyprus as part of the deal.[17]

Two weeks later, the Turks said they would negotiate a new joint defence agreement. It was signed on 26 March 1976, and enabled the resumption of activities suspended in July 1975. It also stipulated that all activities should be carried out jointly by Turkey and the United States, and that all intelligence material be shared. This apparent restriction was not as comprehensive as it sounds, for Turkey was insisting only on the right to assign 50 percent of the personnel – but it could choose not to, letting the United States supply them all. In return, Turkey was awarded $1280 million in military loans, credits and finance deals. It was also loaned a squadron of fighter-bombers.[18]

The new US President, Jimmy Carter, eventually secured an end to the embargo in August 1978. Consequently, Washington signed a new base agreement with Turkey in 1980 and, though it appeared to maintain the restriction on operations to NATO purposes set down in the 1969 and 1976 agreements, unpublished supplementary provisions allowed further mutual agreement on action involving US forces operating 'outside the NATO area'. Also, the Turks did insist that all intelligence information collected through bases in Turkey should be shared with them.[19] By the end of the decade, the division of Cyprus looked far more of a coup for the United States than the damaging split with Turkey over the embargo had made it seem. NATO's southern wing was back together, the Soviets had been kept out of the area, and the balance of power in the Eastern Mediterranean had been successfully shifted in favour of America's most strategically important ally there. In addition, the effective partition of the island had secured a stake in Cyprus for NATO as insurance against British withdrawal, and prevented a feared takeover by the powerful communist movement.

In August 1977, Makarios, having survived so many assassination attempts, died of a heart attack. Among a host of tributes from international leaders were messages of support from Tito and Brezhnev, who praised Makarios's uncompromising efforts to assert Cyprus's independence. But he did not live to see the island reunited. Since then, the two communities have been as divided as ever on the way forward. The Greek Cypriots demand the right to return and reclaim their property in the north, and the freedom to live in or move around any part of Cyprus. But the Turkish Cypriots, who set up their own self-styled republic and have allowed tens of thousands of Turkish immigrants to settle in the north, believe the Greek Cypriots have to be kept out, as a matter of survival.

In 1985, Kenan Attakol, their Deputy President and foreign affairs spokesman, summed up their case: 'We cannot possibly let the Greek-Cypriot refugees come back – if we do, it means bloodshed, we start the vicious circle all over again'. He said that from December 1963 the Greek Cypriots forced the Turkish Cypriots to live on 2 percent of the land for eleven years, making them virtual prisoners in their homes, and harassed them and massacred them in their villages. 'And now the world asks, "Why are you fighting?" We are fighting to be treated as first-class citizens in our own homes. Thanks to Turkey – that came [to our rescue] and watches the border – we are happy, we are free.'[20]

As long as the Cold War continued there was little incentive for the Americans – or the British – to end the division of the island. Throughout the 1970s and 1980s the arms race quickened at a dangerous rate. The SALT I agreement had put a ceiling on the number of nuclear missiles that both superpowers could maintain, but in 1975 the Soviets substantially expanded their ICBM test facilities at Tyuratam, and afterwards continuously upgraded their missiles to enable them to carry more and heavier warheads and improve accuracy. Monitors in Cyprus and elsewhere convinced the Americans that they had achieved great leaps in their capability, and were going way beyond trying to achieve an effective deterrent. They wanted the superiority to be able to fight and win a global nuclear war.[21]

When vital spy stations used to track Soviet missile tests were lost from Iran, Cyprus was the best-placed alternative site. The Stockholm International Peace Research Institute (SIPRI) said in 1980 that it believed a powerful new over-the-horizon radar was being earmarked for Cyprus to spy on cruise missile and ICBM tests in the southern USSR.[22] The three American monitoring stations at Karavas, Mia Milea and Yerolakkos in the Turkish-occupied north of the island had closed in 1975 during the arms embargo row with Turkey, but re-opened in 1978, and a new US station was built on the Karpas pensinsula, according to Richelson and Ball (see Appendix).[23] (However, developments in satellite intelligence monitoring and early warning systems gradually reduced the reliance on ground stations.) A congress report also said NATO needed to find new places to deploy rapid response forces outside the NATO area, because the allies had shown in the Yom Kippur war that they could not be relied upon to risk offending Arab opinion – and Cyprus fitted the bill as a staging post-cum-launch-pad for operations in the Middle East. The report noted that the United States had covertly used Akrotiri for reconnaissance, communications and intelligence-gathering in the past.[24] It may have been no coincidence, therefore, that in the 1980s Turkey built a NATO-standard airport at Lefkonico in northern Cyprus, which Greek Cypriots feared would be used for covert strategic operations as well as to facilitate a future Turkish take-over of the whole island. It allowed Turkey to land up to 9000 troops in between two and three hours.[25]

Little effort, however, was put into reuniting the island, an objective which did not seem to suit the West's strategic interests. A 1987 committee of British MPs, charged with investigating the continued division of the island, found the United States more concerned with maintaining good relations with Turkey and that even their own Government had done little since 1974 to bring the two sides back together. The British Government blocked MPs' attempts to examine how British policy could be changed to help find a solution.[26]

When Ronald Reagan took over in the White House in 1980, he went for broke in the arms race, in an attempt to bring the Soviet Union to its knees through the sheer cost of trying to outpace the Americans. Mobile ICBMs were developed to dodge the Soviet threat to the silos. Five European allies were persuaded to deploy cruise missiles, and Washington announced plans to test 'Star Wars' anti-ballistic missile technology in an attempt to coax the Soviets into a massive and costly programme of research to rival them. The gamble paid off. The Soviets spent so much money trying to match America's nuclear muscle that 37 percent of the communist superpower's budget was swallowed up by defence and the Soviet empire went bust.[27] The collapse of the Berlin Wall and the drawing back of the Iron Curtain heralded a series of dramatic disarmament agreements, which ultimately slashed nuclear arsenals by two-thirds, down to the levels of the 1960s. All multiple warheads were to be scrapped within a decade. The communist threat evaporated.

Subsequently, Cyprus played an important intelligence and logistical role in the Gulf War against Saddam Hussein. But with no Soviet Bloc left for the island to defect to, Reagan's successor, George Bush, declared in 1991 that in the new world order being fashioned after the collapse of communism 'none of us should accept the status quo in Cyprus'. He committed himself to solving the problem 'this year'.

However, the evil genie of inter-ethnic hatred cannot be put back in the bottle that easily. Unleashed with prompting by Eden in the 1950s, encouraged by US-British moves to block re-integration in the 1960s, and solidified by the invasion that the Americans implicitly encouraged in 1974, it continues to this day. Years of on-off talks about troop withdrawals, haggling over where a new dividing line should fall, and whether Cyprus should become a federation or a confederation in which the two sides hardly meet, have come to nothing. Clerides in 1985 admitted, 'Both sides have made mistakes. Our biggest was that when we were in a position of strength we did not give a little more to finish the Cyprus problem. Now the Turks are making the same mistake. They are in a position of strength and they are demanding their pound of flesh.'[28]

In recent years, tension has begun to rise once more, as Greek Cypriots have vented their frustration in demonstrations across the green line and Cyprus's application to join the EU, submitted in 1990 but only now being considered, has threatened to bring matters to a head.

Clerides, elected President of Cyprus in his own right in 1993 and 1997, racheted up the pressure on Washington and London to find a solution by signing a defence agreement with Andreas Papandreou's Government in Athens, in which Greece pledged to provide air, naval and ground support to defend Cyprus from Turkish aggression. Athens then secured a pledge from the EU to begin negotiations on Cyprus's accession, which have now begun. During the signing of the agreement, Turkish Foreign Minister Murat Karaylcin threatened to annex northern Cyprus if the island was admitted to the EU before a political settlement had been agreed.[29] Clerides piled on more pressure by building air and naval facilities on Cyprus for Greek warships and planes, and ordered £400 million worth of Russian surface-to-air missiles, said to be capable of destroying Turkish jets on take-off 90 miles away. Ankara's response was sharp. In 1998, Turkey threatened to blow up the missiles on their launchers, if they ever arrived, or eliminate them on their way, risking war with Greece and Russia. They also threatened a new 1974-style operation. But the Americans – unlike in 1974 – moved swiftly to slap down the threat. The State Department said, 'No country – specifically you, Turkey – shall threaten military force against Cyprus'.[30]

For years the protests along the green line dividing Nicosia have increasingly threatened to explode into violence on the anniversaries of the 20 July landing and the 14 August invasion. For instance, in August 1996 a Greek Cypriot, Tassos Isaac, was beaten to death by Turkish-Cypriot counter demonstrators on the edge of the Turkish-Cypriot zone at Dherinia. Three days later, another Greek Cypriot, Solomos Solomou, was shot dead at the same spot by Turkish security forces after he broke through barbed wire on the edge of the buffer zone and tried to climb a flagpole to tear down a Turkish flag. A refugee, formerly from Turkish-occupied Famagusta, he had known Isaac, and had marched to the buffer zone with hundreds of mourners an hour after Isaac's funeral. He was hit by five bullets in the neck, leg, heart and abdomen.

The trouble began on 11 August, when Greek-Cypriot motorbikers, supported by other protestors, tried to break through the buffer zone at different points along its 112-mile length, to protest at the continuing Turkish occupation of the north. Thousands broke through National Guard and UN lines and squared up to Turkish soldiers and Turkish-Cypriot counter-protestors. Government attempts to prevent the demonstrations were ignored, and troops from the

Turkish side fired on the bikers when they broke through the ceasefire line. UN troops formed a human chain at one point to keep the two communities apart, but the Greek Cypriots started fires and threw stones. More than 50 people from both sides were wounded, and the clashes spread to other areas around the British base at Dhekelia. At Dherinia, an estimated crowd of 1000 demonstrators was confronted by stone-throwing Turkish Cypriots and men wielding clubs and staves, who beat Isaac to death. Since then, streets and squares have been named after Solomou.[31]

Britain's Special Envoy to Cyprus, Sir David Hannay, told the TV programme 'Newsnight' that 'the status quo is not really sustainable, this problem that has festered for so long has a capacity to get worse'. Not even Richard Holbrooke, the successful peace-broker who helped halt the vicious ethnic cleansing in Bosnia, could get the two sides on Cyprus around the negotiating table. He warned that Greece and Turkey's disputes over uninhabited islands in the Aegean were nothing compared to the Cyprus problem. 'If these little rocks nearly exploded,' he said, 'think of a serious island, with serious people and a Berlin-type wall running down the middle of it'.[32] If no agreement is reached, it seems, it will be hard to avoid more bloodshed.

APPENDIX
Interview with Henry Kissinger

When we had pieced together the Cyprus jigsaw, it was obvious that we had to put our allegations to Henry Kissinger, who was Secretary of State and National Security Adviser during this period. We asked for an interview, and he appeared receptive. Brendan O'Malley flew to New York, but when he arrived, Kissinger appeared to cancel the interview.

'Mr O'Malley, I don't think I need to answer any of your questions – all the answers are in my book,' he said bluntly.

He revealed that his latest memoirs were due out the following day in America. When O'Malley protested, Dr Kissinger offered a compromise – read the book for an hour and if there were still any unanswered questions, he might address them. The 1150-page book, *Years of Renewal*, is the third instalment of Kissinger's reflections on his last years in office, starting at the collapse of the Nixon administration but concentrating on the Ford years. A 47-page chapter on the Cyprus crisis portrays the 1974 events as a straight-forward ethnic dispute like the post-Cold War conflicts in Bosnia, Rwanda and elsewhere.

He implies that it was purely a 'cruel twist of fate' that a non-elected President was immediately plunged into the 'maelstrom of Greek-Turkish passions', ignoring America's long history of back-room deals and plotting over Cyprus. For instance, he blamed as a contributing factor the 'weak' system of guarantees of the independence agreements 'brokered by Britain' in 1959. In fact it was Eisenhower who forced Macmillan to give up sovereignty over the island in favour of bases, and it was Washington that secretly negotiated the arrangement, long opposed by the British, for independence to be guaranteed by Greece, Britain and Turkey rather than Macmillan's preference of rule by a tridominium of those three countries. Similarly, Kissinger does not mention US plans, drawn up in February 1964, to allow a limited Turkish occupation of the island and proposals considered by George Ball and Dean Acheson to force Greece and Turkey to divide the island – including one suggestion that the Greeks should declare enosis and then come to a prearranged deal with the Turks to concede a slice of Cyprus for a military base.

He also makes no observation on whether Nixon's deepening military ties with the Athens junta enabled Ioannides to pursue his adventures in Cyprus – though he reveals that when he ordered diplomats to tell Ioannides on the day after the coup that the United States supported Cyprus's independence, the US Embassy reported back that the Greek Colonel was furious. 'One day Kissinger makes public statements regarding non-interference in Greek internal affairs and a few weeks later the USG (US Government) threatens interference,' Ioannides was reported as saying.[1]

In the interview with O'Malley, Kissinger denied that he regarded Archbishop Makarios as the Castro of the Mediterranean, or that there had been any grand design to get rid of him. 'We weren't particularly wild about him. But we didn't have a strategy to get rid of him,' Kissinger said.

Was he not concerned, then, that Makarios would lead Cyprus into the Eastern Bloc? 'We were concerned,' he said, 'not because he was a Castro, but because he overestimated the scope of his action, and he was very confident in his dexterity'. He knew how to play one side off against the other – the super-powers? 'Exactly.'

He also said he did not think Harold Wilson was a Soviet spy, and dismissed Duncan Campbell's claim that he had shut down intelligence links with Britain for a week as punishment for Edward Heath not letting him use the Cyprus bases to help the airlift to Israel in the Yom Kippur War. Campbell told us this was revealed to him by high-level defence sources (conversation with Brendan O'Malley, April 1999), but Heath, while admitting that Britain had refused to allow Nixon to use the bases on Cyprus, claimed that the Americans had respected that decision. He told us he had no recollection of the Americans cutting off intelligence information.[2]

Kissinger's memoirs refer explicitly to the importance of US intelligence sites in Turkey during the Cold War, but not to that of the British or American facilities on Cyprus. Yet in 1974, at a crucial phase in the arms race, when the Soviets threatened future dominance, Cyprus was the site of state-of-the-art over-the-horizon-radar facilities, built by the British but operated by the Americans, which were uniquely capable of monitoring all phases of Soviet nuclear missile test flights from Kapustin Yar and Tyuratam.[3]

State Department papers show that it is normal practice for US diplomatic staff to keep Washington informed of potential political threats to US or Western defence interests. Britain's military Chief of Staff in 1974, Field Marshal Sir Michael Carver, confirmed that, as a result of Harold Wilson's plans for drastic cuts in defence spending, withdrawal from Britain's bases on Cyprus was being considered when Ioannides launched his coup. And Barbara Castle, a minister in Wilson's Government, noted that the Americans later told the British that they feared Britain's plans to withdraw from Cyprus would result in the Mediterranean being turned into a 'Russian lake'. Both Carver and Castle said the abandonment of the Cyprus bases was scuppered after pressure from the Americans. However, Kissinger now denied in the interview that he shared the American concern about the loss of the British intelligence sites and bases. He said, 'I did not think the British would abandon them. It's nothing that is looming in my mind'.

When asked how the Americans could keep using the facilities in the north of Cyprus after the invasion, in a state which they did not recognise, Kissinger said that the Americans had so many bases all over the world, and as long as they continued operating there was no reason for anyone to raise the issue. Nevertheless, someone in Washington did show concern about the fate of those facilities in 1974. According to one report, the Americans sent a jet to Cyprus on 11 May to pick up equipment from their own intelligence stations at Mia Milea and Karavas in anticipation of the invasion, which took place two months later. The report said the US stations in Cyprus were considered vitally important to the secret services of the United States, and they were guarded by specially trained units of the Marines and CIA agents.[4]

The conversation turned to US plans in 1964, devised by US acting Secretary of State George Ball and British Commonwealth Relations Secretary Duncan Sandys, to control a limited Turkish invasion, and the plans of Ball and Acheson, which Komer and Kissinger's patron, McGeorge Bundy, knew about, to let Greece declare enosis and give a slice to Turkey for a military base in a pre-arranged deal. Kissinger denied that his actions were influenced by these schemes. He said he had never heard of them, and stressed that the crisis was 'totally unexpected'. So why did he not pay much attention in his book to the warnings of the coup given by the CIA? Kissinger: 'Look, the CIA, whenever something happens, lists all the warnings; how many of them they put in the presidential [briefings] – I don't know that. All of May I was away.' He was also away between 10 and 18 June.

O'Malley: 'But the first reports came on 3 and 5 June, and you were there in the middle of June; you left on 27 June. Junior officials tried for weeks [to get you to warn off Ioannides]…' Kissinger interrupted: 'Saying what? What did it say?' O'Malley: 'They claimed they had given as strong a warning as they ever do in these circumstances'. Kissinger said he did tell the Ambassador in Greece, Henry Tasca, to warn off the junta. O'Malley pointed out that the warnings were low key because Tasca wasn't in the know, as the CIA was dealing with the junta, not Tasca, and the record showed that Tasca was kept in the dark. 'The CIA didn't tell him?' Kissinger asked. O'Malley said that the Select Committee on Intelligence inquiry was told that Tasca did not warn forcefully, then he went on holiday and it was left to his deputy, who repeated the ill-informed view of the risk to Joseph Sisco, who then decided not to issue a strong warning.

'Why would we possibly want a crisis at this time?' asked Kissinger.

O'Malley: 'What if Ioannides was so unstable and was already provoking a conflict with Turkey in the Aegean over oil, and you wanted to induce it to get rid of him?' Kissinger: 'You find me one document reading that anything like this ever came up and you could make me such a case. Otherwise it's just a journalist's dream.'

O'Malley: 'There were plans in the 1960s that follow that pattern – that you were not involved in – to encourage enosis by the Greeks in order to let the Turks, who would then as a concession, come in under a prearranged deal'. Kissinger said he had never seen such a plan. 'So what if someone came up with the idea that this was some sort of long-held blueprint – as Andreas Papandreou claimed?' Kissinger: 'He would be wrong'.

O'Malley asked about events after the coup – Kissinger said in his account that he didn't want to give Turkey a pretext for going into Cyprus by condemning the coup, yet when the Turks saw that he was stalling efforts at the UN for a motion doing just that it merely reinforced their belief that they would have to go in if they were going to change anything.

'It's easy for someone sitting around, like you, to find some document here, another document there,' said Kissinger. 'I was convinced it would end in a debacle for Greece.' He suggested that he thought US interference would ruin the chances of the junta falling.

In his book, Kissinger says he considered Makarios 'more of a nuisance than a menace'. He writes, 'At no time during my period in office did we take any measure to reduce his hold on power'. However, Callaghan recalled that after the coup Kissinger was 'cool' about letting Makarios return to the island. And Kissinger himself said in the interview that Callaghan 'had the idea of letting the Turks in [to Cyprus] to bring back Makarios, which I thought was nuts'.

Callaghan's political aide, Tom McNally, by contrast remembered British ministers in war-planning meetings considering the placing of the Sixth Fleet alongside British warships, led by assault carrier *Hermes*, in between Cyprus and Turkey to stop an invasion.

Kissinger did not recall being asked to consider this. 'I don't think they [the British] asked us,' he said, insisting moments later that it never happened. 'This was never put... There was no such discussion within our Government.' In fact, in his book he says that on 17 July he told Nixon that the Europeans were clamouring for 'some kind of assault on the Greeks' but he thought Ioannides was 'going to fall anyway'[5] and was more concerned with trying to keep both Greece and Turkey in NATO than taking sides.

On British demands for deterrent action against Turkey, Kissinger said he had an excellent relationship with Callaghan, and held him in very high regard, but he didn't think the Turks were going to accept another humiliation and the junta was isolated. Asked if he meant that because of the culminating Watergate crisis, America could not have copied President Johnson's veto of Turkish action, Kissinger said, 'No, I'm not sure that we would have wanted to either'. He said sending in the Sixth Fleet as Johnson had would have alienated Turkey.

He also thought Britain was unrealistic in demanding that Makarios be brought back. 'Makarios was not found until Tuesday; [Turkish premier Bulent] Ecevit came to London on Wednesday. How on that timetable could anything happen? The British were saying bring Makarios back [and get the Greek officers out]. How were we going to do that in 48 hours?' O'Malley: 'That was the deadline for Turkish military action?' Kissinger: 'Yes'. Instead of proposing military action, he says in his book, he instructed his crisis manager, Joseph Sisco, to put to Callaghan and Ecevit a proposal that Clerides should take over as acting President of Cyprus for six months, when a new election could be held. This would enable a return to constitutional arrangements but keep Makarios out of the way while a new intercommunal arrangement was negotiated for the island.[6] He said in the interview that the first invasion was expected – but the second took him by surprise – and that he asked Sisco to deliver a sharp warning to the Turks saying that 'the US would take the gravest view of Turkish military moves before all diplomatic processes are exhausted'. He admits in his memoirs that he said this had to be done immediately 'because I think we have been waffling and weeping around the place and we have not made clear that we are opposed to military intervention'. Military intervention, Sisco was told to say, would 'not only have serious adverse effects for Turkey in the long run but will be extremely dangerous for the West as a whole'.

Kissinger concedes that America's domestic situation and Greece's recklessness presented Turkey with a unique opportunity in Cyprus.[7] He says that after the invasion started he told Sisco to tell Ecevit that 'we are deeply disappointed the Turkish government did not heed our pleas to exercise restraint'. In the interview with O'Malley he denied Turkish writer Mehmet Ali Birand's claim that when he pushed Ecevit to accept a ceasefire during the first invasion he encouraged him to think his troops could continue moving forward after it. 'Absolutely untrue,' Kissinger said. Similarly, he denied telling Ecevit during the Geneva talks that if he signed up to a settlement he did not have to agree to the part in it saying that Turkish troops should withdraw, but could do what he did at the time of the first ceasefire and ignore it.

One interesting revelation in Kissinger's book is the firm belief of everyone, including himself, who attended the Washington Special Actions Group crisis meeting on 15 July, the day of the coup, that 'the coup had been instigated by the Greek junta in Athens – more specifically by General Ioannides'.[8]

Another is that he regarded Turkey as even more important geopolitically than Greece, and that he 'rejected Callaghan's request to support the threat of a British air-strike against Turkish ceasefire violations'[9] during the second Geneva talks.

He also claims that he proposed a cantonal solution because it would not involve an exchange of populations. Yet maps of the intercommunal make-up of the towns and villages at the time show that not a single canton could have avoided such exchanges.

So did Kissinger have any regrets at all about the way he handled the crisis? 'I have no regrets,' he said, adding that he thought that if he had been at the second Geneva talks the problem would have been solved. O'Malley pointed out that, while he had said that he was too busy at the time because of Watergate, the accounts showed he had an extraordinarily detailed knowledge of where the Turks were positioned.

'Now wait a minute,' Kissinger said. 'Therefore you conclude what? That I colluded with the Turks on the second invasion?' O'Malley: 'You appeared to encourage them, according to reports of what you said to them. You also said you were too busy to be involved.' Kissinger: 'Wait a minute. I was too busy before the crisis started. Once the crisis started I was certainly on top of it. That was my duty.'

In the end, he writes in his memoirs, 'the Ford administration did achieve its most important objective: the eastern flank of NATO, though strained, remained intact... The communal conflict between Greeks and Turks on Cyprus has proved intractable for centuries. However, preserving the general peace and the structure of the Western Alliance on which peace depended were important objectives in their own right'.[10]

NOTES ON THE TEXT

Full details of all works cited here can be found in the bibliography

INTRODUCTION

1 Kissinger, *Years of Upheaval*, p 1188.
2 House of Commons Select Committee on Cyprus, session 1975–6.
3 Interview with Geoffrey Dickens MP, 1985.
4 Appendix 6 to House of Commons Select Committee on Cyprus; interview with Tom McNally, former political aide to James Callagahan.
5 *Guardian*, 2.4.88.
6 *Guardian*, 7.4.88.

CHAPTER 1

1 British Cabinet minutes C 54 245, 21.7.54.
2 Wint and Calvocoressi, *Middle East Crisis*, pp 128-31; *British Interests in the Mediterranean and Middle East*, report by a study group of the Royal Institute of International Affairs, p 27.
3 British Cabinet papers CP56 122, 14.5.56.
4 Porter and Stockwell, *British Imperial Policy and Decolonisation 1938–64*, pp 243–6.
5 *The Sunday Times*, 28.5.89.
6 British Cabinet papers CP51 132, 17.5.51.
7 British Cabinet minutes CM51 36, 22.5.51.
8 See W.R. Louis et al.
9 Porter and Stockwell, *Middle East*, pp 25–30.
10 West, *The Friends*, p 90.
11 West, *The Friends*, p 70.
12 *The Times*, 25.7.55.
13 British Cabinet minutes C57 69.
14 British Cabinet minutes, CP55 94, 25.7.55.
15 British Cabinet minutes C57 69.
16 Reddaway, *Burdened with Cyprus*, p 11

CHAPTER 2

1 British Foreign Secretary's memo on the future of the Italian Colonies, 13.3.46.
2 Vanezis, *Makarios*, p 25.
3 Mayes, *Makarios*, pp 26–35.
4 Grivas, *Memoirs*, pp 13–16.
5 Grivas, *Memoirs*, pp 18–19.

6 Grivas, *Memoirs*, pp 18–19.
7 Mayes, *Makarios*, p 51.
8 British Cabinet minutes CC54 53, 26.7.54.
9 Mayes, *Makarios*, p 53.
10 British Cabinet minutes, C54 245, 21.7.54.
11 British Cabinet minutes, C54 245, 21.7.54.
12 British Cabinet minutes, CC54 53, 26.7.54.
13 Grivas, pp 204–6; Crawshaw, *The Cyprus Revolt*, p 128.
14 Crawshaw, *The Cyprus Revolt*, p 255.
15 Crawshaw, *The Cyprus Revolt*, pp 105, 344.
16 Grivas, *Memoirs*, p 4.
17 Reddaway, *Burdened*, p 73.
18 Grivas, *Memoirs*, pp 15–20.
19 Grivas, *Memoirs*, pp 32, 208.
20 Barker, *Grivas*, p 8; Crawshaw, *The Cyprus Revolt*, p 349.
21 Mayes, *Makarios*, 65.

CHAPTER 3

1 Eden's Memo to British Cabinet C55 93, 5.4.55.
2 British Cabinet papers CP55 33, 11.6.55; British Cabinet minutes CM55 14, 14.6.55.
3 *The Times*, 16.6.55.
4 *The Times*, 21.6.55.
5 Memo to British Cabinet, C55 93, 5.4.55.
6 *The Times*, 20.6.55–25.6.66.
7 Lamb, *The Failure of the Eden Government*, p 131.
8 British Cabinet minutes CM55 18, 28.6.55.
9 British Chiefs of Staff meeting minutes COS55 63, 4.8.55.
10 *The Times*, 2.7.89.
11 British Chiefs of Staff Joint Planning Committee JP55 63, 11.7.55, plus annex.
12 British Chiefs of Staff Joint Planning Committee JP55 63, 11.7.55, plus annex.
13 British Chiefs of Staff Joint Planning Committee JP55 63, 11.7.55, plus annex.
14 British Chiefs of Staff Joint Planning Committee JP55 63, 11.7.55, plus annex.
15 British Cabinet Papers CP55 94, 25.7.55.
16 British Chiefs of Staff meeting COS55 216, 31.8.55.
17 Memo to British Cabinet, C55 93, 5.4.55.
18 *The Times*, 15.7.55–6.8.55.
19 British Cabinet minutes CM55 28, 15.8.55.
20 British Cabinet minutes CM55 29, 26.8.55.
21 British Foreign Office papers FO 371, 12401.
22 Lamb, *The Failure of the Eden Government*, p 132.
23 *The Times*, 2.9.55.
24 British Cabinet minutes, CM55 30, 5.9.55.
25 *The Times*, 8.9.55.
26 *The Times*, 9.9.55.
27 Eden, *Full Circle*, 402.
28 *The Times*, 8.9.55
29 British Cabinet minutes, CM55 36, 20.10.55.

CHAPTER 4

1 British Military Joint Planning Committee, JP55 63, 11.7.55.
2 Calvocoressi, *World Politics Since 1945*, p 222.
3 *The Times*, 28.9.55, 30.9.55.
4 Lamb, *The Failure of the Eden Government*, p 135.
5 Eden, *Full Circle*, pp 404–5.
6 *The Times*, 21–23.11.55.
7 British Colonial Committee, note by Lennox-Boyd, CO926.555, 23.11.55.
8 *The Times*, 25.11.55.
9 *The Times*, 28.11.55.
10 Eden, *Full Circle*, pp 405, 415.
11 *The Times*, 9.12.55.
12 Grivas, *Memoirs*, pp 55–6.
13 British Chiefs of Staff minutes COS56 20, 13.1.56.
14 British Chiefs of Staff minutes COS56 51, 7.2.56; COS56 66, 11.2.56
15 British Chiefs of Staff minutes COS56 51, 7.2.56; COS56 66, 11.2.56; annex to minutes COS56 94, 3.3.56.
16 British Chiefs of Staff meeting annex to minutes COS56 66, 11.2.56.
17 British Cabinet minutes CM56 8, 31.1.56.
18 British Cabinet minutes CM56 16, 22.2.56.
19 British Cabinet minutes, CM56 17, 28.2.56.
20 Grivas, *Memoirs*, p 68.
21 British Chiefs of Staff minutes COS56 104, 13.3.56.
22 *The Times*, 5.3.56; 10.3.56.
23 Hansard, 14.3.56, pp 391–398.
24 British Chiefs of Staff minutes COS56 85, 23.2.56.
25 British Chiefs of Staff minutes, COS56 231, 14.6.56.
26 British Chiefs of Staff minutes COS56 85, 23.2.56; COS56 231, 14.6.56.
27 British Chiefs of Staff minutes COS56 85, 23.2.56; COS56 231, 14.6.56.
28 British Chiefs of Staff minutes COS56 85, 23.2.56; COS56 231, 14.6.56.
29 Hansard, 14.3.56, pp 397–401.

CHAPTER 5

1 Kirkpatrick, *The Inner Circle*, p 262, quoted in Macmillan, *Riding the Storm*, p 95.
2 Macmillan, *Riding the Storm*, p 93.
3 *The Times*, 6.4.56; 9.4.56.
4 *The Times*, 6.4.56; 9.4.56; British Chiefs of Staff annex to minutes COS56 94, 3.3.56.
5 British Chiefs of Staff annex to minutes COS56 160, 20.4.56.
6 *The Times*, 16.1.56.
7 *The Times*, 22.1.56.
8 British Chiefs of Staff annex to minutes COS56 66, 11.2.56.
9 British Chiefs of Staff annex to minutes COS56 20.
10 British Chiefs of Staff minutes COS56 68, 13.2.56.
11 British Chiefs of Staff minutes COS56 9, 9.1.56.
12 British Chiefs of Staff annex to minutes COS56 95, 5.3.56.
13 British Chiefs of Staff annex to minutes COS56 151, 18.4.56.

14 British Cabinet minutes CM56 34, 8.5.56.

15 *The Times*, 28.5.56

16 Barker, *Grivas*, pp 126–7

17 Barker, *Grivas*, pp 126–7

18 *The Times*, 23.4.56.

19 Lamb, *The Failure of the Eden Government*, p 40.

20 British Chiefs of Staff minutes COS56 231, 14.6.56.

21 British Chiefs of Staff minutes COS56 14, 4.1.56.

22 British Colonial Office papers CO926.389, London, 8.6.56.

23 British Cabinet minutes CM56 44, 19.6.56.

24 Macmillan, *Riding the Storm*, p 112.

25 Keightley's despatches in British Prime Minister's Office papers Prem 11/1130.

26 British Cabinet Egypt Committee minutes EC56 43, 6.9.56.

27 Jackson, *Suez 1956*, pp 15, 71; Thomas, *The Suez Affair*, p 142.

28 Nasser interviewed by Erskine Childers for the BBC in 1966, published in *Suez, Ten Years After*, BBC Third Programme series, BBC, London, 1967, p 44.

29 British Colonial Office papers, daily situation reports from Governor Harding CO926/418.

30 British Chiefs of Staff meeting minutes COS56 360.

31 Thomas, *The Suez*, p 71.

32 British Colonial Office papers, CO926/418, Harding's daily situation reports.

33 Lamb, *The Failure of the Eden Government*, p 212, citing British Prime Minister's Office papers Prem 11/1104.

34 Lamb, *The Failure of the Eden Government*, pp 231–41.

35 British Colonial Office papers CO926/418, Harding's daily situation reports.

36 Jackson, *Suez 1956*, pp 66–8.

37 Grivas, *Memoirs*, p 97.

38 Thomas, *The Suez*, p 119.

39 Jackson, *Suez 1956*, pp 63–71.

40 British Colonial Office papers CO926/418.

41 British Prime Minister's Office papers, message to Eisenhower, 5.11.56.

42 Jackson, *Suez 1956*, p 71.

43 Lamb, *The Failure of the Eden Government*, pp 274–9; Jackson, *Suez 1956*, p 100.

44 British Chiefs of Staff minutes COS56 419, 26.11.56.

45 British Chiefs of Staff minutes COS57 220, 11.10.57.

CHAPTER 6

1 Macmillan, *Riding the Storm*, pp 164, 168; British Cabinet minutes and Prime Minister's Office papers CM56 91, 29.11.56; PREM 11.11.35, 29.8.56; CM56 95, 1.12.56; W. Scott Lucas, 'Suez, the Americans, and the Overthrow of Anthony Eden' in *LSE Quarterly*, 1:3, Autumn 1987; Lamb, *The Failure of the Eden Government*, p 279.

2 W. Scott Lucas, 'Suez, the Americans, and the Overthrow of Anthony Eden' in *LSE Quarterly*, 1:3, Autumn 1987, pp 226, 239.

3 W. Scott Lucas, 'Suez, the Americans, and the Overthrow of Anthony Eden' in *LSE Quarterly*, 1:3, Autumn 1987, p 240.

4 British Cabinet minutes CM56 90, pp 91, 92.

5 British Cabinet minutes CM56 90, pp 91, 92.

6   British Cabinet minutes CM56 95.
7   British Cabinet minutes, CM56 96, CM56 98.
8   British Cabinet minutes CM56 99.
9   W. Scott Lucas, 'Suez, the Americans, and the Overthrow of Anthony Eden' in *LSE Quarterly*, 1:3, Autumn 1987.
10 British Cabinet minutes CM57 4, 9.1.57.
11 British Foreign Office papers FO 371/124021.
12 British Chiefs of Staff committee minutes COS56 426.
13 British Cabinet minutes CM56 9C, 12.12.56.
14 Macmillan, *Riding the Storm*, p 176.
15 British Cabinet minutes CM57 2, 8.1.57.
16 Brandon, *Special Relationships*, p 132.
17 British Chiefs of Staff minutes COS56 409, 16.11.56.
18 British Chiefs of Staff minutes COS56 391, 26.10.56.
19 British Chiefs of Staff minutes COS56 448, 21.12.56.
20 US declassified documents, 1989 volume, fiche no. 001094, White House letter, 20.8.54; 001479, 22.6.56, Dulles papers.
21 British Colonial Office papers CO926/626, 13.2.57.
22 British Chiefs of Staff minutes COS56 435; Macmillan, *Riding the Storm*, p 22.
23 Mayes, *Makarios*, p 98.
24 Woodhouse, *Karamanlis*, p 71.
25 British Cabinet minutes CC57 22, 22.3.57.
26 Macmillan, *Riding the Storm*, p 226.
27 Woodhouse, *Karamanlis*, p 71, Averoff, *Lost Opportunities*, p 126.
28 British Colonial Office papers CO926/626, teleg 96 FO to Bermuda delegation.
29 British Cabinet minutes CC57 25 28.3.57.
30 British Chiefs of Staff minutes COS56 20, 13.1.56.
31 Baylis, *Anglo-American Defence Relations 1939–1984*, p 90; Eisenhower, *The White House Years vol. 2: Waging Peace*, p 124.
32 *Hansard*, 1 April 1957, pp 37–58; Baylis, *Anglo-American Defence Relations 1939–1984*, p 90.

CHAPTER 7

1   *The Times*, 18.4.57; Mayes, *Makarios*, pp 104–10.
2   British Chiefs of Staff minutes COS56 426, 30.11.56.
3   British Colonial Office papers CO926/626, telegram, 12.6.57.
4   British Colonial Office papers CO926/626, telegram 586, FO to Paris, 20.6.57; telegram 1319, 21.6.57; Averoff, *Lost Opportunities*, p 141.
5   British Cabinet Minutes C57 161, 9.7.57.
6   Macmillan, *Riding the Storm*, p 660; British Cabinet papers C57 161, 9.7.57.
7   British Cabinet minutes papers C57 161, 9.7.57.
8   British Cabinet minutes CC57 51, 11.7.57.
9   British Cabinet minutes CC57 52, 16.7.57 and C57 161, 9.7.57.
10 British Cabinet minutes CC57 52, 16.7.57.
11 British Cabinet minutes CC57 52, 16.7.57; C57 178, 26.7.57.
12 British Colonial Office papers CO926/627, telegram 811, 12.9.57; telegram 274, Paris to FO.

13 British Colonial Office papers CO926/627.141, account of secret talks between British and US officials.

14 Averoff, *Lost Opportunities*, p 172–3.

15 British Colonial Office papers CO926/627.141, account of secret talks between British and US officials.

16 British Colonial Office papers CO926/627.178.

17 British Cabinet minutes CC58 4, 6.1.58.

18 Foot, *A Start in Freedom*, pp 159–66 and British Cabinet minutes CC58 42, 13.5.58.

19 Reddaway, *Burdened with Cyprus*, p 104.

20 *The Times*, 8.2.58.

21 British Colonial Office papers CO926/627.185; British Cabinet minutes CC58 12, 28.1.58.

22 British Cabinet minutes CC59 14, 4.2.58.

23 Foot, *A Start in Freedom*, p 165.

24 Foot, *A Start in Freedom*, pp 152–3.

25 Macmillan, *Riding the Storm*, pp 666–7.

CHAPTER 8

1   Kaku and Axelrod, *To Win a Nuclear War*, pp 129–30.

2   *The Times*, 21.1.58.

3   British Colonial Office papers CO926/627.207; 213.

4   *The Times*, 9.6.58; Averoff, *Lost Opportunities*, p 229.

5   British Cabinet minutes CC58 47, 10.6.58.

6   British Colonial Office papers, account of NATO negotiations CO926/627.213.

7   British Colonial Office papers, account of NATO negotiations CO926.627.213; 236.

8   British Colonial Office papers, accounts of NATO negotiations CO926/627.236, 16 June, telegram 85; 627.239, telegram 80.

9   British Colonial Office papers, accounts of NATO negotiations CO926/627.236, 16 June, telegram 85; 627.239, telegram 80.

10 British Colonial Office papers, accounts of NATO negotiations CO926/627.236, 16 June, telegram 85; 627.239 telegram 80.

11 *The Times*, 1.7.58.

12 Averoff, *Lost Opportunities*, p 243.

13 British Cabinet papers CC58 55, 14.7.58.

14 Macmillan, *Riding the Storm*, p 520.

15 Maclean, *British Foreign Policy Since Suez*, p 66; Macmillan, *Riding the Storm*, p 517–25.

16 British Colonial Office papers CO926.1015, Sir Hugh Foot on security operations in Cyprus.

17 British Colonial Office papers, accounts of NATO negotiations CO926.628, 26.7.58.

18 British Cabinet minutes CC58 42, 1.5.58.

19 British Colonial Office papers, accounts of NATO negotiations CO926.628, 26.7.58.

20 British Colonial Office papers, accounts of NATO negotiations CO926.628; 29.7.58 telegram 179; CO926.628.303, 31.7.58; telegram 192, 4.8.58.

21 Macmillan, *Riding the Storm*, p 676–8.

22 British Colonial Office papers, accounts of NATO negotiations CO926/628, 5.9.58; CO928/62-8.319; telegrams 223, 1499.

23 British Colonial Office papers, accounts of NATO negotiations CO926/628; telegrams 1499, 241, 22.9.58.

24 British Colonial Office papers, accounts of NATO negotiations CO926/628; telegrams 241/242; document 340/1.

25 Mayes, *Makarios*, p 117.

26 Averoff, *Lost Opportunities*, p 272, quoting interview in the *New York Times*.

27 Grivas, *Memoirs*, p 163.

28 British Colonial Office papers, accounts of NATO negotiations CO26/628; documents 341; 345, 24.9.58; telegrams 1426, 251, 1435.

29 British Colonial Office papers, accounts of NATO negotiations CO26/628; documents 366, 26.9.58; 381; telegram 1399, 28.9.58.

30 British Colonial Office papers CO926/629; documents 404, SD statement, 29.9.58; 415; telegrams 265, 30.9.58; 427; 2946; 1457, 1.10.58; 450.

CHAPTER 9

1 British Colonial Office papers CO926.471, 7.10.58, 459 and 504, 14.10.58.

2 British Colonial Office papers CO926/629.512, 17.10.58; 520, 18.10.58.

3 British Colonial Office papers CO926/630.535, 21.10.58; 568, 26.10.58; 572, 27.10.58.

4 *The Times*, 22.11.58.

5 Averoff, *Lost Opportunities*, pp 273, 283–5.

6 Foreign Office papers FO 371/136387, telegram NY to FO, 5.12.58.

7 Averoff, *Lost Opportunities*, pp 295–6.

8 Foreign Office papers FO 371/136387.

9 Foreign Office papers FO 371/136387, NY to FO, 5.12.58, telegram 8656.

10 Averoff, *Lost Opportunities*, p 299.

11 Averoff, *Lost Opportunities*, pp 302–3.

12 Averoff, *Lost Opportunities*, pp 311.

13 British Colonial Office papers, CO926/630.622, record of meeting at Paris embassy 11.15pm on 16.12.58; telegram from Macmillan and Lennox-Boyd to Foot, 17.12.58.

14 Averoff, *Lost Opportunities*, p 314.

15 British Cabinet minutes CC58 87, 23.12.58.

16 Peter Wright, *Spycatcher*, p 155–9.

17 Peter Wright, *Spycatcher*, p 155–9.

18 Macmillan, *Riding the Storm*, p 693.

19 Macmillan, *Riding the Storm*, p 695–6; Vanezis, *Makarios*, p 52

20 West, *The Friends*, p 75.

21 Bower, *The Perfect English Spy*, p 231.

22 British Colonial Office papers CO926/627.141, 10.57.

23 British Cabinet papers C59 32, 16.2.59.

24 Armacost, *The Politics of Weapons Innovation*, pp 189, 218.

25 British Foreign Office papers, FO371, 144774.

26 Woodhouse, *Karamanlis*, pp 89–91.

CHAPTER 10

1 Foot, *A Start In Freedom*, p 185.

2 Report of Senate Commission, October 1986, Cmnd 9923.

3 West, *GCHQ*, p 99.
4 West, *GCHQ*, pp 99, 274.
5 British Cabinet papers C60 44, 7.3.60.
6 British Colonial Office papers CO926 778, GCHQ MEALF to London, 4.5.59.
7 British Colonial Office papers CO926 778, GCHQ MEALF to London, 4.5.59.
8 British Defence papers, Middle East Defence Secretariat memo, 30.4.59, in CO926/978.
9 British Colonial Office papers CO926/977, 1957; *The Times*, 29.10.85.
10 British Chiefs of Staff meeting minutes COS57 214, 25.9.57.
11 British Colonial Office papers JWPME59, 4.4.59; CO926/977.
12 US State Department papers, 79 295B, Guidelines for Policy and Operations, Cyprus, September 1962, Johnson Library, NSF, NSC History, Cyprus Crisis, December 1963–1967.
13 British Colonial Office papers CO926/977.
14 *The Times*, 14.3.56.
15 British Colonial Office papers CO926/978, Middle East Defence Secretariat memo, 30.4.59.
16 *New York Times*, 17.5.49.
17 Adams and Cottrell, *Cyprus between East and West*.
18 West, *GCHQ*, pp 306–13; *A Matter of Trust*, pp 32; 37.
19 Campbell, *The Unsinkable Aircraft Carrier*, pp 40, 156, 242; *The Times*, March 1956.
20 Treaty of Establishment, exchange of notes between Foot, Makarios and Kutchuk.
21 British Cabinet CC60 30, 10.5.60.
22 British Colonial Office papers, CO926/977, 12.6.57.
23 British Colonial Office papers, CO926/978, Ankara to FO 21.5.59, telegram on conversation between Minister of Defence and Turkish ministers on Cyprus, at Turkish Prime Minister's dinner, 19.5.59; CO926/778/65, FO's JM Addis note, 26.6.59.
24 British Cabinet papers, July 1960, briefing note for Commons debate.
25 British Foreign Office papers, FO371 152929, 27.10.60.
26 British Cabinet papers, CC60 21.
27 *Daily Express*, 24.10.60.
28 *Vima* (newspaper), 13.8.60.
29 British Foreign Office papers FO371 152929, 27.10.60.

CHAPTER 11

1 Oberling, *The Road to Bellapais*, pp 71–6.
2 Mayes, *Makarios*, pp 154–9.
3 US State Department papers, 78 400A, history of Johnson Administration's policy over Cyprus. The US gave $20 million in aid between August 1960 and June 1963.
4 US National Security Council papers 79 274C, 1.6.62, memo from Robert Komer, Senior NSC member, to President; 79 295B, September 1962, State Department guidelines for policy and operations in Cyprus.
5 Reddaway, *Burdened with Cyprus*, p 1940.
6 US government declassified papers, 79 275A, 7.1.63, US official's note.
7 Patrick, *Political Geography and the Cyprus Conflict, 1963–71*, pp 34–8; Reddaway, *Burdened with Cyprus*, p 204.
8 *The Times*, 9.1.64.
9 *The Times*, 23.12.63.

10 *Daily Express*, 28.12.63.
11 British Foreign Affairs Committee, 16.3.87.
12 Carver in Koumoulides (ed.), *Cyprus in Transition*, pp 22–3.
13 *The Times*, 6.1.64.
14 Patrick, *Political Geography and the Cyprus Conflict, 1963–71*, p 50.
15 *Guardian*, 2.4.88; *Turkish Cypriots' Special News Bulletin*, 14.1.64.
16 *Daily Express*, 31.12.63.

CHAPTER 12

1 US State Department papers 79 73B, 30.1.64.
2 US State Department papers 79 72D, 23.1.64, 8.27pm, USUNNY to Secretary of State.
3 US State Department papers 73A 79, 25.1.64, memo of conversation between US and UK officials (Ball, Philips Talbot, William Burdett, Sir David Ormsby Gore and Patrick Wright).
4 Carver in Koumoulides (ed.), *Cyprus in Transition*, p 59; *The Times*, 1.2.64; US State Department papers 78 398B, 25.1.64, meeting attended by Ball, Philips Talbot and Bundy.
5 US State Department papers 78 398A, 26.1.64, memo from Philips Talbot to Ambassadors in Athens, Ankara and Nicosia.
6 Ball, *The Past Has Another Pattern*, p 342.
7 US State Department papers 80 206B, briefing paper for visit of Alec Douglas-Home and Rab Butler, 12–13.2.64.
8 *The Times*, 8.2.64.
9 Kitson, *Bunch of Five*, p 241.
10 Kitson, *Bunch of Five*, p 231–2.
11 *The Times*, 13.2.64, 14.2.64.
12 US State Department papers 81 98A, 11.2.63.
13 US State Department papers 79 72D; US State Department papers 80 206B.
14 Ball, *The Past*, p 345.
15 US State Department papers, 79 73E, 13.2.64, 3.41am, Ball telegram to President, Secretaries of State and Defence and Ambassador Stevenson.
16 Ball, *The Past*, p 345.
17 US State Department papers 79 296B, 13.2.64, 12.36pm, Ball to Rusk.
18 *The Times*, 10.2.64.
19 Ball, *The Past*, p 347.
20 Kitson, *Bunch of Five*, p 234.
21 US State Department papers 78 399B, memo from Benjamin Read, Executive Secretary, to McGeorge Bundy, Special Assistant to President for National Security Affairs, 14.2.64.
22 US State Department papers 78 399B, 14.2.64, memo to Ball from Philips Talbot.
23 US State Department papers 78 399B, 14.2.64, memo to Ball from Philips Talbot.
24 US State Department papers 78 399B, 14.2.64, memo to Ball from Philips Talbot.
25 US State Department papers 78 399B, 14.2.64, memo to Ball from Philips Talbot.
26 US State Department papers 78 399B, 14.2.64, memo to Ball from Philips Talbot.
27 *The Times*, 14.2.64.
28 *Daily Express*, 15.2.64.
29 *The Times*, 7.2.64, 15.2.64.

30 US State Department papers 79 74A, 14.2.64, Rusk to Finletter, permanent North Atlantic Council representative.
31 *The Times*, 18.2.64.
32 US State Department papers 78 398C, 9.2.64, telegram 6077, Ball to US Embassy, Athens, 10.51pm.
33 *Daily Express*, 17.2.64.

CHAPTER 13

1 *The Times*, 17.2.64.
2 *Guardian*, 2.4.88.
3 *The Times*, 22.2.64.
4 *The Times*, 22.2.64.
5 *The Times*, 22.2.64.
6 *Guardian*, 7.4.88.
7 *Guardian*, 2.4.88.
8 Kitson, *Bunch of Five*, p 248.
9 *Turkish-Cypriot Special News Bulletin*, no. 67, 2.3.64.
10 Patrick, *Geopolitical Aspects of Conflict between Communities*, pp 60–3.
11 US State Department papers 79 297A, telegram SD to Ank, Nic, Ath, Lon, 13.3.64.
12 Carver, in Koumoulides (ed.), *Cyprus in Transition*, pp 26–9.
13 *Guardian*, 2.4.88.
14 *Guardian*, 7.4.88.
15 Carver, in Koumoulides (ed.), *Cyprus in Transition*, p 30.
16 Patrick, *Geopolitical Aspects of Conflict between Communities*, p 84.
17 Patrick, *Geopolitical Aspects of Conflict between Communities*, p 87.
18 Mayes, *Makarios*, p 174; Patrick, *Geopolitical Aspects of Conflict between Communities*, p 63.
19 *Guardian*, 2.4.88, 7.4.88.
20 US State Department papers 79 297B, telegram from Ambassador Hare Ankara to SD, 4.6.64, 9.52am, account of talk between Inonu and Hare with Erkin present.
21 *The Times*, 5.6.64.
22 US State Department papers 79 297B.
23 Ball, *The Past*, pp 351–2.
24 US State Department papers 78 399C, 5.6.64, State Department Rusk to US Embassy Nicosia, copied to US embassies in Ankara and Athens, 1.24am.
25 Ball, *The Past*, p 350.
26 US State Department papers 79 298A, 6.6.64, 9.31am, 006162, SD incoming, Hare to Rusk.
27 US State Department papers 79 298A, telegram 2, to Secretary of State in Washington from Ambassador Hare in US Embassy Ankara, 9.56, 6.6.64.
28 US State Department papers 79 297C, 6.6.64, Rusk in SD Washington to Athens, 5.12pm.
29 *Guardian*, 2.4.88, 7.4.88.
30 Carver, in Koumoulides (ed.), *Cyprus in Transition*.
31 *Guardian*, 7.4.88.
32 Ball, *The Past*, p 353.
33 US State Department papers 79 298B, 1.6.64, memo of conversation between President Johnson and Alexander Matsas.

34 Ball, *The Past*, p 353.
35 Ball, *The Past*, p 354.
36 Carver, in Koumoulides (ed.), *Cyprus in Transition*, p 30.
37 Ball, *The Past*, p 357.
38 Reddaway, *Burdened with Cyprus*, p 226, quoting memo, 15.6.64, Papandreou to Johnson.
39 Ball, *The Past*, p 357.
40 *Guardian*, 2.4.88; *The Times*, 17.6.64.
41 *Guardian*, 7.4.88.

CHAPTER 14

1 US State Department papers 79 301A, SD summary of Acheson plans I and II, 13.5.69.
2 *Daily Mirror*, 23.6.64.
3 *Daily Mirror*, 25.6.64.
4 US State Department papers 79 301A, SD summary of Acheson plans I and II, drafted, 13.5.69.
5 US State Department papers 79 301A, SD summary of Acheson plans I and II, drafted, 13.5.69.
6 *The Times*, 9.7.64.
7 *The Times*, 27.7.64.
8 Hart, *Two Nato Allies at the Threshold of War*, p 183, quoting notes of 573th NSC meeting.
9 *The Times*, 4.8.64, 6.8.64.
10 Ball, *The Past*, p 357.
11 US State Department papers 79 299B, telegram Hare in Ankara to SD, 8.8.64, 11.13am.
12 *The Times*, 10.8.64, 11.8.64; Patrick, *Geopolitical Aspects of Conflict between Communities*, p 72.
13 US State Department papers 79 300B, US Ambassador Nicosia to SD and copied to Acheson at Geneva, 9.8.64, 9.58am.
14 *The Times*, 10.8.64.
15 *The Times*, 10.8.64.
16 Ball, *The Past*, p 358.
17 US State Department papers 79 301A, SD summary of Acheson plans I and II, 13.5.69.
18 Ball, *The Past*, p 358.
19 US National Security Council papers 77 297A, Robert Komer and McGeorge Bundy memo for Johnson re Cyprus in advance of NSC meeting, 18.8.64. McGeorge Bundy was Kissinger's Dean at Harvard, and recommended him for his first job in government as an adviser to President Kennedy, though Bundy and Kissinger later fell out.
20 US National Security Council papers 77 297A, Robert Komer and McGeorge Bundy memo for Johnson re Cyprus in advance of NSC meeting, 18.8.64.
21 Hart, *Two Allies*, p 186, quoting Memorandum for the Record, 8.9.64, McGeorge Bundy.
22 US State Department papers 78 400A, Johnson Administration, History of Cyprus Problem.

CHAPTER 15

1 US State Department papers 78 431A, 7–8.12.64, Harold Wilson visit background paper on Near East; 79 302B, SD memo of conversation, 19.2.65, between Ball and French Foreign Minister Couve de Murville; Baylis, *Anglo-American Defence Relations*, p 149.
2 Interview with Brendan O'Malley, 1985.
3 Oberling, *The Road to Bellapais*, p 130.
4 Stern, *The Wrong Horse*, p 33; Mayes, *Makarios*, p 184.
5 Reddaway, *Burdened with Cyprus*, pp 133–4.
6 US State Department papers 79 203A, George Ball paper on British sterling crisis, 6.8.65.
7 US State Department papers 79 203B, briefing on visits of Harold Wilson 5–19.10.1965, points to make to him.
8 British Cabinet papers CC6030, 10.5.60.
9 Leigh, *The Wilson Plot*, pp 103–4.
10 US State Department papers 78 293A, 79 202, US military expenses 1964; Ponting, *Breach of Promise*, pp 48–55.
11 Wilson, *The Labour Government*, p 71.
12 Crossman, *Diaries*, vol. 1, p 574.
13 US State Department papers 78 431B, visit of HW to US, 29.6.66, SD briefing paper
14 Ponting, *Breach of Promise*, p 234–7.
15 Baylis, *Anglo-American Defence Relations*, pp 154–7.
16 Ponting, *Breach of Promise*, pp 56–8.
17 US State Department papers 78 294C, visit of Harold Wilson, June 1967, 29.5.67; 5/5, Rusk memo to President re talks which will take place on 2 June in Washington.
18 Castle, *The Castle Diaries 1964–70*, pp 106, 273.
19 Wilson, *The Labour Government 1964–70*, pp 506–12.
20 Wilson, *The Labour Government 1964–70*, p 613.
21 Castle, *The Castle Diaries 1964–70*, p 354.
22 Stern, *The Wrong Horse*, pp 36–40.
23 Hitchens, *Cyprus*, p 64, quoting Janeway, *Prescriptions For Prosperity*.
24 Woodhouse, *Karamanlis*, p 185.
25 Crossman, *Diaries*, p 449.
26 Hart, *Two Allies at the Threshold of War*, pp 49–52.
27 Hart, *Two Allies at the Threshold of War*, pp 66–67.
28 Hart, *Two Allies at the Threshold of War*, p 93.
29 Hart, *Two Allies at the Threshold of War*, p 82.
30 Leigh, *The Wilson Plot*, p 121.
31 US State Department papers 78 400A, Johnson administration's policy re Cyprus.
32 Stern, *The Wrong Horse*, p 106.
33 US State Department papers 79 295D.

CHAPTER 16

1 White, *Breach of Faith*, pp 63–5.
2 Nixon, *Memoirs*, p 400.
3 Woodhouse, *Karamanlis*, p 191.

4 Hersh, *The Price of Power*, p 140; Stern, *The Wrong Horse*, pp 59–64; *New York Times* 2.8.74.
5 Stern, *The Wrong Horse*, p 67.
6 Hersh, *The Price of Power*, p 140.
7 Hitchens, *Cyprus*, p 128, quoting a letter from Senator George McGovern to the Senate Select Committee on Intelligence.
8 Stern, *The Wrong Horse*, p 84.
9 Stern, *The Wrong Horse*, p 87.
10 Mayes, *Makarios*, p 208.
11 Stern, *The Wrong Horse*, p 88.
12 Hitchens, *Cyprus*, p 70.
13 Attalides, *Cyprus*, p 154, quoting *Ta Nea*, Nicosia, 29.1.73.
14 Mayes, *Makarios*, p 214, quoting Turkish newspaper *Yeni Duzen*.
15 Hitchens, *Cyprus*, pp 73–4, quoting *New Statesman*, 10.3.72.
16 Stern, *The Wrong Horse*, p 89.
17 Interview with Brendan O'Malley 1985.
18 Interview with Brendan O'Malley 1985.
19 Stern, *The Wrong Horse*, p 90.
20 Mayes, *Makarios*, p 223.
21 Polyviou, *Cyprus*, p 129.
22 Stern, *The Wrong Horse*, pp 92–3.

CHAPTER 17

1 Collins and Cordesman, *Imbalance of Power*, pp 48–65.
2 Wiley, *Electronic Intelligence and the Analysis of Radar Signals*, p 1.
3 Richelson and Ball, *The Ties That Bind*, p 177.
4 *SIPRI Yearbook 1980*, p 303.
5 *Observer*, 11.8.74; *Aviation Week and Space Technology*, 5.8.74, 19.8.74.
6 *Observer*, 11.8.74; *Aviation Week and Space Technology*, 5.8.74, 19.8.74; *SIPRI Yearbook 1980*, p 295.
7 *SIPRI Yearbook 1980*, pp 299–302.
8 *SIPRI Yearbook 1980*, pp 293, 307–11.
9 *Aviation Week and Space Technology*, 14.1.74, 25.2.74, 11.3.74.
10 Polmar, *Strategic Weapons*, pp 61, 78.
11 Collins and Cordesman, *Imbalance of Power*, p 51.
12 *Aviation Week and Space Technology*, 22.4.74.
13 Kissinger, *Years of Upheaval*, pp 1011, 1028–9.
14 Morris, *Uncertain Greatness*, p 245.
15 Cline, US HoR Select Committee on Intelligence, 1976, p 871.
16 Kaku and Axelrod, *To Win a Nuclear War*, p 170.
17 Campbell, *The Unsinkable Aircraft Carrier*, p 345.
18 Kissinger, *Years of Upheaval*, p 709.
19 Campbell, *The Unsinkable Aircraft Carrier*, p 345.
20 Leigh, *Wilson*, pp 47–51; Peter Wright, *Spycatcher*, p 362; Pincher, *Too Secret Too Long*, p 474.
21 Leigh, *Wilson*, pp 81–6.
22 Wright, *Spycatcher*, pp 362–4; Leigh, *Wilson*, pp 83–5.

23 Wright, *Spycatcher*, p 365.
24 Interview with Brendan O'Malley, September 1994.
25 Interview with Brendan O'Malley, September 1994.
26 Penrose and Courtiour, *The Pencourt File*, pp 240–5.
27 Wright, *Spycatcher*, p 369.
28 Fairhall, *Guardian*, 29.5.74.
29 Carver, *Tightrope Walking*, p 106.
30 Attalides, *Cyprus*, p 159.

CHAPTER 18

1 US HoR intelligence hearings 1975.
2 Stern, *The Wrong Horse*, p 79.
3 Tasca, US HoR, SC on Intelligence, Hearings, p 1538.
4 Stern, *The Wrong Horse*, pp 94–5.
5 Interview with Brendan O'Malley, 1985.
6 US HoR Intelligence, pp 760, 1554.
7 US HoR Intelligence, 1545.
8 Tasca, US HoR, SC on Intelligence, Hearings, p 1532.
9 Woodhouse, *Karamanlis*, p 204.
10 US HoR Intelligence, p 761.

CHAPTER 19

1 US HoR SC Foreign Affairs, VI.
2 Kissinger, *Years of Upheaval*, pp 1187–1193.
3 US HoR SC Intelligence, pp 743, 914–6.
4 British Foreign Affairs SC, 1976.
5 British Foreign Affairs SC, 1976.
6 Interview with Ian Craig and Brendan O'Malley.
7 Interview with Ian Craig and Brendan O'Malley.

CHAPTER 20

1 Interview with Brendan O'Malley, 1985.
2 US HoR SC on Intelligence, pp 842–52.
3 Morris, *Uncertain Greatness*, p 47.
4 US HoR SC on Intelligence, pp 867–8.
5 *Newsweek*, 19.8.74.
6 Duncan Campbell in *New Statesman*, 2.2.79.
7 Morris, *Uncertain Greatness*, pp 214–25; Ranelagh, *The Agency*, p 520.
8 US HoR SC Intelligence, pp 837–8.
9 Leacacos, 'Kissinger's Apparat', in *Foreign Policy*, no. 5, 1971–2, Winter.
10 US HoR SC on Intelligence, pp 814–27, 849.
11 US HoR SC on Intelligence, pp 822, 830.
12 US HoR SC on Intelligence, p 1546.

13 US HoR SC on Intelligence, pp 1528, 1298.
14 *New York Times*, 2.8.74.
15 US HoR SC on Intelligence, p 1543.
16 Hitchens, *Cyprus*, p 79.
17 US National Security Council papers 77 297A, Robert Komer memo for Johnson re: Cyprus in advance of NSC meeting, 18.8.64.
18 US HoR SC on Intelligence, p 763.
19 US HoR SC on Foreign, p 73.
20 US HoR SC on Intelligence, pp 1536–41.
21 US HoR SC on Intelligence, pp 1536–41.
22 Hitchens, *Cyprus*, pp 80, 100.
23 US CIA papers 78 8B, Post-mortem, January 1975.
24 US CIA papers 78 8C, Memo, and annexe, Post-mortem, 3.3.75.
25 US CIA papers 78 8C, Memo, and annexe, Post-mortem, 3.3.75.
26 US HoR SC Intelligence, p 1544.
27 US CIA papers 78 8C, annex and memo, Post-mortem, 1975. An unconfirmed report in the *Cyprus Mail*.
28 *Cyprus Mail*, 14.8.74.
29 US CIA papers, 78 8C, Memo, Post Mortem, 1975.
30 Tasca, US HoR SC Intelligence, 1567.
31 *New York Times*, 2.8.74.
32 Interview with Brendan O'Malley, 1985.
33 *Guardian*, 22.7.74.
34 Interview with Brendan O'Malley, 1985.

CHAPTER 21

1   Interview with Brendan O'Malley, 1985.
2   Interview with Brendan O'Malley, 1985.
3   Interview with Brendan O'Malley, 1985.
4   Interview with Ian Craig and Brendan O'Malley.
5   *New York Times*, 16.7.74; Birand, *30 Hot Days*, pp 3–4.
6   Interviewed by Ian Craig and Brendan O'Malley, 1986.
7   *New York Times*, 17.7.74.
8   Callaghan, *Time and Chance*, p 338.
9   US HoR SC on Foreign Affairs, August 1974, p 54; *New York Times*, 18.7.74.
10 Callaghan, *Time and Chance*, p 339.
11 *New York Times*, 18.7.74.
12 Interview with Ian Craig and Brendan O'Malley.
13 Wilson, *The Final Term*, p 62.
14 Birand, *30 Hot Days*, p 6.
15 Interview with Ian Craig and Brendan O'Malley.
16 *New York Times*, 18.7.74.

CHAPTER 22

1   Birand, *30 Hot Days*, pp 11–13.
2   Wilson, *The Final Term*, p 62.
3   *New York Times*, 19.7.74.
4   Hitchens, *Cyprus*, p 92, quoting Arnold Smith, *Memoirs*.
5   Dana Adams Schmidt in *Christian Science Monitor*, 19.7.74.
6   *New York Times*, 20.7.74.
7   US HoR SC Foreign Affairs.
8   Callaghan, *Time and Chance*, p 348.
9   Wilson, *The Final Term*, p 62.
10 US CIA Post-mortem.
11 US HoR SC on Intelligence, p 802.
12 US HoR SC on Intelligence, pp 802, 1294–5, 1302, 1546.
13 US HoR SC on Intelligence, p 1301.
14 Birand, *30 Hot Days*, p 16.
15 US HoR SC on Intelligence, p 1302.
16 *New York Times*, 20.7.74.
17 US HoR SC on Intelligence, p 1302.
18 *New York Times*, 6.8.74.
19 *The Times*, 20.7.74.
20 *New York Times*, 21.7.74.
21 Birand, *30 Hot Days*, p 19.
22 US HoR SC on Foreign Affairs, 20.8.74, p 38.
23 US CIA Post Mortem.
24 Interview with Brendan O'Malley, 1985.
25 British Foreign Affairs SC, 1976.
26 Interview with Brendan O'Malley, 1985.
27 Interview with Ian Craig and Brendan O'Malley.
28 Interview with Ian Craig and Brendan O'Malley.
29 Callaghan, *Time and Chance*, pp 341–2.
30 Callaghan, *Time and Chance*, pp 341–2.
31 Interview with Ian Craig and Brendan O'Malley.
32 British Foreign Affairs SC, 16.3.87, p 55.
33 Interview with Ian Craig and Brendan O'Malley.
34 Interview with Ian Craig and Brendan O'Malley.
35 Interview with Ian Craig and Brendan O'Malley.
36 *New York Times*, leader, 19.7.74.
37 Interview with Brendan O'Malley 1985.

CHAPTER 23

1   *Washington Post*, 28.8.74.
2   Interview with Brendan O'Malley, 1985.
3   British Colonial Office papers CO925/628, 5.9.58.
4   *Cyprus Mail*, 13.8.74.
5   *New York Times*, 21.7.74.
6   Birand, *30 Hot Days*, p 25; *New York Times*, 21.7.74.

7   Birand, *30 Hot Days*, pp 30–31.
8   Interview with Ian Craig and Brendan O'Malley.
9   European Commission for Human Rights, pp 111–13.
10 *Daily Telegraph*, 22.7.74.
11 British Foreign Affairs committee, appendix 6.
12 *Guardian*, 22.7.74.
13 *The Times*, 22.7.74.
14 Birand, *30 Hot Days*, pp 33–5.
15 *New York Times*, 27.7.74.
16 *New York Times*, 6.8.74.
17 Birand, *30 Hot Days*, pp 38–44.
18 Callaghan, *Time and Chance*, p 345; Birand, *30 Hot Days*, p 39.
19 Callaghan, *Time and Chance*, p 1192.
20 Birand, *30 Hot Days*, pp 30, 39.
21 US State Department papers, memo to George Ball from Philips Talbot, 14.2.64.
22 Birand, *30 Hot Days*, p 44–5; Callaghan, *Time and Chance*, p 346.
23 *New York Times*, 27.7.74.
24 Birand, *30 Hot Days*, p 52.
25 *Sunday Times*, 21.3.76.
26 *New York Times*, 24–25.7.74.
27 British Colonial Office papers CO926/628, 5.9.58.
28 *New York Times*, 24.7.74.
29 Interview with Brendan O'Malley, 1985.
30 US HoR SC on Intelligence, p 1558.
31 US State Department papers, memo from Philips Talbot to George Ball, 14.2.64.
32 Wilson, *The Final Term*, p 64.

CHAPTER 24

1   Interview with Ian Craig and Brendan O'Malley.
2   UN S/11353,269.
3   Morris, *Uncertain Greatness*, p 274.
4   US HoR SC on Intelligence, p 1295.
5   Birand, *30 Hot Days*, p 60.
6   Birand, *30 Hot Days*, pp 63–5.
7   Birand, *30 Hot Days*, pp 66–7 .
8   Birand, *30 Hot Days*, pp 67–72.
9   *New York Times*, 27.7.74.
10 *Guardian*, 30.7.74.
11 Birand, *30 Hot Days*, p 75.
12 *Hansard*, 31.7.74.
13 Interview with Ian Craig and Brendan O'Malley.
14 *New York Times*, 1.8.74.
15 *Hansard*, 31.7.74.
16 *New York Times*, 5.8.74.
17 *Cyprus Mail*, 6.8.74.
18 *Cyprus Mail*, 8.8.74.
19 *New York Times*, 7.8.74.
20 Woodhouse, *Karamanlis*, p 217.

CHAPTER 25

1 Birand, *30 Hot Days*, p 81.
2 *Guardian*, 14.8.74.
3 Interview with Brendan O'Malley, 1985.
4 *Cyprus Mail*, 10.8.74.
5 *New York Times*, 10.8.74.
6 McNally interview with Ian Craig and Brendan O'Malley.
7 Birand, *30 Hot Days*, p 90.
8 Polyviou, *Cyprus*, pp 167–70.
9 Interview with Brendan O'Malley, 1985.
10 Polyviou, *Cyprus*, p 162.
11 *Cyprus Mail*, 11.8.74.
12 Interview with Brendan O'Malley.
13 *New York Times*, 13.8.74.
14 Interview with Ian Craig and Brendan O'Malley.
15 Birand, *30 Hot Days*, p 94.
16 Interview with Ian Craig and Brendan O'Malley.
17 Callaghan, *Time and Chance*, pp 351–3.
18 Interview with Ian Craig and Brendan O'Malley.
19 Birand, *30 Hot Days*, p 93.
20 Polyviou, *Cyprus*, p 172.
21 *New York Times*, 14.8.74.
22 Interview with Ian Craig and Brendan O'Malley.
23 Polyviou, *Cyprus*, pp 174–5.
24 *Guardian*, 13.7.74.
25 *Cyprus Mail*, 13.8.74.
26 *New York Times*, 16.8.74.
27 Birand, *30 Hot Days*, p 100.
28 Interview with Ian Craig and Brendan O'Malley.
29 Polyviou, *Cyprus*, p 176.
30 Interview with Brendan O'Malley, 1985.
31 Interview with Brendan O'Malley, 1985.
32 Birand, *30 Hot Days*, p 104.
33 Interview with Brendan O'Malley, 1985.
34 Polyviou, *Cyprus*, p 177.
35 Birand, *30 Hot Days*, p 105.
36 Callaghan, *Time and Chance*, p 355.
37 *New York Times*, 14.8.74.
38 Birand, *30 Hot Days*, pp 104–5.
39 *The Times* 181.
40 *Cyprus Mail*, 14.8.74.
41 Birand, *30 Hot Days*, p 111.
42 Polyviou, *Cyprus*, p 183; Birand, *30 Hot Days*, pp 112–114.

CHAPTER 26

1   *The Times*, 15.8.74.
2   *The Times*, 15.8.74.
3   *The Times*, 15 and 16.8.74.
4   *Guardian*, 17.8.74.
5   *The Times*, 16.8.74.
6   *New York Times*, 16.8.74.
7   Woodhouse, *Karamanlis*, p 217; Polyviou, *Cyprus*, p 185.
8   *The Times*, 16.3.74.
9   *The Times*, 16.8.74.
10 *New York Times*, 17.8.74.
11 *Guardian*, 16.8.74.
12 *New York Times*, 17.8.74.
13 *New York Times*, 19.8.74; *Sunday Telegraph*, 18.8.74.
14 UN, S/11353.
15 UN S/11353,400.32 SO.
16 UN S115/114.62.
17 *Daily Telegraph*, 20.8.74.

CHAPTER 27

1   Evidence to 1974 US HoR SC on Foreign Affairs.
2   Speech, 18 August 1974, reproduced in appendix to US HoR Committee on Foreign Affairs, 1974.
3   Richelson and Ball, *The Ties That Bind*, p 323.
4   Interview with Brendan O'Malley, 1985.
5   Report of US HoR SC Foreign Affairs, 19.8.74, and appendix.
6   Interview with Ian Craig and Brendan O'Malley.
7   Callaghan, *Time and Chance*, p 359.
8   *Hansard*, 6.11.74.
9   Carver, *Tightrope*, p 108.
10 US HoR SC Foreign Affairs.
11 *New York Times*, 2.12.74.
12 *Keesing's Contemporary Archives*, 1975, p 27035.
13 Franck and Weisband, *Foreign Policy by Congress*, pp 44–5.
14 *Keesing's Contemporary Archives*, 1975, p 27337.
15 Sulzberger, *The World and Richard Nixon*, p 148.
16 Sampson, *The Arms Bazaar*, p 312.
17 *Keesing's Contemporary Archives*, 1975, p 27450.
18 *Keesing's Contemporary Archives*, 1976, p 27866.
19 Campbell, *The Unsinkable Aircraft Carrier*, p 321.
20 Interview with Brendan O'Malley, 1985.
21 *Aviation Week* and *Space Technology*, 11.8.75, 22.5.78, 14.5.79, 20.8.79, 22.10.79, 25.2.80, 16.6.80, 3.11.80, 7.3.83.
22 *SIPRI Yearbook* 1980, pp 285–302.
23 Richelson and Ball, *The Ties That Bind*, p 323.
24 US Military Installations and Objectives in the Eastern Mediterranean, a report for the Committee on International Relations, 1977.

25 *Jane's Defence Weekly*, 18.4.87.
26 British Foreign Affairs SC, 1987, pp vii–xxiii.
27 'Everyman', BBC1, 9.11.97.
28 Interview with Brendan O'Malley, 1985.
29 *The Times*, 7.2.95.
30 *Guardian*, 10.1.97.
31 *Irish Times*, 12.8.96, *Guardian*, 12.8.96.
32 *Observer*, 18.8.96.

APPENDIX

1 Kissinger, *Years of Renewal*, p 215.
2 Conversation between Sir Edward Heath and Ian Craig, April 1999.
3 *New Scientist*, 7.11.74.
4 *Ekiones*, 27.10.74–9.11.74.
5 Kissinger, *Years of Renewal*, p 212.
6 Kissinger, *Years of Renewal*, p 216.
7 Kissinger, *Years of Renewal*, p 218.
8 Kissinger, *Years of Renewal*, p 207.
9 Kissinger, *Years of Renewal*, p 228.
10 Kissinger, *Years of Renewal*, p 238–9.

BIBLIOGRAPHY

Adams, T.W. and Cottrell, A.J., *Cyprus Between East and West* (The John Hopkins Press, Baltimore, 1968)

Alford, Jonathan, *Greece and Turkey: Adversity In Alliance* (Gower, Aldershot, 1984)

Armacost, Michael A., *The Politics of Weapons Innovation: the Thor-Jupiter Controversy* (Columbia University Press, New York, 1969)

Attalides, Michael, *Cyprus: Nationalism and International Politics* (Q Press, Edinburgh, 1979)

Averoff-Tossizza, Evangelos, *Lost Opportunities: The Cyprus Question, 1950–63* (Aristide D. Caratzas, New York, 1986)

Ball, George W., *The Past Has Another Pattern* (W.W. Norton, New York, 1982)

Barker, Dudley, *Grivas, Portrait of a Terrorist* (The Cresset Press, London, 1959)

Baylis, John, *Anglo-American Defence Relations 1939–1984* (Macmillan, London, 1981)

Birand, M.A., *30 Hot Days* (K.Rustem and Bros, Nicosia, 1985)

Bower, Tom, *The Perfect English Spy* (William Heinemann, London, 1995)

British Interests in the Mediterranean and Middle East (Royal Institute of International Affairs, Oxford, 1958)

Callaghan, James, *Time and Chance* (Collins, London, 1987)

Calvocoressi, Peter, *World Politics Since 1945* (Longman, London, 1984)

Campbell, Duncan, *The Unsinkable Aircraft Carrier* (Paladin, London, 1984)

Carver, Michael, *Tightrope Walking: British Defence Policy Since 1945* (Hutchinson, London, 1992)

Castle, Barbara, *The Castle Diaries 1964–70* (Weidenfeld and Nicolson, London, 1984)

Collins, John M, and Cordesman, Anthony H., *Imbalance of Power: Shifting US Soviet Military Strengths* (Macdonald and Jane's, London, 1978)

Crawshaw, Nancy, *The Cyprus Revolt* (George Allen and Unwin, London, 1978)

Crossman, Richard, *Diaries* (Hamish Hamilton and Jonathan Cape, London 1975–7)

Eden, Sir Anthony, *Full Circle* (Cassell, London, 1960)

Eisenhower, Dwight D., *The White House Years vol 2: Waging Peace, 1956–1961* (Heinemann, London, 1966)

Grivas, George, *Memoirs of General Grivas*, ed. Foley, Charles (Longman, London, 1964)

Foot, Hugh, *A Start in Freedom* (Hodder and Stoughton, London, 1964)

Franck, Thomas M. and Weisband, Edward, *Foreign Policy By Congress* (Oxford University Press, New York, 1979)

Hitchens, Christopher, *Cyprus* (Quartet, London, 1984)

Jackson, Robert, *Suez 1956: Operation Musketeer* (Ian Allan, London, 1980)

Kaku, Michio and Axelrod, Daniel, *To Win a Nuclear War* (Zed Books, London, 1987)

Keesing's Contemporary Archives, Weekly Diary of World Events, (Keesing's Publications, Longman, London, annual)

Kissinger, Henry, *Years of Upheaval* (George Weidenfeld and Michael Joseph, London, 1982)

Kissinger, Henry, *Years of Renewal* (Simon and Schuster, New York, 1999)

Kitson, Frank, *Bunch of Five* (Faber and Faber, London and Boston, 1977)

Koumoulides, John T.A. (ed.), *Cyprus in Transition* (Trigraph, London, 1986)

Lamb, Richard, *The Failure of the Eden Government* (Sidgwick and Jackson, London, 1987)

Leigh, David, *The Wilson Plot* (Heinemann, London, 1988)

Maclean, Donald, *British Foreign Policy Since Suez* (Hodder and Stoughton, London, 1970)

Macmillan, Harold, *Riding The Storm* (Macmillan, London, 1971)

Mayes, Stanley, *Makarios: A Biography* (Macmillan, London, 1981)

Morris, Roger, *Uncertain Greatness* (Quartet Books, London, 1977)

Oberling, Pierre, *The Road To Bellapais* (Columbia University Press, New York, 1982)

Patrick, R.A., *A General System Theory Approach To Geopolitical Aspects Of Conflict Between Communities With Particular Reference To Cyprus Since 1960* (University of London, 1972)

Patrick, R.A., *Political Geography and the Cyprus Conflict, 1963–71* (Contario, 1976)

Penrose, Barry and Courtiour, Roger, *The Pencourt File* (Secker and Warburg, London, 1978)

Pincher, Chapman, *Too Secret Too Long* (Sidgwick and Jackson, London, 1984)

Polmar, Norman, *Strategic Weapons: An Introduction* (Crane Russak, New York, 1982)

Polyviou, Polyvios G., *Cyprus: Conflict and Negotiation* (Duckworth, London, 1980)

Ponting, Clive, *Breach of Promise: Labour In Power 1964–1970* (Hamish Hamilton, London, 1989)

Porter, A. N. and Stockwell, A.J., *British Imperial Policy and Decolonization 1938–64* (Macmillan, London, 1987)

Ranelagh, John, *The Agency: The Rise and Decline of the CIA* (Weidenfeld and Nicolson, London, 1986)

Reddaway, John, *Burdened With Cyprus: The British Connection* (Weidenfeld and Nicolson, London, 1986)

Richelson, Jeffrey T. and Ball, Desmond, *The Ties That Bind* (Allen and Unwin, Australia, 1985)

Sampson, Anthony, *The Arms Bazaar* (Coronet, London, 1988 edition)

Stern, Laurence, *The Wrong Horse* (Times Books, New York, 1977)

Sulzberger, C.L., *The World and Richard Nixon* (Prentice Hall, New York, 1987)

Thomas, Hugh, *The Suez Affair* (Weidenfeld and Nicolson, London, 1966)

Vanezis, Dr P.N., *Makarios: Life and Leadership* (Abelard-Schuman, London, 1979)

West, Nigel, *The Friends* (Weidenfeld and Nicolson, London, 1988)

West, Nigel, *GCHQ* (Hodder and Stoughton, London 1987)

White, Theodore H., *Breach of Faith – The Fall of Nixon* (Atheneum, New York, 1975)

Wiley, Richard G., *Electronic Intelligence: the Analysis of Radar Signals* (Artech House, Mass., USA, 1982)

Wilson, Harold, *Final Term, The Labour Government 1974–76* (Weidenfeld and Nicolson, London, 1986)

Wilson, Harold, *The Labour Government 1964–70: A Personal Record* (Pelican, London, 1971)

Wint, Guy and Calvocoressi, Peter, *Middle East Crisis* (Penguin, England, 1957)

Woodhouse, C.M., *Karamanlis: The Restorer of Greek Democracy* (New York, 1982)

Wright, Peter, *Spycatcher* (Viking, New York, 1987)

INDEX